THE I TATTI
RENAISSANCE LIBRARY

James Hankins, General Editor

VERINO

FIAMMETTA

PARADISE

ITRL 69

UGOLINO VERINO

✦ ✦ ✦

FIAMMETTA

PARADISE

EDITED AND TRANSLATED BY

ALLAN M. WILSON

THE I TATTI RENAISSANCE LIBRARY

HARVARD UNIVERSITY PRESS

CAMBRIDGE, MASSACHUSETTS

2016

Series design by Dean Bornstein

Library of Congress Cataloging-in-publication data

Verino, Ugolino, 1438–1516, author.
Fiammetta ; Paradise / Ugolino Verino ; edited and translated by
Allan M. Wilson.
pages cm — (ITRL ; 69)
Text in English and Latin on facing pages.
ISBN 978-0-674-08862-7 (alk. paper)
I. Wilson, Allan M. (Allan Murray)   II. Verino, Ugolino, 1438–1516.
Fiammetta. English. 2015.   III. Verino, Ugolino, 1438–1516. Paradisus.
2015.   IV. Verino, Ugolino, 1438–1516. Paradisus. English. 2015.
V. Title.   VI. Series: I Tatti Renaissance library ; 69.
PA8585.V45A6 2016
871'.04 — dc23   2015008341

Contents

ॐ∫ℓॐ

Introduction

꙼ꙟꙩꙟ꙼

Ugolino Verino, or de' Vieri, was born on January 15 or 25, 1438,[1] of a family long resident in the Santo Spirito quarter of Florence (2.17.3–6),[2] south of the Arno. A direct ancestor of the same name had twice held the city's highest office of Gonfaloniere di Giustizia (in 1360 and 1364; 2.13.19–20 and note). In his day the family had been prosperous. Three generations later, however, Verino's father, Vieri de' Vieri (1401–80), was open to being labeled poor by a disparager of the poet, though Verino pronounces him nevertheless well-esteemed in the city (2.13.17–18). Verino's mother (substantially younger, it seems, than his father) was Bartolomea di Michele Pescioni, herself from a distinguished Florentine family (both Verino's parents are briefly mentioned at 1.4.77–82). The poet was the second child of eight. His father was already in his mid-thirties when Verino's elder sister, Caterina, was born in 1437. The gap between Verino and his youngest sibling, Salvestro (b. 1457), was nineteen years. Lazzari[3] gives the family tree in an appendix. We are told[4] that Verino's father, a wool trader, was a cultured and studious man. Some earlier members of the family had been apothecaries, but the poet's like-named paternal grandfather had also been involved in the wool trade. Verino's father was *podestà* (mayor) of Castelfranco di Sopra in Val d'Arno in 1448 and one of the *Priori* for September and October 1473. In his eulogy for his revered mother,[5] Verino stresses her very great piety and tells how she wisely and caringly directed her sons to follow "the seeds of nature" in deciding what career best suited them. For two of Verino's five brothers, the choice was trade, and another found his calling in medicine, but when his mother saw Verino "burning with love of the Muses," she encouraged him to pursue that interest.

The young Verino became a pupil of Cristoforo Landino (1424–98), who, with the backing of the Medici (cf. 1.20.29), was in 1458 granted the chair of poetry and rhetoric at the University of Florence. Verino had very high respect for Landino, and his first work, *Flammetta* (= *Fiammetta*),[6] was almost a tribute to his teacher, being a collection of poems about his youthful first love (with various other themes, especially in Book II), greatly influenced by, and often consciously imitating and borrowing from, Landino's own *Xandra*, which had been written in its original form (then comprising fifty-three poems) in 1443/44 but kept from general notice till around 1458–60, when it was recast (with some poems altered in part or omitted), very substantially augmented with material composed since the original *Xandra*, and rededicated to Piero de' Medici (1.20.31–32n). Verino mentions this work of Landino in 1.5.4 and 1.20.29–38, where he expressly describes himself as following in Landino's footsteps (l. 33). Elsewhere, he calls Landino his "venerable teacher,"[7] and in another tribute[8] declares his youth in Landino's debt "as though to a father," lauding him as an illustrious orator, a poet, and a trustworthy interpreter of poets,[9] equally accomplished in Latin prose and verse. Among Landino's works mentioned there, Verino includes his love elegies to Sandra (Alessandra, Latin *Xandra*) "in the manner of Propertius." Some other contemporary Florentine poets too (such as Alessandro Braccesi and Naldo Naldi) aspired, like Verino, to emulate Landino's well-regarded *Xandra* by composing comparable collections of poems. Verino's debts to that work in *Fiammetta* are numerous and substantial, both in terms of larger-scale inspiration and of particular verbal borrowings, occasionally extending to whole or nearly whole lines.[10]

Naturally, Verino draws heavily on Ovid (above all the *Amores*) for themes, expressions, and style, and in places he also reflects Propertius, Tibullus, Vergil, Martial, and occasionally other ancient poets, such as Horace and Juvenal, and (in 2.12) even recalls the prose writer Petronius. We readily see that Verino was well read in his ancient models. He seems to have sent poems to several friends and fellow poets (see, for example, 2.18 and 2.41), sometimes soliciting theirs in return (as 2.7.11–12, 2.18.11–12), and to have shown some to Piero de' Medici (1.19). It appears from 2.17 that Pellegrino Agli saw at least some of Verino's poems and advised on improvements (see also 1.3.5n). Bartolomeo Platina apparently suggested (not too seriously?) that Verino might try translating Homer into Latin verse (2.24.1), though Verino in reply modestly considers Platina much better suited to do so (both Platina and Verino were taught Greek by John Argyropoulos; Verino also had Marsilio Ficino among his teachers). Cherubino Quarquagli seems to have playfully overdone praise of Verino's poetry, and in return Verino lightheartedly treats him as a flatterer (2.23). Though in 2.13.5–6 Verino denies ever hurting anybody in his poems and declares his verses free of "viperish" (that is, malicious-tongued) jokes, some poems in Book II of *Fiammetta* clearly *are* personal attacks (e.g., 2.9, 2.16, 2.28, 2.32, 2.34). Perhaps those attacks (in certain cases revealing some appreciation of Martial) were written later than 2.13.

The content of Book II of *Fiammetta* is much more varied than that of Book I, for it is a miscellany of poems to friends, a few tributes and eulogies, rebuttals of detractors, some contemporary comment, and sundry incidental pieces and oddments, with love poems in the minority. Book II can largely be left to speak for itself, poem by poem. In Book I, however, the principal attention is on Verino's love for an unidentified Florentine girl, the eponymous Fiammetta. She is represented as his first love, and 2.13.11 treats him as enamored of her before his twentieth year had fallen to him (whether that means before it had begun or had been completed; it would start on January 15 or 25, 1457, and end in January 1458).[11] According to the poems, though Fiammetta had, at the high point of their relationship, sworn a solemn oath to Verino in the church of Santa Maria del Carmine never to marry anyone but him (1.27.17–30), he eventually lost her when she honored her father's arrangement that she should marry a man whom Verino contemptuously calls "old Bruno" and (in angry bitterness) represents as physically disgusting and decrepit (1.28).

Though many of the situations in Verino's relationship with Fiammetta as described in the poems reflect elegiac tradition, and 1.2.43–44 probably implies that Verino (like Ovid by his own admission) freely adapted the truth to suit the genre, there is a little external evidence that Fiammetta was indeed a real girl. A copy of Ovid's *Amores* in a manuscript in the Biblioteca Nazionale Marciana at Venice[12] is followed on folio 47 by an elegiac distich in Latin and then by a name in Greek script[13] that identifies the copyist as Ugolino Verino. The distich states, "I copied this out as a flame burned my tender marrow, as radiant love for Fiammetta consumed me." Fiammetta is furthermore treated as real in a poem to Verino seemingly by Francesco Tranchedini, and in a letter Verino compares the resolutely chaste Fiammetta with his addressee's Lelia (both poem and letter are summarized 1.7n). In the former, Verino is urged to *resume* writing of Fiammetta after a substantial period of not doing so, as she has *returned*. That suggests that Fiammetta spent some time away from Florence after Verino became involved with her, something not stated in Verino's own poems. Did he take Tranchedini's advice and pay her renewed attention when she came back? Possibly 1.23.9–12, with its reference to Cupid's having been "doubling" the attack on Verino for three months, may hint that he did, but that is less than clear ("doubling" may mean "intensifying" rather than "renewing"). Naldo Naldi seems to treat Verino's anguish from Fiammetta's non-reciprocation of his love as real (2.26n).

Verino claims attraction at first sight to Fiammetta (1.4.9–20), whom he has secretly many a time observed from a distance (1.4.35–36). Modesty and fear of derision by the crowd have held him back from declaring his feelings, but he is strongly drawn by her beauty, sweet smiles, purity, charming ways, and everything she does (1.4.15–32). He wishes that they could be paired in Spartan-style wrestling exercises or study poetry together (1.4.37–46). He struggles to hide his newly experienced lovesickness from his parents (1.4.75–86). In this confusion he therefore ventures to send his first poem to Fiammetta (or affects to do so), declaring himself her poet (1.4.1–2) and blushingly begging the recipient of his verse-letter, whom he pictures also blushing, to spare him (1.4.95–102). His poems will declare his love, he tells her, but that will be no crime (1.4.103–4). Fiammetta is urged not to fear the short-lived hurt of being slandered by the crowd. Kept secret, the love that he and Fiammetta can share will, he declares, endure till death (1.4.107–10) and beyond (1.6.25–48). Verino represents this falling in love with Fiammetta as happening when he was still in his first, "boyhood" years (1.4.93–94, 2.22.9–10; cf. his words in *Paradise*, preface 3), not yet having had his twentieth year (1.1.17–18n, 2.13.11). The language used of his love-torment, though in part from classical models, is often charged with guilt at succumbing to such emotions. He speaks of his *nequitia* ("badness", whether scandalous behavior, moral failing, or just languishing in lovesickness; 1.4.20n) and of his *dedecus* ("shame" or "turpitude"; 1.4.103). He describes inner conflict over this first stirring of strong sexual attraction to Fiammetta's beauty (1.4.19–28). He speaks of his tears and pain (1.4.19) and of his embarrassingly evident melancholy and infatuated preoccupation (1.4.75–86). Nevertheless, he repudiates slanderous suggestions of carnality and dissipation in his character, declaring his crime, if such at all, as simply having fallen in love (2.13.9–13). He is concerned early in the book to stress to the reader the purity of his morals in reality, though the genre of his writing requires its content (1.2.43–44 and note). (In 2.2.27–32, it may further be observed, he says he cannot, for modesty, describe his second attack of lovesickness — for Lisia, it seems — at all, considering it "disgraceful" for him to confess it.) In 1.29 he represents Fiammetta as so impressed by his restraint in their affair (that is, his respectful acceptance of a nonphysical relationship) that he becomes the foremost among her admirers. Verino wants his readers to understand that this particular love-poet was as much a virgin at the end of his affair with Fiammetta as he was at its beginning, however much he represents himself as inwardly scorched and tortured during the episode.

In physical appearance Fiammetta is represented as beautiful (1.4.101, 1.5.6, 1.6.23, 1.13.13–14, 1.16, 1.17.3–4, 1.18.1–4, 1.28.9, 1.28.13, 2.55.9) and fair-skinned (1.18.9–10, 1.25.47–48, 1.26.24, 1.28.9, 1.30.3, 1.30.5, 1.30.8, 2.55.9). She has yellow hair surpassing Apollo's (1.4.17, 1.30.3), bright, star-like eyes (1.4.15, 1.12.29, 1.13.7–8, 1.30.7), and a sweet smile (1.4.31). She is everything that the old, dwarfish, and ugly (imaginary) Galla, for all her (unsuccessful) recourse to cosmetics, is not (1.17), and, like Landino's Sandra before her (1.5), Fiammetta compares with Roman beauties of old and with goddesses (1.16). Even Verino's second love, Lisia, herself very beautiful, does not quite equal Fiammetta (2.50.37).

It is not only Fiammetta's looks that attract Verino. In his first poem to her, as already observed, he praises her charming ways and purity, and he loves everything she does (1.4.22 and 31–32). Any physical ambitions in Verino's mind are, however, to remain unfulfilled. She is totally chaste. In keeping with the conventions of poetry of unsatisfied passion, she is censured as hard-hearted or cruel, that is, in not being obliging to her tormented lover (1.4.98–100, 1.6.15, 1.10.13–14, 1.14.15–22, 1.18.18, 27–28 and 37–40, 2.50.38), and as haughty, initially spurning Verino (1.10.15–18, 1.28.13–14). When in 1.9.19–22 Verino is the shut-out (would-be) lover enduring the savage elements outside the door of a girl who will not admit him (that is, Fiammetta), he attributes an unconcerned and disdainful sneer to her, addressed to the weather god ("Let him die, since dying is what he wants to do"). Another poem on this (commonly found) theme of rejection of the poet (1.14) includes the added indignant claim that Fiammetta has admitted others to her presence. In 1.23.21–22 Verino thinks her, if not in love with another youth, perhaps too puffed-up with her virginity. When Verino, after a period of acceptance, eventually begins to feel wronged and betrayed, he bitterly labels her perfidious, deceitful, wicked, inconstant, ungrateful, forsworn, and false-hearted (1.6.23, 1.18.15, 1.21.19, 1.27 passim, 1.30.19–34, 2.55.10). Rigidly chaste before marriage, on becoming Bruno's wife, she displays absolute fidelity to him and has no wish to risk being wrongly called an adulteress (1.29, esp. 3–4 and 7–11) by continuing an association (even a nonphysical one) with Verino.

In circumstances, Fiammetta is initially portrayed as a young girl living at the parental home within Florence, protected by her mother (1.10.19–28) and under her father's authority (1.29.17–26), though she has the attention of many youths (1.4.36, 1.6.17 and 47, 1.13.6 and 11–12, 1.21.2, 1.14.2, 1.29.6). Her age is nowhere explicitly stated. In 1.10.19 she "plays with the other girls," watched over by her (supposedly old and faded) mother, who will not let her out of doors with Verino loitering, and there she seems very young, but in other contexts she, not her mother, shuts out Verino while (supposedly) admitting many other admirers (1.14.2; cf. 1.6.19–24 and 47–48, 1.13, 1.18.19–20, and 1.23.16 and 21 for Verino's concerns about rivals), making her seem rather older and less protected. From Verino's wish that he might wrestle with her (1.4.37–40) or study poetry with her (1.4.41–44) we should presumably see her as of an age to be sufficiently credible, physically and mentally, in both activities with a youth then nearly twenty. Though probably, by at least a little way, Verino's junior (as later, by several years, was Lisia), in 1.29 she is given a final speech of some maturity of mind, appropriate to her by then (recently) married status. She seems an educated girl, able to read Latin, though not herself a writer of poetry (1.4.41–58). Her ignorance of the

complexities of civil law (1.29.19–20) is treated as only to be ex-
pected in her sex (all lawyers then being male). She sometimes
attends the cathedral on feast days (1.4.33–36), but as she swears
her oath to marry none but Verino in Santa Maria del Carmine
(1.27.17–30), perhaps, like him, she lived south of the Arno.

We can to some extent follow the course of the relationship
between Verino and Fiammetta, at least as represented in the po-
ems (the professed "facts" of their affair surely include much liter-
ary invention), after the (purported) initial contact in 1.4, already
noticed, and Verino's declared intention (ll. 103–4) to write pro-
claiming his love for her. Seeking a bond between them till old
age, death, and beyond (1.4.109–10, 1.6.25–48), he composes many
poems in praise of Fiammetta. She gives him, he says, poetic pow-
ers denied him by Nature and inspires his verses (1.21.25–36),
which make her beauty all too well known, encouraging rivals
(1.13), and also induce haughtiness toward him in her (1.18.15–17).
Though Fiammetta at one stage playfully snowballs Verino, often
a flirtatious action (1.6.13–16), there are times when she shuns him
and shuts him out, while allegedly receiving many others (1.14,
1.18.10, 18 and 21–36, 1.21.4). Verino complains of her hard-
heartedness toward him (1.18.28) and tells her she will cause his
death (1.18.39–40, 1.23.39–40). He professes himself her slave
(1.10.9–10, 1.14.15, 1.18.27, 1.22.26, 1.25.1–2). Eventually, Fiammetta
consents to be Verino's girl, in a relationship without physical inti-
macy (1.13.5–6n, 1.21.1–14 and 23–24, 1.25.41–42, 1.28.15–16), and,
though her "thousandth" admirer, for a while he is the best re-
garded (1.6.17–18, 1.29.5–6). He wants her to be his only ever love
(1.21.33–36). He has aspirations to marry her (1.27.19, 1.29.1–2n
and 16). She vows in church to wed none but him (1.27.17–26,
1.30.20), but her unrealistic promise is never to be kept.

The end of the relationship is described in the last poems of
Book I. In 1.24 Verino urges himself to think of the scandal and
derision he is attracting and of the suffering his love is inflicting on

him. Like Ovid's Medea, he sees the wise course of action but can-
not resist the foolish one (ll. 23–24). A similar battle between
Verino's heart and head is the theme of 1.25. His heart prevails; he
would far rather be restored to Fiammetta's affections, he vows,
than be a king and have vast riches (ll. 41–48). In 1.26 Erato, the
Muse of love poetry, tells Verino in a dream that he is not fated
ever to "possess" Fiammetta. She must marry another, old Bruno,
and Verino has to accept that; but one day there will be a girl who
will *not* disdain to be his for life. In 1.27 the poet rebukes Fiam-
metta for faithlessness in marrying Bruno and speaks, in his fury,
of not knowing where his young man's anger may lead him (ll.
9–12). The next poem (1.28) is a bitter, disgusted, and jealous pro-
test that the girl who would not have Verino should now consent
to lie in the arms of a revolting old man (as Verino portrays
Bruno). Following that (1.29) is Fiammetta's (reported) reply, ap-
pealing to Verino to accept her changed status and leave her alone,
as further association with him would put her reputation at risk
and hurt her husband, and she will not dishonor her marriage
bond (ll. 3–4, 7–11). She thanks Verino for his restraint toward her
in his great passion, calling that the factor able to induce her to
favor him (ll. 11–14), but she was never truly in a position to marry
him, as she could not have secured her father's consent (ll. 17–22).
She urges Verino to find another girl, one free to be his. Verino
duly agrees to leave Fiammetta alone (ll. 31–32). Nevertheless, in
1.30, still suffering and bitter, he speaks of her being made to pay
one day by Heaven for her treachery, though love checks his anger
sufficiently to ask that her punishment be but light (ll. 21–30). He
declares that Fiammetta will come to regret spurning him and
marrying Bruno and will perceive too late her rejected lover's wor-
thiness (ll. 31–34).

From a few poems in Book II we gather that Verino did recover
from losing Fiammetta (though hurt lingered: cf. 2.49.19–21) and
fall in love again (2.22.49–50; cf. also 2.2.1–6), with another beau-

tiful girl, whom he calls *Lisia* (for Elisabetta), but she died at seventeen (2.50). In 1468, aged thirty, Verino married Piera di Simone di Bartolo Strada, who bore him a single son, Michele (1469–87), and a single daughter, Lucrezia (1475–1546), before dying young in 1477 (when Verino was not quite forty; he never remarried). The well-regarded, scholarly, reflective, abstemious, deeply religious (and somewhat priggish) Michele died at seventeen of a wasting disease, a terrible blow to his father, who himself published his son's book of moral distichs shortly after the boy's death. Verino's concern to keep his beloved Michele from any risk of lapsing from industrious study and godly virtue into idle dissipation can be seen in the fatherly letter reported at 1.4.20n, a revealing insight into the prevailing moral atmosphere and work ethic in the Verino household. Lazzari devotes a whole chapter (6) to Michele.

Something can be deduced from *Fiammetta* of Verino's own character in youth, or at least of how he chooses to portray it. He frequently stresses his own true-hearted faithfulness, in love as in friendship (references 1.30.31–32n). He claims purity of life (references 1.2.43–44n). He fears (or affects to fear) being a scandal and laughingstock for loving Fiammetta (references 1.4.23n, 1.19.15–16n). He rebuts several detractors and slanderers (references 2.46n). He is (reflecting his ancient models) contemptuous of the crowd (references 1.1.11–12n). He is strongly hostile to contemporary male homosexuality, though that antipathy does not preclude admiration for (and imitation of) a homosexual poem by Horace (cf. 2.19n). He is also not so prudish that he cannot write a humorous poem on a brothel (2.12), drawing on relevant contexts in Petronius and Juvenal, and there are indications that he did not recoil from reading Martial, though in *Fiammetta* he ventures only lightly and rather delicately into the genre of sexual lampoons (2.28, 2.32, 2.35, 2.38). He can show modesty and diffidence about his own poetic capacity (cf. 2.26n). His veneration of, and desire to emulate, Landino have already been noticed. Like Landino, he shows himself a reluctant notary, manifestly rating time spent with the Muses far above the tedious earning of a living in the law courts (2.48.15–38). He is close to several other members of Florence's literary circle, such as Piero Vettori (1.10 and 1.28), Cherubino Quarquagli (1.12 and 2.23), Amerigo Corsini (2.10 and 2.27), Lorenzo Lippi (2.11), Pellegrino Agli (2.17 and, I suspect, 1.5), Naldo Naldi (2.26), Bartolomeo Platina (2.24), Andrea Alamanni (2.45), and others (see 1.7 for Tranchedini — Nicodemo or Francesco?), and exchanges poems with a few fellow poets resident elsewhere, such as Nicola Capponi (otherwise Cola Montano, 2.18), Francesco Ricci (2.41), and Agli, as stated above.

The Medici had controlled Florence since before Verino was born. The head of the family, the immensely wealthy banker Cosimo de' Medici, had returned from exile in 1434 to receive the reins of government and assume a position in Florence analogous to that of Augustus Caesar in the Roman principate, where Augustus claimed to be merely the first citizen, but in fact exercised complete personal domination. Verino venerates Cosimo in *Fiammetta* as a great benefactor of his beloved homeland (see especially 2.51, which is a tribute written shortly after Cosimo's death on August 1, 1464, 2.52, and 2.53), and he also speaks in eulogistic terms of Cosimo's gout-ridden son Piero (his eventual successor in power, 1464–69) as a new Maecenas to the poets of his time, analogous to the patron of Vergil and Horace in Augustus' Rome, imagery already used by Landino (1.19.5–6n). Medici patronage of Florence's poets is lauded especially in 1.1.23–28, 1.11.37–56, 1.20.25–32, 2.3.7–10, 2.45.117–42, and 2.51.77–86. Beyond poetry, Verino also proudly celebrates the artistic and other cultural achievements and scholarship then to be seen in Florence and the Medici benefaction to churches (as in 2.8, 2.45.79–116 and 129–32, 2.51.87–118). To Piero's still very young son Lorenzo (the Magnificent) Verino addresses the dedicatory poem of Book I and the first piece in Book II of *Fiammetta*, and he sings his praises in 2.43 to Lucrezia Donati, the literary "mistress" to whom Lorenzo addressed his vernacular love poems. Lorenzo and his brother Giuliano, the two grandsons of high promise in P. 714 and 725–33, are probably eulogized also in *Fiammetta* 1.11.37–56. Piero's brother, Giovanni, is praised too, in 2.45.117–19 (cf. P. 702–21).

Having completed *Fiammetta*, Verino left love poetry behind as a thing of youth. His extensive output thereafter became more serious, often reflecting his devout piety. His *Paradise*, a work in obvious debt for its theme to both Vergil (*Aeneid* 6) and Dante, and influenced a little too by the *Somnium Scipionis*, the "Dream of Scipio" at the end of Cicero's *De Republica*, followed in the late 1460s (ca. 1468, certainly before the death of Piero de' Medici on December 2, 1469; see P. 208–76n), when Verino was somewhere around thirty. His high regard for the deceased Cosimo, his guide in Heaven, is very evident in *Paradise*, and in 702–15 he represents himself as having been a good friend of Cosimo's deceased younger son Giovanni de' Medici. *Paradise* cannot pretend to have any of the depths of Dante, but it provides an interesting and very readable insight into how an intelligent, educated, moral, and religious Florentine could conceive the afterlife (in poetic terms) in the later fifteenth century. It reflects both Verino's classical learning and his Christian piety, as well as serving to venerate Cosimo. A summary of the content of the work is given separately later in this volume (Appendix I).

Space does not permit more than brief notice of Verino's numerous other works, among which the greatest in scale is his *Carlias* ("Carliad"), an epic (in all of fifteen books) recounting the exploits of Charlemagne in legend (in Italy and the Holy Land), finished in its first form in 1480 and dedicated in a revised version to Charles VIII of France in 1493.[14] Verino kept on making changes to the work thereafter till 1506. His *De illustratione urbis Florentiae* (in three books), otherwise *De gloria urbis Florentinae* ("On the Glory of the City of Florence"), surveys Florence's history, illustrious figures (including artists and writers), leading families, and buildings. Verino also composed seven books of epigrams[15] (mostly with moral and religious emphasis). Through them he tried in 1485 to alleviate his strained financial position by taking advantage of the friendly relations that his youngest brother, Salvestro, had developed with the Hungarian king Matthias Corvinus while at his court in the early 1480s. Dedicating the epigrams to Corvinus, Verino, through Salvestro, presented a copy to the king. According to Bartolozzi (quoted by Lazzari, p. 106), Corvinus responded with money for Salvestro to pass on to the poet, but on the return journey Salvestro was captured at sea by the Venetians, robbed, and consigned to the galleys. Thus Verino's recourse to Corvinus for patronage, prompted by his frustration with the disappointing omission of Lorenzo de' Medici, the obvious source of support within Florence, to assist him financially, ended in disaster. The early death of one of Verino's brothers, Pierozzo (1445–80), in his mid-thirties, had also left the poet having to support the many children thus rendered fatherless, severely stretching the limited financial resources at his disposal from working as a notary and from giving some private tuition in poetry and rhetoric (Verino never secured a professorial appointment). Among his pupils was Pietro Ricci, known as Crinito,[16] in 1487 the young scribe of one of the manuscripts (B) of *Paradise*.

Though in youth a venerator and eulogizer of the Medici, in the last years of Lorenzo the Magnificent Verino became sympathetic with the preaching of the Dominican friar Girolamo Savonarola, that vociferous denouncer of moral and religious corruption in Lorenzo's Florence (with its scholarly paganism) and elsewhere. In 1491 Verino dedicated to the friar his *Carmen de Christianae religionis ac vitae monasticae felicitate* ("Poem on the Felicity of the Christian Religion and of the Monastic Life") and in an accompanying letter to Savonarola distinguished true poets (declared both morally uplifting and pleasurable to read by reason of the elegance and structure of their words) from those whom he called wicked and lascivious ones, to be avoided like the plague, who abused the medium, preferring in their paganism to name Jupiter rather than Christ, the thyrsus rather than the cross, and Juno and Bacchus rather than the Virgin Mary and Saint John. He deplored those who had used their poetry to detract from what he saw as Savonarola's holiness. Savonarola wrote back to say what for him constituted true poetry. After Lorenzo's death in 1492 and the expulsion of the Medici in 1494, Savonarola's reforming religious zeal dominated Florence for four years, till he fell in 1498, when he was imprisoned, interrogated under torture, and brought to trial, eventually to be strangled and burned in the Piazza della Signoria. As the friar faced trial, Verino, hitherto one of the Piagnoni (Weepers) or Frateschi (Friar's Followers), as Savonarola's supporters were known, turned upon him with invective, denouncing him as no true prophet and no performer of miracles. How far Verino, who in *Fiammetta* and *Paradise* makes so much of his true-heartedness and faithfulness, acted thus in fear of the consequences for himself if he continued to support the clearly doomed preacher, or how far he had genuinely lost his once strong belief in Savonarola and now felt he had foolishly let himself be misled by him, is debatable. Verino's desertion of Savonarola did not, however, save him from being among those called to account for earlier adherence to the friar's cause. Verino was reprimanded, fined, and debarred from holding public office for three years.

In the remainder of his long life, Verino composed further religious works, in his *Silvae* (in nineteen books) and his paraphrase of the bible (both Old and New Testaments) in hexameter verse. The latter work was dedicated to Lorenzo de' Medici's son Pope Leo X, as was an eight-book work (lost) on vices and virtues, the Christian religion, and true beatitude. Several minor works by Verino (not all extant) are listed by M. E. Cosenza in the entry on him in his *Biographical and Bibliographical Dictionary of the Italian Humanists* (Boston, 1962). They include a panegyric for Ferdinand of Aragon and Isabella of Castile. Verino died in 1516.

This present volume represents a very extensive revision, indeed in large part a rewriting, of separate editions of Verino's *Fiammetta* and *Paradise* that I originally did (privately, as a hobby) in the late 1990s.[17] I am grateful to Professor James Hankins for taking up my offer to recast them for the I Tatti Renaissance Library and for advice on how to prepare this volume. I have also benefitted from many suggestions, especially for felicitous modifications here and there to my translations, made by Professor Leah Whittington in her role as Associate Editor. After working so long alone, it was helpful to me to have a second opinion on some passages, viewed through fresh eyes. I have made very numerous modifications throughout, especially to the notes to *Fiammetta*, where I have incorporated substantial new material, as well as excising or trimming down comments made in my 1998 version. Detected errors and oversights have been corrected during the revision, and some judgments and readings have been reconsidered. The texts of both works are established from my consultation of manuscripts on microfilm, initially in 1997–98 and again (throughout) when revising the material for ITRL in 2012–13. I thank the British Library in London for supplying a microfilm of Additional MS. 16426 for *Fiammetta*, and the Biblioteca Medicea Laurenziana in Florence for supplying microfilms of the manuscripts Plut. 39.42 and Laur. Ashburnham 1703 (1626) for *Fiammetta* and Plut. 26.21 and Plut. 39.40 for *Paradise*. Thanks are also due to several other libraries where I consulted relevant material. These include especially the John Rylands University Library and Chetham's Library, both in Manchester, and the library of the Warburg Institute in London.

NOTES

1. Lorenzo Bartolozzi da Figline in his Latin biography of Verino preserved in manuscript (Cod. Riccardiano 910), cited by Lazzari (p. 32), quotes verses of the poet himself, saying that he was born on the Conversion of St. Paul (January 25), though his birthday is officially recorded as January 15.

2. Unless otherwise stated, references in this Introduction (by book, poem, and line) are to the Latin text of *Fiammetta*. Those to lines of *Paradise* are preceded by P. References ending with an *n* are to notes.

3. See Bibliography.

4. By Bartolozzi. See Lazzari, pp. 25–26.

5. Quoted by Lazzari, pp. 33 and 78 (from Verino, *Epigr.* v.4, ed. Bausi, pp. 430–40). She died in 1477.

6. See 1.4n for the spelling. In this volume I generally use the Italian form of her name, Fiammetta, to refer both to the girl and to the work named after her.

7. In his later *De illustratione urbis Florentiae* (fol. 13, Paris 1583 edition; *Carmina* 10.345). That work is discussed by Lazzari, pp. 382ff.

8. An address to Landino quoted by Bandini (1:176).

9. Landino composed allegorical commentaries on Horace and Vergil in the 1480s and an exposition of Dante in 1481.

10. Because of its very strong influence on Verino's *Fiammetta*, I have frequently cited Landino's *Xandra* in my notes. The Latin text with a translation by Mary P. Chatfield has been published in this I Tatti Library (no. 35, 2008). I have also occasionally taken advantage of having translated (at present just privately) all the poems of Alessandro Braccesi that appear in Perosa's (Florence, 1943) edition to cite a few passages of that poet too. Lazzari discusses Landino on pp. 23 and 37ff.

11. See 1.1.17–18n for discussion of the date of Verino's affair with Fiammetta and of the work named for her, surveyed by Lazzari, pp. 54ff.

12. Venice, Biblioteca Marciana, MS. Marc. Lat. XII 86 [4170] on folios 1–47. See Zorzanello's *Catalogo dei Codici Marciani latini* (Trezzano, 1980–), 2:178; A. Perosa's (Florence, 1939) edition of Landino, xxix; Munari, p. 297.

13. According to Zorzanello, Verino (identified as the copyist also in Latin) oddly makes his name *Ougoulēnous Beroinous* in transliterated Greek form; according to Perosa and Munari, *Ougolēnous Beroinous*. One might have expected *Ougoleinos Bereinos*.

14. *Carlias* (surveyed by Lazzari on pp. 153–85) has been edited by N. Thurn (Munich, 1995), who has further provided it with a commentary, published in 1998 (see Bibliography). Thurn considers that Verino began work on *Carlias* as early as 1465–66. Thurn's edition is reviewed by F. Bausi, *Bibliothèque d'Humanisme et Renaissance* 61 (1999): 803–5. In an elegy (of 1473) addressed to Bartolomeo della Fonte (or Fonzio, 1445–1513) and first published in *Bartholomaeus Fontius: Carmina*, ed. I. Fògel and L. Jahasz (Leipzig, 1932), Politian refers to Verino so (ll. 59–61): "Thus, having [that is, like Landino] already discharged your debts to the Medici family, you now compose your *Carliad*, Ugolino, your *Carliad*, than which there is no work more outstanding in progress in our time in Latium, as far as I can see." In spite of Politian's words there, *Carlias* brought Verino no great acclaim or reward when it eventually came out in its various forms (Bausi thinks the underlying reason was probably that by the 1480s it was not in keeping with prevailing poetic tastes in Florence). In line 36 of the poem already cited, Politian refers to "my Verino," as, it seems, having celebrated Lorenzo de' Medici's victory in the great joust held in Florence on February 7, 1469, where Lucrezia Donati (2.43n) was Queen of the Tournament, and in line 199 Politian names Verino again, as present among a learned gathering listening, it appears, to the Greek teacher Andronicus Callistus. In 1473 the young Politian (born 1454) evidently thought well of Verino. He also wrote a sympathetic epigram on the death of Verino's son, Michele (*Latin Epigr.* 83). *Carlias* includes visits to Hell, Purgatory, and Heaven.

15. These have been edited by F. Bausi (see Bibliography). In 1.3 of these epigrams, Verino stresses to his dedicatee, Corvinus, how these "chaste" poems are free from obscenity, mention Minerva more than Venus, and "sound nothing save Christ." Here, he says, the Muses drink not from (the pagan) Hippocrene, but from baptismal fonts and the waters of the holy Jordan.

16. *Riccio* in Italian = "curly-haired"; *crinitus* = "long-haired" in Latin.

17. See Bibliography. In 1998 I regrettably overlooked Bartolini's 1679 text of *Paradise*. Alerted to that omission by Professor Hankins, I have now taken full account of its readings. I thank both the British Library and the Vatican Library for supplying copies of Bartolini's text.

FIAMMETTA

PARADISE

FIAMMETTA

LIBER PRIMUS

: I :

Ad Laurentium Medicem

Laurenti Medices, Lydi spes certa Leonis,
    hoc tibi devotum suscipe laetus opus.
Exiguo quamvis teneros ludamus amores
    carmine, nec grandis spiritus ore sonet,
5   attamen inserui nonnumquam seria ludis,
    ne levis ex omni parte libellus eat;
et, licet angusta modularer carmen avena,
    saepe pater tuus est et mihi dictus avus.
Hunc tu si dignum Medicos habitare penates
10   duxeris atque tuos inter habere libros,
tunc mala vesani contemnet scommata vulgi
    et Medica vivet tutus in arce diu.
Sin, castigatus penitus, non impleat aures
    atque aliquo infirmus claudicet ille loco,
15 ignoscas, oro, nimium iuvenilibus annis,
    et tantum ingenii semina cerne mei;
nam mihi quinta licet vixdum contingere lustra
    vitae, et iam nobis excidit istud opus.
Quod si Pegaseo nitidus se in fonte libellus

FIAMMETTA

BOOK ONE

: I :

To Lorenzo de' Medici

Lorenzo de' Medici, sure hope of the Lydian Lion,
    accept with joy this work dedicated to you.
Though I playfully tell of tender amours in trivial song,
    and no grand breath sounds from my lips,
yet I have sometimes worked serious matters in with my trifles   5
    to save my book from being entirely frivolous;
and though I may play my song on a narrow reed,
    I have made frequent mention of your father and grandfather.
If you think this book of mine worthy to reside in the Medici
    household
    and fit to have among the volumes in your library,   10
then it will hold in contempt the wicked scoffing of the mad
    crowd,
    and it will long live secure in the Medici stronghold.
But if, when checked through for errors, it should not satisfy
    your ears
    and should limp along lamely anywhere,
pray be forgiving of my very youthful years   15
    and imagine these as but the seeds of my inspiration;
for I am barely yet permitted to reach the fifth lustrum of my life,
    and already I have brought forth this work.
Yet if my little book sparkles blemish free, having bathed in
    Pegasus' fountain,

20   abluit, et nostri si placuere sales,
       tunc dabit ingenio haec tantas fiducia vires
         ut tentem altiloquo grandia ferre pede.
       Per te, Laurenti, laurus Parnassia floret,
         cum faveas doctis, doctus et ipse, viris.
25 Praestitit hoc Petrus et magni clementia Cosmi
         semper, ut egregios tollat ad astra viros.
       Sic Medicum toto nomen celebrabitur orbe,
         nec finem imponet laudibus ulla dies.

: II :

Ad lectorem, quod quisque sequitur
cui est natura aptus

Hos quicumque meos tanges, studiose, libellos,
     contractae frontis pone supercilium.
Lascivis elegis dulces cantantur amores,
     unde suum nomen flebile carmen habet.
5 Saeva Sophocleo cantanda tragoedia versu est,
     magna Maroneis bella sonanda tubis,
ipsa Menandreo gaudet comoedia socco,
     in lyricis Sappho est femina prima modis
(cum lyricis elegos pariter dedit illa sonoros,
10   docta Cupidineos illa referre pedes);
grandius Alcaeus plectro pulsavit eburno,
     non tamen auratam dulcius ille lyram.
Omnia divini non possunt dicere vates;
     uni cuique Deus plusve minusve dedit.

and if my wit has pleased you,   20
then that assurance will give me the confidence of mind
    to attempt to recount grand themes in elevated meter.
Through you, Lorenzo, Parnassus' laurel flourishes,
    since you favor the learned, being learned yourself.
Piero, and great Cosimo too in his kindness, have always made it   25
    their way
    to raise men of exceptional ability to the stars.
So the Medici name will be celebrated all over the world,
    and no day will put an end to its praise.

: II :

To the reader, that everyone pursues the thing
to which he is by nature suited

Whoever you are, studious reader, who will take in hand these
    poems of mine,
    put aside that stern look on your knitted brow.
Sweet loves are sung in wanton elegies,
    and that is how a tearful song gets its name.
Grim tragedy must be sung in Sophoclean verse,   5
    great wars should be sounded with Maro's trumpets,
comedy for its part delights in Menander's slipper,
    while in lyric measures Sappho is the foremost woman
(along with lyrics she gave us sonorous elegies,
    skilled as she was at composing Cupid's measures);   10
Alcaeus struck his golden lyre more grandly
    with the ivory plectrum, but not more sweetly.
Divine poets cannot make every theme their own;
    God has given to each either more or less.

15   Hic melius pugnam canit, aptius alter amorem,
       et pariter laude est dignus uterque sua.
    Historias alius scribit sermone soluto,
       antiquae exscrutans nobilitatis opus.
    Hic nitidis stellis caelatum dicet Olympum
20   et quantum nobis sidera quidque ferant;
    ast alius melius spirantia marmora ducit,
       moreque Iapetidae pollice fingit humum.
    Sunt et Apellea qui pingunt arte tabellas,
       vivida sunt qui nunc mollius aera trahunt;
25   ast alii sacri solvunt aenigmata iuris,
       tristibus enodant vincula caeca reis.
    Ille arma horrendi sequitur Mavortia belli,
       tranquillae et tutae hic otia pacis amat.
    Impiger ad Mauros et nigros currit ad Indos
30   mercator, fugiens pauperis omne malum.
    Deditus hic ruri civilia munera temnit,
       exculti felix ruris amoena colens.
    Quisque suae sequitur naturae semina pronus;
       omnibus hinc rerum discolor usus adest.
35   Quot vivunt homines, tot sunt diversa sequentes;
       velle nec est unum: quod cupis, ille fugit.
    Mi teneros versus Musae tribuere benignae,
       ludereque imparibus mi tribuere modis,
    dum iuvenis, dum sum flagranti pronus amori
40   (ast alios mores cana senecta feret,
    sint licet hi mores mihi nunc quos posset aperta
       quisque bonos solitus fronte probare Cato).

This man sings better of war, another more fitly of love,   15
   and each is equally worthy of his praise.
Another man writes histories in prose,
   poring over the work of illustrious men of old.
This man will tell of the star-chased heavens
   and declare how much and what the stars bring us,   20
whereas another is better at fashioning breathing marbles
   and shaping earth with his thumb like Iapetus' son.
There are those too who paint pictures with Apelles' art,
   and those who now create lifelike bronzes more delicately,
while others unravel the mysteries of sacred law   25
   and untie invisible bonds for sad defendants.
That man pursues Mars' arms of dreadful war,
   this one loves the leisurely ease of tranquil and secure peace.
The tireless merchant speeds to the Moors and the dark-skinned
      Indians,
   trying to escape all the misfortune of being poor.   30
This man scorns civil offices, giving himself to the rural life,
   and happily dwells amid the beauty of the cultivated
      countryside.
Each eagerly follows the seeds of his own nature,
   and so all lead lives unalike in character.
There are as many people pursuing different ends as there are   35
      alive,
   and there is no unanimity of ambition: what *you* wish for, *he*
      flies from.
To me the kindly Muses have assigned tender verses
   and playful composition in unequal measures,
while I am young and inclined to burning love
   (white-haired old age will bring other ways,   40
though I now possess the kind of habits that every Cato
   accustomed to approve virtuous living might wholeheartedly
      smile on).

Mens sincera manet, quamvis scribantur amores;
  materiam talem flagitat istud opus.
45 Quod tua si nostros damnat censura libellos,
  orbae cor dicam tigridis esse tibi.

: III :

Ad librum, quod nimis immature festinet ad lucem

Crede mihi, nimium properas tener ire libelle
  et fugere antiquos, tecta paterna, lares.
Impia nonne times ventosi murmura vulgi?
  Cumque velis, nequeas ipse redire domum.
5 Tristia tam docti peregrini iudicis ora
  non horres, quem sic, officiose, petis?
Vade, sed heu poteras nobiscum tutius esse.
  Deprehensis quotiens flebis, inepte, notis!

: IV :

Ad Flammettam

Ne, Flammetta, tuum mireris carmina vatem
  tam subito sumpta concinuisse lyra.
Non haec Aonides dictant, pia turba, puellae,
  quae iuga Gorgoneo fonte rigata colunt,

8

My mind is pure, though love is my theme;
   the nature of my work demands this subject matter.
And if your censure condemns my poems,   45
   I will say that you have the heart of a tigress robbed of her
      young.

: III :

To his book, that it hastens too prematurely to the light

Believe me, tender little book, you are in too great a hurry to be
      gone
   and to fly your old home, your father's house.
Are you not afraid of the wicked mutterings of the fickle crowd?
   Wish as you may, there would be no returning home for you.
Do you not shudder at the stern face of the "outsider" judge, so   5
      learned,
   to whom you thus head off, all eager to please?
Go, but (alas) you could have stayed here with me more safely.
   How often you will weep, silly thing, once your flaws have
      been detected!

: IV :

To Fiammetta

Do not wonder, Fiammetta, at your poet
   so suddenly taking up his lyre and singing songs to its strains.
It is not the Aonians, that holy band, who dictate these words to me,
   they who dwell on the ridges watered by the Gorgon's fountain;

5 non mihi Parnassi gemino sub vertice Phoebus
   dictitat, aetherii qui regit astra poli,
  sed, mea qui flavis confodit pectora telis,
   purpureus nobis verba ministrat Amor.
  Nam te cum vidi, subito, o pulcherrima rerum,
10 quam sensi ardentes ire per ossa faces!
  Inscius obstupui tanti quae causa furoris
   esset, et insomnis cur ego semper eram,
  donec Acidalia pulcher cum matre Cupido
   dixit, et ardoris reddita causa mei est.
15 Sidereas postquam aspexi tua lumina flammas,
   quae mihi Phoebeae lampadis instar erant,
  cum faciem vidi nitidam flavosque capillos
   (Phoebe, tuas possent qui superare comas),
  principium hinc lacrimae nostrique habuere dolores,
20 nequitiae inde meae tristis origo fuit.
  Me miserum! Quid agam? Magno pudor obstat amori.
   Me sancti mores, me tua forma rapit,
  sed timeo famam, terrent me scommata vulgi.
   Iactor ut in tumidis concita navis aquis,
25 quam gelidus vexat Boreas Eurusque protervus,
   quam rapidus Zephyrus, quam niger Auster agunt.
  Sic agor infelix, variis sic pectora curis
   vexantur, misero non datur ulla quies.
  Ante meos oculos fulgens tua semper imago est,
30 formaque mente mea cernitur usque tua;

it is not Phoebus who dictates to me beneath Parnassus' twofold 5
 peak,
 he who rules the stars of the ethereal sky,
but it is rosy Love, piercing my breast with his golden arrows,
 who furnishes me with words.
For when I saw you, O you most beautiful being in creation,
 how I felt the burning torches instantly pass through my 10
 bones!
I was astounded, not knowing the cause of such madness
 and why I was constantly sleepless,
until handsome Cupid, together with his Acidalian mother, told
 me,
 and the reason for my passion was explained.
The moment I beheld those star-like flames that are your eyes, 15
 which were like Phoebus' torch to me,
the moment I saw your radiant face and flaxen hair
 (which, Phoebus, could surpass *your* locks),
that was when my tears and sorrows had their beginning,
 that was the sad start of my languishing. 20
Woe is me! What am I to do? Modesty stands in the way of my
 great love.
 Your purity of life and your beauty enrapture me,
but I fear for my reputation, and the scoffing of the crowd
 terrifies me.
 I am tossed like a ship thrown on heaving waters,
a ship that the icy north wind and the wanton easterly beset, 25
 and the rushing west wind and the black southerly drive before
 them.
So am I driven in my misfortune, and so is my heart beset with
 diverse cares;
 no rest is permitted me in my wretched state.
Constantly before my eyes is the shining image of you,
 and all the time your beauty is pictured in my thoughts; 30

et dulces risus moresque in cuncta venustos,
    denique quidquid agis, mens mea semper amat.
Seu pia Virgineam cum festis viseris aedem,
    templa Reparatae tunc coluisse iuvat.
35 Ah, quotiens furtim spectavi numquid adesses,
    cum vos urgeret turba proterva procum!
O si, mixta viris Spartanae more palaestrae,
    tractaret varios Tusca puella iocos!
Tunc flava solus tecum luctarer arena,
40   et sine te nullum perficeretur opus.
Seu nos Pieridum studiis aleremur in isdem,
    tunc ego quae legeres carmina multa darem.
Pocula plena daret nobis formosus Apollo,
    Hippocrenaeas combiberemus aquas.
45 Femineas vates non dedignata Thalia est;
    saepe harum lauro cinxit Apollo comas.
Carminibus sacrae cecinerunt multa Sibyllae,
    carmine responsum Pythia virgo dabat.
Ingenuas spretis tractarunt vilibus artes,
50   nec par materiae his defuit ingenium.
Nonne deserta suos docuit Cornelia Gracchos?
    Chrysippum erudiit quam bene docta parens!
Lesbia non Sappho (quid enim lascivius illa est?)
    dulce pharetrati lusit Amoris opus?
55 Versibus haec lyricis fidibus modulata canoris
    dixit et alternos docta puella modos.

my mind ever loves your sweet smiles and manners charming in
    every way;
  in short, it loves everything that you do.
If you should piously visit the church of the Virgin along with
    the festive throng,
  then a worshipper in Reparata's temple it is my delight to be.
Ah, how often I have secretly looked to see whether you were   35
    there,
  when a forward band of suitors was pressing you and the
    others!
O if only Tuscan maids were mixed with the men, as in the
    Spartan wrestling ground,
  and took part in the various games!
Then I alone would wrestle with you on the yellow sand,
  and no exercise would be performed without you.   40
Or if we were being schooled in the same studies of the Pierides,
  then would I give you many poems to read.
Handsome Apollo would give us full cups,
  and we would drink the waters of Hippocrene together.
Thalia has not thought women poets unworthy;   45
  Apollo has often ringed their hair with laurel.
Holy sibyls have made many pronouncements in song;
  it was in song that the Pythian priestess used to give her
    response.
Women have practiced the noble arts, spurning paltry pursuits,
  and they have not lacked the intellect to match their material.   50
Did not the bereaved Cornelia teach her sons, the Gracchi?
  How well their learned mother taught them Chrysippus!
Did not Lesbian Sappho (for what is more wanton than she?)
  amuse herself writing of quivered Love's sweet work?
Learned girl that she was, she sounded forth in lyric verses,   55
  playing on tuneful strings, and composed alternating measures
    too.

Nemo dat huic vitio quod amaverit illa Phaonem,
    vel quia Trinacrias oderit illa nurus.
Sed quid ego haec frustra? Rumpunt suspiria pectus
60   (me miserum!), inque dies saevius urget Amor.
Non Amor est herbis, non est medicabilis arte;
    decipit ille viros, decipit ille deos.
Aeripedes tauros domuit vigilemque draconem
    et messem armatam Phasis iniqua virum.
65 Omnia carminibus superavit praeter Amorem;
    sic scelerum poenas sanguinolenta dedit.
Dulichios Circes mutavit carmine nautas;
    hic lupus, iste ursus, factus et ille leo est.
Philtra Cupidineas minime vitare sagittas,
70   unius pueri nec potuere dolos.
Non opis inventor medicae, deceptus Amore,
    Admeti niveas pavit Apollo boves?
Quis deus et quantus, qui nobis tempora ponit,
    quique altum rapidis aethera currit equis!
75 Hei mihi, nulla cibi est, placidae nec cura quietis;
    somnus abit, lentus crescit in ore cibus.
Saepe mihi genitor, 'Cur es maestissimus?' inquit.
    'En age, dic taciti quae tibi causa mali est.'
Erubui tacuique diu, capitisque dolores
80   post finxi; vetuit dicere vera pudor.
Saepe tuum nomen carae pro nomine matris
    excidit, et verbis prodor ab ipse meis.
Forsitan et, minimo dum nocte sopore quiesco,
    prodidit arcanos inscia lingua sonos.

No one counts it a fault in her that she loved Phaon
    or that she hated the young women of Sicily.
But why do I say these pointless things? My sighs are bursting
    my breast
    (the misery of it!), and with each day that passes Love   60
    oppresses me more cruelly.
Love is not curable by herbs or by healing skill;
    he beguiles both men and gods.
The wicked Phasian girl mastered the brazen-hoofed bulls,
    the watchful dragon, and the armed harvest of men.
She overcame everything with her charms save Love,   65
    and so the bloody murderess paid the penalty for her crimes.
Circe transformed Ulysses' sailors with a spell;
    this man became a wolf, that a bear, and another a lion.
Philters could do nothing to save her from Cupid's arrows
    or the snares of one mere boy.   70
Did not Apollo, the inventor of the healing art, when beguiled by
    Love,
    pasture Admetus' snow-white cattle?
What a mighty god he is, setting the seasons for us,
    and speeding across the high heaven in his swift chariot!
Ah me, I have no care for food or for peaceful repose;   75
    sleep deserts me, food sticks in my mouth.
Time and again my father has said to me, "Why are you so sad?
    Come, tell me the cause of your unspoken misery."
I have blushed, long kept silence, and then pretended a headache;
    shame has forbidden me to tell the truth.   80
Often your name slips out in place of my dear mother's name,
    and I am betrayed by my very own words.
Perhaps too, while I have been asleep at night, enjoying what
    little rest I can,
    my unwitting tongue has uttered secret words.

85 Mens vigilat semper, curisque oppressa diurnis,
    per somnos solita est multa tacenda loqui.
Heu nimis insidiosa meae, Cytherea, iuventae,
    num desunt alii quos tua tela petant?
Quid tibi laudis erit miserum vicisse Verinum
90   arte, Venus? Summum dedecus istud erit.
Tuque, puer Veneris, solus qui saeva Tonantis
    fulmina contemnis, cur mea fata petis?
Parcite, ne moriar primis ego miles in annis,
    vestra sequi ut possim signa, Cupido, senex.
95 Tu quoque, quam mollis fortassis epistola laedet,
    parce: haec insanus scribere cogit amor.
Ardentis iuvenis carmen miserabile tange.
    Ad lacrimas nostras ferrea semper eris?
Tu quoque, Peneia si Daphne immitior esses,
100   flecteris precibus, Flammea Virgo, meis.
Pulchra verecundo tua tinges ora rubore;
    et mea, si nescis, ora pudore rubent.
Carmina, dedecoris quae sint praeconia nostri,
    scribam, sed nullum carmine crimen erit.
105 Hoc Grai atque Itali plures scripsere poetae,
    damnat et hos nemo. Cur ego plectar amans?
Ne falsa insani timeas dicteria vulgi;
    hic tantum biduo rumor acerbus erit.
Si bene celetur, canos adolescet in annos,
110   et nisi mors nostri finis amoris erit.

My mind is ever awake, and, oppressed by daytime cares,   85
    has been wont in my slumbers to say many things that should
      be left unsaid.
Alas, Cytherea, always plotting against my youth,
    are there no others for your shafts to target?
What glory will it bring you to vanquish poor Verino
    with your art, Venus? It will be the height of disgrace.   90
And you, Venus' boy, who alone scorn the Thunderer's
    savage bolts, why do you seek my doom?
Spare me, both of you, do not let me die in my first years as your
    soldier
    so that I may be able to follow your standards, Cupid, in old
      age.
Do you too, Fiammetta, whom perchance my tender missive will   95
    offend,
    spare me; it is mad love that makes me write these things.
Take in hand the pitiable poem of a burning youth.
    Will you be forever iron-hearted to my tears?
Even if you were harsher than Peneus' daughter Daphne,
    you will be moved by my prayers, Flame Maiden.   100
Your fair face will be stained with a modest blush;
    my face too, if you do not know it, is red with bashful
      embarrassment.
I will write poems to proclaim my shameful state,
    but there will be no crime in my song.
Many Greek and Italian poets have penned such verse,   105
    and no one condemns them. Why should I be punished for
      being in love?
Do not fear the baseless chatter of the mad crowd;
    such gossip will sting for but two days.
Should our attachment be well concealed, it will mature all
    through our gray-haired years,
    and nothing but death will be the end of our love.   110

: V :

De Xandra et Flammetta puellis Florentinis

Roma licet iactet pulchras habuisse puellas,
    quarum nunc tantum nomen inane manet,
Cynthia vel Nemesis, Romanae gloria gentis,
    Xandrae cesserunt illa vel illa tamen.
5 At nunc, quae nostro celebrata est carmine virgo,
    Flammetta, Etruscae gloria gentis erit.

: VI :

Quod in horrida hieme amore calescat, ad Flammettam

Iam gelidus Boreas Arninas contrahit undas,
    pigraque Sithonia iam tegit arva nive;
cumque suos sistunt veloces flumina cursus,
    nunc in navali sicca carina latet.
5 Nunc volucres silvis condunt se et carmine nullo
    nec querulis mulcent frondea rura modis.
Stat pecus in stabulis, recubat peronatus ad ignem
    pastor, brumali sidere cuncta rigent.
Me solum flammae rapiunt, me fervidus ignis
10 urit, et in tanto frigore fervet amor.
Sed nimis ah verum sumpsit de nomine flammae
    Flammetta, ardoris maxima flamma mei!

: V :

On Sandra and Fiammetta, Florentine girls

Though Rome may boast that she had beautiful girls,
    of whom all that now remains are empty names,
yet Cynthia or Nemesis, the glory of the Roman race,
    have, both of them alike, yielded to Sandra.
But now the girl who has been celebrated in my verse,   5
    Fiammetta, will be the glory of the Etruscan race.

: VI :

How he is hot with love in harsh winter, to Fiammetta

Now the chill north wind freezes the waters of the Arno
    and covers the dormant fields with Sithonian snow;
and as the rivers halt their swift flowing,
    now the dry hull is safely laid up in the dockyard.
Now the birds hide away in the woods and cheer the leafy   5
    countryside
    with no song or plaintive melodies.
The flock stands in the pens, the rough-booted shepherd reclines
    by the fire,
    and all is frozen stiff in the wintry season.
It is only I whom flames consume and blazing fire burns,
    and amid such intense cold my love glows hot.   10
But, Fiammetta, my passion's mighty flame,
    is alas all too truly named after flame!

Ecce, nive aspersum potuit me quisque videre,
    torqueret pilas cum nivis illa mihi.
15 Saeva nimis, numquam dum torquet dixit amice,
    'Accipe quod gratum munus habere velis.'
Inter mille procos sed cum millesimus essem,
    ultima vix tecum pars in amore fui.
Hei mihi, rivalem nunc hunc, nunc aspicis illum;
20   frigidius glacie tunc mihi pectus erat;
et tamen in gelido caluerunt pectore flammae;
    tempore sic uno frigus et ardor erat.
Non decet esse levem, cum sis formosa, puella;
    tincta verecundo forma pudore placet.
25 Si vis (crede mihi), longum iungemus amorem;
    una fides ambos, unus habebit amor.
Miretur tardo repens pede curva senecta
    felices uno nos simul esse toro.
Etsi Tithoni, Pylii si Nestoris annos
30   vivere Fata sinant, tu mea semper eris.
Non me Mathusalem, non aetas tota Sibyllae
    mutabit, maneas dummodo fida mihi.
Si qua fides rebus Dictaei est danda tyranni,
    nos simul ad virides ibimus Elysios.
35 Est locus irrigui viridis prope fluminis undam,
    frondibus assiduis arboribusque nitens,
quem circum maculis volitat signata cruentis
    pectus iam Prog
nes, ales amica viris,
atque, oblita trucis Tereos, Philomena canoros
40   sub densis umbris concinit ore sonos.

There I was: everyone could see me sprinkled with snow
    when she was throwing snowballs at me.
Cruel girl, as she was pelting me, she never said lovingly,   15
    "Take the welcome gift that you would like to have."
But though I was the thousandth among a thousand suitors,
    I was hardly the least with you in love.
Ah me, now you consider this rival, now that.
    Then my heart was colder than ice,   20
and yet in my chill breast flames blazed,
    so that at one and the same time there was cold and heat.
For all your beauty, it does not become you to be flighty, girl;
    beauty pleases when it is imbued with a bashful modesty.
If you are willing—believe me—we shall love each other long;   25
    one faithful bond, one love will possess us both.
Stooping old age, creeping along on tardy foot,
    will marvel that we are happy together in one bed.
Even if the Fates should permit me to live the years of Tithonus
    or of Pylian Nestor, you will always be mine.   30
The whole lifespan of Methuselah or of a Sibyl
    will not change me, provided that you remain faithful to me.
If one should give any credence to what is said of the Dictaean
      king,
    we shall go together to the green fields of Elysium.
There is a verdant place beside the water of a flowing river,   35
    cheerfully blooming with evergreen foliage and trees,
and round that place, her breast now marked with bloodstains,
    flies Progne, a bird friendly to humankind,
and, forgetting cruel Tereus, Philomena sings out tuneful strains,
    giving voice beneath the trees' dense shade.   40

Has inter fluvialis olor, gratissima Phoebo
    ales, et humani psittacus oris adest.
His nos carminibus silvas habitemus opacas,
    in quibus assiduis murmurat aura sonis,
45 nec quisquam nostros aderit qui turbet amores;
    valle sub Elysia nullus adulter erit.
Sed modo rivales, moneo, depelle protervos;
    fac solus placeam, nam mihi sola places.

: VII :

Ad Laeliam, Tranchedini vatis amicam

Parce tuo vati, precor, o pulcherrima rerum
    Laelia, ne tantum saeviat asper Amor.
Ille tui formam cecinit moresque genusque,
    fama tui ut fines transeat Italiae.
5 Non niger ille dies, non ullum subtrahet aevum
    lucentes oculos, sidera bina, tuos.
Te nunc formosam venturaque saecula dicent,
    vatis eris quoniam carmine nota tui.
Quis nosset Nemesim, quis nunc te, Cynthia, ferret
10   forma caelicolas exsuperasse deas,
si Nautae aut culti tacuissent scripta Tibulli?
    Utraque Lethaeis mersa iaceret aquis.
Candida, disce igitur sanctos adamare poetas,
    et Tranchedino, Laelia, parce tuo.

With them are the river swan, the bird dearest to Phoebus,
    and the parrot that can mimic human speech.
With these songs around us we shall dwell in shady woods
    where a breeze maintains an ever-murmuring hum,
and there will be none present to disturb our love;   45
    in the Elysian valley there will be no adulterer.
Do but drive away forward rivals, I charge you;
    see that I alone please you, for you alone please me.

: VII :

To Lelia, the girl friend of the poet Tranchedini

Have mercy on your poet, I beg you, Lelia, most beautiful being
    in creation,
    so that harsh Love may not deal so cruelly with him.
He has sung of your beauty, character, and birth,
    making fame of you pass beyond the borders of Italy.
Neither the black day of death nor any passage of time   5
    will take away your bright eyes, those two stars.
This present age and those to come will call you beautiful,
    since you will be known through your poet's song.
Who would know of Nemesis or now say that you, Cynthia,
    once surpassed the goddesses of heaven in beauty,   10
if the writings of Nauta or of elegant Tibullus had been silent?
    Both those women would lie submerged in Lethe's waters.
Learn then, fair Lelia, to love holy poets,
    and have mercy on your Tranchedini.

: VIII :

In lenas et avaras puellas

Blanditiis, lenae, miseros lactatis amantes.
　　Foedera cur auro post laceranda datis,
nec iurata movent sanctorum numina divum?
　　Heu, periura audet fallere lingua deos!
5　Fallere lascivae per vos didicere puellae,
　　promissae noctis commaculare fidem.
Per vos saepe suum mater deplorat alumnum
　　plus solito sera nocte redire domum;
periurae ad postes nam dum pernoctat amicae,
10　　pro nato genetrix anxia vota facit.
Coniuge quin etiam tenera persaepe relicta,
　　pervigilat sponsus paelicis ante fores.
Ah, cur, caelestes, formam praebetis avarae?
　　Dulcia cur tanto pocula felle madent?
15　Nunc simulant flentes viridem cecidisse smaragdum,
　　coniugis imperium nunc timet illa sui.
Non ut des orant, utenda sed omnia poscunt.
　　Hoc uno culpam nomine saepe tegunt;
saepeque venturae fallunt in nocte morantes—
20　　O quantis nox est haec vigilanda malis!

: VIII :

On bawds and greedy girls

With your wheedling words, bawds, you dupe poor lovers.
    Why do you make bargains for gold just to tear them up later,
and why do oaths sworn by the sanctity of holy saints mean
        nothing to you?
    Alas, your perjured tongue dares to take the names of deities
        in vain!
Wanton girls have learned through you to practice deceit   5
    and to dishonor the promise of a night together.
Because of you a mother often bewails her darling boy,
    returning home later at night than usual;
for while he spends its duration at the door of his forsworn girl,
    his mother says anxious prayers for her son's safety.   10
More than that, very often a wedded husband leaves his young
        wife
    and keeps vigil before the portal of his mistress.
Ah, why, powers of heaven, do you bestow beauty on a greedy
        woman?
    Why do sweet cups drip with such bitter gall?
Now these girls are in tears pretending that an emerald has fallen   15
        out;
    now one of them fears her husband's tyranny.
They do not ask you to *give*, but press for everything as a *loan*.
    With this one word they often cover up their guilt;
and often, when due to show, they stand up the men who wait in
        the night for them —
    oh, in what great torments must such a night be watched out!   20

Aspera sub gelido miseris stat sidere palla,
 brumali torpent frigida membra Iove,
iam iam ventura deceptus donec ab ortu
 iubaris invisam cogitur ire domum.
25 Quid lacrimare iuvat, quid blandas fundere voces?
  Muneribus solum pandit avara fores.
Nam si grande feras pretium, pandentur aperti
 postes, in Tyrio suscipiere toro.
Tisiphone has agitet sub tristia Tartara lenas
30 et quae prostrato corpore quaerit opes!
 Sint licet in vita, poenas de crimine sumat!
  Sit spes, eventus asperiora dabit!

: IX :

Ad amicum de imperio Amoris

Quid mihi Pierides prosunt, quid pulcher Apollo?
 Quid iuvat Aonios perdidicisse sonos?
Quid iuvat, ad surdam si nos cantamus amicam?
 Quid iuvat incassum carmina tanta dare?
5 Nil bona fortunae prosunt sine amore secundo;
 heu, quantis curis pectora vexat amor!
Quid iuvat Attalico somnum perquirere lecto?
 Pro somno lacrimae fluminis instar eunt.

The poor wretches find their cloaks frozen stiff with the icy
    weather,
  and their chilled limbs go numb with the winter's cold,
till now the dupe, disappointed by the girl he was sure would
    come at any moment,
  is forced by the breaking day's brightness to go off to his hated
    home.
What good does it do to cry or to pour out coaxing words?   25
  The greedy girl opens up only for gifts.
For if you bring her a great sum of money, the doors will be
    thrown wide open;
  you will be welcomed on a bed draped with Tyrian coverlets.
May Tisiphone drive these bawds down to grim Tartarus
  and any girl out to get rich by prostituting her body!   30
Even while they yet live, may that avenger punish them for their
    wrongdoing!
  Let us hope that time to come will inflict harsher retribution!

: IX :

To a friend on the domineering power of Love

What good are the Pierides and handsome Apollo to me?
  What good does it do me to have mastered Aonian verse?
What good is it, if I am singing to a girl who is deaf to me?
  What good does it do to compose so many songs in vain?
Fortune's gifts are useless without success in love.   5
  Alas, with how many cares does love trouble the heart!
What good is it to seek sleep in a bed draped like that of
    Attalus?
  In place of sleep tears flow like a river.

Scilicet insomnis perduces tempora noctis,
10   atque erit ardenti lux odiosa tibi.
Iuppiter, in terris misero quid vivit amante
    durius, aut quod par condicione malum est?
Ludibrium sumus, et nullus miseratur amantem.
    Heu, prima est miseris poena parata viris!
15 Fabula per populum, per compita cuncta volamus;
    designat digitis nos quoque turba suis.
Si quando maestum quatiunt suspiria pectus,
    cum mihi singultu tristia verba cadunt.
Dum queror ad durum fallacis limen amicae,
20   ne promissa rapax irrita ventus agat,
tunc quidem irridens affatur voce Tonantem:
    'Fac pereat, postquam sponte perire cupit.'
Flamina nos gelidi Boreae, pluvialis et Austri,
    intrepidi et patimur fulmina missa Iove.
25 Caeruleus si quando arcus denuntiat imbres,
    tunc neque venturam nos trepidamus aquam;
perque nives altas, per summa cacumina montis
    imus, et hiberno frigore torpet humus,
nosque per ardentes miseri decurrimus ignes,
30   ferventis cum sol astra Leonis adit.
Nullum est discrimen quod non subeamus amantes;
    vah, miser est quem tu, saeve Cupido, premis!
Lurida rimosa tranavit flumina cymba
    ut privet Ditem coniuge Pirithous.

Doubtless you will pass the whole night in wakefulness,
   and the light of day will be hateful to you in your burning   10
      passion.
Jupiter, what creature has a harder life on earth than the poor
      lover,
   or what evil can match his plight?
We are a laughingstock, and no one pities a lover.
   Alas, the worst torment has been devised for us poor men!
We fly, the talk of the town, through the populace and all the   15
      crossroads,
   and the crowd point us out with their fingers.
If ever sighs shake my sorrowful breast,
   sad words fall from me as I sob.
Even as I complain on the hard threshold of my deceitful girl,
   pleading that the wind may not whisk away her promises   20
      unkept,
she just laughs and says to the Thunderer,
   "Let him die, since dying is what he wants to do."
We lovers bravely bear the blasts of the icy north wind and of the
      rain-bringing south
   and endure the thunderbolts launched by Jupiter.
If ever a purple rainbow foretells showers,   25
   then we do not fear the downpour to come.
We go through deep snow and over the highest mountaintops,
   though the ground is stiff with the winter's cold;
and we poor wretches run through blazing fires,
   when the sun draws near the constellation of the scorching   30
      Lion.
There is no danger that we lovers would not face.
   Alas, wretched is he whom you oppress, cruel Cupid!
Pirithous floated over ghastly rivers in a leaky boat
   in order to despoil Dis of his wife.

35 Solus Amor tumidi contempsit Apollinis arcus,
    Herculis et sprevit robora solus Amor.
  Hic Pythona licet torvum, licet ille Leonem
    fixerit, hos potuit vincere solus Amor.
  Ergo Cupidineae vincunt si cuncta pharetrae,
40   cur comes aeternis conqueror esse deis?

: X :

Ad Petrum Vectorium de amore

  Quid iuvat immitis Martis fugitare catervas,
    cum graviora mihi bella Cupido paret,
  si neque lunatis volui me credere castris,
    nam satis hac pugna est dimicuisse mihi?
5 O quantum satius forti succumbere bello
    quam sic ignavi tabe perire mali!
  Nec parere queo, vinclis constrictus Amoris,
    Vectori, monitis, dulcis amice, tuis.
  Infelix tali volui servire puellae
10   morteque servitium durius usque pati.
  Ipse meum flava percussit harundine pectus
    contorsitque faces insidiosus Amor;
  plumbea Flammettae praefixit corda sagitta,
    unde fit ut nullis ardeat illa focis;
15 nec cura hanc tenet ulla mei, sed spernit amorem.
    Me fugit ut rapidos hirta capella lupos,
  ut fugit Hyrcanas nemorosa per avia tigres
    cervus, ut accipitrem Cypria vitat avis.

Love alone held proud Apollo's bow in contempt,   35
    and the only one to scorn the might of Hercules was Love.
Though the one transfixed the grim Python, and the other the
        Lion,
    Love and Love alone could overcome them.
Therefore, if Cupid's quivers are all-conquering,
    why do I complain at keeping company with eternal gods?   40

: X :

To Piero Vettori on love

What good does it do me to fly the battalions of cruel Mars,
    when Cupid prepares worse wars for me,
or if I have refused to trust myself to a crescent-shaped camp,
    since fighting in *this* battle is enough for me?
O how much better to succumb in brave warfare   5
    than to perish from wasting away with this craven affliction!
And yet I cannot follow your advice,
    Vettori, sweet friend, as I am held fast in Love's chains.
Hapless wretch that I am, I *wanted* to be a slave to such a girl
    and ever to endure a servitude harsher than death.   10
Treacherous Love shot my breast with his golden arrow
    and hurled his torches at me.
He pierced Fiammetta's heart with an arrow of lead,
    causing her to burn with no fires;
she feels no care for me, but spurns my love.   15
    She flies me as a shaggy nanny goat flies ravening wolves,
as a stag flies Hyrcanian tigresses through the forested wilderness,
    or as the Cyprian's bird avoids the hawk.

Candida nam teneris ludit cum virgo puellis,
20 additur heu tantis mater iniqua malis.
Ah, quotiens nobis clausit stomachosa fenestras,
 me quoque praesente hanc non sinit ire foras.
Desine, victa situ mater turpique senecta;
 Flammettae ne sis invidiosa tuae.
25 At te mille proci quondam petiere protervi,
 ante tuos postes maxima rixa fuit.
Sic fraudas miserae tempus iuvenile puellae?
 Cur, natura sibi quae dedit, ipsa rapis?
Non est flagitium teneras adamare puellas,
30 dedecus haud Veneri est tempora prima dare,
conveniuntque graves mores gravioribus annis.
 Hoc fateor: senibus turpe daretur amor.
Nunc amet haec, vel se tantum patiatur amari;
 me semper pura noscet amare fide.

: XI :

Visio quaedam

Roscida purpureis surgens Aurora quadrigis
 ad solitum lucis iam properabat iter,
lampade iam crocea Titan spargebat Eoos,
 cum subito haec oculis visa fuere meis:
5 visus eram Aonio recubans dormire sub antro,
 Gorgoneae irriguus qua fluit umor aquae.
Tunc vidi innumeras circum me errare puellas
 quae forma possent aequiperare deas;

For whenever the fair maid is at play with the young girls,
    alas, a hostile mother is added to my many woes.   20
Ah, how many times she has peevishly closed the windows on me,
    and she will not let her daughter go out when I am there.
Desist, mother faded by decay and ugly old age;
    do not be envious of your Fiammetta!
There was a time when a thousand forward suitors sought *you*,   25
    and great quarrels erupted in front of *your* doors.
Would you so cheat a poor girl of her time of youth?
    Why do *you* rob her of what nature has given her?
It is no disgrace to love young girls,
    it is no shame to give one's first years of youth to Venus,   30
and grave conduct becomes graver years.
    This I concede: love would be disgraceful in the old.
Let her love *now*, or let her but allow herself to be loved;
    she will learn that I love her always with pure-hearted
        faithfulness.

: XI :

A vision

Dewy Aurora, rising in her crimson four-horse chariot,
    was already hastening to make her usual light-bringing journey,
and the Titan was already streaming rays from his yellow torch
       on the peoples of the east,
    when suddenly my eyes beheld this vision:
I dreamed that I was reclining in sleep beneath the Aonian cave,   5
    where the gushing stream of the Gorgon's spring has its flow.
Then I saw countless girls wandering around me,
    girls who could equal goddesses in beauty.

vidi et cornigeros Faunos Nymphasque fugaces
10   et Dryades mixtos ludere saepe choros.
Pars citharam pulsant, saltant pars, carmina dicunt;
    quaelibet officio est apta puella suo.
Has inter memini ternas vidisse sorores,
    nil quibus affirmo posse decere magis.
15 Ni fallor, Charites fuerant hae, nam sine zona
    et visa a geminis tertia semper erat.
Aureus interea curru vehebatur eburno
    Phoebus, et in medio constitit ille iugo,
iussit et electas pariter considere Nymphas,
20   namque novem Musis hic comitatus erat.
Tunc et capripedes Satyri timidaeque Napaeae
    atque assurrexit cetera turba sibi.
Ut reor, hic fuerat certe formosus Apollo,
    carmine namque mihi est cognitus ille suo.
25 Quid referam qualis iuvenili in corpore forma
    emicuit, quo nil pulchrius esse potest?
Caesaries illi per cycnea colla fluebat,
    colla tamen cycnis candidiora tegens.
Lumina quid dicam praebentia lumina mundo,
30   ut roseus niveis sit color usque genis,
insignisque auro gemmisque ornatus Eois,
    tinctaque bis Tyrio murice vestis erat?
Ut stetit in medio iussitque silentia, cuncti
    auribus intentis conticuere simul.

I saw also horned fauns, skittish nymphs,
    and dryads merrily performing mixed dances again and again.   10
Some beat the lyre, some danced and sang songs;
    every girl was suited to her role.
Among these girls I remember seeing three sisters;
    nothing, I swear, could be lovelier than they.
Unless I am mistaken, these were the Graces; for one of the three   15
      had no girdle,
    and the gaze of the other two was always on her.
Meanwhile golden Phoebus was riding in a chariot of ivory,
    and, halting on top of a ridge,
he bade chosen nymphs take their places there with him,
    for he was attended by the nine Muses.   20
Then goat-footed satyrs and timid dell nymphs
    and the rest of the gathering stood up to honor him.
This, I am sure, was handsome Apollo,
    for I recognized him by his song.
Why should I recount the beauty that shone forth in his youthful   25
      body,
    than which nothing can be fairer?
His hair was flowing over a swanlike neck,
    yet covering a neck whiter still than swans.
Why should I tell of his eyes that supply light to the world,
    or describe how rosy the color was all over his snow-white   30
      cheeks,
and how his garb was adorned with gold and gems of the east,
    and his raiment twice dyed with Tyrian purple?
When he had positioned himself in the middle of the throng and
      had called for silence,
    all ceased talking as one, according him their full attention.

35 Tunc citharae auratae pulsavit pectine chordas
cumque lyra pariter talia verba dedit: —

'Sunt gemini fratres, Medicum pulcherrima proles,
fulgida qui nostrum nomen in astra ferent.
Nec tales umquam Florentia cernet alumnos,
40 sit licet haec claris nobilitata viris,
nec satis his fuerit maiorum gloria, quamvis
nota sit in multis stirps generosa locis.
Qualis avus proavusque fuit, mora longa referre est,
quilibet istorum sed superabit avos.
45 Dummodo Pieridum dulci raptentur amore,
et nostra cingi tempora fronde velint,
hos tu, Castaliis stillat qua fontibus unda,
educes placido, Calliopea, sinu.
Hinc tibi maior erit nati quam gloria vatis,
50 Ismarii aut nobis gloria magna Lini.
Quare agite, Aonides, vigiles impendite curas,
crescet enim parvo munere vester honor.
Sic per Tyrrhenas celebres cantabimur urbes,
praesertim Tuscus qua tenet arva Leo;
55 nam fore dixerunt Italis caput urbibus illam
ac primum Ausoniae Fata tenere locum.'

Vix haec aurato plectro cantarat Apollo,
visio me pariter destituitque sopor.

Then he beat the strings of his gilt lyre with a plectrum, 35
    and as he played it, he gave voice to these words: —

"There are two brothers, the fairest offspring of the Medici,
    who will carry our name to the gleaming stars.
Florence will never see such nurslings again,
    distinguished though she is for men of high renown, 40
nor will the glory of their ancestors satisfy this pair,
    though their noble stock is famed in many parts.
What manner of men their grandsire and great-grandsire were, it
      would be long to tell,
    but both of them will surpass their forebears.
Should they be seized with sweet love for the Pierides 45
    and wish their temples to be ringed with my leaves,
rear them, Calliope, in your gentle arms,
    where the water drips from the Castalian fount.
From them you will have greater glory than you have from the
      bard you bore
    or than the great glory brought to me by Ismarian Linus. 50
Therefore come, Aonians, apply yourselves watchfully to their
      care,
    for by that small service your honor will grow.
So shall we be sung and famed throughout the Tyrrhenian cities,
    especially in those regions where the Tuscan Lion holds sway,
for the Fates have decreed that that city will head the cities of 55
      Italy
    and have assigned her pride of place in Ausonia."

Scarcely had Apollo delivered this song with his golden plectrum,
    when the vision and my slumber left me together.

: XII :

Ad Cherubinum, cur iocosa scribat

Nuper audentem Veneris Cupido
filius pressit, fidibus canoris
ne canam heroum, Cherubine, laudes
    factaque regum.

5 'Contrahas ventis rapidis phaselum
ne prius ludum tumidae procellae
praebeat quam post erit in minaci
    obruta ponto,'

dixit. 'An Thebae meruere tantum
10 dum canunt pugnas et equos Olympo
monte victores Pelopisque honore
    florea serta?

Ilion Smyrnae cecinere captum;
dixit Aeneam Rutulumque Turnum
15 nobilis linguae decus omne nostrae
    Musa Maronis.

Quid caput prodest furiale saevis
anguibus taetri canis inferorum
scribere et quidquid leve fabulosa
20   Graecia finxit?

Me duce argutam poteris puellam
flectere; et nostris Erycina coeptis
iam favet, sensit quoniam furentes
    illa sagittas.

: XII :

To Cherubino, why he writes frivolous matter

As I was lately venturing the attempt, Venus' son Cupid
restrained me from singing on tuneful strings,
Cherubino, of the exploits of heroes
    and the deeds of kings.

"Shorten sail when rushing winds rage,   5
lest your boat provide sport for the swelling storm
before being overwhelmed and sunk
    in the menacing sea,"

he told me. "Did Thebes gain so much
from singing of fights, of horses victorious   10
by Mount Olympus, and of flowery garlands
    in honor of Pelops?

Smyrna sang of captured Ilium;
the story of Aeneas and Rutulian Turnus
was told by the great glory of our tongue,   15
    Maro's noble Muse.

What good does it do to write of the frightful head
of the Underworld's foul dog, with its savage snakes,
and of all the other trifles myth-telling
    Greece has contrived?   20

Serve under me, and you will be able to sway
a clever girl. Even the goddess of Eryx
now favors my activities, since she has felt
    my raging arrows.

25 Quid novem possent melius Camenae
vel tibi pulcher dare nunc Apollo,
ornet hic quamvis hedera virenti
    tempora vatum?

Ipse Flammettae nitidos ocellos
30 et canes laetas Dryadum choreas,
insequi et Faunos celeres Napaeas
    montibus altis.

Hinc tibi aeternas sine fine laudes
quae colit Cypron genetrix decora
35 et tuum toto volitare nomen
    iam dabit orbe.'

Dixit haec et plura mihi Cupido.
Annuit Phoebus, simul et sorores
quae colunt rupes Heliconis alti
40   dicta probarunt.

∴ XIII ∴

Quod nihil prosint Musae in amore

Quid iuvat ingenium, doctae quid carminis artes?
    Quid prodest Phoebus Pieridumque chorus?
Iam celebris nostris nimis est Flammetta libellis.
    Vah, misero nocuit Musa iocosa mihi!
5 Quam cepi solus quondam, quam solus amavi,
    nunc mihi cum multis est adamanda procis.

What better gift could the nine Muses   25
or handsome Apollo now give you,
however much he decorates the temples of poets
    with green ivy?

You shall sing of Fiammetta's bright eyes,
of the merry dances of dryads,   30
and of fauns swift in pursuit of dell nymphs
    on lofty mountains.

For this you will have eternal praises without end
from my comely mother who dwells on Cyprus,
and she will cause your name now to fly   35
    over all the world."

Cupid told me all this and more besides.
Phoebus nodded assent, and along with him the sisters
who dwell on the crags of lofty Helicon
    approved what had been said.   40

: XIII :

How the Muses are of no avail in love

What good are my genius and the learned arts of poetry?
    Of what avail to me are Phoebus and the band of the
        Pierides?
Now Fiammetta is too well known from my poems.
    Alas, my sportive Muse has done me harm and brought me
        misery!
The girl I once had all to myself and loved as mine and mine alone, 5
    I now must love along with many suitors.

41

Ipse ego sidereos cecini inflammatus ocellos,
    qui primum nostri causa fuere mali.
Dum cupio demens formam celebrare canendo,
10   paene meo erepta est carmine virgo mihi.
Undique nam formam iuvenes venere protervi
    virginis ut cernat turba proterva meae,
et plus quam fama his divinae gloria formae
    fulsit, et hac iurant pulchrius esse nihil.
15 Protinus it rumor totam vulgatus in urbem,
    mox Latiique volans oppida cuncta petet.
Quam mallem formosa minus, nullique placeres,
    hoc possem ut felix solus amore frui.

: XIV :

Ratiocinatio utrum ad eam accedat
a qua est exclusus

Quid faciam? Rursusne petam sua limina pulsus?
    Non mihi si totas pandat iniqua fores,
exclusit quae me multosque recepit amantes!
    Quo, Verine miser, quo periturus abis?
5 Siste! Iterum, infelix, tristem patiere repulsam,
    et quae te perdent asperiora feres.

I myself sang in the fire of my passion of the star-like eyes
    that were first the cause of my affliction.
In my eagerness, mad fool that I was, to make her beauty famous
      by singing of it,
   my girl has almost been snatched from me because of my own   10
    song.
For forward young men have come from all around,
    that impudent mob, to see my girl's good looks,
and, finding the glory of her goddess-like beauty more
      resplendent than reported,
   they vow there is nothing fairer than her loveliness.
At once rumor sets forth and spreads right through the city,   15
    and in its flight it will soon reach all the towns of Latium.
How I wish you were less beautiful and pleasing to none,
    leaving me happily able to enjoy this love alone!

: XIV :

Consideration of whether to go to her
by whom he has been shut out

What should I do? Should I return to her threshold after being
    driven away?
  No, not even if that wicked girl were to throw the doors wide
    open,
seeing how she has shut me out and admitted many lovers!
  Where, poor Verino, where are you going, just to die?
Stop! Unhappy wretch, you will suffer another cruel rejection,   5
    and you will endure harsher hurts that will be the end of you!

Quid faciam? Rapidis ventis mea navis in altum
    inque sinus rapitur, curva Malea, tuos,
nec retinere queo, violenter flantibus Euris.
10   Heu, timet infidas naufraga puppis aquas!
Ore resorbentem fluctus horresco Charybdim;
    latratus metuo, Scylla maligna, tuos.
O ego quam mallem gelidis sub montibus ortus
    aut lapis aequoreis limes adesus aquis,
15 servitium durum quam immitis ferre puellae.
    Quam miser adverso est quisquis amore perit!
Robora tu, silices superas, adamantaque durum,
    tu vincis ferrum ferrea duritie;
nam lacrimae nostrae, nisi ferrea protinus esses,
20   movissentque meae pectora dura preces.
Exstinctum flebis posthac, Flammetta, Verinum,
    et dices, 'Nimium dura puella fui.'

: XV :

Ad Leonardum Beninum

Caesaris magnos referat triumphos
alter et Parthos simul et Britannos
ire conexis humiles catenis
    bracchia vinctos.

What shall I do? My ship is borne off by rushing winds into the
    deep sea
  and into your inlets, curving Malea,
and I cannot hold it back, with easterly blasts violently blowing.
  Alas, my battered vessel fears the treacherous waters!   10
I recoil from Charybdis as she sucks back the waves with her
    mouth;
  I fear your barking dogs, evil Scylla.
O how I would sooner have been born a stone at the foot of icy
    mountains
  or at the edge of the deep, eaten away by the waters of the sea,
than suffer harsh servitude to a cruel girl!   15
  How wretched is any man who pines away with unrequited
    love!
You surpass oak trees, flint, and hard adamant
  and outdo iron, being iron yourself, in your hardness;
for, were you not made of iron through and through, my tears
    and prayers
  would have moved your hard heart.   20
You will weep in time to come for dead Verino, Fiammetta,
  and you will say, "I was too hard a girl."

: XV :

To Leonardo del Benino

Let one man tell of Caesar's triumphs
and of Parthians and Britons together
walking humbled with their arms secured
  in linked fetters.

5 Alter, argutam modulans Thaliam,
   dicat Alcidem superosque reges,
   cantat et flammas vomere e profundo
      ore Chimaeram.

   Hic tuba immensa resonet Tonantem
10 anxium bello et rapidos Gigantes,
   ut feros tandem minitans trisulci
      fulmine trivit.

   Ille vel pugnam populi biformis
   sive describat Danaas phalanges,
15 victaque ut tandem ruerint bilustri
      Pergama bello.

   Delius nam me teneras puellas
   ludere et Bacchum, Veneris sodalem,
   et nemus iussit, Leonarde, frondens
20   dulceque furtum.

   Virgines flavas puerosque pulchros
   et canam Nymphas Charitesque ternas,
   cum pede alterno Satyri choreas
      ordine ductant;

25 atque Flammettae nimios amores
   Cypridos flavae suboles Verinum
   barbiti tensis fidibus referre
      aliger urget.

Let another intone a melodious Muse   5
and tell of Alcides and of kings on high,
and sing of how the Chimaera spews flames
    from the depths of her mouth.

Let this man with mighty trumpet sound forth the Thunderer,
anxious in war, and the fierce Giants,   10
recounting how, menacing them with his three-forked
      thunderbolt,
    he at last crushed those fierce foes.

Let some other describe either the battle of the hybrid race
or the Danaan phalanxes,
and how at length Pergamum fell to its ruin   15
    in a war of twice five years.

For the Delian god has commanded *me* to write
playfully of tender girls, of Bacchus, the companion of Venus,
of leafy woods, Leonardo,
    and of sweet intrigue.   20

I will sing of golden-haired maidens, of handsome boys,
of nymphs, and of the three Graces,
when satyrs with each foot in turn
    perform dances in a line;

and the golden-haired Cyprian's winged offspring   25
prompts Verino to recount his all too deeply felt
love for Fiammetta on his lyre's
    tight-stretched strings.

: XVI :

Tetrastichon sub statua Flammettae

Cedant formosae mihi quae se in vallibus Idae
    iudicio Paridis supposuere deae.
In me congessit quidquid natura decori est,
    in caelo ut dicas pulchrius esse nihil.

: XVII :

In Gallam, anum luxuriosam et turpem

Pumilione minor, cum sit quoque nigrior Indo,
    Flammettae non vult cedere Galla meae.
Turpius hac nihil est, nihil est formosius illa;
    ista senex turpis, candida virgo mea est.
5 Nescio quo studeat pacto formosa videri,
    cum nihil hoc monstro turpius esse queat;
nec quam mane quidem, cum sol tegit astra nitore,
    per mediam velles tu reperire viam:
Alecto e tenebris infernis nempe putares
10   cinctam Tartareis anguibus esse caput.
Non cerussa tuum, non far, non quidquid in herbis
    suci est pallorem, Galla, operire valent;

: XVI :

A four-line poem beneath a statue of Fiammetta

Let the beautiful goddesses who in the valleys of Ida
   submitted themselves to Paris' judgment yield place to me.
Nature has heaped upon me all the beauty there is,
   so that you may say there is nothing fairer in heaven.

: XVII :

Against Galla, a lustful and ugly old woman

Although she is smaller than a dwarf and darker than an Indian,
   Galla is unwilling to yield place to my Fiammetta.
There is nothing uglier than the one, nothing prettier than the
     other;
   Galla is an ugly old hag; my girl, a dazzling white virgin.
I do not know how Galla means to look pretty,   5
   since nothing could be uglier than that monster.
Not even early in the morning, when the sun hides the stars with
     its brightness,
   would you want to meet her in the middle of the street.
You would surely suppose her to be Alecto from the infernal
     darkness,
   her head ringed with Tartarean serpents.   10
Not white lead, not spelt, not all the juice there is in herbs,
   can cover up your sallow complexion, Galla.

contra te facies pugnat deformis et aetas.
　　Stulta nimis, Galla, es, luxuriosa nimis.

: XVIII :

Ad Flammettam, ne tantum formae tribuat

Cur tantum formae tribuis, Flammetta, caducae,
　　cum rapido citius defluat illa Noto?
Non manet aeternum pulchris color iste puellis;
　　heu, nimium fragile est candida forma bonum!
5　Aetate aut morbo languet cito gloria formae,
　　lubrica namque annis deperit ipsa suis.
Ut flos purpureus curvo proscissus aratro,
　　sic una febri labitur iste color.
O utinam fusco potius perfusa colore,
10　dum clausas reseres sic mihi nigra, fores!
O si Medeae norim, si pocula Circes,
　　et quae dira legens Thessala coxit anus;
te postquam nullae duram flexere Camenae,
　　tentarem philtris vincere duritiem.
15　Hei mihi, quid feci? Tribui tibi, perfida, laudes
　　ingentes, quas non auferet ulla dies;
et tu, nunc chartis nostris effecta superba,
　　me flentem ante fores, saeva, manere sinis.

Your ill-favored face and your age fight against you.
    You are too foolish, Galla, too wanton in your lust.

: XVIII :

To Fiammetta, that she should not set such store by beauty

Why do you make so much of perishable beauty, Fiammetta,
    when it passes by more quickly than the speeding south wind?
That color of yours does not last forever in beautiful girls;
    alas, radiant beauty is all too fragile a boon!
Beauty's glory quickly fades with age or disease,   5
    for it slips away and perishes with its own increasing years.
Like a red flower felled by the curved plow,
    so your color fades with a single fever.
O that you were rather utterly swarthy in complexion,
    as long as, with your dark skin, you would unlock your closed   10
        doors to me!
O if only I understood Medea's potions or Circe's
    and the dreadful mixtures picked and brewed by a Thessalian
        crone;
since no Muses have swayed your hard heart,
    I would try to overcome your hardness with philters.
Alas, what have I done? I have bestowed such great praises on   15
        you,
    faithless one, as no day will take away from you,
and yet you, now made haughty by my writings,
    let me wait in tears, cruel as you are, outside your door.

Forsitan alter amor, mihi qui male favit amanti,
20   altera cura tenet, forsitan alter amor.
At mihi sub gelido torpescunt membra Boote;
        vix quantum Ismaria sub nive tristis ager.
Ferrea, non sentis Boream spirare protervum,
        strideat ut flatu iuncta fenestra Cori?
25 Auribus aspideis gemitus, suspiria, fletus
        accipis, et penitus nil tibi cura mei est.
Heu, quis servitio posset durare sub isto?
        Quis posset tanta vivere nequitia,
quam non longa fides movit? Vos sidera testor.
30   Tu, dea silvarum, Cynthia, testis ades;
nam me vidisti vigilantem et saepe gementem
        virginis ante fores nocte silente meae,
et nostrum ex alto caelo es miserata dolorem,
        horrebat vitreo cum mihi palla gelu;
35 fecisti lumen tenebrosa in nocte diurnum,
        nam tenebris maeror saevior esse solet.
Non te luctus edax nec ferrea pectora movit
        pallor qui ex nimio venit amore mihi.
Denique tu miserum coges, Flammetta, Verinum
40   immerita ante diem morte perire tuum.

Perhaps another love, which has not looked kindly on my tender
 feelings for you,
  another care has you in its grip. Perhaps another love.   20
My limbs grow numb under icy Bootes;
 the dismal countryside under Ismarian snow is not nearly so
  frozen.
Iron-hearted girl, do you not hear violent Boreas blow,
 making your fastened window shutters creak with the
  northerly blast?
To my groans, sighs, and sobs you turn ears as deaf as an asp's,   25
 and you have no concern for me at all.
Alas, who could last under such slavery as you impose?
 Who could live under such wicked heartlessness,
which enduring faithfulness has not moved? I call you stars to
 witness.
 Do you, Cynthia, goddess of the forests, be my witness too,   30
for you have seen me keep watch and groan so often
 before my girl's doors in the silence of night,
and from the heavens on high you have pitied my pain,
 when my cloak was stiff with glassy ice;
you have made daylight in the gloomy night,   35
 for sorrow is wont to be more keenly felt in darkness.
My consuming grief has not moved you, Fiammetta, nor has the
 paleness
 that has come from my great love touched your iron heart.
In short, Fiammetta, you will make your wretched Verino
 die a death he does not deserve, before his day.   40

: XIX :

Ad Petrum Medicem

Cum vacuus curis fueris pauloque severis
    amotis, laeta haec carmina fronte leges.
Inter longa iocos admittere seria prodest,
    nec semper curis invigilare iuvat.
5 Quod si forte meos laudabis, Petre, libellos,
    vertice tum feriam sidera celsa meo.

: XX :

Visio de felicitate sui saeculi

Visus eram Fesuli montis recubare sub antro,
    nobile qua Medicum sidera tangit opus.
Tunc nec Lethaeo mersit mea tempora somnus
    rore, nec omnino pervigil ipse fui.
5 Tempus erat, Tereos quo tunc Philomena tyranni
    permemor implebat questibus omne nemus,
pronaque caeruleas iam nox properabat ad undas
    fessaque mergebat astra sub aequoribus,
cum viridi Phoebus redimitus tempora fronde
10   ante oculos subito visus adesse meos.
Obstupui ut crines per candida colla fluebant,
    splendor et in toto corpore quantus erat;

: XIX :

To Piero de' Medici

When you are free from cares and find weighty matters a little
    removed from you,
  pray read these poems with a joyful face.
It does one good to allow jokes a place amid prolonged serious
    concerns,
  and it is not helpful always to be losing one's sleep over cares.
And if you chance to praise my poems, Piero,   5
  then I shall strike the stars on high with the top of my head.

: XX :

A vision concerning the felicity of his times

I dreamed I was reclining in a cave on the hill of Fiesole,
  where the noble villa of the Medici touches the stars.
Sleep did not then immerse my temples in the waters of Lethe,
  nor was I altogether wide awake.
It was the time when Philomena, fully mindful of King Tereus,   5
  was filling the whole forest with her complaints,
and the declining night was now rushing down toward the blue
    waves,
  hiding the weary stars beneath the sea's waters,
when Phoebus, his temples ringed with green foliage,
  suddenly seemed to be there before my eyes.   10
I was astounded to see how his hair flowed over his white neck
  and how great a radiance there was in his whole body.

vestis et ardebat Tyrio sibi murice tincta,
    atque erat Eoo gemma petita salo.
15 Tunc citharam auratam plectro pulsavit eburno
    et placido tales edidit ore sonos: —

'O ter felicem Medicis qui tempore Petri
    inter Sullanidas nomen habere cupis!
Gaudeat Etrusci tellus veneranda Leonis,
20   pro qua Cirrhaei liquimus antra dei,
liquimus Aonios lucos, et Thessala Tempe,
    et quae sunt Graiis nobilitata modis.
Nec Fesulos habitare pudet montesque Mugelli,
    nec pudet Etrusco fonte lavare chorum;
25 nam vivente Petro magnum speramus honorem,
    vatibus Etruscis praemia magna dari.
Haec similis pietas, hic Maecenatis in omnes
    mos fuerat, vates percoluisse sacros.
At nunc Landini, Medicum Petrique favore,
30   cantatur toto nomen in orbe tui,
qui cecinit Xandram, miro inflammatus amore,
    et mox magna Petri dicere gesta parat.
At tu, qui tanti sequeris vestigia vatis,
    haec illi nostro nomine dicta refer.
35 Nec tua Lethaeas mergetur virgo sub undas
    Flammetta, ardoris maxima flamma tui.
Inter et Etruscas cantabitur ipsa puellas,
    et sua post cineres fama superstes erit.'

Haec ubi dicta dedit, Faunos Nymphasque canentes
40   aspexi et toto ducere monte chorum,
donec anhelantes nostrum super aethera Phoebus
    duxit equos, et iam venerat alma dies.

His clothing was ablaze with color, dyed with Tyrian purple,
    and the jewelry he wore was obtained from an eastern sea.
Then he struck his gilt lyre with an ivory plectrum,   15
    and he voiced these words with his gentle lips: —

"O three times blessed are you who desire fame among Sulla's
       sons
    in the time of Piero de' Medici!
Joy to the venerable land of the Etruscan Lion,
    for which I have left the caves of the god of Cirrha,   20
the Aonian groves, Thessalian Tempe,
    and the places made famous in Greek melodies!
I am not ashamed to dwell in the hills of Fiesole and Mugello,
    nor is my dancing band ashamed to bathe in an Etruscan fount;
for, while Piero lives, I hope for great honor   25
    and for great rewards to be given to Etruscan poets.
Maecenas showed a similar regard, and it was his way
    in dealing with everyone to revere holy poets.
Now the name of your Landino, by favor of the Medici and Piero,
    is celebrated all over the world,   30
he who, inflamed by a marvelous love, has sung of Sandra
    and makes ready soon to tell of Piero's great exploits.
Do you, who follow in the footsteps of so great a poet,
    report what I have said here to him in my name.
Nor will your girl Fiammetta, the great flame of your passion,   35
    be immersed in the waters of Lethe.
She will be celebrated in song amid Etruscan girls,
    and her fame will live on beyond her death."

When he had said these things, I beheld fauns
    and nymphs singing and dancing all over the mountain,   40
until Phoebus drove his panting team of horses above the
       heavens,
    and now the kindly day had come.

: XXI :

Ad Flammettam, ne ipsum deserat

Quis fuerat quondam felicior alter amore,
    dum me centenis praetulit illa procis?
Quid meminisse iuvat partes habuisse priores,
    si nunc excluso saevius instet amor?
5 Monstrabar digitis felices inter amantes,
    et mea sors multis invidiosa fuit.
Ut dulce in tuto est veterum meminisse malorum,
    sic magis ex alta sede ruisse dolet.
Numinis adversi nimium securus amavi,
10   incauto unde magis cura nocere solet.
Quis fuit ille meis daemon contraria votis
    numina qui opposuit? Lividus ille fuit.
Felicem quondam multi dixere Verinum,
    nunc Fortuna suam movit iniqua rotam.
15 Mobilis illa quidem est, uno nec firma tenore;
    alternat varias lubrica saepe vices.
Nemo potest recte felix dicique beatus,
    hunc nisi felicem viderit atra dies.
Hei mihi, quid feci? Videor cur, perfida, vilis
20   nunc, Flammetta, tibi? Dic, ubi nostra fides?
En umquam fuit in terris ardentior alter
    et qui maiori norit amare fide?
Ille ego sum quem tu cunctis praeferre solebas,
    quo sine dicebas nil tibi dulce fore,
25 cuius et ingenium sanctis, Flammetta, poetis
    atque ausa es doctis me aequiperare viris.

: XXI :

To Fiammetta, not to desert him

What other man was once luckier in love
   while she preferred me to a hundred suitors?
What good does it do me to recall having held first place,
   if now, shut out as I am from her, love besets me more
      fiercely?
I used to be pointed out among happy lovers,   5
   and my good fortune was a cause of envy for many.
Just as it is sweet in safety to recall former hardships,
   so it hurts the more to fall from a lofty pedestal.
I loved all unconcerned that a deity might set up against me,
   unwariness that usually brings more hurt.   10
Who was the wicked spirit who set the gods in opposition
   to my wishes? He was a spiteful creature.
Once many men declared Verino lucky;
   now hostile Fortune has turned her wheel.
She is fickle indeed and does not hold steady to one course;   15
   slippery in her shifting, she often changes by turns.
No one can rightly be said to be lucky and blessed
   if the black day of death has not seen him in good fortune.
Alas, what have I done, why do I seem worthless now to you,
   false-hearted Fiammetta? Tell me, where is my faithfulness?   20
Was there ever another man on earth more ardent
   or one who knew how to love with greater loyalty?
I am the one whom you used to prefer to all others,
   without whom you used to say nothing would be sweet to you,
he whose genius, Fiammetta, you dared make equal to that of   25
      holy poets,
   going so far as to put me on a par with learned men.

Ingenium et versus quamvis natura negarit,
  laeta dabas versus ingeniumque mihi;
tu mihi praebebas vires sanctumque furorem,
30 te sine Verini muta Thalia foret.
Tu mihi, quaecumque est, tribuisti carminis artem,
  tantus in accensis mentibus ardor erat.
Sis mihi principium, medium, sis finis amoris;
  ne rapiat titulos altera virgo tuos.
35 Tu, Flammetta, meis sola inscribere libellis,
  dummodo te teneat mutua cura mei.

: XXII :

Ad Cupidinem, ne tantum saeviat

Desine iam pharetras, puer, evacuare sagittis
  in me Verinum, saeve Cupido, tuas.
Pone tuos arcus; tibi porrigo pectus inerme;
  pars intacta tuo est vulnere nulla mihi.
5 Spicula quo figes non est locus; omnia telis
  plena tuis. Quid enim nunc, furiose, paras?
Quaere alios iuvenes, alias tibi quaere puellas;
  dum vivam aligeri servus Amoris ero.
Sum, fateor, miles tuus, ambitiose Cupido.
10 Cur laceras pectus militis ipse tui?
Non opus inflammes, uror namque intus et extra;
  Aetnaeis flammis pectora tosta dolent.
Quae requies, quae finis erit, Cytherea, furori?
  Crudelis nati comprime tela tui.

Though nature has denied me creative power and verses,
    you gladly used to bestow verses and creative power upon me.
You used to provide me with strength and holy inspiration;
    without you Verino's Muse would be silent.   30
You provided me with my skill in poetry, such as it is,
    so much ardor was there in my fired-up thoughts.
Be to me the beginning, middle, and end of love;
    let no other girl snatch your glory away.
You alone, Fiammetta, will be the theme of my poems,   35
    so long as you feel a corresponding care for me.

: XXII :

To Cupid, not to be so cruel

Cease now, Cupid, you cruel boy, from emptying
    your quivers of arrows at me, Verino.
Lay aside your bow; I offer you a defenseless breast;
    there is no part of me uninjured by your wounds.
No place is left for you to fix your darts; everywhere is full of   5
      your shafts.
    What are you plotting now, raging tormentor?
Find yourself other young men, find other girls;
    as long as I live I shall be the slave of winged Love.
I am, I admit it, a soldier of yours, ambitious Cupid;
    why do you wound your own soldier's breast?   10
There is no need to set me ablaze, for I am on fire inside and out;
    my breast feels the pain of being scorched with Etna's flames.
What respite, what end will there be, Cytherea, to his fury?
    Check your cruel son's arrows.

15   Vix tegit ossa cutis; pro succo pallor in ore est;
      quaelibet ossa mei dinumerare queas.
  Assiduus luctus turgentia lumina laedit,
     insomnis noctes pervigiloque dies,
  pectora proque cibo maeror macilenta peredit.
20   Ut sit, diva, precor mitior ille mihi.
  Impius ille licet tua per praecordia flavum,
     alma parens, telum torserit asper Amor,
  formosum cum tu, pulcherrima mater, Adona
     ardebas, tibi nec, diva, pepercit Amor,
25 iussa tamen carae faciet genetricis alumnus,
     servitium ut tradat mitius ille mihi.

: XXIII :

De duritie Flammettae, suo infortunio

  An mea me semper simili fortuna tenore
     urgebit? Veniet candida nulla dies?
  Cymba procellosum semper mea curret in aequor,
     in Syrtes rapido praecipitanda Noto?
5 Legibus en ego sum Parcarum natus iniquis,
     ut miser adverso semper amore premar?
  Cur mihi nascenti, Clotho, invidiosa fuisti?
     Anne, deae, livor vos quoque tangit edax?

My skin barely covers my bones; there is paleness on my face in   15
    place of healthy vigor;
  you could count every one of my bones.
Unremitting grief afflicts my swollen eyes,
  I watch out nights and days in sleeplessness,
and sorrow consumes my lean breast for food.
  I pray, goddess, that the boy may be gentler with me.   20
Even though that disrespectful child, cruel Love, shot his golden
    arrow
  through your own heart, kindly parent,
when you, most beautiful mother, were afire for handsome
    Adonis,
  and Love spared not even you, goddess,
yet the child will do his dear parent's bidding   25
  to permit me a gentler servitude.

: XXIII :

On Fiammetta's hardness of heart, his own misfortune

Will my fortune always drive me on this same course?
  Will no bright day of good luck come?
Will my boat always speed into stormy waters
  to be dashed on the Syrtes by the rushing south wind?
Was I born then with the laws of the Fates against me,   5
  so as always to be oppressed to my misery by bad luck in love?
For what reason, Clotho, did you resent me at my birth?
  Does gnawing jealousy touch you too, goddesses?

Purpureis invecta rotis nitidissima pulchrae
10   filia Latonae ter renovata polo est
ex quo saevus Amor flammas geminavit et arcus,
     inque dies vires convaluere suae.
Spes quanto minor est, tanto magis urgeor amens;
14   sic sterilis vana spe mihi gliscit amor.
Quid facis, ah demens? Quid spem nunc nutris inanem?
     Alterius mavult dicier illa viri.
Quid litus curvo frustra proscindis aratro?
     Num segetes laetas tristis arena feret?
Durane blanditiis speras nunc saxa movere,
20   et supplex fastus flectere posse feros?
Aut alium iuvenem (quod nollem) deperit illa,
     aut inflata nimis virginitate sua est.
Rara verecunda est quae non sit virgo superba.
     Pro superis! Mendis rara puella caret.
25 Matronae quis enim fastus tolerare pudicae
     posset? Nulla mihi virgo superba placet.
Intolerabilius quam dira superbia nil est
     quodque magis superis displicuisse ferant.
Sit testis Niobe, in statuam quam vertit Apollo.
30   Pignora bis septem perdidit illa prius.
Si non pampinei vetuisset sacra Lyaei,
     non visus matri Pentheus esset aper.
Si non fugisset Phoebi conubia Daphne,
     non versa in laurum dura puella foret.
35 Discite vos igitur fastus odisse superbae.
     Ponite duritiem, nam nimis illa nocet.

Riding in her shining white chariot, beautiful Latona's supremely
    radiant daughter
  has been renewed three times in the sky   10
since cruel Love doubled his attack on me with flames and bow,
    and his strength has grown mightier each day.
The less my hope is, the more I am driven on in my madness;
    thus my barren love grows on vain hope.
What are you doing, you demented fool? Why do you now feed   15
    empty hope?
  She prefers to be called another man's.
Why do you vainly till the seashore with a curved plow?
  Will joyless sand bear joyous crops?
Do you hope now to move hard rocks with coaxing pleas
  and to sway fierce disdain with supplication?   20
Either she loves another young man, which I would wish not so,
  or she is too proud of her own virginity.
A girl with a sense of modesty who is not also haughty is rare.
  Ye gods! It is a rare girl that is free of faults.
For who could endure the disdain of a chaste matron?   25
  No proud maid pleases me.
There is nothing more intolerable than dreadful pride,
  and nothing that people could say more greatly displeases the
    gods above.
Let Niobe, whom Apollo turned into a statue, bear witness to
    that.
  Before he transformed her, she lost twice seven children.   30
If Pentheus had not forbidden the rites of vine-crowned Lyaeus,
  he would not have been mistaken by his mother for a boar.
If Daphne had not fled union with Phoebus,
  the hard-hearted girl would not have been changed into a
    laurel.
Learn then, you proud girls, to hate disdain.   35
  Put aside hard-heartedness, for it does great harm.

Hoc si nostra fides meruit, miserere precantis,
    Flammetta, ardoris nunc miserere mei.
Iamque extrema legunt mihi saevae stamina Parcae.
40   Ultima, ni properes, lux mea fata feret.

: XXIV :

Ad se ipsum, ut relicto amore sequatur rationem

Stulte, quid in flammas addis nova ligna, Verine,
    heu nimis in damnis ingeniose tuis?
Perdita fortassis ne perdas, omnia perdis.
    En age, tam rapidis contrahe vela Notis.
5 Tempus adest; portus repetat votiva carina;
    iactata in dubio iam satis illa salo est.
Cur plenum curis animum spe pascis inani?
    Irrita nam Zephyri tot tua vota ferunt.
Ah nimis indulges, qui te male perdit, amori;
10   heu nescis, nescis quid sit amare, miser!
Anxia res amor est et curae plenus inanis,
    mortalesque nihil vexat amore magis.
At satius quanto est illis incumbere rebus,
    quae sanare tui tabida membra queant.
15 Fabula non sentis toto ut notissima vulgo
    iactere, et de te compita nulla tacent?
Nemo tuum conviva silet vinosus amorem,
    et tua sunt pleno carmina lecta foro.
Insanus digitis populus te signat euntem,
20   nequitiam ridens damnat et ille tuam.

If my faithfulness has deserved it, have pity on my prayers,
    Fiammetta, and have pity now on my passion.
Already the cruel Fates are gathering the final threads of my life.
    My last day will bring me my death, unless you make haste.   40

: XXIV :

To himself, that he abandon love and follow reason

Foolish Verino, why do you add fresh wood to the flames,
    alas, all too cleverly bringing about your own destruction?
On the chance of not losing what is already lost, you lose all.
    Come, shorten sail before such rushing south winds.
The time is at hand. Let your ship, pledged as an offering, look   5
        for port;
    it has been tossed enough already on an uncertain sea.
Why do you feed a mind full of cares on empty hope?
    For the zephyrs carry away all your many useless prayers.
Ah, you indulge too much the love that wretchedly destroys you!
    Alas, you do not know, do not know what it is to love, you   10
        poor man!
Love is an anxious business and full of empty care,
    and nothing troubles mortals more than love.
But how much better it is to turn your energies to those things
    that have the power to heal your wasting limbs.
Do you not realize how you are the talk of all the crowd,   15
    and how no crossroads is silent about you?
No reveler in his cups fails to speak of your love,
    and your poems have been read in the packed marketplace.
The crazed masses point you out with their fingers as you go by,
    and they laugh as they condemn your disreputable conduct.   20

Quid docti dicent, si plebs tua crimina culpat;
    quid de te gravium turba severa Patrum?
Victa iacet ratio, nam nunc meliora volentem
    me peiora sequi compulit asper Amor.
25   Quis saevi posset contra ire Cupidinis arcum?
    Quis putet armatum vincere posse deum?

: XXV :

Quod amori succumbat ratio

Spes et amor cogunt rursus servire puellae
    iucundoque iterum subdere colla iugo.
Hinc ratio atque animus Veneri contraria surgunt,
    et nimis hostili pugnat uterque modo.
5   Quid fiet de me timeo. Vincetne Cupido?
    Nimirum in nostro pectore victor erit.
Alatus deus est, gravidas gerit ille pharetras,
    aureaque occulte spicula torquet Amor,
nec quisquam vitare potest; prius ossibus haerent
10   fraxineos arcus quam sinuasse putes.
Non missa a Partho tantum letalis harundo
    dum fugit incauti militis ora fodit.
At si quis puerum caecumque vocabit Amorem,
    iudicium sani non habet ille viri.
15   Nemo Cupidineas poterit vitare sagittas;
    nullus ab insidiis tutus Amoris erit.

What will learned men say, if the common folk censure your bad
     behavior?
   What will the stern assembly of venerable Fathers say of you?
My reason is vanquished and prostrate, for, though I now wish to
     follow the better course,
   harsh Love has forced me to follow the worse.
Who could resist cruel Cupid's bow?   25
   Who could imagine himself able to defeat an armed god?

: XXV :

How reason succumbs to love

Hope and love drive me to be once more a slave to my girl
   and again to submit my neck to that pleasant yoke.
On the other side reason and my mind rise up in opposition to
     Venus,
   and the two conflicting forces fight with great ferocity.
I fear what will become of me. Will Cupid prevail?   5
   He will surely be the victor in my heart.
The god is winged, the quivers that he carries are full,
   and he shoots his arrows of gold unnoticed,
nor can anyone avoid them; they are stuck fast in your bones
   before you could suppose him to have bent his ashen bow.   10
Not so deeply does the deadly shaft sped by a fleeing Parthian
   pierce the face of an unwary soldier.
And if anyone calls Love a boy and blind,
   he does not have the judgment of a man in his right senses.
No one will be able to avoid Cupid's arrows;   15
   no one will be safe from Love's ambushes.

Colchida quid referam aeripedes flammamque vomentes
    carminibus magicis perdomuisse boves?
At non ardorem cantatis Iasonis herbis
20   extinxit; crevit tosta per ossa calor.
Tu quoque quae nautas mutasti in monstra Pelasgos
    aurea sensisti praepetis arma dei,
falce nec ad lunam lectum tibi gramen aena
    profuit, et iuvit carmen inane nihil,
25 sed te decepta, licet esses filia Solis,
    sulcavit vitreas callidus hospes aquas.
Quid nunc te memorem, proles generosa Tonantis,
    nempe pharetrato succubuisse deo?
Tu fera Nemaei domuisti monstra leonis
30   Hydraque te metuit Tartareusque canis;
omnia vicisti, tenero nunc servis Amori,
    factus et es servus, qui modo victor eras.
Cur te, Phoebe, canam mutatum turpiter ora
    pastorem vili delituisse casa?
35 Sed quid ego incipio magnos numerare triumphos,
    cum toto notus pervolet orbe puer?
Magne puer, si quis spernat tua regna superbus,
    tam ferus imperium sentiat iste tuum.
Ille tibi iam mitis erit, supplexque rogabit
40   ne faculis uras pectora dura novis.

Why should I mention how the Colchian maid quite subdued
  the brazen-hoofed and fire-spewing bulls with magic spells?
But she could not quench her love for Jason with enchanted
    herbs;
  the fire of love grew and spread throughout her scorched   20
    bones.
You who changed the Pelasgian sailors into beasts
  also felt the golden weapons of the winged god;
herbs gathered by moonlight with a bronze sickle did you no
    good,
  and ineffectual spells availed you nothing,
but you were deceived, though you were the Sun's daughter,   25
  and your cunning guest plowed the glassy waters.
Why should I now recall, noble offspring of the Thunderer,
  that you too succumbed to the god who wears a quiver?
You conquered that fierce beast the Nemean Lion
  and the Hydra, and the dog of Tartarus feared you.   30
You overcame all, but now you serve tender Love,
  and you who were lately a conqueror have been made instead a
    slave.
Why should I sing how you, Phoebus, shamefully disguised
  as a shepherd, hid in a lowly cottage?
But why do I begin to enumerate his great triumphs,   35
  seeing that the boy is well known and flies the world over?
Great boy, if anyone in his pride were to spurn your dominion,
  for all his fierce defiance he would feel your power.
He will soon enough be meek toward you and with humble
    entreaty beg you
  not to burn his hard heart with new-felt torches.   40

O si me vultu aspiceret Flammetta sereno
    et vellet dici quae modo dicta mea est,
tunc ego Persarum ditissima regna recusem.
    Improbus insanas quaerat avarus opes,
45 hic inhiet dulces miserae ambitionis honores,
    iste regat multos; me mea Flamma regat.
Flammea me niveis teneat formosa lacertis,
    et vos cum vestris, regna, valete malis.

: XXVI :

De tristibus somniis

Me miserum, hesterna quae somnia nocte fuerunt!
    Hem, hoc vos nigrae praecinuistis aves,
alteriusque meas subiit canis ater in aedes,
    atque per impluvium decidit anguis humo.
5 Haec quamvis manifesta mei cecinisset haruspex
    signa mali, tantum quis putet esse nefas?
Heu heu, non tantam concepi mente ruinam;
    ducenda est alio nostra puella viro!
Tempus erat quo iam roseis Aurora quadrigis
10   linquebat Phrygii flava cubile senis,
pessima quando quies somno mihi membra rigavit.
    Sint utinam nobis somnia falsa, precor!

O if only Fiammetta were to look on me with serene countenance
    and be willing to be called mine, as lately so she was,
then would I refuse the kingdom of the Persians, for all its vast
    riches.
    Let the wicked money-grubber seek mad wealth,
let this man long for the sweet honors that wretched ambition   45
    pursues,
    and let that other rule over many; let my Flame rule over me.
Let my beautiful Flame Maiden hold me in her snowy arms,
    and goodbye to you, kingdoms, along with the troubles you
    bring.

։ XXVI ։

On sad dreams

What dreams I had to my distress last night!
    Alas, this is what you black birds foretold,
another man's black dog entered my house,
    and a snake fell down to the ground through the skylight.
Although a soothsayer might have declared these to be plain signs   5
    of my misfortune, who would suppose the wrong to be so
    great?
Alas, alas, I did not imagine in my mind a calamity as dire as this:
    my girl is to be married to another man!
It was the time when yellow-haired Aurora in her rosy four-
    horsed chariot
    was now leaving the aged Phrygian's bed,   10
when wicked rest flooded my limbs in sleep.
    May the dreams I saw be false, I pray!

Visa mihi est Erato tristes effundere voces
    (neglecti haec curam semper amantis habet): —

15 'Fata tuis obstant coeptis. Obsistere fatis
    nemo potest hominum; non Deus ipse valet.
Mens Iovis est fatum, fatum est sua firma voluntas,
    et seriem rerum fata vocare potes;
ille Opifex rerum sibimet contrarius esset.
20   Hoc est adversus bella movere deos,
et conere licet, non re potieris amata,
    sed miser incassum tempora longa teres.
Sic visum superis, sic stat sententia Fatis,
    ut nubat Bruno candida virgo seni.
25 Indignum est facinus nec quod mereare, Verine,
    sed tamen o frustra desine, amice, queri;
nos aliam dabimus miro splendore puellam,
    deposito fastu quae velit esse tua,
illiusque toro solusque frueris amore
30   dum sibi (pro superi!) vita superstes erit.'

Vix haec ediderat, gelidos cum sudor in artus
    fluxerat, et pavidi contremuere sinus.
Tunc mea coeperunt vibrari corda timore,
    tristis et e nostro pectore somnus abit.
35 Namque metu est excussa quies, ira atque dolore
    exarsi, nec vox ore retenta mihi est: —

'Cur, ignave, premis mortalia pectora curis?
    Nonne satis fuerat cura diurna, Sopor?

It seemed to me that Erato was pouring out sad words
 (she is always concerned for the slighted lover): —

"The fates stand in the way of your plans. None among men   15
 can oppose the fates; not even God himself has the power.
Jupiter's mind is fate, fate is his firmly fixed will,
 and you can call the fates the unfolding succession of events;
the Maker of all things would be going against himself.
 Such behavior is making war upon the gods,   20
and, try though you may, you will not succeed in making your
  beloved your own,
 but you will wretchedly waste long hours to no end.
So the gods above have decided, and so stands the ruling of the
  Fates,
 that the fair young maid shall marry old Bruno.
It is a terrible outrage and not the treatment you may deserve, 25
  Verino,
 but yet cease, my friend, from futile complaint.
I shall give you another girl of marvelous beauty,
 such a one as will set aside disdain and consent to be yours,
and you alone will enjoy her bed and love
 as long as she (I swear by the gods above!) shall live."   30

She had scarcely uttered these words when sweat flowed over my
  icy limbs,
 and my chest convulsed in panic.
Then my heart began to throb with fear,
 and unhappy sleep departed from my breast.
For my repose was shaken off me by dread, I was set afire with 35
  anger and pain,
 and I did not hold back my voice from my lips: —

"Why, slothful Sleep, do you weigh down mortal hearts with cares?
 Was worry by day not enough?

Cur trepidas falsa deludis imagine mentes
40   atque timere facis saepe quod esse nequit?
Cur terrent sensus phantasmata vana gravatos,
    horrida tam miris cur simulacra modis?
Omnia mentiris, Somne ignavissime, dicta.
    Anne esset tanti nuntia Musa mali?
45 Nec plectrum in dextra, nec barbiton ulla sinistra,
    nec fuit haec Erato, quae mihi visa loqui est;
sed comes una tui Furiarum, tristis Erinys,
    Tartareo venit, pestis amara, lacu.'

: XXVII :

Ad Flammettam, quae nupsit Bruno seni

Ergo deserto tandem, Flammetta, Verino
    nupsisti Bruno, perfida virgo, seni.
Perfida, tam sancti rupisti foedus amoris?
    Deceptis superis sic violata fides?
5 Crede mihi, tanti sceleris dabis, improba, poenas.
    Impia, mene putas talia posse pati?
Facta addam verbis. Tam atrox iniuria posset
    ingenium placidi mite movere viri.
Acer natura atque audax iuvenilibus annis,
10   nescio quid faciam; quo trahet ira, sequar.

Why do you fool anxious minds with false fancy
 and often make us fear what cannot be?   40
Why do vain apparitions strike terror into our slumbering senses,
 and such bizarrely imagined horrors frighten us?
All that you have said is lies, Sleep, you great sluggard—
 could a Muse have been the bearer of such evil tidings?
There was no plectrum in her right hand, nor any lyre in her left, 45
 nor was this Erato that I imagined speaking;
but one of the Furies, a companion of yours, grim Erinys,
 a pestilential scourge, came from the Tartarean lake."

∶ XXVII ∶

To Fiammetta, who has married old Bruno

So, Fiammetta, in the end you have forsaken Verino
 and married old Bruno, you faithless girl.
Faithless deceiver, have you broken the bond of so sacred a love?
 Have you played the gods false and thus dishonored your
  word?
Believe me, wicked one, you will answer for so great a crime.   5
 Impious girl, do you suppose that I can bear such treatment?
I will add actions to words. So outrageous a wrong
 could move even the gentle disposition of a calm-mannered
  man.
Being passionate by nature and having the boldness of youthful
  years,
 I do not know what I shall do; I will follow where my anger 10
  leads me.

Intumuit calidus per fervida pectora sanguis;
    ira et amor nobis cuncta furore replent.
Di meritas poenas tanto pro crimine poscent.
    Tene putas superis verba dedisse deis?
15 Numina sunt testes. Potes hoc, periura, negare,
    an teste infitias ibis, iniqua, deo?
Formula sit testis, quae sacra in Carminis aede
    paene istis verbis rite peracta fuit: —

'Te praeter nullus iunget conubia mecum,
20   cuius nota fides, est mihi notus amor.
Per Numen iuro, cuius densissima ludos
    turba colit, semper tu meus unus eris.
Dum vivam, fidi dicar Flammetta Verini;
    una dies ambos auferet, unus amor.
25 Tu vir, tu coniux, et eris mihi sola voluptas.
    Dispeream, sine te si libet esse mihi.'

Pluraque mendaci dixisti, perfida, lingua,
    et nostrae dextrae dextera nexa tua est.
Tunc prae laetitia lacrimae fluxere per ora
30   et tantum dixi, 'Sint rata verba precor.'
Gaudia (pro superi!) deceptus inania fovi,
    me fore felicem tempus in omne putans.
O leve et infidum, o varium, o mutabile pectus!
    Femina se tanta mobilitate gerit!

My hot blood has risen up throughout my seething breast;
    anger and love quite fill me with fury.
The gods will demand due punishment for so great a crime.
    Do you imagine that you have deceived the gods?
The deities are witnesses. Can you dispute that, perjurer,   15
    or will you attempt denial, unjust girl, even when a god is
        witness?
Let the contract that was solemnly made in almost these words
    in the holy church of the Carmine be witness: —

"No man will marry me apart from you,
    whose faithfulness and whose love are well known to me.   20
I swear by the Divinity whose festival celebrations
    this dense throng observes, that you will always be my one and
        only man.
As long as I live, I shall be called faithful Verino's Fiammetta.
    One and the same day and one love will bear off both of us.
You will be my man, my husband, my only joy.   25
    May I perish, if I want to live without you."

And you said more, faithless girl, with your lying tongue,
    and your right hand was clasped in mine.
Then tears flowed over my face in delight,
    and I said only, "I pray your words may turn out to be truly   30
        spoken."
Duped as I was, I cherished (O gods above!) joys that were vain
        delusion,
    imagining that I would be happy for all time.
O frivolous and faithless, O inconstant and fickle heart!
    A woman behaves with such changeability!

35 Nulla fides usquam est; iuranti nemo puellae
    credat: cum verbis mobile pectus habent.
Promptum aliud verbis, aliudque in pectore clausum est;
    mella gerunt linguis, dira venena latent.

꞉ XXVIII ꞉

Ad Locterium Neronium amicissimum

Men' lacrimare vetas, et talis adempta puella est
    nobis, et turpi Flammea nupta seni?
Vah, mihi decrepitus quidam praefertur adulter.
    Men' siccis credis talia ferre genis?
5 Immittat potius mea per praecordia ferrum
    quam, Flammetta, miser priver amore tuo!
Me iugulet potius — fuero sibi mitior hostis —
    illius quam tu nupta ferare senis!
Tune illum tanges niveis formosa lacertis
10   et non pollutas credis habere manus?
Tune fovere sinu squalentia membra pedore
    tam molli poteris, stulta puella, senis?
En, ubi mollities formosi pectoris illa est?
    Oris ubi inflati verba superba? Iacent!

There is no trustworthiness anywhere; let no one believe a girl's   35
    oath:
    girls have hearts as unreliable as their words.
They tell you one thing, while another is shut away in their heart.
    They have honey on their tongues, but dreadful poisons are
    concealed underneath.

: XXVIII :

To his very good friend Lottieri Neroni

Do you tell me not to weep, when such a girl has been taken
    from me,
    and my Flame Maiden married to an ugly old man?
Alas, a decrepit adulterer is preferred to me.
    Do you think I can bear such a hurt with dry cheeks?
May he rather drive steel through my heart   5
    than I be deprived to my misery of your love, Fiammetta!
May he rather cut my throat — I shall be a gentler enemy to
    him —
    than I endure your being that old man's bride!
Will you in your beauty touch him with your snow-white arms
    and not believe yourself to have defiled hands?   10
Will you be able, foolish girl, to fondle his old man's frame,
    foul with corruption, in your soft embrace?
Why, where is that delicacy of feeling you have within your
    beautiful breast?
    Where now are your proud lips' disdainful words? Forgotten!

15 Heu, tibi tam cari non amplius ipsa Verini
      dicere? — Et lacrimas fundere tune vetas?
   Me Scythicis releget potius Florentia terris,
      publicet et nostras denique fiscus opes,
   quam nostram tangat turpissimus ille puellam!
20   Avertant tantum numina sancta nefas!
   Desine, Locteri, sapientia fundere verba
      frustra, nam nimis est imperiosus Amor.
   Te bona dicentem nosco, peioraque cogor
      turpiter, insano victus amore, sequi.
25 Quid faciam? Finem nequeo praescribere amori;
      exitium infelix subsequor ipse meum.
   Sed tamen enitar paulatim pellere labem
      tam tristem monitis, dulcis amice, tuis.

                    ∶ XXIX ∶

                  Ad Flammettam

   Quid mihi dixisti? 'Infelix, discede, Verine.
      Me coniux alter, me tenet alter amor.
   Rumpere ne tentes socialia vincula taedae,
      ne sponsam alterius sollicitare velis.
5 Dum licuit tempusque tulit salvoque pudore,
      inter mille procos tu mihi primus eras.

Alas, will you no more be called your dear Verino's girl?   15
 And *you* tell me not to stream tears, Lottieri?
May Florence rather banish me to Scythian lands,
 and the treasury then confiscate all my wealth,
than that ugliest of creatures touch my girl!
 May the holy powers of heaven avert such a sin!   20
Cease, Lottieri, to pour forth words of wisdom
 to no avail, for Love is too domineering a tyrant.
I realize that you advise me well, and yet I am compelled
 shamefully to follow the worse course, overcome by mad love.
What am I to do? I cannot put an end to my love;   25
 in my misfortune, I am pursuing my own death.
But yet I will, by your advice, sweet friend,
 strive little by little to get over so sad a blow.

: XXIX :

To Fiammetta

What have you said to me? "Go away, hapless Verino.
 Another husband has me for his wife, I am bound by another
  love now.
Do not try to break the conjugal bonds of the marriage torch,
 do not seek to tempt another man's bride.
While it was permitted, when the time was right, and without   5
  impropriety,
 you were the foremost among a thousand suitors in my eyes.

Vir, mihi ni cedas, nostro laedetur amore,
    et te propter erit fama sepulta mei,
et falso turpis te propter adultera dicar.
10   Deprecor, alterius cede, Verine, toro.
Ardenti ut quondam fueras in amore modestus,
    quae mentem potuit flectere causa meam,
sic tua nunc prosit, dilecte, modestia nobis;
    profuit illa tibi, prosit et illa mihi.
15 Nulla dies nisi mors disiunget foedera lecti.
    Ne doleas; non tu vir, sed amator eras.
Verba puellarum quae sunt sub iure parentum
    ad iam promissum nil valuere torum.
Non ego civilis cognovi aenigmata iuris
20   (scire tamen mulier quaelibet ista potest?).
Nescia promisi, sed quid promittere quivi,
    actibus his genitor si neget ipse fidem?
Aut bene cede volens seu invitus tempora perdes,
    gratia sicque tuis non erit ulla malis.
25 Quaere aliam, nulli quae sit promissa marito,
    quae possit semper firmior esse tibi.
Illa quidem, nostri si quid tibi restat amoris,
    curam adimet, curam cum dabit illa tibi.
Truditur ut clavus clavo, sic ignis ab igne,
30   sic deletur amor priscus amore novo.'

Discedam, quamvis abs te discedere nollem;
    hinc tamen imperium me iubet ire tuum.

My husband will be hurt by our love, if you do not give way to
    me,
  and my reputation will be buried on your account,
and through you I shall falsely be called a foul adulteress.
  I beg you, Verino, accept the claims of another man's bed.   10
As once you were modest in your ardent love—
  and that was how you swayed my mind—
so now, beloved, may your restraint serve my advantage;
  it served you well, may it serve me well too.
No day save death shall sunder my marriage bond.   15
  Do not grieve; you were not my husband but my lover.
The words of girls who are under their parents' authority
  have no force with regard to a marriage already promised.
I do not know the mysteries of civil law
  (yet can any woman know them?).   20
I made my promise in ignorance, but how could I promise,
  if my father for his part refused to confirm the arrangement?
Either be content to yield willingly, or you will waste your time if
    you refuse,
  and that way you will get no thanks for your sufferings.
Look for another girl, one who is promised to no husband   25
  and can be ever more steadfastly yours.
She will take away your care, if any trace of your love for me
    remains,
  when she is the one to cause you care.
As nail is driven out by nail, so is fire by fire,
  and so is an old love killed off by a new love."   30

I will go away, though I would rather not leave you;
  yet your command bids me be gone from here.

: XXX :

Ad Flammettam

Quid faciam? Quo me vertam? Discedere cogis;
    ad te me facies ista redire iubet,
me flavi crines retinent et eburnea colla.
    Me miserum sine te vivere posse putas?
5 Quam bene puniceus lactenti in corpore nitor
    fulget! Et hanc formam linquere posse putas?
En, ego sidereos ut linquam credis ocellos?
    Sperasti ah tantum, candida virgo, nefas?
En, alium imperiosa iubes me quaerere amorem?
10   Quo sine te pacto vita futura mea est?
Unica tu requies nostri, Flammetta, laboris,
    solamen tristis sola doloris eras.
Pectore sola meo poteras depellere curas,
    tu vere poteras gaudia sola dare.
15 In te spes vitae, mors in te nostra manebat;
    sors mea pendebat sorte, puella, tua.
Quis mihi deserto, quod erit solamen, amicus?
    Quis pellet curas, gaudia quisve dabit?
Contra fas divum tu, contra iura virorum
20   a iam promisso pellis, iniqua, toro.
Si nescis, deus est testis, deus ultor amantis;
    deceptus verbis non ego solus eram.

: XXX :

To Fiammetta

What shall I do? Where shall I turn? You make me go away;
   that face of yours bids me return to you,
your yellow hair and ivory neck hold me back.
   Do you think that I can live without you, wretch that I am?
How splendidly the rosy bloom glows on your milky body!   5
   And you think that I can leave this beauty?
Do you really believe that I can leave your star-like eyes?
   Alas, did you hope for such a crime, fair maid?
Do you imperiously bid me seek another love?
   How can my life go on without you?   10
You, Fiammetta, were the only respite from my suffering,
   you alone were comfort for my sad pain.
You alone could drive the cares from my breast,
   truly you alone could give me joy.
My hope of life rested with you, my death rested with you;   15
   my fate hung on your fate, my girl.
What friend shall I have, deserted as I am, to be a comfort to me?
   Who will drive away cares, or who give joy?
Against what the gods lay down as right, and against the laws of
     men,
   unjust girl, you drive me away from a marriage already   20
     promised me.
In case you do not know it, a god is my witness, the god who
     avenges a lover;
   I was not the only one deceived by your words.

Quas mihi tu poenas, si non mortalia temnunt
    numina, sed meritas, Flammea Virgo, dabis!
25 Ultrices iras graviora in tempora differt,
    non impune feres verba dedisse deo.
Non omnes subito peccantes fulmine perdit
    Iuppiter, eventus acta probare solent.
Vos precor, o superi, sim quamvis laesus ab illa,
30   sit tamen huic causa poena remissa mei!
Si non decipior, fidum sprevisse Verinum
    plorabis, cum nos alter habebit amor.
Tunc quotiens dices, 'Erat hic, hic dignus amari.'
    Damnabis fastum stultitiamque tuam.

How you will pay for what you have done to me, if the powers of
    heaven
  do not despise mortal affairs, and deservedly so, Flame
    Maiden!
A god puts off his avenging wrath only till a harsher time of   25
    reckoning;
  you will not escape punishment for playing a god false!
Jupiter does not destroy all sinners with an instant thunderbolt;
  subsequent events are commonly his judgment on our acts.
I pray you, powers above, though I have been hurt by her,
  yet let her punishment be remitted for my sake.   30
If I am not deceived, Fiammetta, you will rue spurning faithful
    Verino
  when another love possesses me.
Then how often you will say, "He was the one who deserved my
    love."
  You will condemn your disdain and your folly.

LIBER SECUNDUS

: I :

Ad Laurentium Medicem

Qui modo, Laurenti, miro inflammatus amore,
    Flammettae lusi carmina multa meae,
grandia nunc ausum tragico cantare cothurno
    me vetuit prolis facta Cupido tuae.

5 'Tune audes,' inquit, 'Medicum describere gesta,
    gesta Maroneis vix referenda sonis?
Perque Thetim audebas fluviali currere lembo
    quae foret aequoreis mersa phaselus aquis?
Linque haec, Aeschyleis quae sunt ornanda cothurnis,
10   unus et aligeri miles Amoris eris.
Ne pigeat castris meruisse Cupidinis aera;
    hinc poterit tolli nomen ad astra tuum.
Sub duce me multi aeternum sunt nomen adepti,
    quorum perpetuo fama perennis erit.
15 Nos quoque Phoebeum vati inspiramus amorem,
    et dat Apollineo nunc Venus ore loqui.
Callimachus querulo formosam carmine Lydem
    et cecinit Sappho docta Phaona suum.
Lusisti infamem, miserande, Lycorida, Galle;
20   dixisti Nemesim, culte Tibulle, tuam.
Cynthia carminibus blandi est celebrata Properti,
    Nasonis versu pulchra Corinna viget,

BOOK TWO

: I :

To Lorenzo de' Medici

I who of late, Lorenzo, inflamed with marvelous love,
　　playfully penned many poems of my Fiammetta,
now ventured to sing in tragic buskin of the grand deeds of your
　　　　line,
　　but Cupid forbade me.

"Do *you*," he said, "dare describe the exploits of the Medici,　　　5
　　exploits scarcely to be recounted in Maro's tones?
And were you making so bold as to speed across the sea in a river
　　　　boat
　　that would have sunk in the open waters?
Leave these themes, which should be grandly treated in
　　　　Aeschylean style,
　　and be a soldier of winged Love.　　　　　　　　　　　10
Do not be ashamed to earn your pay in Cupid's camp;
　　such service will enable your name to be raised to the stars.
Under my command many have won eternal renown,
　　and their fame will endure for ever.
I breathe Phoebus' love into a bard as well,　　　　　　　　15
　　and Venus gives the power to speak now with Apollo's lips.
Callimachus sang of fair Lyde in plaintive song,
　　and learned Sappho of her Phaon.
Pitiable Gallus, you told of ill-famed Lycoris;
　　you, polished Tibullus, spoke of your Nemesis.　　　　　20
Cynthia was celebrated in pleasing Propertius' poems;
　　beautiful Corinna lives on in Naso's verse.

Lesbia, praedocti modulis cantata Catulli,
    gaudet ab extrema posteritate legi.
25 Nomine pastoris formosum lusit Alexim
    qui cecinit Phrygii tristia bella ducis,
ast niveam Lalagem Venusina natus in urbe
    dixit, et hic alios carpere doctus erat.
Divino Laurae Tyrrhenus amore Petrarca
30   cantavit Gallae lactea colla suae.
Per me turba viget clarorum maxima vatum
    quae nunc Lethaeis mersa lateret aquis.
Et te militiae volitantis taedet Amoris,
    et pudet in castris signa tulisse meis?
35 Me duce cum magno superi meruere Tonante,
    et quisque illorum praemia magna tulit.
En age, materiam dabimus tibi versibus aptam,
    et Medicum maior gesta poeta ferat.
Iurgia, blanditiae, lacrimaeque precesque minaeque—
40   est elegi proprium carminis istud opus.
Te minime ignavum formosae virginis ardor
    nec tota residem stertere nocte sinet.
Errat, desidiam si quisque vocabit amorem;
    credite, nullus amans desidiosus erit.'

45 Nunc me, Laurenti, aggressum maiora, Cupido
    dicere nequitiam compulit ipse meam.

Lesbia, hymned in erudite Catullus' strains,
    rejoices to be read by furthermost posterity.
He who sang of the grim wars fought by the Phrygian leader   25
    wrote in lighter vein, under a shepherd's name, of handsome
        Alexis,
while he who was born in the city of Venosa told of snow-white
        Lalage
    and was adept too at censuring others.
Tyrrhenian Petrarch, in his divine love for Laura,
    sang of his French lady's milky neck.   30
Through me very many famous poets yet live on
    who might now be forgotten, submerged in the waters of
        Lethe.
And are *you* weary of being a soldier of winged Love
    and ashamed of bearing standards in my camp?
Gods above, the mighty Thunderer among them, have served   35
        under my command,
    and each of them has gained great rewards.
Come, I will give you fit material for your verses,
    and let a greater poet recount the exploits of the Medici.
Quarrels, blandishments, tears, prayers, and threats—
    that is the proper business of elegiac poetry.   40
Passion for a beautiful maid will keep you very far from inactive
    and will not allow you to snore lazily in slumber all night long.
Anyone who ever calls love idle languishing is wrong;
    believe me, all you people, no one in love will be an idler."

Now, Lorenzo, in spite of my attempt at greater themes,   45
    Cupid has compelled me to tell of my own folly.

: II :

Ad Cupidinem, ne amplius eum vexet

Emeritum cur me rursus tua castra, Cupido,
    militiae cogis signa superba sequi,
principis atque iterum iurare in verba fidelem
    me numquam aligeri deserere arma dei?
5 Cur ita vexatur qui iam dediscit amare
    imbellis miles, proelia saeva pati?
Sunt tibi Tyrrheni iuvenes multaeque puellae,
    viribus atque annis turba petenda tibi.
His tu militibus Thylem superabis et Indos,
10   infidos Mauros Sauromatasque truces.
Quin et caelicolas vinces ipsumque Tonantem,
    ad vincla et supplex porriget ille manus.
Quin tibi Gradivus victricia porriget arma,
    privignoque ferox serviet ille suo.
15 Nobilis ista tuos comitetur turba triumphos,
    dique gerent vinctas post sua terga manus.
Maxime rex hominum cantabere, *maxime divum,*
    quisquis *Io,* magna voce, *triumphe!* canet,
maternaeque trahent felicia plaustra columbae;
20   sed ne militibus sis ferus ipse tuis.

: II :

To Cupid, that he trouble him no more

I have done my time in your ranks, Cupid. Why do you compel
  me
    again to follow your camp and the proud standards of your
    service,
and once more to swear an oath of loyalty to my prince
    never to desert the arms of the winged god?
Why is an unwarlike soldier troubled so, one who is now trying   5
  to forget
    being in love and enduring fierce battles?
You have many Tyrrhenian young men and many girls to choose
    from,
    all suitable recruits for you in their vigor and youth.
With them as your soldiers you will conquer Thyle and the
    Indians,
    the treacherous Moors and the fierce Sarmatians.   10
More than that, you will conquer the gods of heaven and the
    Thunderer himself,
    and he will offer his hands to chains as your suppliant.
Furthermore, Mars will surrender his victorious arms to you,
    and that fierce warrior will serve his stepson.
That distinguished band of captives will follow in your triumphs,   15
  and gods will be paraded with their hands bound behind their
    backs.
You will be hymned *King most mighty of men and gods*,
    everyone will sing *Hurrah for victory!* with loud voice,
and your mother's doves will pull the happy wagons;
    but do not be savage to your own soldiers.   20

Nescio cur victo fias crudelior hoste,
    curque omnes tractes condicione pari.
Blanditiis primo incautos deprehendis amantes,
    decipis et stultos calliditate puer;
25   quos postquam illecebris vicisti armatus inermes
    servitio horrendo, saeve Cupido, premis.
Non possum, licet ipse velim, narrare furorem,
    obstat scribenti nam pudor ipse mihi.
Quod licitum est aliis, nobis est turpe fateri;
30   nostra erit hoc uno littera manca loco.
Nam bene dum rapidae flammae celantur amoris,
    exstingui poterit dissimulatus amor.
Me miserum, quantae vexant mea pectora flammae!
    Me miserum, quantis ignibus urit Amor!
35   Hoc superi videant et, qui me perdidit unum,
    saevus Amor, nullum crimen inesse mihi.
Obiciet crimen nemo mihi praeter amorem,
    nam sine labe mihi candida vita fuit.

: III :

Ad librum Curiam Florentinam petentem

Atria Tyrrheni petis, ambitiose, Leonis;
    heu nimium sordent tecta paterna tibi!
Illic invenies multos, lascive, Catones;
    illic tractantur seria, parve liber.

I do not know why you turn crueler once your enemy has been
    vanquished
  and why you treat all your victims with the same ruthlessness.
First you catch lovers off their guard with enticing blandishments,
    and you deceive the foolish with cunning, though you are but
    a boy.
After you have conquered them with allurements (you armed   25
    when they are not),
  you oppress them, cruel Cupid, with a frightful servitude.
I cannot describe my passion, even should I wish to do so,
  for shame prevents me from writing of it.
What was allowed to others is disgraceful for me to admit;
  my poetry will be lacking in this one regard.   30
For, provided that the consuming flames of love are well hidden,
  it will be possible for dissembled love to be quenched.
How wretchedly I suffer! What great flames torment my breast,
  and with what great fires Love burns me in my misery!
May the gods above and cruel Love, who has been my particular   35
    destruction,
  see that there is no guilt in me.
No one will cast any charge in my face save that of love,
  for my pure life has been without blemish.

: III :

To his book as it heads for the senate house of Florence

Full of aspirations, you head for the halls of the Tyrrhenian Lion;
  alas, your father's roof is not good enough for you!
There, you wanton thing, you will find many Catos;
  there serious matters are dealt with, little book.

5 Quo properas, lascive? Mane! En, non te pudet unde
    cogeris nulla pulsus abire mora?
    At me defendet Laurentius, inquis, amicus,
      ut sperem gravibus posse placere viris.
    Gloria magna mei fuit et tutela libelli
10   vatibus Ausoniis semper amica domus.

: IV :

De nuptiis Lisiae Pictiae et Benedicti Biliocti

Alma Venus, nostris et tu Saturnia coeptis
    Iuno fave, et curva pulcher Apollo lyra.
Nunc vos, Pierides, casto date carmina vati,
    quae iuga Gorgoneis uda tenetis aquis.
5 Non hic Bellonae Martisque ferocia bella
    pallidus in media nocte poeta canit,
candida sed caro cum coniuge Lisa canetur.
    Adsis, cincte comas, o Hymenaee, tuas.
Quod felix faustumque precor. Procul esto, Megaera,
10   vipereas atro cincta dracone comas.
His adsis placido thalamis, Concordia, vultu;
    ambos unus amor servet et una fides.
Insignes forma, insignes virtutibus ambo
    iungant perpetui foedera sancta tori.

Where are you dashing off to, you wanton thing? Stay! Why, are   5
    you not ashamed
  to go where you will be instantly rebuffed and sent on your
    way?
But my friend Lorenzo will defend me, you say,
  and so I am hopeful of being able to please the grave
    gentlemen.
The house that is ever friendly to Ausonian poets
  has been my little book's great glory and protection.   10

: IV :

On the wedding of Lisa Pitti and Benedetto Biliotti

Kindly Venus, and you, Saturn's daughter Juno,
  and handsome Apollo with your curved lyre, favor my
    undertaking.
Now do you, Pierides, furnish your chaste bard with songs,
  you who dwell on the ridges moistened by the Gorgon's
    waters.
Not here does a pale poet sing in the middle of the night   5
  of the fierce wars of Bellona and Mars,
but fair Lisa will be my theme, along with her dear husband.
  Come join us here, Hymen, your hair ringed with a garland.
I pray for what is lucky and auspicious. Keep well away, Megaera,
  your viperous hair wreathed with black snakes.   10
Be you present at this marriage, tranquil-faced Concord;
  let one love and one bond of loyalty preserve both husband
    and wife.
Outstanding in looks and virtues as both are,
  may they join the holy bonds of an everlasting marriage.

15   Felices ambo, qui vos genuere parentes
      gaudia sub tacito pectore quanta ferent!
   Cum iuvenes longa praecedent ordine pompa,
      candida cum niveo nupta vehetur equo,
   cumque tubis festos cantabit tibia ludos,
20   cum restim iuveni mixta puella trahet,
   suspendet ramum ad speculam frondentis olivi
      rusticus, et niveas sparget ubique rosas,
   udaque tum multo madefactus tempora Baccho
      dicet inornatos ore canente sonos.

: V :

Eulogium Alberae puellae sub porticu attritae

   Quam dira, heu, miseris fati mortalibus instat
      sors! Heu, quam magnum porticus ausa nefas!
   Omnia, me miserum, sibi vult Fortuna licere.
      Pro, tantum terris, di, prohibete nefas!
5   Porticus annoso ligno suffulta rigebat,
      quod carie attrivit longa senecta malo.
   Rusticus hic imbrem atque aestus vitare solebat,
      nam Tusca hanc quartus signat ab urbe lapis.
   Venerat huc multis comitata Albera puellis,
10   infelixque, illic dum manet, illa perit.

Happy pair, what joys your parents, who brought you into the   15
    world,
  will feel within their silent breasts!
When young men go in line before you in a long procession,
  when the radiant bride rides on her snow-white horse,
when flute joins with trumpets to sound forth the festivities,
  and when girls mingle with youths in trailing out the rope,   20
the countryman will hang up a branch of leafy olive at his upper
    window,
  sprinkle snow-white roses all around,
and then, his moistened temples befuddled with much wine,
  give voice to unembellished strains as his lips open in song.

: V :

Eulogy for the girl Albiera, crushed beneath a portico

How dreadful, alas, is the doom of death that bears down on
    wretched mortals!
  Alas, how great a sin a portico has dared commit!
Fortune (how it pains me!) wants total license for herself.
  O bar such great wickedness, gods, from our earth!
A portico stood supported on old wood   5
  that long passage of time wore away with accursed rotting.
Here the peasant was accustomed to escape from rain and heat,
  for the fourth milestone from the Tuscan city marks its
    position.
Albiera had come here accompanied by many girls,
  and while tarrying in the place she unluckily met her end.   10

Porticus ingentem traxit collapsa ruinam.
    Pignora dum protegit, concidit ipsa parens.
Concidit et caro vitam servavit alumno,
    carior et nati quam sua vita fuit.
15 Crudeles, quid vos truncastis stamina, Parcae?
    An vestra infecit pectora livor edax?
Quid pietas, quid forma tibi, quid profuit aetas,
    quin cito tu Lethes flumina nigra bibas?
Quid lacrimae, quid vota pii valuere mariti,
20   quid, quod eras Scalae vatis amica tui?
Te tamen Elysios praestantior umbra recessus
    nulla petet. Ditis coniuge maior eris,
filia sit quamvis Cereris neptisque Tonantis,
    et licet inferni nupta sit illa Iovis.

∶ VI ∶

Epitaphium Alberae puellae

En poteris siccis me cernere, lector, ocellis?
    Numne piis lacrimis ora rigare gemens?
Perlege marmoreo tumulo hoc miserabile carmen,
    nam causam et nomen littera maesta docet.

The portico collapsed and brought much of the structure
    crashing down.
  The mother perished protecting her offspring.
She perished and saved her dear boy's life;
    her son's life was dearer to her than her own.
Cruel Fates, why did you cut short her threads?   15
  Did consuming jealousy infect your hearts?
Of what help to you, Albiera, were your piety, beauty, and youth
    in saving you from drinking so soon the black waters of Lethe?
Of what avail were the tears and the prayers of your loving
    husband
    or the fact that you were your poet Scala's ladylove?   20
Yet no shade more supremely beautiful than you will seek the
    Elysian retreats.
  You will surpass Dis' consort,
though she is the daughter of Ceres and the granddaughter of the
    Thunderer,
    and though she is the bride of the Jupiter of the Lower World.

: VI :

Epitaph of the girl Albiera

What, reader, will you be able to look on me with dry eyes?
  Do you not sigh, and is your face not damp with tears of
    compassion?
Read through this pitiable poem on my marble tomb,
  for its sad message tells you the cause of my death and my
    name.

5   Vix me bis denos numerantem porticus annos
     dum ruit Elysias compulit ire domos.
  Alberae fuerat nomen mihi. Lector amice,
     ne pigeat tumulo collacrimare meo.

: VII :

Ad Clio, ut Romae reliquias et
Petrum Caponium visat

Reliquias Romae, docto comitata Capone,
     Clio, refer, quondam quae caput orbis erat.
Dic, an Aventinum montem pharetrata Diana
     servat? An Esquilias numina prisca tenent?
5   An Capitolina se Iuppiter ornat in arce?
     Numne Palatinus Phoebus in aede sua est,
  an versa in cineres miranda potentia Romae est?
     Heu, nunc sub tanta diruta mole iacet!
Nullane tantarum maneant vestigia rerum,
10   ut mala marmoreas obruat herba domos?
  Singula conspicies veterum monumenta Quiritum,
     postque salutato, Musa, recede Petro.

When I barely counted twice ten years a portico collapsed   5
    and made me go to dwell in Elysium.
My name was Albiera. Kindly reader,
    be not loath to shed tears at my tomb.

ː VII ː

To Clio, that she visit the remains of
Rome and Piero Capponi

In the company of learned Capponi, bring back word, Clio, of
    the remains of Rome,
    the one-time capital of the world.
Tell me, does quivered Diana keep safe the Aventine Hill?
    Do old-time deities occupy the Esquiline?
Is Jupiter honored in splendor on the Capitoline citadel?   5
    Is Palatine Phoebus in his temple,
or has Rome's awe-inspiring might been turned to ashes?
    Alas, she lies now in ruins beneath such a mass of rubble!
Do no traces of such great glories remain,
    so that wicked grass overwhelms the marble houses?   10
Pray look upon all the monuments of Rome's citizens of old,
    and then, Muse, bid Piero farewell and return to me.

: VIII :

De Apollonio pictore insigni

Maeonides quondam Phoebeae moenia Troiae
    cantarat Graiis esse cremata rogis,
atque iterum insidias Danaum Troiaeque ruinam
    altiloqui cecinit grande Maronis opus;
5   sed certo melius nobis nunc Tuscus Apelles
    Pergamon incensum pinxit Apollonius,
Aeneaeque fugam atque iram Iunonis iniquae
    et mira quassas pinxerat arte rates
Neptunique minas, summum dum pervolat aequor,
10   a rapidis mulcet dum freta versa Notis.
Pinxit ut Aeneas, fido comitatus Achate,
    urbem Phoenissae dissimulanter adit;
discessumque suum, miserae quoque funus Elissae,
    monstrat Apolloni picta tabella manu.

: IX :

Ad Ciprianum

Quod sis nobilium procerum conviva frequenter,
    esse illis carum te, Cipriane, putas,
perque forum medium quod deducaris ab illis,
    haec fieri forsan credis honore tui.

: VIII :

On the distinguished painter Apollonio

The Maeonian once sang of how the walls of Phoebus' Troy
    were consumed by Greek funeral pyres,
and the Danaans' trickery and Troy's fall were once more
    the theme of the grand work of lofty-speaking Maro;
but Apollonio, a Tuscan Apelles, has surely now   5
    better depicted Pergamum in flames for us,
and he has also painted with marvelous skill Aeneas' flight,
    hostile Juno's anger, the battered ships,
and Neptune's threats, as he flies over the surface of the sea,
    calming waters set heaving by the rushing south winds.   10
He has depicted how Aeneas, accompanied by faithful Achates,
    secretly goes to the Phoenician woman's city;
and Aeneas' departure and poor Elissa's death too
    are shown in a picture painted by Apollonio's hand.

: IX :

To Cipriano

Because you are frequently a guest-at-table of the noblest men,
    you suppose, Cipriano, that you are highly regarded by them,
and the fact that they escort you through the middle of the
        marketplace
    perhaps leads you to believe all this is done out of respect for
        you.

5   Delectas illos, non tu, Cipriane, probaris;
     nam quis stultitias posset amare tuas?

: X :

Ad Amerigum Corsinum de puerorum vitando concubitu

  Hoc est cur teneras sectaris, amice, puellas,
     et tua cur nullus pectora flexit Athis:
  scilicet umbrosae silvae te tristis imago
     terruit horrendo vaticinata sono,
5   *Utatur si quis Phrygii Ganymedis amore,*
     aeterno infelix igne cremandus erit.
  Nunc quicumque sapit talem vitabit amorem.
     Heu quanta est illis poena parata viris!
  Iudice Corsino, moneo, vitate cinaedos:
10   spurcius his nihil est nec capitale magis.

: XI :

Ad Laurentium Lippum

  Desine Laurenti tantas facunde querelas
     fundere de iusto, desine velle queri.
  Nam precibus fortes, donis flectuntur avari
     (sic esca incautas callida fallit aves),
5   sed qua praecipue possit ratione moveri
     nescimus stultus, qui ratione caret.

You amuse them, Cipriano, you are not well thought of;   5
   for who could love your displays of foolishness?

: X :

To Amerigo Corsini on shunning sleeping with boys

The reason why you pursue young girls, my friend,
   and why no Attis has swayed your heart,
is no doubt that the grim image of the shadowy wood
   has struck terror into you, warning you in words of dreadful
      import,
If anyone should indulge in the love of a Phrygian Ganymede,   5
   the wretch shall surely be burned in the eternal fire.
Now anyone with sense will shun such love.
   Alas, how great a punishment is in store for those men!
Follow Corsini's judgment, I advise you all, and shun catamites:
   there is nothing fouler than they, nor do any criminals more   10
      deserve death.

: XI :

To Lorenzo Lippi

Leave off pouring out so many righteous complaints, eloquent
   Lorenzo;
   stop seeking to voice protests:
for brave men are swayed by prayers, and greedy men by gifts
   (that is how the cunning bait tricks unwary birds),
but by what method a fool can best be influenced   5
   is a mystery to us, as he has no method in his madness.

: XII :

De quodam rustico qui intravit lupanar Florentinum

Nescius Etruscum intraret cum forte lupanar
    rusticus et nomen quaereret inde viae,
'Intus adest quod quaeris,' inquit nonaria, 'mecum
    i, sequar,' atque addit postibus illa seram.
5 Ille, ubi se clausum sensit nil tale verentem,
    credidit extremum lucis adesse diem;
cellula nam fumo squalebat nigra lacernae
    et paene obscuri carceris instar erat.
Atque ubi se contra venientem Thaida cernit,
10   extimuit gelido pallidus ille metu.
Hic fugit, illa instat dextra attrectare paventem.
    Dum fugit exclamat, 'Numina, fertis opem!
Obsecro, fertis opem misero, vicinia!' clamat.
    'Heu, heu! quae patior, carcere quove premor!'
15 Huc ebrii veniunt lenones, huc meretrices,
    huc calidi lustri cetera turba ruit.
Thaida circum instant, resonat clamore lupanar,
    cognita sed cunctis res fuit illa ioco.
Rusticus egressus meretrici iurgia multa
20   intulit, inde cita proripuitque fuga.

: XII :

On a certain rustic who entered a Florentine brothel

When a countryman unwittingly chanced to walk into an
    Etruscan brothel
  and to inquire from there the name of the street,
a ninth-hour-girl said, "I've got what you're looking for in here;
  lead the way, I'll follow," and set the bar in place on the door.
The rustic, upon perceiving himself quite unexpectedly shut in,   5
  thought that the last day of his life had come;
for her tiny cubicle was filthy black with the smoke of the lamp
  and was almost like a dark dungeon.
And when he saw this Thais advancing upon him,
  he was scared pale in the face with ice-cold fear.   10
He fled, while she strained in pursuit to grasp her terrified quarry
    with her right hand.
  As he fled, he screamed out, "Powers of heaven, help me!
I beg you, help a poor wretch, all you neighbors here!
  Alas, alas, what an outrage I suffer, and what a prison I'm
    trapped in!"
Drunken pimps came on the scene, prostitutes appeared,   15
  and the rest of the hot bawdy house's company rushed up.
They pressed round the Thais, and the brothel resounded with
    shouting,
  but everybody realized it was all just a joke.
The rustic emerged, heaped many reproaches on the prostitute,
  and made off from the place in a hasty escape.   20

: XIII :

Ad Braccium Martellum

Cur, Martelle, meos carpis sine crimine mores,
    vita mihi semper si sine labe fuit?
Innocuum cur me laceras? Tua pectora cur sic
    tanto odio flagrent non tibi causa mei est.
5 Te numquam nostro, nec quemquam, carmine laesi,
    vipereisque caret littera nostra iocis.
Doctior est alius, sed me non castior ullus;
    non lasciva mihi sed proba vita fuit.
Dilexi, fateor, succensus amore, puellam.
10   Sunt vitae haec, si sunt, crimina magna meae,
    et nondum nobis bis denus contigit annus.
    Si tamen est quidquam, causa feretur amor.
Si Cato, si nigris revocetur Curius umbris,
    non carpet mores ille vel ille meos.
15 In te Pierides, ni desinis, arma capessent;
    in te tela simul ferre coactus ero.
Nec me despicias quia sim de paupere natus
    patre: tamen carus civis in urbe sua est.
Quin etiam proavus Tusci vexilla Leonis
20   bis rexit, tanto dignus honore, meus.
Contemnas quamvis Musas et Apollinis artes,
    te dicet linguae quilibet esse malae.

⁚ XIII ⁚

To Braccio Martelli

Why, Martelli, do you carp at my blameless character,
   if my life has always been without blemish?
Why do you wound me when I am guiltless of any offense?
    There is no reason that your heart should burn with such
      hatred of me.
I have never hurt you or anybody else with my poetry,   5
   and what I write is free of viperish jokes.
There are others more learned than I, but none more chaste;
   my life has not been lascivious but pure.
Fired by love, I have cared for a girl, I admit.
    These are my life's great crimes, if they are such at all,   10
and I have not yet attained my twentieth year.
    If, however, there is anything amiss, the cause will be said to
      be love.
If Cato or Curius were recalled from the dark shades,
    neither the one nor the other would find fault with my
      character.
The Pierides will take up arms against you, unless you desist,   15
   and I shall be forced to do the same along with them.
Do not despise me on the grounds that I was born of a poor
    father:
   he is yet a well-esteemed citizen in his city.
Moreover, my great-grandfather had charge of the Tuscan Lion's
    standards
   on two occasions and was worthy of so great an honor.   20
Though you may despise the Muses and Apollo's arts,
   everybody will say you have a wicked tongue.

: XIV :

Ad Iustum amicum

O mihi iucundos inter numerande sodales
 Iuste, Fluentini maxima fama soli,
det tibi longaevae felicia tempora vitae,
 det tibi candentes Parca secunda dies.
5 Iusta precor, superi; pro Iusto debita posco;
 sint rata pro Iusto debita vota precor.

: XV :

Ad eundem

Non dubito quin te felix ego dicar amico;
 dispeream, mihi si carior alter adest!
Quam bene conveniunt Verino nomina Iusti:
 Verinus Iusto verus amicus erit.

: XVI :

In Philippum maledicum

Saepius inquiris, 'Quid scis?' me carpere tentans.
 Hoc unum scio, te scire, Philippe, nihil.

: XIV :

To his friend Justus

O one to be counted among my delightful companions,
    Justus, greatest glory of the Florentine state,
may Fate smile on you and grant you happy times in a long life,
    grant you bright, sunny days!
What I pray for is just, gods above; I ask for Justus what is his   5
    due;
    I pray that my due wishes for Justus may be granted.

: XV :

To the same

I do not doubt that I shall be called lucky to have you as a friend;
    may I perish, if I have any other dearer!
How well the name of Justus fits with that of Verino!
    Verino will be a true friend to Justus!

: XVI :

Against the slanderer Filippo

Many a time you ask me, "What do you know?" when trying to
    carp at me.
    One thing I *do* know is that you, Filippo, know nothing.

: XVII :

Ad Peregrinum Allium

Ne forte ignores ubi sim vel nescius erres,
    accipe quae dicent carmina pauca tibi.
inter Tyrrhenas Florentia nobilis urbes
    me genuit, nostrae hic gentis origo fuit,
5 atque ubi sunt veteres sedem posuere penates,
    Spirituae classis non procul aede mei.
Sed non hac causa nobis responsa dedisti,
    Musa sed illoto venerat illa pede,
et nimium petulans, quae se Permessidos unda
10   non prius abluerat, iam rapuisset iter.
Et nunc Castalio nondum perlota liquore
    tristia tam docti iudicis ora tremit.

: XVIII :

Ad Montanum vatem

I nunc, Montano defer mea carmina vati,
    hunc salvere meo nomine, Musa, iube.
Munera grata solent auri magis esse poetis,
    Montano sed erunt carmina grata magis.
5 Divitias cupidus petit, ambitiosus honores,
    mortale est quidquid mobile vulgus amat.

: XVII :

To Pellegrino Agli

In case you happen not to know where I am, or unwittingly err,
   here are a few verses that will tell you.
Florence, noble among Tyrrhenian cities,
   gave me my birth, here was my family's origin,
and my household gods of old set up their seat where they are   5
     now,
   not far from the church of my quarter of Santo Spirito.
But it was not for this reason that you gave me your responses,
   but that Muse of mine had come with foot unwashed
and had too impudently ventured forth in haste
   without first bathing in the stream of Permessis.   10
Even now, having not yet been thoroughly washed in the
     Castalian waters,
   she quakes before the stern face of so learned a judge.

: XVIII :

To the poet Montano

Go now, Muse, take my poems to the poet Montano,
   and greet him in my name.
Gifts of gold are normally more pleasing to bards,
   but poems will please Montano more.
The greedy man wants riches, the ambitious man honors;   5
   everything beloved of the fickle crowd is mortal.

Quid melius Musis, quid Apolline dulcius exstat,
    per quem post cineres vita secunda datur?
Ad vatem propera nostros deferre libellos;
10   laeta fronte meos perleget ille iocos.
Carminibus comitata suis ad nostra redibis
    scrinia, montano plena, Thalia, sale.

: XIX :

Ad puerum formosum

Utere labenti fugitivae munere formae,
    nam numquam redeunt qui periere dies.
Lanugo niveas iam vestiet horrida malas.
    Tunc male praeteritos flebis abesse dies.
5 Tunc quam sit durum cognosces fallere amantem.
    Carmina tunc quanto nostra dolore leges,
'Cur mihi non redeunt transacti tempora floris?'
    et dices. 'Cur mens non fuit ista mihi?'

: XX :

Ad tumidum et inflatum

Cum nec nobilior nec te sit doctior alter,
    cum tibi sit procerum sedula turba comes,
miraris cur non tibi turba assurgat eunti,
    et tibi cur meritus non tribuatur honor.

What is there better than the Muses or sweeter than Apollo,
    through whom we are given a second life after death?
Hasten to take my poems to the poet;
    he will read through my jokes with a joyful face.   10
Return to my book-chest, Thalia, accompanied
    by poems of his, full of "mountain" wit.

⦂ XIX ⦂

To a beautiful boy

Make use of the passing gift of fleeting beauty,
    for days that have been lost never return.
Very soon now bristly down will clothe your snow-white cheeks.
    Then you will tearfully rue that days gone by are no more.
Then you will learn how cruel it is to disappoint a lover.   5
    Then with what great pain will you read my poems and say,
"Why does the time of my spent youth not return?
    Why did I not think then as I do now?"

⦂ XX ⦂

To a proud and puffed-up man

Since there is none nobler or more learned than you,
    and you have an attentive band of leading men accompanying
        you around,
you wonder why the crowd does not rise to you as you go along
    and why deserved honor is not paid you.

5 Crede mihi, astuta est nimium Florentia, quae te
   sic aspernatur stultitiasque tuas.

: XXI :

Epitaphium egregii civis Benini Florentini

Ille ego sum Tusci quo consultore Leonis
   publica res summo constabilita loco est.
Iustitiam et mores colui, pietatis amator;
   sola mihi virtus unica cura fuit.
5 Candida me Petrum servant nunc templa Beninum:
   hoc claudit tumulo candidus ossa lapis.

: XXII :

Ad Cupidinem nimium saevientem

Ergo ero quem semper figant tua tela, Cupido,
   et miser adverso semper Amore premar?
Hei mihi, nulla dies niveo signanda lapillo
   defluet? Infelix en ego semper ero?
5 Aut moriar vitae primis exstinctus in annis,
   aut mihi mitis erit qui modo saevit Amor.
Me miserum, adversis Fatis genuere parentes;
   principium infaustum Parca maligna dedit!

Believe me: Florence, which thus spurns you   5
    and your follies, has too much sense.

: XXI :

Epitaph of the eminent citizen Piero del Benino of Florence

I am he by whose counsel the state of the Tuscan Lion
    was firmly established in pride of place.
I cherished justice and right conduct and was a lover of godliness;
    virtue was my one and only care.
A white shrine now shelters me, Piero del Benino;   5
    in this tomb white stone encloses my bones.

: XXII :

To Cupid in his excessive cruelty

Shall I, then, always be a target for your arrows to pierce, Cupid,
    and in my misery be oppressed by having Love always against
      me?
Ah me, will there be no day to mark with a snow-white pebble?
    Shall I then always be unlucky?
Either I shall die, killed off in my first years of life,   5
    or else Love, who now is cruel, will be gentle to me.
To my woe, my parents brought me into the world with the Fates
    against me;
    a malign Fate gave me an inauspicious beginning!

Quid sit amor iam tum noram puerilibus annis
10   (necdum gustaram dulcia furta puer)
cum deus armatus mihi bella paravit inermi,
    torsit et ardentes nostra per ossa faces.
Egregiam palmam nempe hanc duo numina divum
    me puero victo tunc meruere dolis!
15   Me Cytherea petit certique Cupidinis arcus
    telaque in exitium vix numeranda meum.
Sed quisnam poterit vitare Cupidinis arma,
    et quis ab insidiis tutus Amoris erit?
Cuncta videt, quamvis caecus, puer, omnia vincit,
20   armatos superat nudus et ille deos.
Forte per Haemonios campos, Pythone perempto,
    ibat siderei qui regit astra poli,
et, caede exultans, puerum contempsit Amorem,
    et tumido indignos protulit ore sonos:
25   'Tune meos titulos rapis, ambitiose Cupido?
    Conveniunt forti fortia tela deo.
Pone arma; haec nostrae sunt convenientia dextrae.
    Femineos mollis quaere Cupido procos.'
Talibus exarsit dictis Cythereia proles.
30   'Spicula quid possint experiere mea,'
dixit. Fraxineos curvavit fortiter arcus,
    transilit et medium flava sagitta iecur.
Ah, quantis curis miser est vexatus Apollo,
    illum dum Daphne virgo pudica fugit!

I learned what love is already in my boyhood years
    (and I had not then tasted sweet amours, being but a boy)   10
when the god prepared to make war on me, he with his weapons
        against me unarmed,
    and hurled burning torches through my bones.
It was a glorious victory, to be sure, that two deities won then
    by defeating me, a boy, with their wiles!
Cytherea assails me, and Cupid's unerring bow,   15
    and his arrows almost past counting, shot for my destruction.
But who will be able to avoid Cupid's arms,
    and who will be safe from the ambushes of Love?
The boy is all seeing, though blind, and all conquering,
    and he vanquishes gods in arms, though naked himself.   20
By chance he who rules the constellations of the starry heaven
    was making his way through the fields of Haemonia after
        slaying Python,
and, exulting in his kill, he treated the boy Love with contempt,
    and came out with unfitting remarks from his pride-elated lips.
"Do *you* usurp *my* honors, ambitious Cupid?   25
    Brave weapons befit a brave god.
Lay down your arms; it is *my* right hand that should wield such
        weapons.
    Find yourself womanish suitors to prey upon, effeminate
        Cupid."
Cytherea's child flared up at such words.
    "You shall experience what my darts can do!" he said.   30
Mightily he bent his ashen bow,
    and a golden arrow passed through the middle of his quarry's
        liver.
Ah, with how many cares poor Apollo was vexed,
    while the chaste maid Daphne fled him!

35   Me miserum, quanti veniunt in amore dolores,
     durius in terris ut sit amore nihil!
   Pro superi, tantum mortalia pectora vexat,
     vexat, pro, tantum perniciosus Amor!
   Quanta quidem miseros insania turbat amantes!
40   Mutantur quanta mobilitate leves!
   Rectius amentes quam dicere possis amantes,
     expers est omnis nam rationis amans.
   Et meliora vident et deteriora sequuntur.
     Quid facias? Saevo mens sub Amore iacet.
45   Prudentes pereunt, sed quid prudentia prodest?
     Indomitus captis mentibus haeret Amor.
   Difficile est primos vitare Cupidinis ictus,
     pectora sed numquam capta furore carent.
   En age, semper eris Veneris nova praeda, Verine?
50   Non satis ad flammas Flammea Virgo fuit?
   Uror ut accensis fervet Liparea caminis,
     fulminis Ignipotens dum rude tractat opus,
   cum defessa movet crudelis membra Typhoeus,
     fumiferos caelo cum vomit Aetna focos;
55   utque leves stipulae ventis spirantibus ardent,
     arentes postquam pastor inussit agros,
   sic pectus nobis ferventi exaestuat igne,
     flammaque dum tegitur, convalet illa magis.
   Hoc pudor, illud amor, vetat hic, iubet alter adire,
60   nam studet hic famae, quod iuvat alter habet.
   Sic anceps vertit mens in contraria pectus.
     Hei mihi, quid faciat non videt ullus amans,

Woe is me, how many pains come in love,   35
  so that there is nothing on earth crueler than love!
Ye gods! So much does ruinous Love torment mortal hearts,
  so much, alas, does he torment them!
What great insanity indeed disturbs wretched lovers!
  With what great inconstancy the fickle creatures change!   40
You would more correctly call them out of their minds than in
    love,
  for every lover is devoid of reason.
They see the better way and yet follow the worse.
  What are you to do? Your mind lies in cruel Love's power.
Wise men pine, and what good is their wisdom?   45
  Indomitable Love clings to their captive minds.
It is difficult to avoid Cupid's first blows,
  but hearts once captured are never free of raging passion.
Come, will you always be Venus' latest prize, Verino?
  Was the Flame Maiden not cause enough of flames?   50
I am as much afire as Lipara is hot with blazing forges,
  when the fire lord shapes the half-made form of a thunderbolt;
when cruel Typhoeus stirs his tired-out limbs,
  and Etna spews forth smoky fires to the sky;
and as the flimsy grasses blaze with the breath of the winds   55
  after a shepherd has set the dry fields alight,
so my heart burns with a blazing fire,
  and while the flame is hidden, it grows in strength the more.
Shame prompts one course, love another; the one forbids an
    approach, the other urges it;
  for the one is concerned with reputation, but the other has   60
    delight to offer.
Thus my vacillating mind steers my heart this way and that.
  Ah me, no man in love sees what he does,

si sibi purpurei pensum est aut cura pudoris;
    pectore namque uno pugnat uterque ferox.
65 Sed pudor, ut cuncta, indigno succumbet Amori,
    deque meis spoliis bina trophaea feret.

⋮ XXIII ⋮

Ad Cherubinum

Cedant scriptores nobis Venusinaque tellus,
    Romanae quamvis sit decus omne lyrae,
cedat et Alcaeus nobis et mascula Sappho,
    dulcius haec quamvis, grandius ille sonet,
5 et Thebae et Smyrnae cedant et Mantua nobis,
    lugeat et posita victus Apollo chely.
Ne mirum sit, me tanto Cherubinus honore
    affecit, quoniam sic Cherubinus ait.
Nescio cur tantum laudet, nisi doctus haberi
10   et voluit notus laudibus esse meis.
Laudibus aetherias iam iam volitabit in auras,
    si modo tot laudes iam superesse queunt.
Laudari cupio, cupio quoque semper amari,
    blandus adulator sed procul omnis eat.

if he has any thought or concern for red-faced shame;
    for in one heart, in fierce contention, those two forces, love
      and shame, do battle.
But shame, like all things, will succumb to unworthy Love,   65
    and he will win twofold trophies from spoils taken from me.

: XXIII :

To Cherubino

Let writers yield place to *me:* let the land of Venosa yield,
    though he is the whole glory of the Roman lyre;
Alcaeus too, and manly Sappho,
    though he sounds more sweetly, she more grandly;
let Thebes yield to me, and Smyrna, and Mantua;   5
    and let Apollo lay down his lyre and grieve in defeat.
To save any wonder at my meaning, Cherubino has bestowed
      such honor on me,
    since Cherubino speaks of me in those terms.
I do not know why he praises me so much, unless he wanted to
      be thought learned
    and to be famous through his praises of me.   10
Through his praises he will at any moment fly off to the air of
      heaven,
    if only he can still have so many praises left in him.
I want to be praised, and I want always to be loved too,
    but may every smooth-talking flatterer get far away from me.

: XXIV :

Ad Bartholomaeum Platinensem de traductione Homeri

Maeonios quid me cogis traducere cantus
    (non est haec umeris sarcina danda meis),
quem Grai atque Itali vix libavere poetae
    Pieriae unde fluit lucidus umor aquae?
5 Carminibus nostris forsan, dum ludimus ignes,
    effugiet nigros nostra puella rogos,
et forsan celebris Tyrrhena per oppida curret
    Flammetta, ardoris maxima flamma mei.
Magnos magna decent. Ego dicar lusor amoris,
10 tu referes grandi grandia verba lyra.
Smyrnaei melius divina poemata vatis
    Romano poteris ipse referre pede.

: XXV :

De muscipula quae infantem strangulavit

Quid rapidae maius tigres Libycique leones
    audebunt, Veneris cum ferus urget amor?
Sive fame, aut ira cum fervida corda tumescunt,
    hoc canis auderet quae rabiosa nefas?

: XXIV :

To Bartolomeo Platina on translating Homer

Why do you press me to translate the Maeonian's poems?
    That burden is not to be entrusted to *my* shoulders.
From those works there flows a clear stream of Pierian water
    that the Greek and Italian poets have scarcely sipped.
Perhaps, while I write playfully of love fires, in my poems   5
    my girl will escape the black grave of oblivion,
and perhaps much report of Fiammetta, my passion's mighty
        flame,
    will speed through the Tyrrhenian towns.
Great matters are suited to great men. *I* shall be called a playful
        poet of love;
    you will revive those grand words with your grand lyre.   10
You will be better able to reproduce in Roman measures
    the divine poems of the bard of Smyrna.

: XXV :

On a rattrap that strangled an infant

What greater act of savagery will ferocious tigers and Libyan
        lions dare,
    when fierce lust drives them on?
Whether out of hunger, or when her seething heart swells with
        rage,
    what rabid bitch would dare commit such a heinous crime?

5   Strangulat infantem muris raptator edacis
      atque avido pueri viscera dente fodit.
   Quid magis infandum vel quid crudelius umquam
      Tyrrhenus Tusca vidit in urbe Leo?

⫶ XXVI ⫶

Ad Naldum Naldinum de invido

Baccare frondenti ut cingam mea tempora suades,
    nam daphnaea mihi, Nalde, corona nocet.
Hoc verum fateor, quia non sum munere Phoebi
    dignus ut exornent laurea serta comas;
5   invideat si quis studiis, doctissime, nostris,
     invideat cunctis sed sine fine miser.
Nemo sibi solus careat livore beatus —
    indoctus, pauper, turpis, ineptus, iners.
Invideat, doleat, stupeat quoque, mordeat ungues,
10   et crepet hic tandem, lividus invidia.

⫶ XXVII ⫶

Ad Amerigum Corsinum

Miraris, longo cum sis de stemmate natus,
    et titulis multis sit tua clara domus,
et facunda tibi non desint verba diserto,
    cur fugit amplexus candida Lisa tuos.

A trap for the voracious rat has shut fast on an infant   5
    and pierced the boy's entrails with its greedy tooth.
What more unspeakable or crueler thing
    did the Tyrrhenian Lion ever see in the Tuscan city?

ː XXVI ː

To Naldo Naldi on a jealous man

You urge me to ring my temples with the leafy nard plant, Naldo,
    for a laurel crown does me harm.
I admit it is true that I am not worthy through Phoebus' gift
    of having a garland of laurel adorn my hair;
but if anyone were to be jealous of *my* poetic efforts, most learned   5
    Naldo,
    the poor fellow would be endlessly jealous of everyone.
Not a single "lucky" soul would escape his jealousy —
    not the unlearned, the poor, the ugly, the inept, the sluggish.
He would be resentful, pained, and aghast, he would chew on his
    nails,
    and he would grumble away, livid with jealousy.   10

ː XXVII ː

To Amerigo Corsini

You wonder, since you are born of an old noble line,
    your house is distinguished with many titles,
and you are not wanting for eloquent words, being an articulate man,
    why fair Lisa flies your embraces.

5   Indignum exclamas facinus, Corsine, puellae,
      quae te tam doctum nolit habere virum.
   Crede mihi, nimium fastus amor odit avitos;
      nobilibus solus cedere nescit amor.
   Aut avidam numquam tentasti munere Lisam?
10   Munere, crede mihi, vincitur omnis amor.
   Sed, tamquam sapiens, haec tu deperdere non vis,
      sed solum hanc tentas fallere blanditiis.
   Ad limen frustra surdae cantabis amicae,
      incassum iactans nomina prisca patrum.

⁝ XXVIII ⁝

In Franciscum nequam

Producas quod tu ad multam convivia noctem,
     scilicet excusas, 'Fecerat ista Cato.'
Quod nudos inter iaceas, Francisce, cinaedos,
     hoc vitium patriae dicis habere tuae.
5   Dic tamen unde tibi sit tanta superbia, cum te
     pauperior tota nullus in urbe fuit
nec magis infamis; dic unde superbia tanta est,
     nomina cum minime dicere possis avi.

You protest loudly at the undeserved outrage that the girl   5
    commits, Corsini,
  in refusing to have so learned a fellow as you for her man.
Believe me, love thoroughly hates haughty pride in one's
    ancestors,
  love alone does not know how to defer to rank.
But have you never tried out greedy Lisa with a gift?
  All love, believe me, can be won with a gift.   10
Yet in your "wisdom" you are unwilling to incur such expense,
  but try to turn her head merely with flatteries.
You will sing in vain at the threshold of a girlfriend deaf to you,
  as you vaunt to no purpose the ancient names of your
    forebears.

: XXVIII :

Against the wicked Francesco

For your drawing out banquets till late in the night
  no doubt you make the excuse, "Cato did the same."
As for your lying between naked catamites, Francesco,
  you say it is a vice you share with all your countrymen.
Yet tell me where you get your great arrogance,   5
  since there has been none poorer than you in the whole city
nor anyone more disreputable; tell me where your arrogance
    comes from,
  since you are quite unable to name your grandfather.

: XXIX :

Ad Locterium Neronium

Carmina cum nequeat, quidam vult carpere mores;
    invidus ut placeant carmina nostra dolet.
Hoc ideo de me quaedam tibi crimina finxit:
    a te, Locteri, quod prober ipse, dolet.
5 Nunc ego laudari magis, et magis opto probari,
    ut crepet et doleat lividus ille magis.

: XXX :

Cur aurum palleat

'Nimirum,' Cynicus dixit, 'cur palleat aurum,
    namque dolis omnes insidiantur ei.'

: XXXI :

Ad Nerium Be.

Quod placidam requiem, quod molles carpere somnos
    non possis quereris, nec vigilare die.
Nunc tibi causa instat cari commissa sodalis,
    nunc tua res angit teque relicta domus,

: XXIX :

To Lottieri Neroni

Unable to find fault with my poems, a certain person is out to
    reproach my behavior;
   the jealous fellow is upset at how my poems please.
It is for this reason then that he has trumped up certain
    allegations about me to you:
   he is upset that I meet with your approval, Lottieri.
Now I want to be praised more and approved more   5
   to make that jealous backbiter grumble and grieve more.

: XXX :

Why gold is pale

"It is no wonder," said the Cynic, "that gold is pale,
   for all have scheming designs to lay hands on it."

: XXXI :

To Neri Be.

You complain that you cannot get any peaceful rest or soft slumber,
   and that you cannot stay awake during the day.
Now the conduct of a dear friend's cause, entrusted to you, is on
    your mind;
   now your own business and the house you have left behind
    make you worry;

5 nunc dulces vexant saevae ambitionis honores,
  te forsan pulchrae virginis ardor habet,
 nunc te sollicitat tumido quae gurgite multis
  mercibus et gaza puppis onusta natat—
 et miraris adhuc, nequeas quod ducere somnos
10 et placidae quod non otia mentis agas?
 Immo ego mirarer si, tantis excite curis,
  in media *posses* stertere nocte, Neri.
 Fac cupias metuasque nihil, mediocriter omnes
  dilige, sed vitii conscius esto tui.
15 Ducere sic somnos poteris placidamque quietem,
  si nihil exoptes, dulcis amice, nimis.

∶ XXXII ∶

In Petrum hypocritam

 Quid fronte obducta et tetrica me, Cretice, voce
  corripis et fundis tristia dicta, Petre,
 ac Zenona mihi rigidum tristesque Catones
  obicis et quidquid Stoica verba sonant?
5 Sis tamquam Curius, Decius, Numa, Fabriciusque,
  Chrysippum verbis te simulare cupis.
 Dic mihi, cum molli quid agebas, Petre, cinaedo,
  deprehendit coniux cum furibunda simul,
 damnaretque tuos, hypocrita perfide, mores?
10 Quid tibi tunc animi, quid tibi mentis erat?

now the sweet rewards of relentless ambition unsettle you;   5
   perhaps love for a beautiful girl has you in its grip;
now a ship sailing on a heavy sea laden with many wares
   and with much treasure troubles you—
and do you still wonder that you cannot sleep
   and that you do not have the relaxation of a mind at peace?   10
It would be more of a marvel to me if, agitated by so many cares,
   you *could* snore away in the middle of the night, Neri.
Make sure that you long for nothing and dread nothing, and love
     all people moderately,
   but be conscious of where there are failings in yourself.
The way you will be able to sleep and enjoy a good night's   15
     peaceful rest
   is by wishing for nothing, sweet friend, *too much*.

⁞ XXXII ⁞

Against the hypocrite Piero

Why do you reprove me with knitted brow and harsh voice,
   Piero Cretico, pour out stern words,
and hurl strict Zeno and stern Catos at me
   and all that Stoic teaching has to say?
As though you were Curius, Decius, Numa, and Fabricius,   5
   you seek to make yourself out to be a Chrysippus, the way you
     talk!
Tell me, what were you up to with that effeminate catamite, Piero,
   when your furious wife caught you together
and denounced your behavior, you faithless hypocrite?
   What nobility of soul or loftiness of mind had you then?   10

Desine vel Curium vel te simulare Catonem,
    et sis qui semper Sardanapalus eras.

: XXXIII :

Delphicum Oraculum

O quantum sapere est, et se cognosse secundum est!
    In tripode aurato hoc Delphica templa docent.
Virtutis vitiique tui sortisque locique
    sis memor, et meritis ne tibi plura velis.

: XXXIV :

Ad Ciprianum For.

Infidum, vafrum, pravum, mutabile pectus
    vitavi Libycis anguibus usque magis.
Hi ratione carent et pressi crura remordent,
    ingenium pravum cum ratione nocet.
5 Quo fallat pacto partes rem versat in omnes,
    perniciem semper cogitat ille tuam.
Hoc etiam verum cum tu fateare, requiris
    conventus fugiam cur ego saepe tuos.

Stop making yourself out to be a Curius or a Cato,
  and be the Sardanapalus that you always were.

The Delphic Oracle

O how great a thing it is to be wise, and to know oneself is next
    best!
  The Delphic temple teaches this on its golden tripod.
Be mindful of the good and the bad in you, of your lot, and of
    your place,
  and do not want more for yourself than your deserts.

: XXXIV :

To Cipriano For.

The untrustworthy, sly, wicked, and inconstant heart
  I have always avoided more than Libyan snakes.
Serpents are devoid of reason and bite people's legs when stood
    on,
  whereas a wicked nature does harm with deliberate intent.
A person like that goes to every length to work out ways to   5
    deceive
  and is always devising your ruin.
Even though you admit this to be true,
  you ask why I often shun meetings with you.

Si non dissimulas, si non vis stultus haberi,
10 noscere perspicue hoc tu, Cipriane, potes.
Ars tua, crede mihi, nostra ludetur ab arte,
  et tibi profuerit dissimulare nihil.

⁚ XXXV ⁚

Ad Nerium Boncianum de Perusino

Uxorem quare Perusinus ducere nolit,
  res est in promptu: femina nulla placet,
et tamquam Libycos mulieres effugit angues,
  et vellet potius quaelibet ipse pati.
5 Si quando illarum misero est ad proelia ventum,
  longior illa anno nox sibi visa, Neri, est.
O quae vota facit! Veluti deprehensus ab Austris
  cum mare turbatur navita vovet aquis,
per Stygias undas, per numina cuncta deorum
10 uxorem iurat ducere nolle, Neri.
Quid faciet, dicis? Num caelebs ipse manebit?
  Hoc quoque posse negat. Quam, Perusine, sapis!
Denique quartanam potiorem coniuge ducit:
  quartanam postquam sentiat, ille cupit.

If you are not dissembling and do not want to be considered a
    fool,
    you must know that very clearly, Cipriano.   10
Your art, believe me, will have sport made of it by *my* art,
    and it will do you no good at all to dissemble.

: XXXV :

To Neri Bonciani on Perugino

The reason why Perugino will not take a wife
    is plain to see: no woman pleases him,
and he flies women as he would Libyan snakes
    and would rather suffer any fate than marry.
If it has ever come to "battles" with that sex for the poor fellow,   5
    that night has seemed longer than a year to him, Neri.
O what vows he makes! Just as a sailor, caught by south winds
    when the sea is stirred up, makes pledges to the waves,
Perugino swears by the waters of Styx and by the sanctity of all
    the gods
    that he will not take a wife, Neri.   10
What will he do, you say? Surely he will not remain celibate?
    He says he cannot do that either. How wise you are, Perugino!
In the end he takes an "every fourth day" woman rather than a
    wife;
    knowing she is "every fourth day," he desires her.

: XXXVI :

Ad invidum innominatum

Invide, quod nostros carpas non curo libellos;
  non tamen ipse meo carmine notus eris.
Barbara quod tamquam vel sint puerilia dicas;
  non tamen ipse meo carmine notus eris.
5 Insidias nostrae quod tendas, invide, vitae;
  non tamen ipse meo carmine notus eris.
Sardoniis quamquam est tibi risus tristior herbis,
  non tamen ipse meo carmine notus eris.
Lethaeisque tuum nomen mandabitur undis,
10   et nulli nostro carmine notus eris;
  et licet adversis tu nostris, invide, rebus
    laeteris, nulli carmine notus eris.
Et tibi profuerit nihil irritasse Verinum,
    neve voti tui, livide, compos eris.
15 Ignotus moriere, tacent mea carmina nomen;
    sed doleo quod tu non moriare cito.

: XXXVII :

De milvo famelico

Cum frustrum carnis portaret parvulus infans,
  paene trucis milvi praeda novella fuit;
nam cum despiceret liquido procul aere carnem,
  carnem cum puero sustulit ille rapax,

∶ XXXVI ∶

To an unnamed jealous man

Jealous creature, I do not care that you carp at my poems;
   you will still not be granted fame through my verses.
For all that you call them barbarous or puerile,
   you will still not be granted fame through my verses.
No matter that you make plots against my life, jealous creature;   5
   you will still not be granted fame through my verses.
Though you have a smile more bitter than Sardinian crowfoot,
   you will still not be granted fame through my verses.
Your name will be consigned to the waters of Lethe,
   and you will be known to none through my verses;   10
and though you take delight in my misfortunes, jealous creature,
   you will be known to none through my verses.
Provoking Verino will do you no good at all,
   and you will not get what you wish for, jealous man.
You will die unknown, my poems make no mention of your name;   15
   my regret is that you are not quick about dying.

∶ XXXVII ∶

On a famished kite

When a tiny little infant was carrying a chunk of meat,
   he was nearly the latest prey of a fierce kite;
for, espying the meat below from far off in the clear air,
   it rapaciously snatched up the meat and the boy with it,

5   sed puer a nimio fuit hic vix pondere tutus.
      Ad quid cogis aves, imperiosa fames?
    Consenuit forsan Ganymedis forma cinaedi,
      utque alium raperes a Iove missus eras?

⁚ XXXVIII ⁚

In Franciscum paediconem

Non ita servavit serpens vigil aurea poma
    ne mala Hesperidum carperet unca manus,
vellera Phrixeae pecudis nec Martius anguis
    sic custodivit flammigerique boves,
5   quam Ganymedeum asservas, Francisce, cinaedum:
    noctes atque dies unica cura tibi est.
Discedis nusquam, lateri tu semper adhaeres,
    si stet, si pergat, dormiat aut vigilet.
Zelotypus patruum, fratres ipsumque parentem
10   ne faciant quod tu saepe verere facis.
Ignosco. Puer hic tibi se pro coniuge praebet,
    et merito coniux sit tibi casta cupis.

but the boy was only just saved by being too heavy.   5
    To what lengths do you drive birds, tyrannical hunger?
Perhaps the beauty of Jupiter's catamite Ganymede has faded
      with the years,
    and you were sent by the god to carry off another?

∶ XXXVIII ∶

Against the sodomite Francesco

Not so well did the watchful serpent keep the golden apples safe,
    in case a clasping hand should pluck the fruits of the
      Hesperides,
nor so closely did Mars' dragon and the fire-breathing bulls
    guard the fleece of Phrixus' ram,
as you, Francesco, watch over your Ganymedean catamite: 5
    he is your sole care night and day.
You never leave him, you cling constantly to his side,
    whether he is standing, walking, asleep, or awake.
In your jealousy you are afraid that your uncle, brothers, and even
      your father
    may do what you often do yourself.   10
I pardon you. This boy offers himself to you in a wife's role,
    and you quite rightly want your wife to be chaste.

: XXXIX :

In Lurcum

Cum tibi Tartarei spiret gravis halitus oris,
  vermibus ut putida est quadriduana caro,
alia cur etiam male olentia, Lurce, vorasti,
  an perdas ut me, tam male pastus, ades?
5 Non homines solum, posset corrumpere caelum
  spiritus iste tuus, perdere posset aves.
Non miror quod nunc crassetur pestis in urbe,
  noxia perserpat tabida membra lues:
quemcumque alloqueris quam primum peste peribit,
10 optima profuerit nec medicina sibi!
Tam gravis internis de faucibus halitus exit,
  aequoreas phocas ut maculare queat.
Accedas hostes propius, vitabis amicos;
  me potius sitiens vulneret anguis Afer!

: XL :

Ad amicum discedentem

O iucunda quies, o dulcis cura sodalis,
  quo sine me raptim carpere tendis iter?
Qui tecum Libycas ausim percurrere Syrtes,
  et caecos scopulos, curva Malea, tuos,
5 nudus Hyperboreos tecum gelidosque Triones
  atque ausim Indorum currere in Oceanum,

: XXXIX :

Against Lurcus

Seeing that you have the noisome breath of a mouth as rank as
 Tartarus,
 like meat on the fourth day that is rotten with worms,
why have you also eaten foul-smelling garlic, Lurcus,
 or are you here, after such a vile repast, to be the death of me?
That breath of yours could not only lay humankind low   5
 but pollute the heavens too and kill birds.
I do not wonder that plague is now rampant in the city
 and that deadly infection is spreading through wasting bodies:
anyone you talk to will perish of plague in no time at all,
 and the best medicine will be of no help to him!   10
So noisome a breath emerges from the depths of your jaws
 that it could foul the seals in the sea.
Get closer to your enemies and keep away from your friends;
 I would rather have a thirsting African snake bite me!

: XL :

To a departing friend

O delightful recreation, your friend's sweet care,
 where are you planning suddenly to dash off to without me?
I, who would boldly speed with you through the Libyan Syrtes
 and through your hidden rocks, curved Malea,
and would as boldly journey naked with you to the Hyperboreans, 5
 to the icy Triones, and to the Indians' ocean,

ad nigros Mauros atque ultra moenia Thyles
    tendere non fugerem, dulcis amice, simul.
Non me terrerent maris aut discrimina terrae;
10   fert amor illud onus, fit minor ipse labor.
Non tantum Pylades carum dilexit Orestem,
    nec tantum Oebalium Castora frater amat,
abs te nec tantum est dilectus Scipio, Laeli,
    nec tantum a Xerxe est qui prius hostis erat,
15 Thesea vel tantum nec amavit Thessalus heros,
    nec quicumque alius clarus amicitia est.
Di tibi dent facilem cursum celeremque regressum;
    ad nos quam primum fac rediturus eas.
Omine felici, carissime, vade, sodalis,
20   et procul absentis sis memor usque mei.

: XLI :

Ad Musam ut Mediolanum petat et Franciscum
Rictium suo nomine alloquatur

Bedriacos campos et celsa palatia magni
    Sfortiadae nostro nomine, Musa, pete.
Ne stupida horrescas postes intrare superbos
    et mira auratos arte subire lares;
5   ne ducis invicti, qui quamvis alter in armis
    sit Caesar, timeas ora videre sacra;
nutritusque licet patria est Galeactius arte,
    ille tamen Musis semper amicus adest.

would not shrink from traveling with you, sweet friend,
   to the black Moors and beyond the walls of Thyle.
Perils of sea or land would not frighten me;
   love bears that burden, and the hardship itself is made less.   10
Not so much did Pylades love his dear Orestes,
   not so much does his brother love Oebalian Castor,
nor was Scipio so fondly regarded by you, Laelius,
   nor his former foe by Xerxes,
nor did the Thessalian hero so much love Theseus,   15
   nor did anyone else famed for friendship feel so warmly.
May the gods grant you an easy journey and a swift return;
   see that you come back to me as soon as possible.
Go, and good luck be with you, my dearest friend,
   and be ever mindful of me, though far apart from you.   20

: XLI :

To the Muse, that she make for Milan and
address Francesco Ricci in his name

Seek in my name, Muse, the plains of Bedriacum
   and the lofty palace of the great son of Sforza.
Do not, overwhelmed by awe, shrink from passing within the
      proud portals
   and entering a residence gilt with marvelous skill;
do not fear to set eyes on the august face of the invincible duke,   5
   though he is another Caesar in arms;
and, though Galeazzo has been brought up in his father's art,
   yet he is ever a good friend to the Muses.

Illic invenies veterem fidumque sodalem,
10   cuius tu tanges officiosa manus,
et verbis nostris sibi dicito mille salutes:
     dimidium vitae est Rictius ille meae.
Hic est qui nostros solitus laudare libellos
     et lepidos hilari fronte probare iocos.
15   Hic quoque Pegaseis doctus non horret ab undis;
     hospitio vatis suscipiere, Clio.
Cum sciet unde venis vel quis te miserit istuc,
     te manibus subito, te geret ille sinu.
Inter delicias spectati carmen amici
20   Franciscus noster semper habere solet.

: XLII :

Ad Federigum Donatum, ne Amoris
illecebris capiatur

Quid iuvat insano tantum indulgere furori,
     quid teneris annis noscere quid sit amor?
Heu, fuge principium, scintillas effuge primas;
     te quantis posthac ignibus uret Amor!
5   Nascentes facile exstinguit medicina dolores;
     dum licet, evita praepetis arma dei.
Principiis est blandus Amor ducitque volentes,
     hos donec laqueis vinxerit ille suis.
Post rapit invitos nimium violenter amantes
10   et vinctos centum nexibus urget Amor.

There you will find an old and faithful companion of mine.
   Courteously take hold of his hands   10
and bid him a thousand wishes of good health from me:
   that man Ricci is half of my life.
He it is who is accustomed to praise my compositions
   and approve my witty jokes with a cheery expression.
He too is a poet and does not recoil from Pegasus' spring;   15
   you will be received with a bard's hospitality, Clio.
Once he knows where you come from and who has sent you
      there,
   he will straightaway carry you around in his hands and pocket.
Considering a poem by a well-regarded friend among his joys
   is always the way of my Francesco.   20

: XLII :

To Federico Donati, that he not be trapped
by the allurements of love

Why does it please you to give in so much to mad passion
   and to know in your tender years what love is?
Alas, fly its beginning and its first sparks;
   with what great fires Love will burn you hereafter!
Medicine easily extinguishes pains at their onset;   5
   avoid the winged god's weapons while you can.
At first Love is gentle and leads willing victims
   until he has secured them in his snares.
Then Love hustles lovers away with great violence against their
      will
   and drives his captives along bound with a hundred knots.   10

Sub quo servitio, sub quo, Federige, tyranno,
    si non hunc vites, vita futura tibi est!
Sit licet insignis forma, sit candida virgo,
    et superet Tuscas Elisabetta nurus,
15 ne tamen insanos sentire Cupidinis ignes
    et mala ne gratis tanta subire velis.
Toxica quanta bibes, quantos patiere dolores!
    Heu, nescis, nescis quid sit amare, puer!
Iurgia quid referam, quid verba minantia amicae,
20   quem fastum, nota est cui sua forma, gerit?
Si dura est, quando voto potieris amoris?
    Incassum misero tempora longa fluent.
Quo poteris tristes animo perferre repulsas?
    Quae frustra implores numina quosque deos?
25 Sin facilis fuerit, iuvenes et mollis ad omnes,
    sollicito numquam pectore laetus eris.
Quoscumque aspicies rivales esse putabis,
    innocuas rodes saepe dolore manus,
promissaque tibi saepe alter nocte fruetur.
30   Longa nimis multis nox erit ista malis.
Tu tamen interea nutries spem tristis inanem.
    'Nunc veniet,' dices; alter habebit eam.
Quae cernes oculis, quibus exagitabere dictis,
    et quae non possum dicere plura feres!

Under what servitude and under what a tyrant, Federico,
   unless you avoid him, will your life be lived!
Though Elisabetta is outstanding in looks and a beautiful girl,
   surpassing all other Tuscan young women,
yet do not consent to feel Cupid's mad fires   15
   and undergo such great ills for no return.
What powerful poisons you will drink, what great pains you will
   suffer!
   Alas, you do not know, boy, you do not know what it is to be
   in love!
Why should I mention the quarrels, your girlfriend's threatening
   words,
   and the haughtiness displayed by a woman who knows her   20
   own beauty?
If she is hard of heart, when will you gain love's desire?
   A long time will flow by to your misery with no result.
In what frame of mind will you be able to bear her cruel rebuffs?
   What forces of heaven and what gods will you call upon in
   vain?
But if she is easy natured and affable to all young men,   25
   you will never be happy in your anxious heart.
All the men you see you will consider rivals,
   you will often gnaw your unoffending hands in anguish,
and often another will enjoy a night promised to you.
   That night will be all too long with its many woes.   30
Yet you meanwhile will sadly nourish empty hope.
   "She will be coming now," you will say, but another will have
   her.
What sights you will witness! What upsetting words you will
   hear!
   And you will endure more that I cannot say.

35 Optabis miseram quotiens abrumpere vitam,
  adversosque deos saepe querere miser!
  Milia quanta feres curarum, quanta laborum!
    Tunc quantis lacrimis carmina nostra leges!
  'Ah, cur non volui fido parere Verino?' —
40   sed tunc incassum — saepe querere miser.
  Flumina nulla tuas poterunt exstinguere flammas,
    ossibus accensis cum furet asper Amor.
  Non somni, non cura cibi placidaeque quietis
    ulla tibi fuerit, totus Amoris eris;
45 et cum privatis cessabunt publica rebus,
    maxima cum magno damna pudore feres.
  Quid dicent cari qui te genuere parentes,
    quid tibi germanus, quid tibi cara soror?
  Et tibi quo dulces poterunt prodesse sodales,
50   cum Venus arbitrio te reget alma suo?
  Cum tua mortifero tabescent corda veneno,
    sanabit tantum quae medicina malum?
  Nequitiasque tuas reticebunt compita nulla
    et fies vulgi fabula nota levis.
55 Quid tibi profuerit doctum legisse Platonem,
    quid tibi Aristotelis, quid Ciceronis opus?
  Nec te Calliope, nec te defendet Apollo,
    nec te Hippocrenes turba canora sacrae,
  Castaliis quamvis sis enutritus in antris,
60   inque caballino merseris ora lacu.

How often you will wish to end your miserable life,   35
    and many a time you will wretchedly complain of the gods
        being against you!
How many thousands of cares and hardships you will endure!
    With how many tears will you read my poems *then!*
"Ah, why would I not listen to trusty Verino?"
    you will often complain in your misery, but then to no avail.   40
No rivers will be able to put out your flames
    once cruel Love is raging in your blazing bones.
For sleep, food, and quiet peace you will have no care;
    you will be all Love's.
Your public affairs will be neglected along with your private ones,   45
    you will bear great losses along with great shame.
What will the dear parents who brought you into the world say?
    What will your brother and your dear sister say to you?
And how will your sweet friends be able to be of any help to you,
    once bountiful Venus rules you at her whim?   50
When your heart is wasting with the deadly poison,
    what medicine will heal so great an evil?
No crossroads will be silent about your scandalous misdoings,
    and you will become the talk of the light-minded crowd.
What good will it do you to have read learned Plato,   55
    Aristotle's work, or Cicero's?
Neither Calliope nor Apollo will defend you,
    nor will the tuneful band of holy Hippocrene,
though you have been reared in the Castalian caves
    and have immersed your lips in the nag's pool.   60

⁝ XLIII ⁝

Ad Lucretiam Donatam, ut Laurentium Medicem amet

Gloria sis quamvis Tuscae, Lucretia, gentis,
    aequiparesque ipsas nobilitate deas,
nec tua Tyndaridi concedat forma Lacaenae,
    aetherio tantum fulget in ore decus,
5 sis nive candidior, sis formosissima tota,
    exstet ut in toto pulchrius orbe nihil,
sis facie insignis quamvis, et crine soluto
    ipse tuis pulcher cedat Apollo comis,
sidereas quamvis vincant tua lumina flammas,
10   et tua sint astris aemula labra poli,
vincat ebur nitidum quamvis tua lactea cervix,
    et superent roseae Punica mala genae,
os minimum dentesque pares candore micantes
    et risum Iuno vellet habere tuum,
15 et Tyrio niveus perfusus rideat ostro
    vultus, nativus sit color usque genis,
et planae scapulae, nihil ut sit rectius illis,
    bracchia non tacta candidiora nive,
parva mamillarum niveo sit pectore forma,
20   nec nimium pinguis nec macilenta nimis,
Tyrrhenas collo superes tenus usque puellas,
    nullaque ad exiguos vertice menda pedes,

: XLIII :

To Lucrezia Donati, that she love Lorenzo de' Medici

Though you are, Lucrezia, the glory of the Tuscan race,
    and equal the very goddesses in nobility,
though your beauty is no less than that of the Spartan daughter
      of Tyndareus,
    so much radiance shines in your heavenly visage,
though you are whiter than snow and all supremely lovely,   5
    so that there is nothing fairer in the whole world,
though your face is striking, and in free-flowing locks
    handsome Apollo himself yields to your hair,
though your eyes surpass the flames of stars,
    and your lips rival the stars of heaven,   10
though your milky neck eclipses shining ivory,
    and your rosy cheeks outmatch pomegranates,
and Juno would wish to have your tiny mouth, your perfectly
      matching teeth,
    gleaming with whiteness, and your smile,
though your snow-white face is brightly suffused with the redness   15
      of Tyrian purple,
    and the color all over your cheeks is natural,
though your shoulder blades are so flat that nothing could be
      straighter,
    your arms whiter than untouched snow,
the breasts on your snowy bosom small,
    neither too plump nor too thin,   20
though you surpass other Tyrrhenian girls all the way up to your
      head,
    and have no fault from your top down to your tiny feet,

et quamvis victae cedant tibi voce Sirenae,
    et Charites choreis, cedat et ipsa Venus,
25 sit roseo vultu divina infusa venustas,
    fecerit ut manibus Iuppiter ipse suis,
incessusque tuos quamvis soror ipsa Tonantis,
    denique quidquid habes vellet habere tui,
atque pudicitiae exemplar Lucretia cedat,
30   cuius habes nomen, moribus illa tuis,
et quamvis omni penitus sis parte beata,
    ut te felicem quisque vocare queat,
non tamen idcirco talem contemnere amantem
    debes, sed magis hic ultro petendus erat.
35 Si te divitiae capiunt, ditissimus hic est
    (divitias, moneo, nulla puella velit:
divitiis periere viri, periere puellae;
    Alcmeonis mater testis avara mihi est.)
Si te nobilitas titulis insignis avorum
40   tangit, quis Medice est nobilitate prior?
Non fuit in populo generosior ulla Quiritum
    stirps neque tam claris nobilitata viris.
Si mores, si forma placet, iuvenilis et aetas,
    iudice te, iuvenis pulcher et ipse probus.
45 En age, non alius tota praestantior urbe
    est iuvenis, si non saevus adesset amor.
Hunc quoque Castaliis Musae nutriere sub antris,
    et totum hunc fovit Calliopea sinu.
Hunc, saeva, immiti patieris amore perire?
50   Et quis te iuvenis dignior alter erat?
Hic te dilexit salvo, Donata, pudore,
    et famam laesit fabula nulla tuam.

though the Sirens yield, vanquished, to you in voice,
    and the Graces in dances, and Venus herself yields to you,
though divine loveliness is infused on your rosy face,   25
    as if Jupiter himself made it with his own hands,
though the Thunderer's very sister might want to have your walk,
    to have all your qualities, in fact,
though the famous Lucretia, that paragon of chastity,
    whose name you have, yields place to your virtuous character,   30
and though you are entirely blessed in every part,
    so that everyone may call you fortunate —
yet you should not on that account hold such a lover in contempt,
    but rather he ought to have been actively sought.
If riches win you, he is very rich   35
    (yet I advise no girl to desire riches:
both men and girls too have perished because of them;
    the greedy mother of Alcmaeon is my proof of that).
If nobility distinguished with ancestral titles touches you,
    who is before Medici in nobility?   40
There has been no line of better pedigree among our people
    nor one ennobled by such illustrious men.
If character, good looks, and youthful years please,
    in your own judgment he is a handsome young man and
        honest too.
Come, there is no other youth more outstanding in the whole city,   45
    even were he not fiercely in love with you.
The Muses too have fostered him in their Castalian caves,
    and Calliope has nurtured him completely in the folds of her
        lap.
Cruel girl, will you allow him to perish of painful love?
    And what other young man will be worthier of you?   50
He has loved you, Donati, without impropriety,
    and no slander has injured your reputation.

: XLIV :

De Corvino glorioso

Omnia Corvinus noster se scire fatetur
    et probat exemplis omnia nosse suis;
dives et antiqua ducit de stirpe parentes,
    fastidit si qui nobilitate carent.
5 Virtutes canit ille suas, aliena reprehendens,
    crimina et obducta fronte nefanda notat;
sed melius nescisse fuit, tanto quam parta labore
    perdere tam fatua garrulitate sua.
Ergo erit is vates poteritque disertus haberi,
10   si nullum carpit, vel sua facta tacet.

: XLV :

De laudibus poetarum et felicitate sui
seculi ad Andream Alemannum

Etsi non longo fuerim tibi cognitus usu,
    nostra sed incepit nuper amicitia,
officio es veteris tamen usus, amice, sodalis,
    muneris et potero non meminisse tui?
5 O meritas possem, Andrea, tibi reddere grates!
    Di referant, nobis sit voluisse satis.

: XLIV :

On the boastful Corvinus

Our Corvinus declares that he knows it all
    and demonstrates that omniscience by his conduct.
He is rich and traces his parentage from ancient stock;
    he turns up his nose at all who lack noble blood.
He sings his own virtues, censuring what others do,   5
    and he reproves unspeakable offenses with a scowling frown;
but it would have been better not to know than to destroy the
      fruits
    of so much hard work by such fatuous prating as his.
Therefore he will make a poet and be able to be considered
      eloquent,
    if he carps at no one or keeps quiet about his own   10
    achievements.

: XLV :

To Andrea Alamanni, on the praises of poets
and on the felicity of his time

Even though I have not been known to you by long acquaintance,
    and our friendship has begun only lately,
yet you have acted toward me like an old companion, my friend,
    and shall I ever be able to forget your kind service to me?
O that I could give you the thanks you have deserved, Andrea!   5
    May the gods repay you; let the wish to do so be enough for
    me.

Non tamen officii fuero, si Nestoris annos
    fata mihi dederint, immemor ipse tui.
Si tibi non opibus, potero prodesse canendo:
10   non nihil ad famam carmina culta valent.
Interdum vates misero tribuere salutem,
    nonnumquam laudem carmen opemque tulit.
Cum Niciae classem cepit Trinacria pubes,
    tunc stilus Euripidis contulit altus opem;
15 nam pius, Euripidis recitatis versibus, hostis
    captivos gratis iussit abire domum.
Cum veteres Thebas Pelei fregere phalanges,
    et rueret magnae funditus urbis opus,
parcere Pindaricis domibus clementia regis
20   et proli iussit, si qua superstes erat.
Movit nonne Solon elegis ad bella Pelasgos,
    cum capitale foret de Salamine loqui?
Stultitiam sapiens prudenti pectore finxit;
    illo sic tandem est insula capta modo.
25 Ter victi Spartae Tyrtaeo vate fugarunt
    Messenios, pravo cum foret ille pede.
Quid referam Alcaei pulsos ex urbe tyrannos
    carminibus, terris bellaque gesta mari?
Hoc duce libertas patriae est, hoc vate, parata,
30   qui totiens caeso victor ab hoste redit.
Mantua, Caesareae quondam data praeda cohorti,
    civibus est vatis carmine tuta sui.

I shall not for my part, however, be unmindful of your kindness,
    even if the fates grant me the years of Nestor.
If not with wealth, I will be able to help you by my singing:
    polished songs are not totally powerless to bring fame.   10
Sometimes poets have brought well-being to one in wretched
      plight;
    on occasion a song has brought praise and help.
When the Sicilian forces captured Nicias' fleet,
    then Euripides' lofty pen brought aid;
for the foe, out of respect at hearing Euripides' verses recited,   15
    bade the prisoners go home without ransom.
When the Pellaean's phalanxes subdued ancient Thebes,
    and the great city's buildings were being leveled to the ground,
the king in his mercy gave orders to spare Pindar's house
    and any surviving descendant there might be of his.   20
Did not Solon stir the Pelasgians to war with his elegies,
    though it was a capital offense to speak of Salamis?
Wise man that he was, he prudently feigned stupidity,
    and so in that way the island was finally taken.
The thrice-beaten men of Sparta routed the Messenians with the   25
      help
    of the poet Tyrtaeus, even though he had a lame foot.
Why should I mention tyrants driven out from the city
    through Alcaeus' songs, and wars waged by land and sea?
With this man as both leader and bard, his homeland's liberty
      was secured,
    when he so often returned victorious after slaughter of the   30
      enemy.
Mantua was once given over as booty for Caesar's army,
    but it was saved for its citizens by its poet's song.

    Incertum est igitur ne magis prosintne iuventne,
       sed mixta vates utilitate iuvant.
35 Quis dubitabit adhuc patriae prodesse poetas,
       quis vates dignos stultus honore neget,
    per quos post mortem virtus aeterna futura est,
       nec simul interitu cuncta perire sinunt,
    per quos posteritas cognoscet facta priora,
40   per quos florebunt maxima gesta ducum?
    Omnia cum tacite rodat damnosa vetustas,
       vatibus a sacris abstinet illa manus.
    Argentum atque adamas longo consumitur usu,
       carius et si quid mobile vulgus amat.
45 Aspice Romuleam, qua nil conspectius umquam
       urbe fuit, vulsam protinus esse solo.
    Marmorea haec quondam multis ditata trophaeis
       urbs fuerat, nunc est antra habitanda feris.
    Ludit in humanis rebus Fortuna maligna,
50   et quaecumque libet tollit, et alta premit.
    Vilibus in rebus tantum est concessa potestas,
       tangere res sacras non tamen illa potest.
    Idcirco sanctos timet haec violare poetas,
       res quia divina est carminis ille furor.
55 Nam vates, maius reliquis scriptoribus, ipsi
       inscribunt serae posteritatis opus,

It is uncertain, therefore, whether poets benefit or delight us
    more,
  but there is an element of service mixed in with the pleasure
    they give.
Who will still doubt that poets are of benefit to their homeland   35
  or will foolishly deny that bards are worthy of honor,
when through them a person's distinction will live on forever after
    death,
  and they do not allow all one's achievements to perish at the
    grave;
when through them posterity will learn of the deeds of days gone
    by,
  and through them the glorious exploits of commanders will be   40
    remembered still?
Although the destructive passage of time silently gnaws away all
    else,
  it stays its hands from holy poets.
Silver and a diamond are worn away by long use,
  along with anything of greater value that the fickle crowd loves.
See how Romulus' city (and a more glorious sight there has never   45
    been)
  has been torn down right to the ground.
It was once a city of marble, enriched with many trophies;
  now it is caves for wild beasts to inhabit.
Malign Fortune makes sport of human affairs,
  and she raises up whatsoever she pleases, abasing what is   50
    exalted.
Power is granted her only in matters of little worth;
  she cannot, however, touch sacred things.
For that reason she fears to harm holy poets,
  because the ecstatic inspiration of song is god given.
For poets, more than all other writers,   55
  compose works for posterity long after them,

unde datum est vati numen, quod mentibus insit
    vis vehemens, sine qua non bene crescit opus.
Unde etiam Graeci pariter dixere poetam
60   quod scriptore omni nobiliora facit.
Noctua sed doctas, credo, mittetur Athenas;
    stulte, quid aequoreis fluctibus addis aquas?
Si non est carmen, certe est laudanda voluntas,
    si non eloquii, plenus amoris ero.
65 Non tantum Pylades carum dilexit Orestem
    quam colo amicitiam, docte Alamanne, tuam.
In me non tantum patuit tua magna librorum
    copia, sed multis profuit illa viris.
Nunc ego felici laetor me tempore natum,
70   cum sit honor meritis non minor ipse suis,
praemia cum magnis maiora laboribus adsint.
    Nunc artes nutrit gloria vera bonas;
nunc dulcis labor est, fallunt cum praemia nullum;
    Pieridum studiis nunc vigilare iuvat,
75 quae bis quingentos Latio iacuere per annos,
    cum nostram pressit barbarus hostis humum.
Vix tandem Tuscus longo post tempore Dantes
    reddidit Ausoniis haec celebranda viris.
Sic artes aliae subito viguere repertae,
80   imperium crevit cum tibi, Tusce Leo.
Cum tu vicinos felici Marte tyrannos
    vicisti, inque dies cum tibi crescit honor,
creverunt pariter vires et copia fandi,
    doctorumque hodie est maxima turba virum.

and therefore divine power is granted to bards, to be a mighty
    force in their minds,
  without which their work fails to prosper.
Thus it is that the Greeks too have likewise spoken of the poet
  as producing nobler creations than every other writer.   60
But, I believe, I shall be sending an owl to learned Athens;
    Verino, you fool, why do you add water to the waves of the
      sea?
If my poem does not deserve praise, certainly the intention
    behind it does;
  if not full of eloquence, I shall be full of love.
Not so much did Pylades love his dear Orestes   65
  as I revere your friendship, learned Alamanni.
Your abundant library of books has not only been open to me
  but of service to many men.
I rejoice that I was born now in a happy time,
  when honor is not less than its deserts,   70
when greater rewards attach to great labors.
  Now true glory nourishes the fine arts,
now labor is sweet, when no one is disappointed of rewards;
  now it is a pleasure to work late in studies of the Pierides,
who were neglected in Latium for twice five hundred years,   75
  while a barbarian foe oppressed our land.
At long last Tuscan Dante finally succeeded in restoring
  these praiseworthy pursuits to the people of Ausonia.
So too other recovered arts have suddenly blossomed
  with the rise of your power, Tuscan Lion.   80
Now that you have vanquished neighboring tyrants in successful
    wars,
  and day by day your glory waxes,
power and skill in speaking have grown side by side,
  and today there is a great multitude of learned men.

85 Sunt qui naturae causas, qui sidera norint,
   ut Iove Saturni frangitur ira senis,
  mitigat ut Martem Iubar, sidusque perustum
   Mercurii fures eloquiumque parit.
  Sunt qui mensuram Oceani novere profundi,
90   pendeat ut tellus inter utrumque polum,
  solis ut antipodes alterna luce fruantur,
   religio Christi hoc perneget ipsa licet;
  conanturque Deum nonulli noscere, quamvis
   humanis maius viribus hoc sit opus;
95 quique bonos mores urbi domuique sibique
   praebeat est hodie; vivat ut iste precor.
  Est qui fallaci cogat sermone fatentem
   dicere constrictus quae minime ipse putat.
  Innumeras artes hodie florere videmus,
100   saecula per Latium quae latuere decem.
  Nunc Zeuxis rediit, qui quondam pinxerat uvas
   ad quas deceptae saepe volastis aves;
  nunc alter Phidias rediit, nunc alter Apelles,
   picturam quorum vivere nempe putes.
105 Spirantem hic Pario vultum de marmore ducit,
   aera alius fundit, fingit at ille rota.
  Praeterea florent aliae sine nomine multae,
   quas lucro intentum vulgus ubique colit.
  Pace mihi liceat vestra dixisse, priores,
110   temporibus cedant Aurea Saecla meis.
  Quando fuit recti aut aequi reverentia maior,
   quando magis culta est cum pietate fides?

There are those who know the workings of nature and the stars,   85
   how the anger of old Saturn is countered by Jupiter,
how the Morning Star tempers Mars, and how Mercury's
    scorched star
    gives us thieves and eloquence.
There are those who have learned the measure of the deep ocean,
   how the earth hangs between the two poles,   90
and the antipodes enjoy the sun's light in their turn,
   though the very religion of Christ may quite deny it;
and some try to come to know God,
   though that is a task too great for human powers.
There is a man today who promotes good behavior   95
   in his city, his house, and himself: I pray that he may live long.
There is a man who compels another by deceptive argument
   to admit under constraint of logic what is not at all his own
    belief.
We see countless arts flourishing today
   that have been neglected in Latium for ten centuries.   100
Now Zeuxis has returned, he who once painted the grapes
   to which you deceived birds often flew.
Now another Phidias has returned and another Apelles;
   you would think a picture of theirs truly alive.
This man brings forth a breathing face from Parian marble,   105
   another casts bronze, while that man works at the potter's
    wheel.
Many other arts without a name flourish besides,
   arts that the vulgar crowd cultivate everywhere in pursuit of
    gain.
May I be permitted to say it with your leave, men of earlier days,
   the Golden Age would yield place to my times.   110
When was there greater respect for what is right and fair,
   when was good faith, along with piety, more venerated?

Horrida, devictis vicinis, bella quiescunt.
    An licuit pace hac prosperiore frui?
115 Erexit propter tales Florentia cives
    urbibus Ausoniis altius ipsa caput.
Nam quis par Medici Cosmo, natisque duobus
    moribus, ingenio, nobilitate fuit,
aut quis divitiis est largior usus opimis?
120   Hac re nos superis possumus esse pares.
A meritis homines laudavit prisca vetustas,
    a sera factos posteritate deos.
Vulcanum Lemnos, Naxos te, Bacche, Minervam
    Attica, Cretenses excoluere Iovem.
125 Hyperiona Phryges, coluit te Roma, Quirine,
    a quo Sullanidae gentis origo fuit.
Hinc, Alamanne, tuum, Medicum genus inde creatum
    inter Iuleos forsan habebis avos.
Virginibus merito sacris quot templa dicavit
130   nobilium Medicum religiosa domus!
Larga manus Medicum quot nubere fecit egenas,
    castum ut servarent (maxima causa) torum!
Sed tu, magnanimi Cosmi generosa propago,
    praecipue es magno dignus honore, Petre.
135 Maecenas Tuscis alter nunc natus in oris,
    doctorum ingeniis, ingeniose, faves.

Frightful wars are at rest, our neighbors conquered.
    Has it ever been permitted to enjoy peace more prosperous
        than this?
Because of such citizens Florence herself has raised her head   115
    higher than all the other cities of Ausonia.
For who has been the equal of Cosimo de' Medici and his two
        sons
    in character, genius, and nobility,
or who has been more generous in his use of great wealth?
    Through such benefaction we mortals are able to equal those   120
        in heaven above.
Olden times praised men for their merits,
    men who were made gods by later posterity.
Lemnos worshipped Vulcan; Naxos, you, Bacchus;
    Attica, Minerva; the people of Crete, Jupiter.
The Phrygians worshipped Hyperion, and Rome worshipped   125
        you, Quirinus,
    from whom derived the race of Sulla's sons.
Perhaps you will find your own family, Alamanni, sprung from
        one line,
    and that of the Medici from another, among ancestors of Iulus'
        blood.
How many churches has the house of the noble Medici,
        observant of religion,
    fittingly consecrated to holy virgins!   130
How many needy girls have the Medici's generous hands enabled
        to marry,
    allowing them to keep a chaste bed, the best of causes!
But you, Piero, noble offspring of great-souled Cosimo,
    are especially worthy of great honor.
A second Maecenas born now on Tuscan shores,   135
    a man of genius yourself, you favor the geniuses of the learned.

Gloria Tyrrhenae es, Medices, verissima gentis,
    sospite quo doctis praemia semper erunt.
Hic inopes opibus iuvitque favore poetas,
140   et vatum vati maxima cura sibi est.
Vos ego consortes studii, quibus altior exit
    ore sonus, precor, hunc concelebrate virum.

: XLVI :

Contra Invidiam

Livor edax, audes tam sanctos carpere mores,
    et de me cunctis crimina ficta loqui?
Quid nisi virtutum corrumpere praemia tentas,
    subque boni specie tu scelus omne facis?
5 Cumque aliquem virtute vides ad sidera tolli,
    protinus haec tristis causa doloris erit.
O monstrum horrendum, Furiarum pessime, Livor,
    Tartareos inter digne manere lacus!
Rumpis amicitias, armas in proelia fratres,
10   foederis humani solvis, inique, fidem.
Tristia finitimos populos impellis ad arma;
    nequitiae, Livor, semina cuncta seris.

You, Medici, are the truest glory of the Tyrrhenian race;
    while you are safe and well there will always be rewards for the
       learned.
This man has helped impoverished bards with wealth and favor,
    and he has the very greatest concern for poets, being a poet   140
       himself.
I beg you fellow poets of mine, from whose lips
    loftier speech sounds forth, join in celebration of this man.

: XLVI :

Against Jealousy

Consuming Jealousy, do you dare slander such pure morals as
    mine
    and make false accusations about me to everyone?
What do you ever do except try to destroy the rewards of virtue
    and commit every kind of wicked act under the pretense of
       good?
And whenever you see someone being raised up to the stars by   5
    virtue,
    the sight will instantly be the cause of bitter pain to you.
O horrendous monster, worst of Furies, Jealousy,
    deserving to dwell amid the lakes of Tartarus!
You break up friendships, you arm brother to do battle with
    brother,
    you dissolve trust, wicked thing, in our bonds with one   10
    another.
You drive neighboring peoples to grim arms;
    you, Jealousy, sow all the seeds of wrongdoing.

Iustus Aristides, Spartam detrusus ad urbem,
    iustitiae accepit praemia saeva suae;
15 quique rebellantes iuvenis devicit Hiberos,
    cui nomen posthac Africa victa dedit
    (namque ferum Poenum et saevae Carthaginis arces
    contudit), exilium praemia saeva tulit.
    Quid referam sancti victricia signa Camilli?
20   Quid ducis invicti tanta trophaea loquar?
Hic tamen, Invidia cara deiectus ab urbe,
    ingratae patriae contulit exul opem.
Sed quid victoris dicam Themistoclis arma?
    Hunc quoque Livor edax misit in exilium.
25 Si premor Invidia, non miror: carpere divos
    audet, et alterius pallet iniqua bonis.
    Quid magis horrendum, quae belua taetrior ista?
    Sed poenas sceleris sustinet ipsa sui!
Roditur infelix, rebus vexata secundis,
30   nec lacrimas maestis continet illa genis.
Dentibus infrendens, sic qua ratione nocere
    possit pestifera callida mente parat.
Cogitat exitium, meditatur et usque ruinam;
    Tartareum spirat virus ab ore suo.
35 Pascitur in tenebris luctu et serpentibus atris,
    et sibi pro suco est pallor in ore teter.
Sanguine vipereo latum cratera coronat;
    noxia pro liquida toxica potat aqua.

When Aristides the Just was banished to the city of Sparta,
    it was a cruel reward he had for all his justice;
and he who as a youth subdued the warring Spaniards   15
    and was thereafter named for conquered Africa
(for he crushed the fierce Punic foe and the citadels of cruel
      Carthage)
    suffered exile as his cruel reward.
Why should I mention the victorious standards of revered
      Camillus?
    Why should I speak of that invincible commander's many   20
      trophies?
He was, however, cast out of his dear city through Jealousy
    and brought help to an ungrateful homeland as an exile.
And why should I speak of the arms of victorious Themistocles?
    Consuming Jealousy drove him too into exile.
If I am beset by Jealousy, I do not wonder: it dares to slander   25
      saints
    and turns pale, wicked as it is, at the blessings enjoyed by
      another.
What is more horrendous? What monster is fouler than this?
    But it suffers punishment for its own evildoing.
It gnaws itself in wretchedness, vexed by the successes of others,
    and cannot hold back tears from its sad cheeks.   30
Gnashing its teeth, the crafty thing schemes
    in its pernicious mind to find some way to cause harm.
It ponders destruction and constantly meditates on how to bring
      about ruin;
    it breathes Tartarean poison from its lips.
It feeds in darkness on grief and on black serpents,   35
    and there is a foul paleness on its face in place of healthy vigor.
It fills a broad mixing bowl to the brim with vipers' blood;
    it drinks noxious poisons in place of flowing water.

Anxia perpetuis macrescunt pectora curis,
40   et sua non umquam lumina somnus habet.
Tisiphone comes atque ardens Discordia bello est:
   et dolor est illi gratus, et ipse metus.
Tempora Lethaeis Mors pallida cincta tenebris
   praecipue cordi semper amica suo est.
45 Pernicie exultat, laetaturque improba damnis;
   hoc fruitur tantum pestis iniqua bono.
Felle madent caros carpentia verba sodales,
   quoque nocere queat cogitat usque modo.
Obsit ut haec nobis, turpes vulgavit amores;
50   sed mens pro factis stat mihi pura bonis,
et detractorum rumores spernit iniquos,
   namque meae vitae conscia testis adest.
Illa susurronum contemnit murmura falsa,
   nec curat vulgi scommata dura levis,
55 quos modo non verbis, sed re confutet aperta,
   multum adeo vitiis abstinuisse iuvat;
crimine sed sperat poenas graviore daturum,
   qui carpsit vitae candida facta meae.

∶ XLVII ∶

Epitaphium Donati Cochii iurisconsulti, civis Florentini

Quantum Sulpicio debent civilia iura
   et quantum, Muci Scaevola docte, tibi,
tantum Donato Cochio debere fatentur.
   Civilis vere iuris amator eras.

Its anxious heart wastes with constant cares,
    and sleep never comes to its eyes.   40
Tisiphone is its companion, as is Discord, burning for war;
    and anguish is pleasing to it, and so too is fear.
Pale Death, temples girt with Lethe's darkness,
    is ever especially dear to its heart;
it exults in calamity and wickedly rejoices in loss;   45
    that is the only delight the malicious pest takes.
Words that slander dear comrades drip with gall,
    and it incessantly contemplates how it can do hurt.
To cause me mischief it has spread talk of shameful loves,
    but my mind is pure, in keeping with my good conduct,   50
and spurns the malicious rumors of detractors,
    for it stands witness to the truth of my life.
It holds in contempt the false mutterings of whisperers
    and pays no heed to the harsh scoffing of the frivolous crowd,
whom it could prove wrong not only by words but by plain fact,   55
    as it delights so much in abstaining from vices;
but it hopes that he who has defamed the unblemished conduct
      of my life
    will pay the penalty for his grave offense.

: XLVII :

Epitaph of the jurisconsult Donato Cocchi, citizen of Florence

As great a debt as civil law owes to Sulpicius
    and to you, learned Mucius Scaevola,
it acknowledges owing to Donato Cocchi.
    Truly you were a lover of civil law.

5　Tu quoque philosophos noras, et Curia semper
　　consilio in dubiis casibus usa tuo est.

∶ XLVIII ∶

Visio qua monetur ne lucri aviditate
dulces Musas relinquat

Memnonis aetherio pulcherrima mater Olympo
　　iam fessa oceanos compulit astra lacus,
cum subito ante oculos nostro consistere lecto
　　et tales Erato est fundere visa sonos: —

5　'Tune potes dulces, Verine, relinquere Musas?
　　　　Tune potes nostros spernere, amice, choros?
　　En, cui daphnaeam Nymphae intexere coronam?
　　　　En, cui porrexit pulcher Apollo lyram?
　　En, cui Pegasides sacrum gustare liquorem
10　　　concessere deae Calliopeque parens?
　　Et tua Tyrrhenas inter Flammetta puellas
　　　　aeternum per me nomen habere potest.
　　Me duce felices inter numeraris amantes
　　　　purpureusque tibi me duce favit Amor.
15　Ah, nunc verbosas velut unus rabula leges
　　　　insanique potes iurgia ferre fori?

You also knew the philosophers, and the Senate   5
 in doubtful circumstances always availed itself of your counsel.

: XLVIII :

A vision in which he is advised not to forsake
the sweet Muses in pursuit of gain

Memnon's beautiful mother was now driving the weary stars
 from the sky of heaven to the pools of Ocean,
when suddenly I imagined that before my eyes Erato stood by my
  bed
 and addressed these words to me: —

"Can *you*, Verino, forsake the sweet Muses?   5
 Can *you*, friend, spurn our dances?
What, even though the nymphs have woven you a crown of
  laurel?
 Even though handsome Apollo has given you a lyre?
Even though the goddesses of Pegasus' fountain and their mother
  Calliope
 have permitted you to taste the sacred water?   10
It is through me that your Fiammetta is able
 to have a name renowned forever among Tyrrhenian girls.
It is by my guidance that you are counted among lucky lovers,
 and by my guidance that rosy Love has favored you.
Ah, are you able now, like some pettifogging lawyer,   15
 to endure wordy laws and the squabbles of the mad forum?

Ferre potes litum strepitus turbamque latrantem?
 Tu potes in tanta vivere barbarie?
Ad quid non auri cogit scelerata cupido?
20 Mortales ad quid, sordide quaestus, agis?
O vanas hominum mentes, o pectora caeca
 quae sint pro multis sollicitata malis!
Turbida qui fragili percurrunt aequora cymba,
 qui nec praecipites extimuere Notos,
25 non horrent letum digitis vix quinque remotum,
 sed pelagi illudunt monstra nefanda trucis,
quique natant avidis mergendi piscibus esca,
 quos voret horrendo Scylla maligna sinu —
tantus amor nummi et crescendi cura peculi est,
30 ut properent celeres ad sua fata dies.
Sacra fames auri infecit (pro Iuppiter!) omnes,
 ut sacer Aonidum praetereatur honor.
En age, si vitae tibi cura est ulla futurae,
 et dulcis laudis pectora tangit amor,
35 divitias alii per mille pericula quaerant;
 quae sint fortunae, mobile vulgus amet.
At tu, Pieridum miro perculsus amore,
 carmina Apollineo da celebranda choro.'

Dixit et in tenuem dilapsa per aera fugit,
40 discessu argutae sed sonuere lyrae.

Are you able to bear the din of lawsuits and suffer barking-toned
    ranters?
  Can you live amid that degree of barbarism?
To what folly does the wicked lust for gold not impel people?
  To what lengths, squalid moneymaking, do you drive mortals?   20
O deluded minds of humankind, O blind hearts,
  to be so anxiety ridden over many troubles!
Those who speed over stormy seas in a fragile bark
  with no fear of the rushing south winds
and do not shudder at death when scarcely five fingers' width   25
    removed,
  but scoff at the unspeakable monsters of the cruel deep,
and who sail as food for fishes that long to pull them under
  and as prey for evil-hearted Scylla to devour in her dreadful
    clutches —
so great is their love of money and their concern to add to their
    wealth,
  that they hurry on the swiftly passing days to their deaths.   30
The accursed hunger for gold has — ah Jupiter! — infected all,
  so that the holy honor of the Aonians is passed over in
    disregard.
Come, if you have any concern for your future life,
  and the love of sweet praise touches your heart,
let others seek wealth by facing a thousand dangers,   35
  and let the fickle crowd love things subject to the whim of
    fortune.
But do you, spurred on by wondrous love of the Pierides,
  supply songs to be hymned by Apollo's band."

She spoke, and, slipping away, vanished into the thin air,
  to the sound of tuneful lyres as she departed.   40

: XLIX :

Ad Nicolaum Beninum et Ginevram eius amasiam

Liber eras quondam nostrique illusor amoris,
    aligeri spernens regna superba dei.
Nunc te deiectum nec grandia verba sonantem
    depressit niveis flava Ginevra comis,
5 et tua bis centum religavit bracchia nodis,
    et libertatis spes tibi nulla datur.
I nunc et saevos contemne Cupidinis arcus;
    infelix nostras experiere vices.
Nec iam pallorem nostro mirabere vultu,
10   nec cur tam lentis ignibus urar amans,
atque una decies hora deponere vitam
    et cupies quaevis tu sine amore pati.
Sed doleo miseretque tui; sum expertus amorem,
    aurea quid possint praepetis arma dei.
15 Nam miserabilius nihil invenietur amante,
    durius in terris vivit amante nihil.
Fac igitur parcas, formosa Ginevra, Benino,
    ut tibi purpureus parcere possit Amor.
Neglecti deus est aliquis, deus ultor amantis;
20   contempti poenas det licet ille mei.
Non potes exemplis tangi propioribus ullis.
    Hoc natura iubet: si quis ametur amet.
Si tua non cedit Spartanae forma Lacaenae,
    attamen ante alios iste petendus erat.

: XLIX :

To Niccolò del Benino and Ginevra, his ladylove

Once you were free and scoffed at my being in love,
    scorning as you did the proud tyranny of the winged god.
Now with her snowy locks flaxen-haired Ginevra has brought
      you low,
    leaving you downcast and blustering no more grand words,
and she has bound your arms with two hundred knots,   5
    with no hope of freedom granted you.
Now go and scorn Cupid's cruel bow;
    unhappy man, you will experience my plight.
You will wonder no longer at the paleness in my face
    nor why in my love I am burned by such slow fires;   10
and you will want to lay down your life ten times in one hour
    and to suffer any hardships to be freed from love.
But I grieve and pity you; I have known love
    and what the golden arrows of the winged god can do.
For nothing will be found more wretched than a lover;   15
    nothing on earth has a harder life than one in love.
See therefore that you spare Benino, beautiful Ginevra,
    so that rosy Love may be able to spare you.
There is a god, a god who avenges the slighted lover;
    he is entitled to make someone answer for contempt of *me*.   20
You cannot be swayed by any closer examples.
    This is nature's command: anyone loved should return that
      love.
If your beauty does not yield place to that of the Laconian
      woman of Sparta,
    your suitor was nevertheless more eligible than all other men.

25   Sunt sibi divitiae, generoso est sanguine cretus,
      dicier ut felix huius amore queas.

: L :

Eulogium Lisiae, pulcherrimae puellae
quam mire deperibat

Ergo per Elysios sine me, mea Lisia, campos
     tam celeri perges funere rapta mihi?
Te nimium, heu, teneris Parcae rapuere sub annis;
     pro, superi tantum sustinuere nefas!
5 Crudeles divi, crudelia numina Parcae,
     tam subito quid vos hanc rapuisse iuvat?
Quid iuvat—immitum respondeat una sororum—
     veloci filum subsecuisse manu?
Vix ternis lustris binos haec addidit annos;
10   ibit ad infernos non reditura lacus.
Dic, ubi, Phoebe, tui latuerunt carminis artes,
     exanimes possunt quae revocare viros?
Heu, pia formosae et morientis verba puellae
     flectere tam duras non potuere deas!
15 Irrita quin etiam templis mea vota fuerunt,
     flectere Tartareum quae potuere canem.
Nec prece nec lacrimis nec carmine motus Apollo est:
     en, frustra curam vatis habere ferunt!
Parcite, caelestes, et tu mihi, candide lector,
20   impia si laedunt carmina nostra deos.

He has riches and is sprung from noble blood, 25
    so that you can be spoken of as fortunate in his love.

: L :

Eulogy for Lisia, a very beautiful girl with
whom he was madly in love

Will you then make your way across the Elysian Fields without
      me, my Lisia,
    snatched from me by so speedy a death?
The Fates have snatched you away, alas, in all too tender years;
    ah, the gods above presumed so great a sin!
Cruel gods, and cruel powers, you Fates, 5
    why does it please you to snatch this girl away so suddenly?
Why does it please you—let one of the pitiless sisters reply—
    to cut her thread of life with a hasty hand?
She scarcely added two years to three lustra,
    yet she will go to the lakes below, never to return. 10
Tell, Phoebus, where were your song's skills
    that can call people back from the dead?
Alas, the pious words of a beautiful dying girl
    were not able to sway goddesses so hard of heart!
Equally fruitless were my prayers in the churches, 15
    prayers that could have swayed the dog of Tartarus.
Apollo was not moved by prayer, tears, or song;
    see how idly people speak when they say that he cares for a
      poet!
Forgive me, denizens of heaven, and you, good reader,
    if my impious verses offend the gods. 20

Aut superi non sunt aut non mortalia curant;
    falluntur stulta credulitate viri.
Lisia, ten' potuit, Stygiis adoperta tenebris,
    mors rapere, et sanctae nil valuere preces,
25   vota nihil miserae matris, nil vota sororis,
    nil lacrimae fratris, nil pia vota patris?
Quod magis admiror, viridis nil profuit aetas
    quin cito Tartareas illa subiret aquas.
Nil valuit, quamvis esset sibi candida forma,
30   posset quae magnum sollicitare Iovem.
Ecce iacet feretro sine vita corpus inane.
    Quis poterit lacrimas ore tenere pias?
Sed quis non flendo crudelia sidera dicet,
    aspicere hoc tantum quae potuere nefas?
35   Quis non infestis contundet pectora palmis?
    Quis non immites dixerit esse deos?
Haec erat in terris Flammettae forma secunda,
    durior ista tamen, mitior illa fuit.
Quid faciam? Quo me, Verine miserrime, vertam?
40   Haec, adimens curas, gaudia quanta dabat!
Spiritus hic defit tantum narrare dolorem.
    Dicite, Parnassi turba canora sacri!
Ne querulis pudeat disponere carmina nervis
    ut reddat maestos barbiton icta modos.
45   Inferias tali meritas conferte puellae,
    qualem vix aetas protulit ulla patrum.
Spargite nunc passos per cygnea colla capillos,
    et lacrimae innumerae maesta per ora fluant,
purpureisque rosis innectite lilia busto,
50   rideat ut verno tempore semper humus,
et laurus circum vireat nativaque myrtus,
    desuper assiduo carmine vernet avis,

Either there are no powers above or they do not care for mortals;
    men are deceived by their foolish credulity.
Lisia, was Death, veiled in Stygian darkness, able to carry you off,
    and did holy prayers have no effect,
nor the intercessions of your poor mother and sister,   25
    your brother's tears, or your father's pious pleading?
What I wonder at more, her green youth did nothing
    to save her from a swift descent to the waters of Tartarus.
Though her beauty was sufficient to tempt great Jupiter,
    it was of no help to her.   30
Behold, she lies on a bier, an empty, lifeless corpse.
    Who will be able to hold back tears of pity from his cheeks?
But who, as he weeps, will not call the stars cruel
    that were able to look upon such a crime?
Who will not beat his breast with pounding palms?   35
    Who will not declare the gods unkind?
This girl was on earth a beauty second only to Fiammetta;
    she, however, was harder of heart, this girl was gentler.
What shall I do? Where shall I turn, O most wretched Verino?
    How many joys she used to give me, taking away my cares!   40
Breath fails me here to recount such great pain;
    speak, tuneful band of holy Parnassus!
Do not be ashamed to set songs to plaintive strings,
    so that the striking of my lyre may sound mournful measures.
Offer deserved rites in death to such a girl   45
    as scarcely any age of our ancestors has produced.
Now spread your hair loose over your swanlike necks,
    let countless tears flow over sorrowful faces,
and interweave lilies with red roses for her tomb,
    so that the earth may always smile with springtime,   50
and let laurel and native myrtle flourish about the sepulcher,
    from overhead let a bird salute the spring in constant song,

suspiretque pius praeter sua busta viator
et madidis oculis disticha nostra legat: —

55 *Lisia sum, lector, teneris exstincta sub annis,*
quae Florentini fama decoris eram.

: LI :

Eulogium in funere clarissimi viri Cosmi
Medicis, civis Florentini, 'Patris Patriae'
a Senatu Plebeque dicti

Sic mala Fata bonos rapiunt, nec parcitur ulli.
Posse igitur sanctos credo perire deos;
ergo instat cunctis indevitabile fatum,
ut possint etiam numina sancta mori.
5 Tene Pater Patriae, potuit, sanctissime Cosme,
Atropos audaci corripuisse manu?
Parca maligna tuam valuitne invadere vitam?
Quis deus huic tantum iuris habere dedit?
Dicite, Pierides, sacras quae Gorgonis undas,
10 et nigrum colitis fronde virente nemus;
dicite, Pierides, nostro date carmina Cosmo
certatim, et tantum concelebrate virum.
Nunc magni oris opus, nunc totum Helicona, Camenae,
pandite, ut exiguo crescat in ore sonus.
15 Hic vos infernis potuit revocare tenebris,
cum vestrum fuerit semper ubique decus.

and let the pious wayfarer sigh beside her tomb
   and read with moist eyes this couplet of mine: —

I am Lisia, reader, cut off in my tender years,   55
   who was the glory of Florentine beauty.

: LI :

Eulogy on the death of the most distinguished gentleman
Cosimo de' Medici, citizen of Florence, called "Father
of his Country" by the Senate and the People

Thus the wicked Fates carry off the good, and none is spared.
   And so I believe that holy gods can perish;
death then inescapably menaces all,
   so that even holy deities can die.
Was Atropos able, most revered Cosimo, Father of your Country,   5
   to snatch you away with presumptuous hand?
Had a malign Fate the power to move against your life?
   What god permitted her to have so much right?
Speak, Pierides, who dwell by the Gorgon's holy waters
   and inhabit a wood dark with green foliage;   10
speak, Pierides, vie with one another to sing songs in honor of
      our Cosimo
   and join in celebration of so great a man.
Now I need a mighty voice, now, Muses, throw open all of
      Helicon,
   so that the sound may swell on my feeble lips.
This man could have recalled you from the darkness below,   15
   since he was always everywhere your glory.

Tunc sic illacrimans, nulla redimita corona,
    emisit querulos Calliopea sonos: —

'Heu, Tuscis quantum est terris splendoris ademptum!
20   Occidit Ausonii gloria quanta soli!
Pectora maesta suis tundat Florentia palmis;
    orbata heu quanto est patria sancta viro!
Curia maesta Patrum ploret sanctusque Senatus,
    certatim et lacrimis irriget ora piis.
25 Et pueri iuvenesque fleant, matresque nurusque;
    parvulus in cunis vagiat ipse puer.
Fundite, Sullanidae, lacrimas populariter omnes,
    et nihil, heu, tanta non sit in urbe dolens.
Quam demissa iuba est, nullusque in crinibus exstat,
30   nullus in Etrusci fronte Leonis honor,
sed iacet et maestis rugitibus aera pulsat
    et notat insanis unguibus ora Leo!
Heu, quanta Etruscis instare pericula cerno!
    Tyrrhenae quantum decutientur opes!
35 Namque fere omnis decoquet argentaria mensa,
    credat ut iratos Lydus habere deos.
Sed Medices Cosmus si tempore viveret illo,
    non premeret Tuscas tanta ruina domos,
nam quod non vidit magni sapientia Cosmi,
40   mortales omnes hoc latuisse putem.
Pace mihi liceat priscorum dicere, talem
    non produxerunt saecula cuncta virum.
Divitiis, fama, ingenio, virtute, fideque
    huic nemo ex priscis aequiperandus erat.

Then, weeping and ringed with no crown,
  Calliope delivered this plaintive lament: —

"Alas, how much of its splendor has been taken from Tuscany!
  How great a glory of the land of Ausonia is no more!   20
Let Florence beat her sad breast with her palms;
  alas, how great a man his sacred homeland has lost!
Let the House of Fathers and venerable Senate lament in sadness,
  and let each vie with each to wet his cheeks with tears of fond
    respect.
Let boys and young men weep, and mothers and daughters-in-   25
  law too;
  let even the tiny baby in the cradle wail.
Pour forth your tears, you sons of Sulla, all as one people,
  and let there be nothing, alas, in so large a city that is not
    grieving.
How crestfallen the Etruscan Lion is: there is no proud bearing
  in his mane or on his face,   30
but the beast lies dejected, startling the air with mournful roaring
  and scarring his cheeks with madly rending claws.
Alas, what great dangers I perceive menacing the Etruscans!
  How great a blow Tyrrhenian resources will suffer!
For almost every banking house will become insolvent,   35
  causing the Lydian to suppose the gods are angry with him.
But were Cosimo de' Medici still alive at that time,
  such great ruin would not oppress our Tuscan homes,
for what the wisdom of great Cosimo did not see,
  to my mind would have escaped the notice of every mortal.   40
If I may be permitted to speak without offending our forebears of
  old,
  all the centuries gone by have not produced such a man.
None of the men of former days can be counted his equal
  in wealth, fame, genius, virtue, and good faith.

45 Saepe licet tristem decantet Sparta Lycurgum;
    Neocliden quamvis Attica laudet humus;

[*The text is faulty here.*]

    et tu qui Veios armis, pietate Faliscos
      iussisti Aeneadum subdere colla iugo;
    Fabricius quamvis Pyrrhi contempserit aurum,
50   pauper et incompta Curius ille coma;
    arma Iovi quamquam suspendit opima Feretrio
      Claudius, et Poenos contudit ense feros;
    quamquam exsultantem Libycis iuveniliter armis
      contrivit lenta Maximus ille mora;
55 Scipiadas licet, tribuit quibus Africa nomen,
    inseruit superis maxima fama deis;
    seque licet iactent tristi gravitate Catones,
      et Scauri insignes aedilitate ferant;
    sis ternis quamvis clarus, Pompeie, triumphis,
60   et nomen Magni traxeris inde licet;
    devicit Gallos Caesar, subiecit Hiberos,
      et Mauri quamquam contudit arma Iubae —
    non tamen hos poteris magno componere Cosmo.
      qui talem poterunt aequiperare virum?
65 Hi sunt nimirum praeclari fortibus armis,
    uni sed numquam tanta fuere bona.
    Hic fuit ex omni recte virtute beatus,
      et tamen heu Lethes pocula nigra bibit.
    Plangite, Castaliae, infestis nunc pectora palmis,
70   et nunc maestitiae conscia signa date,

Though Sparta may often sing of stern Lycurgus,   45
   though the land of Attica may praise Neocles' son.

[*The text is faulty here.*]

and you who compelled Veii with arms and the Falisci with your
     piety
   to bow the neck to the yoke of Aeneas' sons;
though Fabricius held Pyrrhus' gold in contempt,
   as did that penniless Curius with his unkempt hair;   50
though Claudius hung up the *spolia opima* in honor of Feretrian
     Jupiter
   and crushed the savage Carthaginians with his sword;
though the famous Maximus wore down with long delay a foe
   who was exulting in Libyan arms with youth's martial spirit;
though the great fame of the Scipios, to whom Africa gave her   55
     name,
   won them a place among the gods above;
and though the Catos boast of their stern severity,
   and the Scauri enjoy distinction through the aedileship;
though you, Pompey, are famed for three triumphs,
   and owe to them the name *Magnus*;   60
though Caesar conquered the Gauls, subdued the Spaniards,
   and crushed the Moor Juba's arms —
yet you will not be able to compare these men to great Cosimo.
   Who will be able to equal such a man?
These worthies are distinguished for brave arms, to be sure,   65
   but there have never been so many good qualities in one and
     the same man.
He was truly blessed with every virtue,
   and yet, alas, he has drunk Lethe's black waters.
Now beat your breasts with pounding palms, Castalians,
   make now the mourning signs of sorrow,   70

crinibus et sparsis flentes celebrate, Camenae,
    nunc Medicis Cosmi triste ministerium.
Delius ecce suam citharam deponit Apollo,
    vixque potest lacrimas ille tenere genis;
75 nec lugere deum est, sed luctus cogit acerbus
    laurea de niveis demere serta comis.
Hic sacros coluit vates, hic aurea nobis
    Caesaris Augusti saecla redire dedit.
Egregios illa non tempestate poetas
80   maiori affecit Caesar honore meos
quam Medicum proles scriptorem amplectitur omnem,
    nec desunt doctis praemia digna viris.
Non sic Tuscus eques nostros veneratus alumnos
    vatibus Aoniis praemia tanta dedit,
85 quam Medices Cosmus, nostri tutela decori,
    dona dedit doctis, doctus et ipse, viris.
Hic quoque philosophos multa gravitate verendos
    fovit, grammaticos fovit et historicos.
Necnon astrologos et amavit rhetoras omnes
90   et quicumque alia nobilis arte fuit.
Dicite, caelestes caeli qui templa tenetis,
    quis vobis dederit munera plura pius,
verius aut Christi quis religionis amator
    exstiterit. Divos aequiperasse puto.
95 Hic est qui cunctis construxit partibus orbis
    aere suo aeternis candida templa deis,
quae dispersa simul si tu componere velles,
    vix caperent Phrygii moenia celsa Remi.
Quid dicam Marci reverendi numinis aedem,
100   quam Medices Cosmus condidit aere suo?
Pro dolor! Hic nobis, hic diversoria Musis
    condiderat, variis tota referta libris.

and now celebrate, you Muses, tearful and with streaming hair,
    the sad rites of Cosimo de' Medici.
Behold, Delian Apollo now lays down his lyre
    and can scarcely hold back tears from his cheeks;
grieving is not a thing gods do, but bitter grief makes him   75
    remove the laurel crown from his snowy hair.
Cosimo cared for holy poets and caused the golden age
    of Augustus Caesar to return for us Muses.
Caesar did not more highly honor
    my leading poets in his time   80
than the Medici line embraces every writer,
    nor do learned men go wanting for worthy rewards.
The Tuscan knight did not honor my nurslings so much
    and did not give so many rewards to Aonian bards
as Cosimo de' Medici, the guardian of our glory,   85
    gave to learned men, being a learned man himself.
He also fostered philosophers venerable for their great authority,
    as he did grammarians and historians too.
Furthermore he loved astrologers and all rhetoricians
    and anyone else who was ennobled by distinction in some art.   90
Tell, you heavenly ones who dwell in the temples of heaven,
    what pious man has given you more gifts,
or who has more truly been a lover of the religion of Christ?
    I believe he has equaled the saints.
He is the one who constructed gleaming churches   95
    to the eternal gods at his own expense in all parts of the
        world.
If you put those scattered buildings together in one place,
    Phrygian Remus' lofty walls would scarcely contain them.
Why should I mention the church of venerable Saint Mark,
    which Cosimo de' Medici built at his own expense?   100
Oh sorrow! This same man founded lodging places for us Muses,
    quite filled with books of all kinds.

Aonii montes, et Thessala cedite Tempe,
    et loca quae Graiis sunt celebrata modis.
105   Cedant magnifici Luculli splendida tecta,
    marmoream quamvis struxerit urbe domum,
mole licet grandi tumidum constraverit aequor,
    aequarit montes et iuga celsa licet.
Nam si quam Fesulis Medices in montibus aedem
110   struxerit aspicies, illa minora putes.
Quod si Laurenti mirum splendore lacunar,
    et totum templi conspiciatur opus,
nullus erit qui non Capitoli praeferat arci
    hoc, quo nil toto pulchrius orbe reor.
115   Atria quid referam Fesulis suffulta columnis
    luminibus stupidis suspicienda viris?
Me citius tempus quam copia deseret ipsa.
    Hunc quis divinum non putet esse virum?'

Dixerat, et magno pectus constricta dolore
120   conticuit, mediis exanimata choris.

Tempus erat rapido cum terra ardore dehiscit,
    et sicca arescunt arva perusta siti,
cum per Nemaei ferventia terga Leonis
    ductaret celeres sol rubicundus equos,
125 ultima cum Cosmo Parcae sua fila legebant.
    Extremum Medices novit adesse diem.

Yield place, Aonian mountains and Thessalian Tempe,
  and all the parts that have been celebrated in Greek measures.
Let magnificent Lucullus' splendid villas yield place too,   105
  though he built a house of marble in the city,
paved the swelling sea with a great causeway
  and leveled mountains and lofty ridges.
For if you see the church that Medici built in the hills of Fiesole,
  you will deem Lucullus' buildings inferior.   110
And should eyes be set on San Lorenzo's panel ceiling, marvelous
    in its splendor,
  and the whole construction of the church,
there will be none who would not prefer it to the Capitoline
    citadel;
  I think there is nothing more beautiful than it in the whole
    world.
Why should I mention the halls supported on Fiesolan columns   115
  to which men must look up with astounded eyes?
Time will fail me sooner than the abundance of things to say.
  Who would not think this man divine?"

She had spoken, and, with her heart choked with great grief,
  she fell silent, breathless in the midst of her troop.   120

It was the season when the earth gapes open with the scorching
    heat,
  and the parched fields wither with dry thirst,
when the red Sun was driving his swift team
  toward the burning back of the Nemean lion.
That was when the Fates were gathering in the last threads of   125
    Cosimo's life.
  Medici recognized that his final day had come.

Advocat egregium natum proceresque verendos
    languidus, et sacro sic dedit ore sonos: —

'Vixi, et quod tribuit spatium natura peregi.
130   Desinite impositas exsuperare colos.
Mors sua quemque manet, mortales nascimur omnes;
    omnibus inferni est ianua aperta Iovis.
Vos igitur, proceres, et tu, carissime fili,
    (sit patriae sanctae maxima cura, Petre),
135 publica privatis semper potiora putetis,
    tollere si Tuscum vultis ad astra decus.
Exstirpate malos, iustos attollite cives;
    praemia sint meritis cuique parata suis.
Sic poterit celsos Astraea relinquere caelos
140   et vestros iterum sic habitare domos.
Tollite civiles omnes ex urbe furores;
    sit procul insanae seditionis amor.
Exitiale odium subito sedate, priusquam
    suscitet ingentes parva favilla focos.
145 Non de divitiis certet cum divite dives,
    cum possit plures continuare domos;
iustitia sed enim conetur vincere iustum
    iustus; sic fortem vincere fortis amet.
Aemula virtutis nempe haec certatio prodest,
150   inflammat cives ad meliora suos.
Sitque animus liber, nullique obnoxia culpae
    mens, ut quod verum est, cernere pura queat.

He called his illustrious son and the city's most eminent men
    as he was failing in strength, and he spoke to them thus from
        his august lips: —

"I have lived my life and I have completed the span that nature
    has allotted me.
    Stop trying to overcome ordained destiny.   130
Death awaits each of us, we are all born mortal;
    the infernal Jupiter's door is open to all.
Therefore you, leading citizens, and you, my dearest son
    (may your greatest care, Piero, be for your sacred homeland),
always consider public affairs more important than private,   135
    if you wish to raise Tuscan glory to the stars.
Root out the wicked and exalt the good citizens.
    Let there be rewards for each man according to his deserts.
So Astraea will be able to leave the high heaven
    and dwell again in your homes.   140
Banish all civil conflict from the city;
    let love of mad sedition keep far away.
Be swift to calm deadly hatred
    before a tiny spark can ignite huge blazes.
Let not the rich citizen compete with the rich for riches,   145
    although he could string together a row of houses,
but let the just man try to outdo the just in justice,
    and let the brave man likewise long to surpass the brave.
Such competing rivalry in virtue is surely valuable:
    it fires a city's citizens to better things.   150
And let the soul be free, and the mind guilty of no sin,
    so that, being pure, it may be able to see what is true.

Horrida sanguinei vitetis semina belli;
    pacis honoratae semper ametis opus.
155 Sumere cuique licet, sed bello imponere finem
    non cuicumque licet, non nisi victor erit.
Exitus est dubius; Mars est communis, et hora
    urbibus insigni clade ruina datur.
Externus sed si vos contra insurget hostis,
160   ut Florentinos depopuletur agros
    (ut Piccininus, quem nos constravimus armis,
    et quisquis Tuscum terruit imperium),
tunc vos, conducto potius, seu milite Lydo,
    pellite, ne priscis degeneretis avis.
165 Vincatis ratione hostes, superetis et armis,
    Lydius ut multo crescat honore Leo.
Debellate malos, subiectis parcite, tota
    ut vestris cedat finibus Ausonia.
Numina sancta favent iustis, odere superbos;
170   felicem nullum per scelus esse sinunt.
Has artes retinete, quibus Florentia possit
    per decus Ausoniis reddere iura viris.
Nunc postquam vitam caelestia fata reposcunt,
    non mea marmoreus contegat ossa lapis,
175 nec longa incassum ornetis mea funera pompa.
    Quod terrae, ipsi reddite corpus humo.

Avoid the dreadful seeds of bloody war;
    ever love the work of honored peace.
Anyone can begin a war, but not everyone can put an end to one,   155
    not, that is, unless he emerges the victor.
The outcome is in doubt; Mars can favor either side, and in an
        hour
    cities can suffer ruin in signal defeat.
But if an outside enemy should rise up against you
    to despoil the lands of Florence   160
(such as Piccinino, whom we laid low with arms,
    and whoever has struck terror into the Tuscan dominions),
then do you, preferably with hired soldiers or else with Lydian
        troops,
    drive off such a foe, lest you degenerate from your ancestors of
        old.
Defeat the enemy by planning and prevail by arms,   165
    so that the Lydian Lion may grow with much honor.
Bring down the wicked and spare the vanquished,
    so that all of Ausonia may submit to your sway.
The holy gods favor the just and hate the proud.
    They allow no man to be happy through crime.   170
Preserve these arts, so that through them Florence may be able
    in glory to lay down laws for the men of Ausonia.
Since Heaven's decree now demands back my life,
    let not a stone of marble cover my bones,
nor let a long procession embellish my funeral to no purpose.   175
    Restore my body, made of earth, to the same soil from which
        it came.

Credite marmoreis etiam data fata sepulcris;
    nos immortales gloria sola facit.'

Vix haec ediderat, gelidos cum spiritus artus
180   liquit, et Empyrii sidera celsa petit.

: LII :

Epitaphium Cosmi Medicis, clarissimi viri

Hic situs est Cosmus, Tyrrhenae gloria gentis,
    quo Florentinum floruit imperium.
Ditior hoc nullus nec magnificentior alter,
    nec par consilio iustitiaque fuit.

: LIII :

Aliud pro eodem

Quantum vix patriae Ciceroni Roma parenti,
    et quantum debet Sparta, Lycurge, tibi,
tantum se Medici debet Florentia Cosmo,
    nam maior non hoc ille vel ille fuit,
5   quem plebs, quem proceres *Patriae* dixere *Parentem*,
    qui duro dederit tempore pace frui.

Believe that even tombs of marble have an ordained end;
   glory alone makes us immortal."

Scarcely had he said these words, when his spirit left his icy
    frame
   and sought the stars of the Empyrean on high.   180

: LII :

Epitaph of Cosimo de' Medici, most distinguished gentleman

Here lies Cosimo, glory of the Tyrrhenian race,
   under whom the power of Florence flourished.
No other was richer than he nor more magnificent
   nor his equal in wisdom and justice.

: LIII :

Another for the same

Rome scarcely owes as much to Cicero, the father of his country,
   and Sparta to you, Lycurgus,
as Florence owes to Cosimo de' Medici,
   for neither the one nor the other was greater than he,
whom the common people and the leading men alike called *Father*   5
    of his Country
   for having permitted it the enjoyment of peace in hard times.

: LIV :

De infelicibus signis et portentis illius anni

Saeva nimis Tuscum terrent portenta Leonem.
    Plebs timet, attonita est Curia sancta Patrum.
Quot periere viri! Quantum grassata per urbem,
    quantum per nostros tabida pestis agros!
5 Maximaque annonae tenues penuria cives
    pressit, macrescunt pallida membra fame,
hostibus ut macies possit miseranda videri,
    possit et immites illa movere feras.
Decoxere Patres; clausa argentaria mensa est,
10 qua multum Tuscum floruit ingenium.
Occidit una salus, nostris moderator habenis,
    Cosmus, Tyrrheni maxima fama soli.
Quo maior iactura fuit quam cetera damna!
    Hoc cive amisso gloria quanta perit!
15 Alme Pater Patriae, nunc te cognoscimus omnes,
    cum terret nostras sors inimica domos.
Ensis eras clipeusque tuis, terrorque propinquis
    regibus et populis hostibus unus eras.
Quid faciat, quo se vertat Florentia mater?
20 Tam multis mentes obstupuere malis.
Civibus at nostris Medicis spes unica Petri
    restat, qui miseros non sinet esse suos.
Consilio atque opibus cunctis succurrit egenis,
    hortaturque omnes spe meliore frui.

: LIV :

On the unlucky signs and portents of that year

Portents all too frightful terrify the Tuscan Lion.
    The common folk are afraid; the august Council of Fathers,
        astounded.
How many people have perished! How widely wasting plague
    has raged through our city and through our countryside!
A great shortage of corn sorely afflicts our lean citizens,   5
    and their pale bodies thin with famine,
so that their emaciation would seem pitiable to enemies
    and would move savage beasts.
The Fathers have gone bankrupt; the banker's table,
    at which Tuscan genius has so excelled, is closed.   10
Our one salvation, the guider of our reins, Cosimo,
    the greatest glory of the Tyrrhenian land, is dead.
How much greater a loss was that than all our other hardships!
    How great a glory has perished with that citizen gone!
Kindly Father of your Country, now we all know your worth,   15
    when hostile fate strikes fear into our homes.
You were sword and shield to your countrymen and a terror
    to neighboring kings and enemy peoples.
What is Mother Florence to do? Where is she to turn?
    Our minds are stunned by so many woes.   20
But one hope is left to our citizens in Piero de' Medici,
    who will not let his people remain in misery.
He helps all the needy with his counsel and wealth
    and urges all to be more hopeful.

25 Sed tu Sullanidas maiore urgente periclo
       servasti semper, Iuppiter, incolumes.
     Fac tandem cesset series tam longa malorum,
       Florentem populum neve perire sinas.

: LV :

Ad Venerem et Cupidinem de imponendo
fine teneris versibus et amori

     Tempus adest elegis teneris imponere finem
       et Medicis Petri gesta referre mei.
     Aurea cede Venus, tuque, o formose Cupido,
       vestraque de campo vellite signa meo.
5   Area maior equis iam nunc pulsetur anhelis,
       non sunt imbelli grandia danda lyrae.
     Carminibus blandis insanos lusimus ignes,
       dum sterili ieci semina tristis humo,
     cum me torreret Flammettae candida forma,
10   carminaque ingratae milia multa dedi.
     Iam satis est. Erato, versus genialis, abito,
       vosque Cupidinei turba valete chori.
     Haec cecinisse sat est, viridis dum pertulit aetas
       intonsas vario nectere flore comas,
15   atque coronatus convivia lauta peregi,
       dum licuit Veneri tempora prima dari.
     Iam satis insani fuimus nova fabula vulgi;
       alma, recede meis nunc, Cytherea, libris.

But you, Jupiter, have always kept Sulla's sons safe   25
    when great peril threatens.
Grant that at last so long a succession of evils may come to an
    end,
    and do not allow the Florentine people to perish.

꞉ LV ꞉

To Venus and Cupid, on putting an end
to amatory verses and love

The time has come to put an end to tender elegies
    and recount the exploits of my Piero de' Medici.
Withdraw, golden Venus, and you too, handsome Cupid,
    and pull up your standards from my plain.
Let my panting horses now pound a greater racing ground;   5
    grand themes must not be assigned to an unwarlike lyre.
I have playfully told of the mad fires of passion in soft strains,
    while in sadness I cast seed on barren ground,
while Fiammetta's fair beauty scorched me,
    and I gave the ungrateful girl many thousands of poems.   10
Now it is enough. Erato, jovial verse, away with you,
    and goodbye to all of you that make up Cupid's band.
It is enough to have sung of these things while my green youth
    allowed me to weave my unshorn hair with diverse flowers,
and I indulged in sumptuous banquets with a garland on my   15
    head,
    while it was permissible for my first years to be given to Venus.
Now I have been the latest scandal for the mad crowd's gossip
    long enough;
    depart now, kindly Cytherea, from my books.

Me residem increpuit graviter crinitus Apollo:
20   'En, tu nugarum semper amator eris,
semper et imbelles ludes, lascive, puellas,
    mollis et ad curas nate poeta leves?
En age, materiam Medices in carmina praebent
    quae sit Maeonio digna furore cani.'

Long-haired Apollo has rebuked me as I sit idle, saying,
    "What, will you always be a lover of trifles,   20
and will you always write playfully of unwarlike girls,
    you lascivious lad, you soft-natured poet born for lightweight
        cares?
Come, the Medici supply such material for poems
    as would be worthy of being sung with Maeonian rapture."

PARADISUS

Si quondam nostrae lusus placuere iuventae,
    nec tibi lascivi displicuere sales,
qui teneros elegos lusi puerilibus annis,
    dum merui castris, saeve Cupido, tuis,
5 hunc lege, Laurenti, graviori carmine librum,
    materia vires exsuperante meas.
Regia magnanimi nunc est cantata Tonantis,
    versibus heroicis intonuere poli,
astrorumque faces cecini sedesque beatum
10   divorumque hortos sidereumque nemus.

PARADISUS

Fraternis radiis nitido fulgebat Olympo
filia Latonae rapidisque invecta quadrigis
lampade lustrabat tenebrosa silentia noctis,
omnia cum placidum carpunt animalia somnum
5 et duras tristi ponunt e pectore curas.
  Ast ego, quanta meos maneant discrimina cives
et quantas Latio caedes Bellona minetur
insomnis mediae meditabar tempore noctis;
dumque animo dubio, celeri dum mente revolvo

PARADISE

Preface to Lorenzo de' Medici

If once the playful poems of my youth pleased you,
    and my lascivious wit did not offend,
when I composed tender elegies in my boyhood years,
    while serving in your camp, cruel Cupid,
then read this book, Lorenzo, in more serious verse,   5
    its subject matter exceeding my powers.
Now the greathearted Thunderer's palace has been my theme,
    the skies have resounded forth in heroic verses,
and I have sung of the stars' torches, the dwelling places of the
        blessed,
    the gardens of the saints, and the wood amid the stars.   10

PARADISE

Latona's daughter was shining from the bright heaven
with her brother's rays and, riding in her swift four-horse chariot,
was lighting up the dark stillness of night with her torch,
at the time when all creatures take peaceful sleep
and put hard cares from their sad hearts.   5
But as for me, I was sleepless at midnight, pondering the
        magnitude
of the dangers facing my fellow citizens and the scale of the
        slaughter
that Bellona was threatening to inflict on Latium;
and as, with uneasy heart and racing thoughts, I reflected on the
        devastation

10 vastari Italiam et pulchros cultoribus agros
  et miseras tantis viduari civibus urbes
  ut grave Martis opus sub mille pericula tractent,
  spiritus ecce meus sopito corpore visus
  ardua sublimis caeli super astra volare.
15   Cernere tunc licuit propius miracula toto
  quae sunt sparsa polo. Furiosi bracchia Cancri
  horret adhuc animus saevumque videre Leonem,
  Herculeae dextrae Nemea quem in valle peremit
  nodosum robur longo certamine victum.
20 Saevit adhuc oculis et Phoebi torridus aestu
  vertitur in rabiem. Longum perterritus Anguem
  vitavi, magnam caeli qui corpore partem
  occupat immani, gemino porrectus ab axe.
  Te quoque qui vexit stellantis cornua Tauri,
25 Europa, ingentes animo fecere timores.
  Terruit aetherias magno clangore per auras
  armiger ipse Iovis pennis crepitantibus ales,
  ne puer ut quondam raptarer Troius Ida.
  Inde venenatis horrendus Scorpio chelis,
30 per devexa poli gradiens irasque minasque
  effundens, pavidam implevit formidine mentem;
  impastusque diu, crocitans circumque supraque,
  me rostro et pedibus terrebat Corvus aduncis.
  Parte alia Chiron, telo metuendus acuto,
35 aetheriam audacter peragrabat semifer arcem.

of Italy, the emptying of her fair fields of cultivators,   10
and the bereaving of her wretched cities of so many citizens
to take on the stern work of Mars and face a thousand perils,
behold, once my body had settled into sleep, I dreamed that my
    spirit
flew aloft beyond the high stars of heaven.
    Then I was permitted a closer view of the strange wonders   15
that are scattered all over the sky. My mind still shudders at
    seeing
the furious Crab's claws and the fierce Lion
that the knotty club wielded by Hercules' right hand slew in the
    Nemean vale
after the beast had been vanquished in a long struggle.
It still has ferocity in its eyes, and scorched by Phoebus' heat,   20
it is driven to madness. In terror I evaded the long Serpent
that fills a great part of the sky with its vast body
as it stretches out from the twofold Pole.
The horns of the starry Bull that carried you,
Europa, also caused my mind great fear.   25
Jupiter's arms-bearing bird terrified me too with the loud noise it
    made
in the ethereal heavens with its flapping wings, in case I should
    be carried off,
as once the Trojan boy was from Ida.
Then the Scorpion, frightful with its poisoned claws,
descending the slope of the sky and pouring out anger and   30
    menaces,
filled my fearful mind with dread; and the Raven,
long unfed and cawing around and above me, terrified me
with its beak and curved talons. From another quarter
the half-bestial Chiron, dauntingly ready with his sharp arrow,
was boldly traversing the ethereal citadel.   35

Hos inter pulcher candenti pectore Cygnus
sidereas miris replebat questibus auras.
Hinc Aries, hinc Hydrus erat, viridesque dracones
vibrabant saevis horrentia sibila linguis.
40 Terribili quoque adhuc saevas venator Orion
ense feras mediis velox urgebat in astris.
Longa nimis numerare mora est immania monstra,
in toto passim quae vidi errantia caelo.
      Tunc vero extimui ne me comprehenderet ignis,
45 namque videbatur stellis ardentibus aether
comburi, et totus fumare est visus Olympus.
Sidereo at postquam steteram sublimis in axe,
unde aer liquidus Neptuniaque arva videri,
unde urbes poterant et tristia Tartara Ditis,
50 despexi in terras et regna iacentia late,
quae fuscus Maurus colit, et quae nigrior Indus,
qui colit occiduam Thylem montesque Rhipaeos,
quaeque iacent inter parvo discrimine terrae.
Me miserum, parvi brevis est angustia mundi!
55 Vix instar puncti visa est telluris imago!
Hei mihi, Tyrrheni quam parva potentia regni est,
paenituitque tuae, mater Florentia, sedis!
Non altae turres, montis non ardua moles,
templa Reparatae celsas aequantia nubes,
60 qua nec maiori se homines testudine iactant,
nec poterant celsae spectari moenia Romae.
Pertimui, barathro ne praecipitata profundo
orbis et antiqui desisset forma videri.
Heu, scelus ad tantum potuit discordia demens
65 pro tali imperio et dominandi insana cupido

Between them the beautiful white-breasted Swan
was filling the starry air with wondrous laments.
On this side was the Ram, on that the Hydra, and green snakes,
their savage tongues quivering, emitted dreadful hisses.
With terrible sword the hunter Orion too was still   40
swiftly harrying fierce beasts amid the stars.
It would take too long to recount the frightful monsters
that I saw roaming here and there all over the sky.
    Then indeed I was sorely afraid that I might catch fire,
for the ether seemed to be ablaze with burning stars,   45
and the whole of heaven appeared to be smoking.
But when I had alighted high above in the starry sky,
at a place from which the clear air, Neptune's fields, the cities,
and Dis' grim Tartarus could be seen, I looked down
on the earth below and on the wide-spreading realms   50
that the dusky Moor and the swarthy Indian inhabit,
or where dwellers in western Thyle and in the Rhiphaean
        Mountains live,
and on all the lands lying between that merge into one another.
What a tiny area the little world covers, it distressed me to note!
The earth that met my eyes seemed scarcely the size of a dot.   55
Ah, how small a territory the Tyrrhenian state controls,
and I felt pained, mother Florence, for your seat!
I could make out no high towers, no mountain's steep mass,
nor Santa Reparata's church rising up to the clouds on high
(and men can boast of no bigger dome than that),   60
nor the walls of lofty Rome. I very much feared
that even the ancient world itself had been cast down
into the depths of the Pit and was no more to be seen. Alas, have
        mad strife
and the insane desire for domination been able to lead men into
        the error
of committing crimes of such enormity for such an empire   65

ducere transversos — minimo pro iugere terrae —
iustitiae et recto torquere a limite cives?
Talia dum lacrimis iactarem maestus obortis,
quam tenues vexent mortalia pectora curae,
70 percussit nostras divini carminis aures
concentus, subitoque poli miro ordine visi
in gyrum flecti. Phoebus contrarius illis
volvitur et miseris sic praebet lumina terris
unde homines pecudumque genus variaeque volucres
75 crescendi vires ducunt et noxia vitant.
    Dicite, Pierides, sanctosque inflate furores;
nunc mihi Parnassi totos aperite recessus!
Si mereor, divae, vestrum praebete favorem!
Crescat in ore sonus! Nam nos maiora paramus
80 dicere, nec teneri nobis luduntur amores.
Spiritus alme, precor, nostro succurre labori,
ignis ut inspiret divini pectus amoris
sanctus, et altisono cantem mysteria versu.
Regia magnanimi nunc est referenda Tonantis;
85 quosque frui aeterno divos feliciter aevo,
atriaque ipsorum tectis miranda superbis
quae vidi, narrate, deae (vos omnia nostis),
namque meo scitis falsum nil carmine fingi.
    Aurea sex gradibus caelo pendebat ab alto
90 ad centrum terrae longe demissa catena,
qua tellus ponto, qua se ligat ignibus aer,
qua sphaerae ac vertex alti est connexus Olympi,
omnia ne ruerent vasta divulsa ruina.
Haec super aeterni miranda palatia Regis
95 me stupidum tenuere diu, dum singula cerno.

—for a tiny plot of land—and to divert citizens
from the right path of justice? While I was sadly
thinking these thoughts, tears welling up,
and reflecting what petty cares trouble mortal hearts,
the harmonious singing of a divine song struck my ears,   70
and suddenly the heavens seemed to revolve amazingly.
Phoebus came round to face them and so provided the poor
        lands of earth
with the light from which humankind, the race of cattle,
and the various birds draw the strength to grow
and by which they avoid what is harmful.   75
    Speak, Pierian goddesses, and breathe holy inspiration into me;
now open up to me all the recesses of Parnassus!
If I deserve it, goddesses, show me your favor!
Let the sound swell on my lips! For I make ready to speak of
        greater things,
and it is not tender love that I playfully make my theme.   80
Kindly Spirit, I beg you, assist my labor,
so that the holy fire of divine love may inspire my breast,
and I may sing of mysteries in high-sounding verse.
Now I must describe the greathearted Thunderer's palace;
and do you, goddesses (you know all), tell   85
of the saints I beheld happily enjoying eternal life
and of their astounding halls that I saw with their proud roofs,
for you are aware that I tell no lies in my verses.
    A far-descending golden chain was hanging in six steps
from high heaven to the center of the earth.   90
By it the earth is tied to the sea, and the air to the fires,
and by it the spheres and high heaven's pole are linked together
to prevent everything from being wrenched apart and crashing
        down in an immense fall.
Above these, the marvelous palace of the eternal King
held me in amazement as I long surveyed each detail.   95

217

Non mihi si totidem linguis mille ora sonarent,
tantarum vix pars rerum millesima posset
describi: humanae possunt non omnia vires.
Vestibulum solido centum ex adamante columnae
100   sustentant late et longe, quibus aurea basis
subiacet, et totidem credas lucescere soles.
Aurati postes, argentea limina, portae
postibus affixi miro fulgere pyropi.
Vincebant flammas, et erat mirabile visu
105   ordine quo nexi fuerant viridesque smaragdi
inter amethystos positi rubrosque hyacinthos.
Partim adamas plana, partim quoque cuspide acuta,
ut solis flammae portis radiabat in illis,
milleque praeterea gemmae conchaeque rotundae,
110   quae candore nives possent superare recentes;
nec poteram aeriae fastigia cernere turris,
tantum se moles spatium tollebat in altum.
Etsi non esset magni super ardua caeli,
sidera dixisses ipsum superare cacumen.
115   Postquam introgressus primi fastigia tecti,
mirabar parvis emblemata picta lapillis,
divinaque faber variaverat arte lacunar.
Paene imitatus erat spirantibus aethera signis,
sumque iterum ignitum visus mihi cernere caelum.
120   Candidus at paries, mira spectabilis arte,
vincit ebur nitidum, lactentia marmora vincit,
et lapidum tenues iunctura excluderet ungues.
Haec ego suspiciens stupidis dum miror ocellis,
attonitusque diu circum dum singula lustro,

Not if I had a thousand mouths sounding with as many tongues
could I tell even the thousandth part of such great things;
human powers cannot do everything. Far and wide
a hundred pillars of solid diamond hold up the vestibule,
each of them standing on a plinth of gold,   100
and you might suppose as many suns to be shining.
The doorposts were made of gold; the entrance steps, of silver;
and the doors shone with a wonderful covering of gold-bronze
    affixed to the posts.
They were brighter than flames, and it was marvelous to see
how intermingled green emeralds   105
had been inset among amethysts and red hyacinth-stones.
The diamond, partly smoothed off and partly sharp-edged,
sparkled on those doors like the sun's flames,
as did a thousand gems and round pearls besides,
able to surpass fresh snow in whiteness;   110
nor could I see the battlements of the airy tower,
so high did its massive structure rise.
Even were it not located above the great heaven's heights,
you would have said its top stood higher than the stars.
    On passing beneath the roof of the entrance portico,   115
I marveled at the mosaic pictures made with small pebbles,
and the craftsman had decorated the ceiling with a skill that was
    divine.
He had almost reproduced the ether with lifelike stars,
and I was given the impression that I was looking again on the
    fire-lit sky.
A white wall striking in appearance through its wonderful art   120
surpassed gleaming ivory and milky marble, and the joining
of the stones would not permit the insertion of thin fingernails
    between them.
As I looked up and admired these sights with astounded eyes,
and as I long surveyed each glory in amazement,

125 vidi alios postes, ubi sunt conclavia divum,
   tramite qui ducunt recto ad penetrale Tonantis.
   Auratum limen valvae, crystallina porta,
   ex adamante fuit vectes, argentea claustra,
   atque incisa notis fuerant duo carmina magnis:
130 *Atria fas nulli est mortali intrare deorum*
   nec nisi qui meritis divino est dignus honore.
   His super astabat vultu facieque rubenti
   candentemque ferens gladium torvusque satelles,
   qui geminis bifores utrimque amplectitur alis.
135 Tunc vero ardebam penitus cognoscere divos,
   atque Dei faciem coramque videre beatos,
   reddere quos miseros nulla infortunia possunt.
   Accessi tetigique fores ac supplice voce
   aetheriae divinus erat qui ianitor arcis
140 oravi ut liceat caelestia tecta subire;
   quod si edicta Dei, si lex vetuisset Olympi,
   semiaperta tamen reseretur ianua nobis,
   ut possim e foribus Caelestis Numinis aulam
   angustisque sacros rimis lustrare penates.
145   Sic ego. Sic arcis divinae est ianitor orsus:
   'Parcarum quamvis nondum compleveris horas,
   restet adhuc multum et nendum de stamine Clotho,
   nec tua purgarint virtutes pectora labe,
   sitque nefas magnum impurum contingere purum,

I saw another doorway where the saints' chambers are,   125
a doorway leading by a direct path to the Thunderer's sanctum.
The threshold of the entrance door was made of gold; the door,
    of crystal;
the bolt, of adamant; the bars, of silver;
and two verses had been inscribed in large letters:
No mortal is permitted to enter the halls of the gods   130
nor anyone not worthy of divine honor through deserving acts.
On watch here stood an attendant with ruddy face and
    countenance
menacingly bearing a bright-bladed sword,
spanning the double door on either side with his two wings.
Then my whole being burned with desire to know the saints,   135
to look on God's countenance, and see the blessed ones face to
    face,
those whom no misfortunes can make wretched.
I approached and touched the double door,
and in suppliant voice I begged the divine doorkeeper
of the ethereal citadel to let me enter heaven's palace;   140
but if God's edicts, if heaven's law, forbade it,
I asked that the door might yet be eased half-open for me,
so that I might survey the Celestial Power's hall from the doorway
and view the holy abode through a narrow crack.
    So I pleaded, and so the doorkeeper of the divine citadel   145
    responded:
"Though you have not yet completed the hours that the Fates
    allot you,
and there yet remains much of your thread for Clotho to spin,
and though your virtues have not purged your heart of fault,
and it is a great sin for the impure to have contact with the pure,
    yet I do not believe

150   non tamen aetherias credo sine numine divum
      repseris in sedes per tanta pericula tutus.
      Siste gradum donec quae sit sententia poscam
      magnanimi Iovis, an possis admittier intro.'
        Iam redit, et subito resolutae cardine valvae
155   ingentem fecere sonum, magnusque remugit
      aether, et intremuit totius machina mundi,
      non secus ac quondam, ventis agitantibus imbres,
      dissiliere poli crepitumque dedere tremendum.
      Tunc mihi siderei patefacta est ianua Regis.
160   Protinus obstupui cecidique in limine demens,
      tantum divino fragrabat nectare sedes
      magna Iovis. Prorsus quidquid Panchaia felix,
      India, vel totus quidquid tulit orbis odoris
      sedibus ex illis — vel plus — spirare putasses.
165   Lux etiam longe Phoebea lampade maior,
      divorum facie quae sancto ardebat amore,
      effulsit nostrique hebetavit lumina vultus,
      non aliter quam si ferventis Apollinis orbem,
      cum purus sine nube dies aestate serena
170   illuxit terris, spectarem lumine fixo.
        Forsitan et Regis faciem vultumque superni
      nosse voles, lector, solio quo Iuppiter alto
      iura daret meritosque deis conferret honores.

that you could have made your way to the ethereal dwelling   150
    places of the saints
in safety through such great perils without divine help.
Wait here while I ask what greathearted Jupiter's will is,
and whether you may be admitted within."
  By and by he returned, and suddenly the doors swung open on
    their hinges,
making a loud noise; the great ether resounded,   155
and the structure of the whole of the heavens shuddered,
just as happens when sometimes, as the winds drive rain before
    them,
the sky bursts asunder and gives a fearful crash.
Then was the entrance door of the King amid the stars laid open
    to me.
I was instantly overwhelmed, and I fell in distraction upon the   160
    threshold floor,
so powerful an aroma of divine nectar did the great abode of
    Jupiter emit.
You would have thought that the perfume of all the fragrances
that rich Panchaia, India, or the whole world has ever
produced — or more — was issuing from those halls.
A light too, far greater than Phoebus' torch,   165
which burned brightly on the countenances of the saints from
    holy love,
shone forth and dimmed my eyes,
just as if I were gazing with a fixed stare
on blazing Apollo's orb, when in the calm of summer
a cloudlessly clear day has dawned upon the earth.   170
  Perhaps, reader, you will wish also to know the face and
    countenance
of the supernal King and from what high throne Jupiter was
    laying down laws
and conferring deserved honors upon the gods.

Non potuere pati mortalia lumina tantum
175   splendorem; cecidi quotiens spectare volebam.
Si tu contuleris quidquid splendoris ubique est —
sidereas flammas, lunam, solemque diurnum —
prae facie illius iuraveris esse tenebras
obscurae noctis, cum caelum nubila condunt.
180   Dum sic, mentis inops, penderem limine in ipso,
tunc veneranda meas subito vox attigit aures:
    'Surge age, nec dubita postes intrare superbos!
Pelle metum! Aeterni dedit hoc sapientia Regis,
hoc tibi fatorum series concessit, ut, ante
185   quam tuus exutus terrestris carceris artus,
spiritus aetherias Divini Numinis aedes
visitet, atque ipsos mireris in aethere divos,
qui factis meruere suis post funera caelum.
Me duce carpe viam.' Dixit dextramque timentis
190   prendit et hoc dubiam confirmat pignore mentem.
Pone tamen lento comitor vestigia passu;
nam vocem agnovi, sed erat mutata figura.
Candida vestis erat, multo contexta labore
(Cecropiae dicas confectam Palladis arte),
195   et facies illi terso fulgentior auro,
sed iuvenilis erat, triginta circiter annos.
At pariter similes omnes aetate videntur.
Dispar erat fulgor, tamen est stola candida cunctis.
Mutuus ardentes tanta caritate revinxit
200   et mirandus amor laetantes fronte serena.

My mortal eyes could not bear brilliance so great;
I fell down whenever I wanted to look.   175
If you combined together all the brightness that exists anywhere
— the stars' fires, the moon, and the sun that shines by day —
you would swear that in comparison with God's face
they are the darkness of shadowy night, when clouds hide the sky.
As I was thus tarrying, benumbed in mind, there on the   180
    threshold,
a venerable voice suddenly came to my ears.
   "Come, arise, and do not hesitate to enter the proud portals!
Away with fear! This privilege the Eternal King in his wisdom
    has granted you,
and this the course of destiny has conceded, that before your
    spirit
has sloughed off the body of its earthly prison,   185
it may visit the heavenly seat of the Divine Power,
and you may marvel at the very saints in the ether,
who by their works have earned heaven after their deaths.
Make your way forward with me as your guide."
   He spoke, and took my right hand in my fear, by that token   190
    reassuring my hesitant mind.
I followed his steps with a slow tread behind,
for I recognized the voice, but his figure had changed.
His clothing was white and had been woven with much labor
(you would declare it finished with the skill of Cecropian Pallas),
and his face gleamed more brightly than polished gold,   195
but he was young, about thirty years old,
and everyone else there seemed alike in age.
They did not all have the same gleam, yet all wore a white robe.
A marvelous love for each other has bound them together,
ablaze with such great benevolence, evincing joy on their serene   200
    brows.

Infecit nullus caelestia pectora livor,
quisque sua contentus agit feliciter aevum
sorte, nec ullius meliori invidit honori.
Tunc animus miro scire haec optabat amore
205 scitarique ducem causas splendoris et aeui.
Ut faciem agnovi, 'Patriae lux inclita nostrae,
dic, venerande pater,' dixi, 'sanctissime Cosme,
cur urbi incubuere tuae discrimina tanta,
cur tantas caedes, cur tanta incendia cives
210 instituere mali, cur vertere funditus urbem,
quam tu servasti tranquilla pace tot annos,
foederibus ruptis crudelis turba parabat?
Consiliis atque aere tuo quos saepe fugasti,
isti in perniciem ducunt urbisque ruinam;
215 externos hostes addunt civilibus armis.
At Petrus ille tuus, patriae spes unica nostrae,
extorsit praedam rabioso ex ore luporum;
incolumes cives, miseram servavit et urbem.
Profuit afflictis summo in discrimine rerum
220 fortiter ipse nepos pulchris Laurentius armis.
Artibus imperium quam longe extendet avitis!
Quo tibi nil timeo, Florentia, sospite; quo tu
florebis, vero "felix" cognomine dicta.'
    Sic ego. Sic Cosmus divino est ore locutus:
225 'Exsulibus quamvis comitatus Colleo nostris
Flaminiae populetur agros, Asturque rebellis
fugerit ad Venetos abrupto foedere demens,
perfidiae poenas sceleratas imbuet auctor

No jealousy has poisoned their heavenly hearts;
each passes his time happily, content with his own lot,
without any feeling of envy for any other's higher honor.
Then my mind longed with wondrous passion to know these
    mysteries
and to ask my guide the reason for the people's radiance and   205
    youthful age.
As I recognized his face, I said, "Distinguished light of our
    homeland,
tell me, venerable father, most august Cosimo,
why have such great perils beset your city?
Why have wicked citizens started so much bloodshed and so
    many fires?
Why was the complete overthrow of the city   210
that you preserved in tranquil peace for so many years
the aim of a cruel band who broke their agreements?
Men whom you often drove away with wise counsels and with
    your own money,
they draw in, to the destruction and ruin of the city,
and they add foreign enemies to civil arms.   215
But that Piero of yours, the one hope of our homeland,
wrested the prey out of the wolves' mad jaws
and kept his fellow citizens and his poor city safe and sound.
In the greatest moment of crisis your grandson Lorenzo
bravely aided the afflicted with a fine show of arms.   220
How far he will extend his sway by his grandsire's arts!
While he lives I have no fear for you, Florence;
under him you will flourish, then truly called *fortunate*."
    So I spoke, and so Cosimo answered with his divine lips:
"Though Colleone, accompanied by exiles of ours, may lay waste   225
the lands of Flaminia, and the mad rebel Astorgio
may have broken his agreement and deserted to the Venetians,
that instigator of treachery will be made to pay for his crimes

cum sua vastari tam pinguia culta videbit,
230 ingentem abduci praedam, vallisque Lamonae
viderit infelix raptari hominesque pecusque;
insultetque licet castris et territet armis
Marcicola et nostris minitetur moenibus hostis,
credat et Italiae cunctis dominarier oris
235 si Florentinos Romana a stirpe nepotes,
quos nulli populi, nulli domuere tyranni,
sub iuga misisset, nescit quid vivida virtus
possit in Etruscis, quos nulla pericula terrent,
non labor assiduus, non hostes mille fatigant.
240 Si totus contra armatus contenderit orbis,
Marte satis minime cedet fiducia Tuscis.
Pro Florentinis Deus est, et numina cuncta
attollunt humiles, deponunt arce superbos.
Foederibus ruptis vix tandem suscitat arma
245 Martia Romanae Sullanus stirpis alumnus.
Quin Rex Ferrandus, Tusci pars maxima belli,
mittet opes magnas, nobis socia agmina iungens.
Ut natum Lydi pro libertate Leonis
tantus amor nostri est in aperta pericula mittat.
250 Parte alia victor sociis Galeactius armis
Gallica terribili populabitur oppida bello.
Forsitan Alpino descendet ab aggere, magnum
agmen agens, hostis quondam, nunc factus amicus,
adsueta bellis comitatus gente Philippus.

when he sees his rich lands being devastated
and booty taken in plenty, and the Lamone's unhappy vale   230
witnesses its men and cattle being seized.
And though the foe who venerates St. Mark may assault our
    camps,
terrify us with arms, and threaten our walls, and believe himself
    lord
over all the shores of Italy, should he but succeed
in sending the Florentine grandsons of Roman stock,   235
whom no nations, no tyrants have subdued, under the yoke,
he knows not what spirited valor can accomplish in the
    Etruscans,
whom no dangers frighten, and neither constant toil
nor a thousand enemies wear down.
Should the whole world contend against them in arms,   240
 the Tuscans, sons of Mars, will never lose their self-confidence.
God is for the Florentines, and all the powers divine raise up the
    humble
and cast down the proud from their citadel.
Only after the treaty has been broken does the Sullan nursling of
    Roman stock
reluctantly take up Mars' arms as a last resort.   245
Moreover, King Ferrante, the foremost champion of the Tuscan
    cause,
will send us great support, adding allied columns to our army.
So great is his love for us that he will dispatch his son
to face the dangers of open battle for the liberty of the Lydian
    Lion.
From another quarter the victorious Galeazzo with his allied arms   250
will despoil the Gallic towns in a terrible war.
Perhaps Filippo will descend from the Alpine heights,
leading a great column, a one-time enemy now turned friend,
in company with his war-seasoned people.

255   Mantua quin etiam iustam consurget in iram;
     inflammata odiis, gladium destringet in hostes.
     Necnon magnanimus coniunget castra Robertus
     et dux Urbini, belli cui summa gerundi
     mandetur, pietate bonus, praeclarior armis,
260   qui nunc in bellis Latio est Sertorius alter.
     Et dubitatis adhuc, cives, cum gente nefanda,
     cum duce praedone, et cum desertoribus urbis,
     saepe lacessiti, tam iusta capessere bella?
     Quin etiam impleri Tyrrhenum navibus aequor
265   Illyricosque sinus celsas percurrere puppes
     aspicies (credas Ossam Taurumque revulsos,
     aut Alpes mediis fluitantes dixeris undis)
     ut ratibus Venetum turritis ostia claudant.
     Quas meruere dabunt abrupto foedere poenas.
270   Exstirpate metus et duras pectore curas
     ponite. Certa manet iam nunc victoria Tuscis,
     et sero optabit supplex post proelia pacem,
     qui modo nascentis flammas exstinguere belli
     posset, sed caeco mavult contendere Marte.
275   Ausoniam heu miseram ferro flammisque ruentem!
     Sed meliora dabit summi Regnator Olympi.
       'Sic memini quondam, dum pristina vita manebat,
     ultima cum nobis legerent sua fila Sorores,
     et mors iam Stygiis circum me serperet umbris,
280   cum circumstarent proceres, et turba senilis
     circumfusa torum lacrimis lugeret obortis:
     "Iustitiam imprimis colite et vitate nefandum
     ac civile odium. Meritis bene munera dentur.
     Exstirpate malos, totum ne perdat ovile
285   inficiatque pecus turpi porrigine porcus.

Mantua too will rise up in just wrath   255
and, inflamed with hatred, draw sword against the foe.
Great-souled Roberto will join forces with Urbino's leader,
just the man to be entrusted with the supreme direction of the
    war,
virtuous in piety and outstanding in arms,
who in the field is now another Sertorius to Latium.   260
And do you still hesitate, citizens, when many times provoked,
to take up so just a war with an unspeakable people,
a brigand commander, and deserters of your city?
Moreover, you will see the Tyrrhenian Sea filling with ships
and swift craft speeding over the Illyrian Gulf   265
(you might suppose Ossa and Taurus torn away,
or you could speak of the Alps floating in the midst of the waves)
to close harbors to the turreted ships of the Venetians.
They will pay the penalties that they have deserved for breaking
    the treaty.
Rid yourselves of fear, and put hard cares from your hearts.   270
Even now victory is already assured to the Tuscans,
and too late will that foe sue for peace after battle
who could have quenched the flames of the conflict at its birth,
but prefers to hazard the uncertain outcome of war.
Alas, poor Ausonia plunging to ruin with sword and flames!   275
But highest heaven's Ruler will grant better times.
    "I recall once giving this advice, while still in my former life,
when the Sisters were spinning their last threads,
and death was now creeping about me with Stygian shadows,
when the leading men were standing round, and the elders,   280
thronging about my bed, were grieving, their tears welling up:
'Above all cultivate justice, and avoid unspeakable civil hatred.
Let rewards be given to those who have served well.
Root out evil men, lest one pig may destroy the whole sheep pen
and infect the flock with his ugly mange.   285

Esse Deum memorem iusti iniustique putate,
qui volet exacte rationem exquirere rerum.
Non aurum, non te Ciceronis lingua tuetur,
non tibi consultus nodosa aenigmata solvet.
290 Non vi, non precibus, non victus munere, Iudex
regali solio, Tyrio sublimis in ostro,
supplicium miseris, virtuti praemia reddet.
Omnes qui fuerint quacumque ex gente creati,
cum suprema dies perituro illuxerit orbi,
295 ante thronum venient et Iudicis ora tremendi;
crimina nec poterunt celari, cuncta patebunt,
et nihil infitias quidquid peccaveris olim
ire miser poteris, dictum, factum, atque putatum.
Codice divino scriptum scelus omne legetur.
300 Vae misero, quem iusta Dei sententia damnet!
Quam foret utilius, si numquam munera vitae
gustasset, numquam vidisset sidera caeli!
O vox terribilis, vox, inquam, horrenda Tonantis,
cum terrore malos sub tristia Tartara pellet:
305 *Ite, mali, in tenebras procul hinc, procul ite, maligni,*
spe sine ut aeterno cruciatu torreat ignis.
At bonus aetherii fiet novus incola caeli:
Ad dextram venias, divinae legis amator,
nectare ut aeterne felix sine fine fruaris!"
310 'Haec ego nequiquam supremo in funere vitae
irrita iactavi ventis portanda sub auras.
Tunc timui patriae ventura pericula, namque
perfida progenies, Medicum quae crevit honore,
ex humili iam facta potens, ex paupere dives,

Reflect that there is a God who remembers the just and unjust,
who will wish to make a precise reckoning of your conduct.
Neither gold nor Cicero's tongue can protect you,
no skilled lawyer will unravel knotty obscurities for you.
Unswayed by violence, prayers, or any gift, the Judge   290
on his royal throne, sublime in Tyrian purple,
will dispense punishment to the wretched and give rewards to
    virtue.
All those sprung from whatever race will,
when the last day dawns on the doomed world,
come before the throne and gaze of the dread Judge,   295
and crimes cannot be concealed, all will be plainly known,
and you will not be able to deny any sin, poor wretch,
that you have ever committed in word, deed, and thought.
Every wrongdoing, recorded in the divine book, will be read.
Woe to any wretch whom God's just sentence may damn!   300
Far better for him, had he never tasted
the gifts of life, never seen the stars of the sky!
O terrible voice, dreadful voice, I say, of the Thunderer,
when he shall drive the wicked down to grim Tartarus, saying,
Get you far from here, you wicked ones, to the darkness, get you far from   305
    here,
you wrongdoers, for fire to scorch you in eternal torment without hope!
But the good man will be made a new dweller in ethereal heaven:
Come you to my right hand, you lover of divine law,
happily to enjoy nectar for evermore without end!'
  "These words I vainly uttered on the last, dying day of my life   310
only for them to be borne away into the air by the winds.
I feared then for the perils to come for my homeland;
for a treacherous family grown prominent through honor shown
    them by the Medici,
a family now made powerful from humble origins, and rich
    instead of poor,

315　exitiale odium memori sub pectore servans,
　　　exitium nato quaerens patriaeque sibique,
　　　sollicitum quoque me his degentem reddidit astris,
　　　atque Deum supplex, ut tot discrimina pellat,
　　　eripiat rapidis Florentia moenia flammis,
320　oravi. Nutu dedit hoc Regnator Olympi.
　　　Quin etiam poenas solvet scelerata propago,
　　　et quicumque armis prodet civilibus urbem
　　　infelix luet aeterne sub Tartara poenas.'
　　　　　Haec ubi dicta dedit, caelestes ordine miro,
325　hinc cherubim seraphimque choros ostendit ovantes
　　　(scintillas totidem dicas ardere micantes),
　　　qui prope caelestem posuere sedilia Regem,
　　　aurea et invicti praecordia summa Tonantis
　　　(nam propiora tenent) noscunt, si noscere possunt;
330　ardentemque ferens princeps archangelus hastam
　　　aurea servabat celsi subsellia Patris,
　　　gemmatisque cohors alis (mirabile visu)
　　　lauta ministrabat sanctis convivia divis;
　　　nec numerare queas oculos radiantibus alis
335　et miras facies, nobis vix credere dignas.
　　　Corpora non fuerant, tenues nec dixeris umbras.
　　　Qualia saepe solent miris insomnia visis
　　　perplexam mentem et sopitos ludere sensus,
　　　cum ieiuna fames seu turpis crapula corpus
340　prosternit, clauditque gravantia lumina somnus,
　　　sic mirae errabant vario splendore figurae.

harboring murderous hatred in unforgetting hearts   315
and seeking destruction for my son, their homeland, and
    themselves,
caused anxiety to me too, though I live amid these stars,
and as a suppliant I begged God to dispel so many dangers
and snatch the walls of Florence from the consuming flames.
The Ruler of heaven granted this request with a nod.   320
What is more, the wicked line will pay the penalty,
and whoever gives up his city to civil war will to his misery
answer for it for all eternity in Tartarus."
    After speaking these words, he revealed the denizens of heaven
    to me in wondrous array.
On this side he showed me exulting choirs of cherubim and   325
    seraphim
(you would declare them as many gleaming sparks ablaze),
who have set their seats of gold next to the celestial King
and know the invincible Thunderer's supreme heart
(for they hold the nearest place), if know it they can;
and a prince-archangel, bearing a burning spear,   330
guarded the high Father's golden throne,
while a cohort with bejeweled wings (marvelous to see)
served sumptuous banquets to the holy saints.
You could not count the eyes on their radiant wings
or describe their wonderful faces, scarcely credible to me.   335
They were not physical bodies, nor would you call them
    insubstantial shades.
Like such dreams as are often accustomed to delude the
    perplexed mind
and slumbering senses with strange sights,
when either hunger from fasting or shameful inebriation
prostrates the body, and sleep closes heavy eyes,   340
so went about the wonderful figures in their diverse splendor.

Prima tenet seraphim, summi sapientia Regis,
igneus et cherubim una thronique verendi.
Hi nullo aspiciunt medio Dominoque fruuntur.
345 Inde potestates virtutesque insuper omnes
ordine composito sedes tenuere secundas.
Angelus hos sequitur, caelestis nuntius aulae.
Nam Rex omnipotens cherubim, cherubimque secundis,
hi mandata tibi, tu defers, angele, nobis.
350 Sic a supremo fas est descendere ad imum.
    At monstrum horrendum mira formidine mentem
percussit trepidam, calido ut sine sanguine vultus
albus, et horrentes steterint in vertice crines.
Vox mihi lapsuro mediis in faucibus haesit.
355 Cui capita assistunt torvis horrentia formis,
et septem linguas septenaque porrigit ora,
et totidem signis impressum bellua librum
servabat, cuius fuit hoc in cortice carmen:
Viventum liber est quibus est promissus Olympus.
360 Caelicolum nulli fas est aperire libellum,
sed Deus altitonans (opus innarrabile) claves
inclusas retinet solvitque tenacia vincla.
Purgatum postquam scelus est, super aethera purus
spiritus aeterno est caeli functurus honore.
365   Nec procul attonita renovarunt mente pavorem
quattuor horrendis diversa animalia formis.

The seraph, the wisdom of the King most high, holds first place,
and together with him the fiery cherub and the venerable thrones.
These behold the Lord and enjoy his presence with none in-
    between.
Next down, the powers and, with them, all the virtues   345
hold the second rank in the hierarchy.
The angel, the messenger of the celestial court, follows them. For
    the almighty King
gives commands to the cherubim, and the cherubim to those of
    second rank;
these last pass them down to you, angel, and you pass them down
    to us.
That is the right descent from the highest to the lowest.   350
   But a terrifying monster struck wondrous dread into my
    fearful mind,
so that my face, drained of hot blood, turned white,
and the hair on my head stood on end.
My voice stuck in the middle of my throat as I was on the point
    of fainting.
A beast that had heads bristling with frightful shapes   355
and stretched out seven tongues and seven mouths
was guarding a book impressed with as many seals,
on the cover of which was this inscription:
This is the book of the living who have been promised heaven.
None of the dwellers in heaven may open this book,   360
but (in a procedure that cannot be described) high-thundering
    God
keeps the keys shut away and undoes the fastening chains.
Once purged of sin, the pure spirit is ready
to enjoy the eternal honor of a place in heaven beyond the ether.
   Nearby, four diverse creatures of frightful form   365
renewed the fear in my astonished mind.

Nam leo, terribilis villoso tegmine, saevis
unguibus acer erat, qualem Gaetulia creavit,
aut, Acheloe, tuis potasti, corniger, undis;
370   hinc truculenta bovis facies, spectabilis inde
angelus humano vultu, fulgentibus alis.
Hos super astabat pennis miranda volucris—
armiger illa Iovis, ni me sententia fallit.
Quattuor hos iuxta divi (mirabile visu)
375   astiterant, quorum terso fulgentior auro
vultus erat, risusque decens in fronte serena.
Vicissent nitidum radiantia lumina solem,
aut candore nives quae mox cecidere recentes
talis fluxa tenus superasset palla decoris.
380   At divina cohors caelique exercitus omnis
partim hymnos partimque leves agitare choreas
flectereque in gyrum, saltantes ordine miro.
Hi laudes Domini cantabant voce sonora,
fecerit ut caelum, terramque crearit et undam,
385   utque leves ignis volitare per aethera flammas
de nihilo, ut dederit variis animalia formis.
Pars habitat terras, pars umida regna profundi,
pars liquido pictis se librat in aere pennis.
Possit ut id fieri, terram secrevit ab undis
390   aeraque ardenti nitidum divisit ab igne.
Fecerit utque globum lunae, quae mense peragrat
per bis sena suis radiantia signa quadrigis.
Ut, Cytherea, tuum rutilanti lumine sidus
lascivos, hilares, pulchros, levitatis amicos,
395   producatque choris habiles ac versibus aptos.

For there was a lion, terrible with shaggy mane and ferocious
    with savage claws,
one such as Gaetulia has spawned, or whose thirst
you, horned Achelous, have quenched with your waters.
On this side was the fierce glare of an ox; on that, an angel   370
of striking appearance with a human face and gleaming pinions.
Above them was a bird with marvelous feathers
— the arms bearer of Jupiter, if I am not mistaken.
Next to them stood four saints, a wondrous sight.
Their faces were brighter than polished gold,   375
and there was a beautiful smile on their serene countenances.
Their radiant eyes would have bettered the shining sun,
while the robe that flowed to each man's elegant ankles
would have surpassed newly-fallen snow in whiteness.
    But the divine cohort and all heaven's host   380
in part sang hymns and in part performed light dances
and circled about, tripping along with amazing skill.
They sang the praises of the Lord in sonorous voice,
telling how he created the heaven, the earth, and the sea,
how he made quick flames of fire fly through the ether   385
from nothing, and how he gave the world animals in their various
    forms.
Some creatures live on the land, some in the moist realms of the
    deep,
some balance on painted wings in the clear air.
To achieve his purpose, he separated the land from the sea
and divided the bright air from the burning fire.   390
Then they told how he made the globe of the moon,
in a month traversing twice six radiant signs in her four-horse
    chariot.
They sang how your star, Cytherea, with its rosy glow,
brings forth lusty, blithe, beautiful people,
friends of levity, fitted for dancing and suited to poetry.   395

Quin et Atlantiades velox, licet ille galero
tectus, Apollineos non quit vitare calores,
credat ut a solis radiis ignobile vulgus
combustum, cum iam rutilo vanescat Olympo.
400 Astutum, varium, et prompto Cyllenius ore,
et nimium lucri cupidum producit alumnum.
Formosus mediis ut temperet omnia Phoebus
impositus sphaeris et lustret lampade terras;
ut citharae auratae resonanti pollice chordas
405 pulset, et ad sonitum cuncti moveantur Olympi;
ut teneras frondes et flores vere nitenti,
aestibus intensis canas producat aristas,
impleat autumnum maturis largiter uvis,
ut bruma australes penitus concessit ad oras.
410 Mavortisque ardens animosa irritet ad arma
sidus, et insanis agitet mortalia bellis,
audaces moresque feros pugnaque superbos
et furere ardenti vesanos procreet ira.
Utque benigna viris Dictaei stella tyranni
415 fulgeat et sanctos producat lucida mores.
Ut grave Saturni miseris mortalibus astrum
triginta tandem cursum vix expleat annis.
Ni Cytherea Venus, rutilo ni Iuppiter igne
obsistat sidusque senis perfringat iniqui,
420 omne malum terris curva se falce daturum
portendit, iunctusque bonis sic temperat astrum.

Furthermore, Atlas' speedy grandson, though shielded
by a leather hat, cannot avoid Apollo's heat,
so that the ignoble crowd believe him burned up by the sun's rays
when he vanishes from view in a now-reddening sky.
The Cyllenian god disposes his nursling to be shrewd,   400
changeable, ready tongued, and too eager for gain.
They sang how handsome Phoebus, set in the midst of the
    spheres,
tempers all and lights up the earth with his torch;
how he strikes the strings of his golden lyre with resounding
    thumb,
and all the heavens are moved at the sound;   405
they told too how he brings forth tender leaves and flowers in the
    bright spring
and white ears of corn in the intense heat of summer,
and how he fills autumn full with ripe grapes,
when the winter has retired far off to southern shores.
They sang how Mars' burning star stirs us to spirited arms   410
and harries mortal life with mad wars,
producing bold and fierce-natured men, proud in battle,
and crazed to a frenzy in blazing wrath.
They sang too how the Dictaean King's star shines in goodwill
    for men
and in its brightness produces morally upright natures;   415
and how Saturn's star, burdensome to wretched mortals,
barely completes its orbit at long last in thirty years.
If Cytherean Venus and Jupiter with his glowing fire did not
    oppose him
and counter the wicked old man's star,
he threatens to inflict every kind of woe on Earth with his curved   420
    scythe,
and it is only through being joined with good forces that he
    tempers his planet.

241

Necnon divinum tanta dulcedine carmen
cantabant, notulis vix enarrabile miris,
attonito ut similis, sine motu, lumine fixo,
425 perstarem. Arrectas concentus carminis aures
ceperat, ut seraphim referebat voce canora,
principio ut varia depinxit imagine caelum.
Ne foret hoc vacuum, miro est splendore creatus
angelus et simili comites fulgore micantes.
430 Utque superba cohors, regnis detrusa supernis,
immensas sine fine dabit sub Tartara poenas,
quae summo aequiperare Deo Regi Patrique
ausa fuit, crudele nefas, immane nefandum.
Caelicolae ast alii divina voce canebant,
435 post caelum et terras ut primum effinxerit Adam
de limo, humanos ne saeva superbia natos
tollat humo inflatos, homines rapiatque feroces,
ut neget esse Deum aut praesentia numina temnat
(sed tamen ille sua similem sub imagine fecit,
440 ne tota humanis iaceat mens obruta rebus);
deque viri latere uxorem sibi fecerit Evam,
his animam partem divinae inflaverit aurae.
Primum immortales ambo sine crimine nati,
post errata tamen mortem subiere parentes,

The angels proceeded to sing a divine song of such sweetness,
barely describable by reason of its wondrous notes,
that like one thunderstruck I stood motionless with fixed gaze.
The harmony of the song had me listening with rapt attention,   425
as the seraph recounted in tuneful voice
how in the beginning God painted the sky with a variety of
    shapes.
Lest it should be empty, the angel was created with his marvelous
    luster,
as were his companions shining with like brightness.
And the choir sang how the proud cohort that was thrust down   430
    from the kingdom
up above will suffer immeasurable punishment without end in
    Tartarus.
That band dared to challenge God most high, the King and
    Father,
a cruel sin and a monstrous act of wickedness.
   Other heaven dwellers sang with divine voice
how, after the sky and the earth, God first fashioned Adam   435
out of mud, for fear that overweening arrogance should so puff up
humans beings born from the earth, and make them so fiercely
    headstrong,
that in their presumption they would deny the existence of God
    or despise divinities
there in presence with them (but God yet made man in his own
    likeness, lest his mind
should be totally crushed and dispirited, overwhelmed by human   440
    concerns).
And they sang how from the man's side God made him a wife in
    Eve
and breathed into them part of his divine breath as a soul.
At first the humans were both born immortal without sin,
but after their wrongdoings our parents became subject to death,

445 unde necesse fuit mortalia cuncta perire.
  Nam quaecumque globo lunaeque sub orbe creantur
  inferius primum crescunt, post aucta senescunt.
  Haec voluit parere viris Rex magnus Olympi.
  Quidquid alit tellus — pisces, animalia, plantae,
450 saxaque diversis terrae pretiosa metallis —
  aut hominem oblectant aut praestant commoda vitae.
  Natus et ipse Deo, caelestia regna moretur,
  si modo fatales virtutibus egerit annos.
   Custodes gemini miseris mortalibus adsunt.
455 Hinc bonus, inde malus trahit in contraria pectus
  ambiguum. Spectare bonus caelestia regna
  admonet, et vanos vitae mortalis honores
  spernere, virtutemque sequi per mille labores.
  Ille alter vitiis tentat corrumpere mentem.
460 Nunc magnas ostentat opes, nunc ditia regna,
  nunc suaves epulas, Veneris nunc dulcia furta.
  Sic hominem vario dubium certamine turbant.
  Ipse sed, arbitrio liber, deflectit habenas
  frenaque anhelantum spumantia volvit equorum.
465 Nunc altos montes cursumque intendit ad astra,
  et nunc, illecebris captus, percurrit apertum
  aequor et evitat rupes atque invia saxa.
   Necnon altisono referebant carmine Throni
  ut genus humanum miro dilexit amore
470 ille Opifex summus rerum mundique Creator.

making it inevitable that all mortal creatures must perish;   445
for all things created on earth beneath the sun's ball and the orb
of the moon at first grow and then, when their growing is done,
    become old.
These the great King of heaven willed should obey humankind.
All things that the earth produces — fish, beasts, plants,
and precious stones in the various mines within the ground —   450
either delight man or provide advantages to him in life.
Born as he is himself of God, an abode in the celestial kingdom
    can be his,
if only he has passed his allotted years in virtue.
    Poor mortals have two guardians: on one side a good,
on the other a bad, pull man's wavering heart in opposite   455
    directions.
The good guardian advises man to look toward the heavenly
    kingdom,
spurn the vain honors of mortal life,
and follow virtue through a thousand hardships.
The other tries to corrupt his mind with vices,
now showing him great wealth, now rich kingdoms,   460
now delicious feasts, now Venus' sweet intrigues.
Thus they vex the hesitant man with a conflict of urges.
But, having freewill, it is he who controls the reins
and directs the foaming bits of his panting horses.
Now he steers his course for the high mountains and the stars,   465
and now, ensnared by allurements, he speeds over the open sea,
trying to avoid the reefs and impassable rocks.
    Furthermore the thrones told in high-sounding song
how the Maker most high of all things and Creator of the
    universe
cared for the human race with marvelous love.   470

245

Nam quia siderei permansit ianua caeli
clausa diu, nullaeque animae super astra volabant,
mortali quamvis defunctae corpore vitae,
et, dum vixerunt tenebroso carcere limi
475   inclusae, semper leges hominumque Deique
servarint, nullo macularint crimine vitam,
his tamen obstabant primi delicta parentis.
At Deus omnipotens, cui servit machina mundi
caelestisque cohors, cui caeli regia paret,
480   humanam sumpsit pura de Virgine formam,
cum foret Augusti sub nutu Caesaris orbis.
Non dedignavit terras Regnator Olympi
immixtusque habitare viris sub imagine servi,
vivere ter denos cum mille laboribus annos
485   orbe quidem medio, ne ignoraretur ab ullo
factus homo. Immensi quantus fuit ardor amoris!
Rex aeternus erat servus mortalis, et aeque
mendicus, qui dives erat. Cruciatibus insons
se dedit et vili terra mutavit Olympum.
490   Aeternis tenebris ne gens humana periret,
assumpsit multo periturum verbere corpus,
seque neci tradi voluit, reseraret ut altum
humano generi pretioso sanguine caelum.
Ut cruce suspensum gemini cinxere latrones,
495   qui furtis, qui caede cruces meruere nefandas,
dic, homo, dic, ingrate, mihi, Divina Potestas
quid meruit, cum se ligno transfixit acerbo
impia Iudaeae immitis periuria gentis?

For, because the starry heaven's door long remained closed,
no souls flew beyond the stars,
though they were done with the mortal body of life;
and though, while they lived shut in their dark prison of mud,
they always kept the laws of men and God   475
and stained their lives with no wrong,
yet their first father's sins stood in their way.
But Almighty God, whom the whole structure of the universe
and the celestial cohort serve, and whom heaven's palace obeys,
took human form, being born of a pure Virgin,   480
when the world was under Augustus Caesar's sway.
The Ruler of heaven did not disdain the earth and did not scorn
to dwell among humankind in the form of a slave,
living thrice ten years with a thousand hardships, made a man
in the midst of our world, lest he should be unknown by any.   485
How great was the warmth of his boundless love!
The eternal King was a mortal slave, and in the same way he who
        had been rich
was a beggar. He gave himself up to tortures,
though innocent of guilt, and exchanged heaven for the paltry
        earth.
Lest the human race should perish in eternal darkness,   490
he assumed a body that would perish with many a lash,
and he was willing to be delivered up to death in order to open
high heaven to the human race through his precious blood.
When two robbers flanked him as he hung on the cross,
men who by thefts and murder deserved their unspeakable   495
        crosses,
tell me, ungrateful man, tell me, what did the Divine Power
        deserve,
when the wicked perjury of the cruel Jewish race
pierced him through on the bitter wood?

Cantabant, veluti portas reclusit Averni
500   victor, ut ingressus sanctas detraxerit umbras,
et secum aetherias tandem ut duxisset ad arces,
felices animae summo ut potirentur Olympo,
utque vias aliis posthac patefecerit alti.
Quin etiam alterno modulantes carmine voces,
505   angelicas mira implebant dulcedine sedes,
non secus ac quondam finxerunt Orphea vates,
pulsantem dulces aurato pectine chordas,
immites flexisse feras et flumina cursu
firmasse et duras movisse in montibus ornos,
510   infernos adiisse lacus. Cui ianitor Orci
cum tria porrigeret venienti Cerberus ora,
ad sonitum citharae vigilantia lumina clausit.
Pulsabat pariter citharam pariterque canebat,
si modo Tartareas potuisset flectere leges
515   ut secum Eurydicen superas adduceret auras.
Si licet humanis divum componere rebus,
talia caelestes edebant carmina throni.
Ut sunt bis seni Divino Ardore repleti
discipuli atque, eius vestigia tanta secuti,
520   Doctoris leges totum sparsere per orbem.
Tunc mala cessarunt sculptorum oracula divum,
tunc fraudes victae, et patefactae daemonis artes.
Haec et plura chori resonanti voce canebant,
omnia sed turbae non sunt vulganda profanae,
525   et vetat ipse Deus mysteria cuncta referre.
    Dum biberem attonitus suspensis auribus ista,
dux mihi Cosmus ait, 'Restant tibi plura videnda

They also sang how, once he had opened the gates of Avernus
in victory, he entered and brought forth the holy shades,   500
and how at length he took them with him to the ethereal citadel,
so that the happy souls might possess high heaven,
and how he laid open the pathways of the world above to others
    thereafter.
Indeed, modulating their voices in alternate song,
they filled the angelic abodes with wonderful sweetness,   505
just as poets say that Orpheus once,
striking dulcet strings with a golden plectrum,
swayed cruel beasts, made rivers stand fixed in their course,
moved hard ash trees on mountains,
and journeyed to the infernal lakes. And when Orcus' gatekeeper   510
Cerberus presented three mouths to him on his approach,
the dog closed his watchful eyes at the sound of Orpheus' lyre.
Orpheus kept striking his lyre and singing all the while,
in the hope that he might prove able to bend Tartarus' laws
so as to bring Eurydice back with him to the air above.   515
If it is permissible to compare the divine to the human,
such were the songs to which the celestial thrones gave voice.
They told how the twice six disciples were filled with the Divine
    Ardor
and, following in their Teacher's great footsteps,
spread his laws throughout the world.   520
Then the wicked oracles of graven gods fell silent,
then deceptions were defeated, and the devil's arts exposed.
These things and more the choirs sang in resounding voice,
but all may not be divulged to the profane crowd,
and God himself forbids the telling of every mystery.   525
    While I was drinking in their songs with attentive ears, all
    amazed,
my guide Cosimo said to me, "More things remain for you to see,

dum licet et fas est caelestia visere regna,
mortali quondam raro concessa videri.
530 Me duce festina, tibi cunctas ordine miro
ostendam causas tanti splendoris et aevi,
cur omnes nivea florent in veste iuventa.
    'Hos paene innumeros, solio quos cernis eburno,
candida gemmatis redimitos tempora sertis,
535 veste frui in nitida ambrosiis et nectare divos —
hi peperere suis virtutibus atria caeli.
Hic quia servavit castos cum coniuge mores,
alterius nullos thalamos violavit adulter.
Hic quia paupertatem animo sic pertulit aequo
540 ut, quamvis multis rebus mendicus egeret,
nil tamen optabat placide nisi ducere vitam.
Hic quia se nulli mulieri miscuit umquam
sed caelebs vixit, tali dignatus honore est.
Hic quoniam aere suo multis subvenit egenis,
545 non animo infecto, populi ut sibi quaereret auram;
clam dabat egregiae solum virtutis amore.
Ille autem, insignis contemptis fascibus urbis,
contemplans caelum, silvestri se abdidit antro.
Ille sacras divis construxit funditus aedes;
550 hic alimenta dedit ruituraque templa refecit.

while it is permitted and lawful for you to visit the celestial
    kingdom,
a sight but rarely ever granted to a mortal.
Follow my lead and hurry along, and I will wondrously reveal to   530
    you
all the reasons for their radiance and age—
why all bloom with youth in snow-white raiment.
   "These saints whom you see almost without number on ivory
    thrones,
their fair temples ringed with jeweled garlands,
enjoying ambrosia and nectar and clad in shining raiment—   535
these have won the halls of heaven by their virtues.
This one did so because he lived chastely with his wife
and violated no other man's bedchamber in adultery;
this one because he bore poverty with such equanimity
that although, being a beggar, he lacked many things,   540
yet he wished for nothing other than to lead his life in peace.
This man was thought worthy of such honor because he never
    lay with any woman
but lived celibate; this other, because he helped
many needy people with his money. He did not act
with tainted motives, to court the acclaim of the people,   545
but used to give in secret merely from his love of outstanding
    virtue.
That man, scorning a magistrate's office in a distinguished city,
hid himself away in a forest cave in contemplation of heaven.
That man built holy churches for the saints from the very
    foundations;
this other gave funds for maintenance and restored churches in   550
    danger of falling down.

Iste, in honore Dei, primae post sidera noctis
sedabat tenui ventris ieiunia victu,
ut nunc ambrosiis caelo saturetur in alto.
Hic res urbanas perituraque regna reliquit
555   et patriam et dulces cara cum coniuge natos;
omnia dimisit vitae caelestis amore.
Is, Dominum iusto quoniam est veneratus honore,
servavit praecepta Dei legesque superbas,
nunc fruitur caelo felix semperque fruetur.
560   Ille Dei verbum multas vulgavit in urbes,
et resides populos vitiis ad templa deorum
hortando precibus, terrendo voce minaci,
eloquio tandem sancto, ad meliora reduxit.
Ille parum lucens, gradibus quem cernis in imis
565   fronte quidem laeta summum spectare Tonantem,
Tartarei horrendo solum terrore flagelli
abstinuit vitiis. Alti est nunc incola regni.
Haec veneranda cohors, nitido fulgentior auro,
quae viridi palma florentia tempora cinxit,
570   dum Christi nomen celebrat, profitetur, adorat,
corpora suppliciis tribuit lanianda tyranni.
Haec vera est fidei martyr. Non dira Neronis
constantes potuere viros tormenta movere,

This one, in honor of God, used to settle the hunger in his
    stomach
with meager nourishment taken only after the stars of first night
    had appeared,
so that now he is sated with ambrosia in high heaven.
This other left behind city affairs and kingdoms doomed to
    perish,
his homeland, and sweet children, along with his dear wife,   555
and gave up all out of longing for the celestial life.
This one, because he venerated the Lord with just honor
and kept God's commandments and excellent laws,
now happily enjoys heaven and always will.
That other man spread the word of God to many cities and   560
    brought
lapsed peoples back from vice to the temples of the gods
by urging them with entreaties, by terrifying them with menacing
    voice,
and finally by employing holy eloquence, so turning them once
    more to better things.
The man over there with a faint brightness — the one you see on
    the lowest steps
gazing on the Thunderer most high with a happy face —   565
abstained from vices only out of dreadful fear
of Tartarus' scourge. He is now a dweller in the realm on high.
This venerable company of people, gleaming more brilliantly than
    bright gold,
whose flowery temples are ringed with green palm leaves,
while they celebrated the name of Christ, professing him and   570
    adoring him,
gave up their bodies to be mangled by a tyrant's tortures.
They are true witnesses of their faith.
Nero's dreadful torments could not shake men of such constancy,

et quamvis avidae torrerent pectora flammae,
575 mens invicta magis divino ardebat amore.
Ignes, arma, famem, frigus, ludibria, caedes
aequo animo victrix vitiorum turba ferebat.
Quos autem miro cernis candore micantes
ac propiore Deo et sublimi in sede locatos,
580 hi miseras viduas carisque parentibus orbos
foverunt, patriae qui commoda publica rebus
duxerunt potiora suis, potirentur ut astris;
praemia qui iustis poenasque dedere malignis,
Astraeam intrepidi totum coluere per aevum,
585 debita cuique suae tribuentes munera vitae.
Hic, patriae ingenti laudis perculsus amore,
largiter expendit magni patrimonia census.
Post etiam, saevos patriae ut depelleret hostes,
per medias acies hostiliaque arma cruentus
590 suscepit pulchram crudeli in vulnere mortem.
Eripuit miseram hic bellis civilibus urbem.
Cum fureret populus, cum belli dira cupido
redderet insanos ad impia proelia cives,
sedavit placidis flagrantia pectora dictis.
595 Sed, ne te fugiat, nihil est acceptius ipsi
qui mare, qui terram, ex nihilo qui cuncta creavit,
quam servatores patriae, quorum aurea serta
cinxerunt multis radiantia tempora gemmis.

and, even though greedy flames were scorching their breasts,
their unconquered minds burned all the more with love of God.   575
The band that prevailed over vices endured fires, weapons, hunger, cold,
mockery, and execution with equanimity.
These men, however, whom you see shining with wondrous brilliance
and placed on a high seat nearer to God,
looked after wretched widows and children bereft of their dear   580
     parents
and held the public good of their homeland
above their own interests, so that they might attain the stars.
They gave rewards to the just and dispensed punishments to the
     wicked
and fearlessly honored Astraea all their days,
bestowing on each person the due rewards of his life.   585
This man, stricken by great longing for his homeland's praise,
generously spent an inheritance of great value,
and thereafter, in the attempt to drive fierce foes from his
     homeland,
drenched with blood in the thick of battle and amid enemy arms,
met a noble death from a cruel wound.   590
This man rescued his poor city from civil wars.
When his people were raging with fury, and a dreadful desire for
     war
was making his fellow citizens mad for wicked battles,
he calmed their blazing breasts with words of peace.
But, in case it may escape you, nothing is more agreeable to the   595
     one
who created the sea, the land, and all things else from nothing
than saviors of their homeland; golden garlands
radiant with many gems have ringed their temples.

Hos omnes summi collustrat gratia Regis,
600   ut sol germanam totumque illuminat orbem;
sed qui corporeo caelestem carcere vitam
duxit et a vitio sine fraude abhorruit omni,
ille Deo propior maiori lumine fulget.
Pro meritis minus hic, longe magis ille relucet.
605   Sorte sua quisque est laetus, livore fugato.
    'Forsan et inquiris cur una est omnibus aetas.
Non infans curvusque senex, non debilis ullus;
sunt validae cunctis iuvenili in pectore vires.
Hac aetate Deus (namque est perfectior omni)
610   sponte cruci voluit figi mortemque subire,
ut possent homines, aeterna morte redempti,
vivere perpetuo iuvenes feliciter aevo.
Pulchrum namque mori est iuvenili in tempore, quando
sint plenae vires, vigeantque in pectore sensus.
615   Credendum tunc est, felici morte beatum,
defunctum vita summo placuisse Tonanti.
Quid nisi plena mali vita est, nisi plena laborum?
I nunc, longinquo te mille doloribus aevo
serva, ut fortunae infelix ludibria solvas.
620   Quin et corporibus divinus praemia Iudex
contribuet, tantos quae sustinuere labores
mortalis vitae regni caelestis amore,
cum tuba supremi ciet ad praetoria Regis
defunctas animas vitae fatalibus annis.
625   Tunc sibi quisque suum corpusque animumque resumet,
praemia seu capiat pariter cum corpore poenas.

The grace of the King most high illuminates all these people,
as the sun lights up his sister and the whole world;   600
but he who led a heavenly life in his bodily prison
and recoiled without deceit from all vice,
is nearer to God and shines with a greater light.
In proportion to their deserts, this man shines less, that man far
        more.
Each is happy with his lot, with no feelings of jealousy.   605
    "You may also want to know why all are the same age.
None is an infant or crooked elder, none an invalid,
but all have sturdy vigor in their young breasts.
It was at this age that God (for he is more perfect than all others)
chose to be crucified and suffer death   610
so that humankind might be redeemed from death eternal
and live happily in everlasting youth.
For it is a fair thing to die in young adulthood,
when strength is at its peak, and the senses are unimpaired in
        one's breast.
We must believe that a man who has departed life at that age,   615
in the blessing of a fortunate death, has pleased the Thunderer
        most high.
What is life but full of woe and full of toil?
Go now and by living a long life preserve yourself for a thousand
        pains
to be the unhappy butt of fortune's mocking sport.
Indeed, the divine Judge will grant rewards to bodies   620
that have sustained such great hardships
of mortal life out of longing for the celestial kingdom,
when the trumpet shall summon to the supreme King's palace
souls that have completed their allotted years of life.
Then each will take up again his own body and spirit,   625
whether he receives rewards or punishments along with his body.

257

Cui Deus aetherias habitandas destinat arces,
ille reviviscet iuvenis fulgentior astris.
Cui tenebrosa palus Stygii continget Averni,
630   debile et obscurum sumet corpusque senile,
sed tamen aeternis misere durabile poenis.
Felix qui poteris leges implere supernas!
Candide, perpetuo caeli fungeris honore.
Non hic fortunae miseros violentia reddit;
635   non morbo infirmi, non longa aetate senescunt.
Quattuor in partes non hic distinguitur annus.
Aeternum ver est, sed nullis nubibus aether
nigrescit, nullus caelestes irrigat imber,
nec tonitru divos horrendo fulmina terrent.
640   Quippe absunt rapidi venti frigusque calorque;
maxima temperies hic est, totumque per annum
egregios servant fructus pomaria caeli.
Semper habet flores, pomis est semper onusta
arbor, ut a nimio curventur pondere rami
645   (mirandum visu!); lectoque renascitur alter
et subito miro fructus mitescit odore.
Sed ne suspensum tanti admiratio pomi
te teneat, dubiusque animi fortasse requiras,
anne cibum divi capiant et pocula siccent,
650   accipe, nam paucis perstringam arcana deorum.
Illustrata Dei felicia corpora luce,
quae, leviora Noto, nullis sunt subdita poenis,
quidquid et ante orbem Divina Potentia fecit,
virtutes, cherubim, seraphim, mentesque supernae,
655   siderei tantum Regis splendore fruuntur.

He to whom God assigns a dwelling place in the ethereal citadel
will live again in youthfulness, brighter than the stars.
He to whom the gloomy marsh of Stygian Avernus is allotted
will assume a feeble, lusterless, and aged body,   630
yet one wretchedly durable for suffering eternal punishments.
Happy are you who will be able to satisfy the laws above!
Shining bright white, you will enjoy the perpetual honor of
　　heaven.
Not here do the ravages of fortune make people wretched;
they are not ill with disease, nor do they grow old with the   635
　　passing of time.
Here the year is not divided into four parts.
Spring is eternal, and the sky darkens with no clouds;
no rain drenches those who dwell in heaven,
nor does thunder frighten the saints with its dreadful peal.
There are no speeding winds, there is no cold, no heat;   640
there is very great mildness here, and throughout the year
Heaven's orchards keep their choice fruit.
The tree is always in flower and is ever laden with its crop,
so that its branches are bent with the immense weight
(a marvelous sight to see!); and whenever a fruit is plucked,   645
　　another is produced
and instantly ripens with a wonderful aroma.
But in case wonder at such a fruit tree keeps you in doubt,
and in your uncertainty of mind you perhaps seek to know,
whether the saints take food and drain cups, listen,
for I will briefly tell you the secrets of the gods.   650
The happy bodies illumined by God's light,
which, lighter than the south wind, have been subjected to no
　　punishments,
and all the beings that the Divine Power made before the world
— virtues, cherubim, seraphim, and the supernal minds —
delight only in the splendor of the King amid the stars.   655

Hic cibus, hoc nectar mentem cum corpore pascit;
non opus, aetherio ut fiat decoctio ventri.
Corporibus minime vires alimenta ministrant
perfectis, nullum quae sunt passura dolorem.
660 Nam cibus aerias, si quisquam forte comedit
poma, velut fumus, subito se vertit in auras.
Caelestes tantum exornat pomaria mensas.
En age, me sequere ad magni plantaria Regis.'
      Dixit, et aetherii tunc ianua panditur horti.
665 Ingredimur, divum magna comitante caterva,
qui flores passim variorum mille colorum,
aut curvis ramis redolentia poma legebant,
marmoreasque vias circum pomeria lustrant
caelicolae, ast alii dulci sermone vagantur,
670 laudantes inter se ingentia facta Tonantis,
quanta malis sit poena, viris quae gloria iustis.
Dum nexas mira frondes testudine cerno,
aurea sub viridi pendentia fornice mala,
carpebant lepores florentia prata fugaces,
675 et timidi passim, posita formidine, dammae
inter capreolos ludebant gramine denso,
et mille annorum praelongis cornibus ingens
currebat cervus, cuius si cornua cernas,
annosae ramos brumali frigore quercus
680 dixeris, ad terram cum frondes iecerit Eurus.
Denique mille meis oculis animalia numquam
visa pererrabant silvas saltusque Deorum.
Ast aberant rabidae tigres saevique leones,
non lupus insidias niveo tendebat ovili,
685 non aderant ursi turpes, non letifer anguis,

This food, this nectar feeds the mind along with the body;
an ethereal stomach has no need of digestion.
Food supplies no strength to perfect bodies
that will experience no pain.
For if anyone chances to eat the fruit, the food   660
instantly changes, like smoke, into airy breezes.
The orchards merely decorate the celestial tables.
Come, follow me to the great King's gardens."
    He spoke, and then the gate of the ethereal garden opened.
We entered, accompanied by a great throng of saints,   665
who were everywhere gathering flowers of a thousand varied hues
or plucking fragrant fruit from curving branches;
the inhabitants of heaven strolled around the perimeter on
        pathways of marble,
while some wandered in sweet discourse, praising to each other
the Thunderer's great deeds, recalling how severe   670
the punishment is for the wicked and what glory comes to
        righteous men.
As I beheld foliage entwined in a wonderful dome
and golden apples hanging beneath a green arch,
skittish hares were cropping the flowery meadows,
timid deer, freed of their dread,   675
were everywhere playing among roebuck on the thick grass,
and a huge stag a thousand years old with exceedingly long
        antlers
ran swiftly by. If you saw his antlers, you would say they were
branches of an ancient oak in the cold of winter,
when the east wind has cast the leaves to the ground.   680
Indeed, a thousand creatures that I had never set eyes on
were roaming the woods and glades of the gods.
Yet fierce tigers and savage lions were nowhere to be found,
no wolf was preparing to ambush the snowy sheepfold,
there were no ugly bears, no deadly vipers,   685

serpentesque absunt alii quos Africa gignit
tosta siti et solis magnis ardoribus usta.
Sed pulchrae mitesque ferae caelestia prata
carpebant. Subito crescebat in aequore gramen.
690 Pinguis humus suberat multique umoris abundans.
Quid referam plenos divino nectare fontes?
Purior electro per levia saxa fluebat
umor, et irrigui manabant undique rivi,
et non incisae sudabant balsama silvae,
695 stillabatque udo pretiosus cortice sudor,
qualem non habuit Iudaeae regius hortus.
Mortua si cuius tetigisset corpora liquor,
posset ab infernis animam revocare tenebris,
rursus ut aetherias vivendo carperet auras.
700 Haec dum felices caperent solatia divi,
lustrarentque hortum per amoena virecta canentes,
obvius ecce mihi insignis pietate Ioannes,
egregia Medicis Cosmi de stirpe creatus.
Qui, postquam iusto est veneratus honore parentem,
705 ad me conversus veterem compellat amicum,
apprensaque manu, nobis dedit oscula centum.
'O fautor Medicum, duroque in tempore fidus,
Verine, o vero vere cognomine dictus,
quae virtus super astra tulit, cum carcere nondum
710 corporeo exemptus fatalem impleveris horam?
Impetus ille sacer fortassis ad aethera vexit
Pieridum, quarum miro perculsus amore
ludere coepisti carmen lactentibus annis?

or other snakes that Africa spawns,
a region parched by drought and scorched by the sun's great heat.
None but beautiful and gentle wild creatures grazed the celestial
    meadows.
The grass immediately grew back on the plain.
There was fertile earth beneath, well supplied with moisture.   690
Why should I mention the springs full of divine nectar?
Water purer than amber flowed over smooth rocks,
streaming rivulets poured forth on every side,
trees exuded fragrant balm without being cut,
and from their damp bark dripped a precious gum   695
such as the royal garden of Judaea never had.
If its liquid had been applied to dead bodies,
it could have called back a soul from the infernal darkness
to breathe the ethereal air again in life.

    While the happy saints partook of these comforts   700
and traversed the garden, singing their way through its lovely
    greens,
behold, there before us was Giovanni, outstanding in piety,
born of the illustrious line of Cosimo de' Medici.
After he had paid his father the proper respects,
he turned to me and addressed me as an old friend,   705
taking me by the hand and giving me a hundred kisses, saying,
"O faithful supporter of the Medici even in a time of difficulty,
Verino, O truly called by a true surname,
what virtue has borne you beyond the stars, when you have not
    yet been freed
of your bodily prison and reached the appointed hour of your   710
    death?
Perhaps the sacred power of the Pierian goddesses has carried
    you to the heavens?
It was because you were struck by a marvelous love for them
that you began to toy with writing verse in your suckling years.

Quid faciunt urbis duo lumina clara nepotes?
715   In caelumne parant patriis virtutibus ire?'
     Dixerat haec Medices, cum lumina fixa parumper
continui, tandemque meo vox excidit ore.
'Tune ille Etruscae es quondam spes altera gentis?
Liquisti heu quanto moriens discrimine cives!
720   Sed Deus omnipotens, caelo miseratus ab alto,
reddidit incolumes cives urgente periclo.
Desine fata Dei caecasque inquirere sortes,
nam me caelicolum voluerunt visere sedes
antea quam Lachesis mihi fila novissima rumpat.
725   At gemini ad caelum, Medicum pulcherrima proles,
ire viam affectant omni virtute nepotes.
Qui quamquam teneris — vix pubescentibus — annis
nunc sint, cura tamen prudensque in corde virili
est animus doctique senis prudentia velox.
730   Urbis uterque senex habeat Florentis habenas,
expleat et genitor Saturni saecula terna,
ne navim mediis vexatam deserat undis,
quam prius attingat portum secura procellae.'
     Dum sic iremus, referentes multa vicissim,
735   siderei magnam partem lustravimus horti.
Silva erat in medio, multa densissima lauro,
et viridi frondens myrto platanoque virenti,
multaque pinus erat, plures sine nomine frondes,
quas voluisse Deum solum caelestibus hortis

What are the city's two shining lights, the grandsons, doing?
Are they preparing their way to heaven through their father's   715
    virtues?"
   Medici had finished speaking, whereupon for a little while
I held my eyes fixed, and at last my voice fell from my lips.
"Are you the one who was once the other hope of the Etruscan
    race?
When you died, alas, in what a crisis you left your citizens!
But Almighty God took pity from heaven above   720
and preserved the citizens unharmed in their pressing peril.
Inquire no further into God's will and the hidden fates;
for they have wished me to visit the abode of the dwellers in
    heaven
before Lachesis breaks my last threads.
As for those two grandsons, the fairest offspring of the Medici,   725
they are aspiring to make the skyward journey by the display of
    every virtue.
Though they are now in tender — barely adolescent — years,
yet in grown men's hearts they have circumspection, levelheaded
    good sense,
and the quick-thinking wisdom of a learned elder.
May both in old age hold the reins of the city of Florence,   730
and may their father live out three ages of Saturn;
may he not desert a troubled ship in the midst of the waves,
before it can reach harbor safe from the storm."
   Making our way thus and exchanging many remarks,
we traversed a large part of the garden amid the stars.   735
There was a wood in the middle, thick with abundant laurel
and leafy with green myrtle and verdant plane,
and there was many a pine, and more trees without name,
which we must believe God wanted only in his celestial gardens.

740 credendum est. Quae nec violenti verbera Cori
nec gelidi Boreae stridentia murmura curant
nec nimium solem aut urentia frigora frondes;
toto namque viret ramis frondentibus anno
silva, nec arescit longa vitiata senecta,

745 nec ponit frondes, tineis arrosa medullas.
Non usus hominum metuunt saevasque secures
annosae, excelsos tollunt ad sidera ramos.
Qualis Aricinae quondam sacrata Dianae
silva ingens fuerat, ramis tangentibus astra.

750 Fons sacer in medio large manantibus undis
perpetuae venae mollissima prata rigabat,
quem patulis sursum ramis contexerat ilex.
Quin etiam volucres tectae nemoralibus umbris
implebant virides mira dulcedine lucos.

755 Psittacus, humanam modulatus carmine vocem,
arbore punicea, gemmas imitantibus alis,
vincere certatim niveum tendebat olorem.
Mille modis dulces variabat gutture cantus
quae scelus Hismarii passa est crudele tyranni

760 Cecropide Philomela prius Pandione nata;
ac plures aliae variae pictaeque volucres,
in terris numquam nostroque sub aere visae,
vicissent ipsas cum Phoebo carmine Musas.
Illinc vultur edax aberat rapidaeque volucres

765 et bubo informis cornixque odiosa Minervae.
Maxima turba virum silvis errabat in istis
(sive fuere viri quondam, dum vita manebat),

Those trees pay no heed to the lashings of the violent northwest   740
    wind,
the strident moaning of the chilly north,
excessive sun, or leaf-scorching frosts;
for the wood is green all year round with leafy branches,
and it does not wither rotted with great age
or drop its leaves gnawed to the core by worms.   745
The ancient trees do not fear mankind's abuse and savage axes,
but raise their branches high toward the stars,
like the vast grove once consecrated to Diana of Aricia,
whose boughs reached to the heavens. In the heart of the wood
a sacred fountain moistened the softest meadows   750
with the wide-streaming waters of its ever-flowing course.
A holm oak had covered over the fount with a canopy of
    spreading branches.
What is more, birds concealed in the forest shadows
were filling the green thickets with wonderful sweetness.
A parrot, mimicking the human voice in song,   755
perched on a red-colored tree, with wings like gems,
was zealously striving to better the white swan.
Warbling her sweet song with her throat, in a thousand
    variations,
was Philomela, once the daughter of Cecropian Pandion,
she who endured the Ismarian king's cruel outrage;   760
and many more varied and painted birds besides,
never seen on Earth in our air, would have defeated
the very Muses, along with Phoebus, in song.
There the rapacious vulture was absent, as were birds of prey,
the ugly owl, and the crow hateful to Minerva.   765
    A great crowd of men was wandering in those woods
(or they were men once, while they still lived),

fronte quidem fusca, multosque induta colores,
dissimilis veste et variis quoque dissona linguis.
770   Non tamen ullus erat maeror, sed luce carebat
divina ac splendore dei quo cetera fulget
caelestis pubes; homines iam vivere credas.
    'Dic age, sancte pater, quae gens est incola silvae
sidereae? Cur est varios vestita colores?
775   Dissona cur multis linguis, nec frontibus ullus
splendor inest? Caecis errat tenebrosa latebris?
Pallida cur tristis maeror non inficit ora?'
    Tunc dux ore sacro, cuius Florentia quondam
cuncta sua erexit virtute per oppida nomen,
780   protulit haec: 'Omnes diversis partibus orbis
progeniti, vitiis atque omni labe carentes.
Sola fides Christi, qui est unus imagine terna
Rex (Pater ac Natus, quos iungit Spiritus Ardens),
qui semper gignit, semper procreatur ab illo,
785   nec prior hic aut ille fuit, sed semper eodem
tempore (principiis caruere et fine carebunt),
quem nec cognovit (quantum mortalia possunt
pectora nosse Deum) turba haec, nec stulta negavit—
sola fides tantum, sine qua non itur ad astra,
790   Aeterni fuscos privavit lumine Regis.
Non tamen infernas meruerunt crimina poenas.

with dusky faces, and dressed in many colors,
dissimilar in their clothing, and dissonant too in their diversity of
    tongues.
They showed no sadness, but they lacked the divine light   770
and the brightness of a god, with which the other occupants of
    heaven shine;
you would suppose them to be men still alive.
    "Come tell me, venerable father, what people are these who
    dwell in the wood
amid the stars? Why are they clad in various colors,
why do they speak in many different tongues, and why is there   775
    no brightness
in their faces? Do they go about in darkness in unseen hiding
    places?
Why does sad sorrow not mar their pallid countenances?"
    Then from his august lips my guide, by whose capable
    direction
Florence once raised her name high in every town,
gave this reply: "All were sired in diverse parts   780
of the world, free of vices and of all fault.
Only faith in Christ, who is the one King in three persons
(the Father, the Son, and the Ardent Spirit joining them
    together),
who is ever begetting and ever begotten of his sire,
nor was one before the other, but they have always existed at the   785
    same time
(they had no beginning and will have no end),
whom this group of people neither knew (as far as mortal hearts
can know God) nor foolishly denied—
only that faith, without which none can go to the stars,
deprived these dusky folk of the eternal King's light.   790
But their sins did not deserve infernal punishments.

Est locus electus sine poena inglorius illis.
Illic infantes habitant, quos funus acerbum
abstulit, et nullo macularunt crimine vitam,
795 antea quam sanctus purgatos laverit umor.
Quem tu palliolo tenui sua corpora tectum
conspicis errantem densae sub tramite silvae,
sustulit anguigenas armis ad sidera Thebas,
cum captiva diu Spartae Thebana iuventus
800 servisset. Madidae testantur funera Leuctrae:
non fuit Argorum virtute insignior alter,
qui totiens armis palantes fuderit hostes,
quique veru tantum patrimonia liquerit unum.
Aspice Pelopidam, laeva qui semper amico
805 suppeditavit opes, quo nullo Echionia proles,
hoc tamen excepto, se plus iactaverit armis.
Quem posito cernis diademate veste gregali
marmoreo in dextra cum falce sedere recessu,
cum periturus erat dux sive exercitus alter,
810 pro populo rex se vovit mortemque subivit.
Qui subter viridem platanum spatiatur ad undam
irrigui fontis, testis Marathonia laudis
terra suae est, vivitque suum per saecula nomen.
Qui cubito innixus multas sub pectore curas
815 evolvit, patria ingratae pepulistis Athenae.
Quo duce mille rates devicit Graecia victrix,
innumeros hostes, et Persica contudit arma.

There is a special place for them — without glory but without
    punishment.
That is the abode of infants whom a premature death carried off,
and who had defiled their life with no wrongdoing,
before holy water could wash them pure of sin.   795
He whom you see with his body covered by a thin cloak
wandering by the path of the dense wood
raised snake-born Thebes to the stars with his arms,
when the captive young men of Thebes had long served Sparta.
The corpses of blood-drenched Leuctra bear witness: 800
no other among the Argives was more outstanding in valor and
    virtue,
a man who routed his scattering foes in battle so many times,
and left as his patrimony only one spit.
Behold Pelopidas, who always supported his friend at his left.
In no one more than in him did the Echionian race   805
glory in arms, with the exception of that one other.
He whom you see, his crown laid aside, in common garb,
sitting in a marble recess on the right with a sickle,
when either leader or army was doomed to perish,
king as he was, pledged his own life for his people and underwent 810
    death.
As for the man who walks beneath the green plane by the water
    of the flowing fountain,
the battlefield of Marathon is witness of his praiseworthiness,
and his name lives down through the centuries.
The man who leans on his arm and turns over many cares in his
    heart
you drove from his homeland, ungrateful Athens.   815
Under his command Greece victoriously defeated a thousand
    ships
and countless foes and crushed Persian arms.

Ille, sub umbrosa qui nunc sedet anxius ulmo,
imposuit cunctis censum sine fraude Pelasgis,
820   Fabricio similis, quondam quem Graecia iustum
dixit, et aeternum meruit cognomen habere.
Cerne sub ingenti quercu cui forma leonis
oblongi paene est, qui caspide fulget acuta.
Attulit hic sanctos mores multosque triumphos
825   in tua, devictis inimicis, regna, Virago.
     'Parte alia nemoris Romanos cerne potentes,
qui totum peperere suis virtutibus orbem.
Difficile est numerare omnes, nam maxima turba est,
et plures cecidere viri sine nomine vulgi,
830   quorum nunc famam delevit prisca vetustas.
Ostendam paucos. Illum qui fronte severa
irarum tantam volvit sub pectore molem
aspice; nam doctus sapienti pectore Brutus
Romulea immites exegit ab urbe tyrannos,
835   et dulces natos pro libertate trucidat
intrepidus, nusquam deflectens lumina, consul.'
     Nec procul hinc aberat populi cognomine vero
qui monte excelsas popularis diruit arces.
Hos iuxta Serranus erat, qui plurima bella
840   confecit paucis populo victore diebus.
     'Ille aurum Gallos pendentes pondere iniquo
dispulit et patriae victricia signa reduxit.'
     Illic Cursor erat, pedibus pernicibus audax.
fortior an miles vel dux praestantior armis
845   extiterit dubitant, nec adhuc discernere posses.

He who now sits anxiously beneath the shady elm
imposed a tax without fraud on all Pelasgians,
a man like Fabricius, one whom Greece once called *The Just*,   820
and who earned that appellation as his everlasting surname.
See under the huge oak the man who looks almost like a lion
with an elongated head, whose pointed helmet flashes with light.
He brought upright morals and many triumphs
to your state, defeating your enemies, Warrior Maiden.   825
   "In another part of the wood behold the mighty Romans
who won the whole world by their valor.
It is difficult to recount them all, for they make up a very large
      crowd,
and many nameless men of common rank have fallen
whose fame the passage of time has now obliterated.   830
I will show you a few. Behold that man there who, with severe
      brow,
turns over so great a store of wrath in his heart;
for learned Brutus in his wisdom
drove out the cruel tyrants from Romulus' city
and as consul unflinchingly butchered his sweet sons in liberty's   835
      name
without turning his eyes from the sight."
   And not far away was a man truly named for the people,
who in his devotion to them demolished his towering residence
      on the hill.
Next to them was Serranus, who brought so many wars to an end
in victory for his people within a few days.   840
   "That man drove off the Gauls who weighed gold unfairly
and brought back victorious standards for his homeland."
   Over there was Cursor, bold in his swiftness of foot.
Whether he was a braver soldier or a more outstanding leader in
      arms
people are uncertain, nor could you decide even now.   845

Necnon Corvinus lucis errabat in istis,
vertice cuius erat (visu mirabile) corvus.
    'Manlius ille ferox metuenda (cerne) securi;
victorem natum populo spectante necavit,
850 namque suo iniussu contra pugnaverat hostem.
Omnes hi Fabii, silvae qui in parte suprema
delegere locum, Romanae gloria gentis,
augendo patriam vitam excoluere modestam,
sed longe virtute duo capita alta ferebant.
855 Etruscos devicit avus populosque Latinos;
ipse nepos rabiem Poenorum saepe morando
Hannibalemque ferum victriciaque arma repressit.
Aspice Fabricium incomptum Curiumque propinquum,
quos non argenti corrupit pondus et auri,
860 elixam solum contentos rodere rapam.'
    Nec procul Attilius fidei plenissimus illo
forte loco densa subter consederat umbra.
    'Tres illi egregii, crudelia vulnera passi,
servando patriam Decii cecidere sub armis.
865 Cui flammam rutilare vides et lambere crines
innocuam, amissos victor servavit Hiberos.
Hic binis castris defesso milite Poenos
reliquiis cladum nocte exspoliaverat una.
Scipiadae, exitium saevae Carthaginis ambo,
870 cincta gerunt viridi florentia tempora lauro,
turbaque per totum lucum miratur euntes.
Ille est Poenorum clades, qui, rege superbo
Gallorum caeso, in templum tulit arma Feretri.'

Corvinus too was wandering in those groves,
and on his head there was (strange to tell) a raven.
  "That man is Manlius (see him there), fierce with his terrible
      ax;
he executed his victorious son as the people looked on,
for the youth had fought an enemy without his command.   850
All the Fabii here, the glory of the Roman race,
who have chosen a place in the highest part of the wood,
ennobled a modest life by advancement of their homeland,
but two bore their heads especially high because of their prowess.
The grandfather conquered the Etruscans and the Latin peoples;   855
the grandson, by many times delaying the fury of the
      Carthaginians,
checked fierce Hannibal and his victorious arms.
Behold unkempt Fabricius and close by him Curius,
men whom no amount of silver and gold corrupted,
men content to gnaw only on boiled turnip."   860
  Not far away Atilius, a man of abundant good faith,
had chanced to sit down in that place beneath dense shade.
  "Those three illustrious Decii, after suffering cruel wounds,
fell in arms to save their country. That man
on whose head you see a flame harmlessly glow   865
and lick his hair, saved the lost Hiberians by his victory.
With tired soldiers, in two camps within a single night
he despoiled the Carthaginians of what was left from their
      defeats.
The two Scipios, both of them the destruction of savage
      Carthage,
have their flowery temples ringed with green laurel,   870
and the throng admires them as they go throughout the grove.
That man is the scourge of the Carthaginians, he who slew
the Gauls' proud king and bore his arms into the temple of
      Feretrian Jupiter."

Illic Rutilius pauper durique Catones
875 per nemus umbrosum tristi se fronte ferebant.
'Quem silva in tanta vix conspicis, optimus olim
creditus, Idaeam Matrem susceperat hospes.
Alter Brutus erat; cerne ipsum a tramite laevo
Flectentem et densi luci interiora petentem.'
880 Dum celeramus iter per amoena virecta beatum,
dum silvam saltusque vagi lustramus Olympi,
venimus ad fontem, de quo nitidissimus amnis
manabat. totum peragrando gurgite caelum.
Non ita tam liquidis Peneius irrigat undis
885 Haemoniae apricas valles et Thessala Tempe
aut Aganippeus laudatus carmine liquor,
quem Musae et Graii totiens hausere poetae.
Fons erat in medio luco, quem candida circum
lilia purpureaeque rosae croceique coloris
890 milleque praeterea flores (mirabile visu)
sponte sua, aeterne, nullis cultoribus horti,
spirando suavem cingebant undique odorem.
Forte duos illic vadentes passibus aequis
cerno, sed ora sono agnovi discordia linguae.
895 At laevam Graius, dextram Romanus habebat.
Illum Roma potens quondam est mirata loquentem,
flexerat hic doctas quocumque volebat Athenas
eloquio rapidi montani fluminis instar.

Over there impoverished Rutilius and the severe Catos
were proceeding stern faced through the shady grove.   875
 "That man whom you can scarcely see in so big a wood, once
   deemed
to be the most virtuous of men, received the Idaean Mother as
   her host.
There was a second Brutus: see him turning off from the left-
   hand path
and making for the interior of the dense thicket."
 As we hastened our journey through the lovely greens of the 880
   blessed
and traversed in our wanderings the wood and glades of heaven,
we came to a fountain from which there issued a brilliantly
   sparkling stream
that wound its course through the whole of the sky.
Not with such clear waters does Peneus' river irrigate
Haemonia's sunny valleys and Thessalian Tempe;   885
not so clear is Aganippe's stream, celebrated in song,
which the Muses and the Greek poets have so many times
   imbibed.
The fountain was in the midst of a grove,
and round it white lilies, red roses, and ones of yellow hue,
and (marvelous to tell) a thousand flowers besides   890
clustered eternally of their own accord, with no one tending the
   garden,
breathing a sweet scent on every side.
I chanced to espy two men walking there with matching strides,
but from the sound of their voices I detected that they spoke
   different languages.
On the left was a Greek, on the right a Roman.   895
At the latter's speeches mighty Rome once marveled;
the former used to sway learned Athens whichever way he wished
with eloquence like a swift-flowing mountain river.

'Aspice,' Cosmus ait, 'tres illo in vertice collis,
900   qui vario inter se referunt sermone diserti
codicibus magnis divina volumina iuris.
Atticus ille Draco, longam qui in pectore barbam
mulcet, qui torvis oculis, qui fronte severa est,
humano saevas descripsit sanguine leges.
905   Spartanis alter tribuit sua iura Lycurgus,
civibus atque usum flaventis sustulit auri,
insanas et opes, cunctorum alimenta malorum,
eripuit. Regno sic mansit paupere dives
Sparta, sine invidia, nulli virtute secunda.
910   Tertius est Solon, qui ditis munera Croesi
sprevit, et ante obitum felices esse negavit.'
    Ingens silva fuit, praedensis horrida ramis.
Vix radii solis, cum fervida terga Leonis
Phoebus adit, densam possent penetrare sub umbram,
915   si super empyrium currus volitaret Olympum
Titanis, radiosque super torqueret Apollo.
Hac multi egregii passim regione poetae
ibant ornati frondenti tempora lauro.
Longe alios virtute duo superare videntur,
920   sed Graius dextram, laevam Romanus habebat;
ambo tamen paribus concordes passibus ibant.
    'Ille senex cecinit fumantia moenia Troiae
Dulichiumque ducem longis erroribus actum.
Hunc alium tantum produxit Mantua vatem.
925   Cerne novem lyricos citharas pulsare canoras,
et veste et lingua Graios. Certare videntur

"Behold," Cosimo said, "the three men on that hilltop
who in varied discourse are eloquently discussing   900
divine books of law set out in great tomes.
Athenian Draco there, he who strokes the long beard resting on
    his chest
— the one with the fierce eyes and severe brow —
wrote his savage laws in human blood.
The second, Lycurgus, gave the Spartans their laws   905
and took away the use of yellow gold from his fellow citizens,
removing the folly of wealth, the food that feeds all woes.
Sparta thus remained rich in a poor realm,
free of jealousy, second in prowess to none.
The third man is Solon, who scorned rich Croesus' gifts   910
and declared no men fortunate till dead."
    There was a huge wood bristling with very dense branches.
The sun's rays would scarcely be able to penetrate beneath the
    thick shade
when Phoebus approaches the Lion's hot back,
even if the Titan's chariot flew atop the empyrean heaven,   915
and Apollo shot forth his rays up above.
Everywhere in this region many outstanding poets were going
    about
with their temples decorated with leafy laurel.
Two seemed far to surpass the others in excellence.
It was a Greek on the right, a Roman on the left,   920
yet both were proceeding harmoniously with matching steps.
    "That old man sang of the smoking walls of Troy
and of the Dulichian leader driven in long wanderings.
Mantua brought forth this other great poet.
Behold the nine lyric bards striking their tuneful lyres,   925
Greeks by both clothing and speech. They seem to be competing
    in song,

carminibus, sed longe alios supereminet omnes
Pindarus; ut flumen vena de divite manat.
Lesbius Alcaeus loca proxima, tertia Sappho
930   obtinet, et digno quisquis manet ordine vates.'
       Nec procul his meditans secreto in vertice collis
Flaccus erat, credasque iterum describere versus.
    'Illi autem Latio nati, quos ordine terno
ire per hanc silvam ridentes cernis opacam,
935   alterno longam pepererunt carmine famam.
Ovidius loca prima tenet; post ambo sequuntur,
ingenio ac virtute pares, cum vate Tibullo
Nauta.' Et Callimachus post istos avia solus
lustrabat, victumque elegis doluisse putares.
940   Arbor erat nemore in medio latissima ramis.
Frondibus illa suis complerat iugera centum.
Illic purpureis evinctos crura cothurnis
aspicio et longo venerandos syrmate vates.
    'Dic mihi, Cosme pater, quae turba est illa verenda?
945   Agnoscone viros? cur Graecis omnibus unus
Romanus mixtus tanto est dignatus honore?'
    Tum dux ore sacro nobis haec talia fatur:
'Illum quem Tyrio fulgentem cernis in ostro
ante omnes tragicos Graii dixere, Sophoclem.
950   Aeschylus ille senex, tanto certamine victus,
excessit patria Siculasque advertit ad oras.
Necnon Euripides, sublimi carmine vates,
praemia prima sibi non reddi pertulit aegre.
Hic noster Seneca est, doctrina et moribus unum
955   humanae specimen vitae, quem dira Neronis
cum multis aliis saeve tormenta necarunt.'

but Pindar far surpasses all the others;
he flows like a river from a rich source.
Alcaeus of Lesbos holds the second place, Sappho the third,
and then come the remaining poets in order of merit."   930
    And not far from these, meditating on a secluded hilltop, was
        Flaccus,
and you would believe him to be composing verses again.
    "Those men of Latin birth, whom you see
passing through this shady wood in laughter three abreast,
have won long-lasting fame in alternating verse.   935
Ovid holds the first place; after him follow both Nauta and the
        bard Tibullus,
evenly matched in ability and worth." Behind them
Callimachus was traversing trackless regions alone,
and you would think him in grief at having been surpassed in
        elegies.
    There was a very wide-spreading tree in the heart of the wood. 940
It filled a hundred acres with its foliage.
There I saw poets with legs clad in red buskins
and venerably dressed in long robes.
    "Tell me, father Cosimo, what estimable band is that?
Do I know the men? Why is only one Roman mixed in   945
with all the Greeks and thought worthy of so great an honor?"
    Then my guide made me this reply from his august lips:
"Him whom you see shining in Tyrian purple, Sophocles,
the Greeks pronounced above all other tragedians.
That old man, Aeschylus, defeated in this great rivalry,   950
left his homeland and repaired to Sicilian shores.
What is more, Euripides, a poet of sublime verse,
took it badly that first prizes were not given to him.
This is our Seneca, in erudition and character
a very model of human life, whom Nero's harsh torments   955
cruelly killed along with many others."

Pone duo errabant diversa in parte poetae
obscuri nemoris, quorum, si rite recordor,
unus cantarat tumido civilia versu
960   bella per Haemoniam et totum dispersa per orbem,
alter grandiloquo Romae et Carthaginis arma
carmine descripsit Latii Libyaeque ruinam.
      'Illi autem, viridi quos stare sub ilice cernis,
tam torvis oculis vates, tam fronte minaci,
965   corruptos vitiis secuerunt carmine cives.
Lucilius primus vitiorum acerrimus hostis,
Persius hos inter libro est mirabilis uno;
his coniunctus erat praeclarus alumnus Aquini.
Nullus in hoc numero est vates de gente Pelasga.'
970   Sed procul astabant nullo discrimine mixti
cum Grais Itali; quorum mihi nomina Cosmus
designans digitis, 'Comicos, en aspice,' dixit,
'hic doctus Varro, multa ille Terentius arte est,
saevus Aristophanes facieque minante Cratinus.
975   Hic lepidus Plautus. Facundum cerne Menandrum.
Ille senex gravis est petulantis fama Tarenti.
Eupolis iste minax, ventosique Accius oris.'
      Multi praeterea fuerant, quos dicere longum est.
Dux sacer admonuit tempus non esse terendum.
980   'Acceleremus iter, non hac in parte moremur.
Dum tibi fata deum concedunt visere caelum,
omnia percurras oculis ac mente reponas.'
      Lucus erat densus myrto lauroque virenti.
Texerat in morem camerae spinosus acanthus,
985   atque hederae errantes iucundam desuper umbram

Behind these men two poets were wandering in a different part
of the dark wood, of whom, if my memory serves me right,
one sang in bombastic verse of civil wars
scattered over Haemonia and throughout the whole world,   960
while the other described in grandiloquent song
the arms of Rome and Carthage and ruin of Latium and Libya.
    "Those bards over there whom you see standing under a green
        holm oak,
with such piercing eyes, such menacing brows,
censured vice-corrupted fellow citizens in their verse.   965
Lucilius was the first mordant enemy of vices;
Persius is remarkable among these satirists because of a single
        book.
To them was joined the famous nursling of Aquinum.
There is no poet of the Pelasgian race within this number."
    But some distance away Italians were standing mixed together   970
with Greeks. Cosimo pointed them out to me with his fingers
as he named them, saying, "Behold the comic poets.
This is learned Varro, over there is the highly skilled Terence,
and there too are savage Aristophanes and Cratinus with his
        threatening look.
Here is witty Plautus. Behold eloquent Menander.   975
That stern old man is insolent Tarentum's glory.
This is menacing Eupolis, and that is windy-mouthed Accius."
    There were many others besides, whom it would take a long
        time to name.
My august guide warned that we should not waste time.
    "Let us hurry on, not tarry in this area.   980
While the fates of the gods allow you to see heaven,
look over everything and store it all in your mind."
    There was a grove dense with myrtle and green laurel.
A spiny acanthus had covered it over in the manner of an arch,
and wandering ivies provided pleasant shade   985

praebebant. Dulces pendebant vitibus uvae,
non quales avibus praedam labrusca racemos
ferre solet silvis densis aut saepibus altis.
Fons lucentis aquae recta de rupe fluebat.
990   Undique cingebant nativo marmore sedes
divinos latices, pluresque sedilia circum
praestantes animae magnam fecere coronam,
palmiferae fuerat quos inter gloria Memphis,
quem stupet Aegyptus, verus qui paene propheta
995   exstitit arcani, Mosis iucundus amicus.
     'Quem laeva cernis citharam pulsare canorum
et dulcem suavi modulari carmine vocem
hunc Rhodopes saevae laniarunt rupe parentes,
mystica belligeris qui Thracibus orgia primus
1000   attulit, ut castae celebrent trieterica matres.
Ille Sinus Calabros, Samiis licet ortus in agris,
incoluit, quondam quae Graecia Magna vocata est.
Hic nostram posuit variis animalibus umbram
purgari donec sine sordibus aetheris alti,
1005   venerat unde prius, caelestia regna revisat.
Hic Dion Archytasque una, Platonis amici,
disserere inter se dulci sermone videntur.
Ille Syracusis, hic est Archyta Tarenti.
Qui fronte est hilari, lateri qui iunctus adhaeret
1010   Pythagorae Samii dextra laevaque Biantis,
Pythius hunc vere sapientem dixit Apollo.
Pro scelus infandum! Gelidae exstinxere cicutae.
Ast illum, qui te dudum miratur euntem,

from above. Sweet grapes hung on vines,
not such clusters as the wild vine is accustomed to bear
as plunder for birds in dense woods or on high hedges.
A fountain of clear water flowed from a sheer-faced crag.
On all sides seats of native marble surrounded   990
the divine waters, and many highly distinguished souls
formed a great circle around the seats.
In this crowd was the glory of palm-bearing Memphis,
he who was the marvel of Egypt and almost a true prophet
of hidden mysteries, the agreeable friend of Moses.   995
    "The man you see on the left striking a tuneful lyre
and modulating a sweet song with his dulcet voice,
savage mothers tore apart on Rhodope's crag.
It was he who first brought mystic rites to the warring Thracians,
causing chaste matrons to celebrate the triennial festival of   1000
    Bacchus.
That man over there, though born in Samian lands, lived on the
    Calabrian Gulf,
which at one time was called Greater Greece.
He maintained that our soul is purged in the bodies of various
    animals
until, without polluting the high heaven,
it can return to the celestial realm whence it originally came.   1005
Dion here, and Archytas with him, friends of Plato,
can be seen holding sweet discourse with each other.
Dion is from Syracuse; Archytas, from Tarentum.
The man with the jovial face walking alongside
Samian Pythagoras on his right and Bias on his left,   1010
is he whom Pythian Apollo declared truly wise.
Ah unutterable crime! Chilling hemlock ended his life.
But speak to the man over there who has been gazing at you in
    wonder

et sua qui nusquam radiantia lumina flectit,
1015   quique umeris latis longe supereminet omnes,
alloquere. Est Plato, similem cui nulla tulerunt
saecula, cui rerum sensum natura reclusit,
ut quod mortali licitum est cognoscere norit.'
His animus miro dictis ardebat amore
1020   compellare virum et dextram coniungere dextrae,
sed pudor et tanti tenuit reverentia vatis.
At prior ille inquit, 'Nate o melioribus annis,
cum verbum Christique fides totum occupat orbem!
Christicolis nunc lux ablatis clara tenebris
1025   fulget, et aeterni portam reseravit Olympi.
Felices animae, quibus haec in tempora nasci
contigit, et meritam vitam nunc ferre per auras!
Quid non tentavit mea mens, dum vita manebat,
inquirens totum diversis partibus orbem,
1030   quid Druides Galli, Samii quid littera vatis,
ambiguique Tagis caecum quid proferat omen,
quid dixere Magi, nudus quid protulit Indus,
dum contemplatur nigranti pectore caelum,
quidquid et invenit Phoenicis gloria gentis,
1035   qui numero ex isto contra sedet (aspice), Thales.
Quid Chaldaeorum doctrina recondita, quidquid
repperit Aegyptus, multis vix legimus annis.

as you go along, the one who never averts his radiant eyes from
    you,
and who towers far above all the others with his broad shoulders.   1015
He is Plato (no other age has produced his like),
to whom the universe has revealed its meaning,
granting him knowledge of what it has been permitted a mortal
    to know."
   At these words my mind was burning with a marvelous
    longing
to approach the man and take his right hand in mine,   1020
but modesty and reverence for so great a seer held me back.
He in fact spoke first: "O man born in better years,
when the word and faith of Christ have taken hold throughout
    the world!
Now that darkness has been dispelled, the light shines clear for
    Christ's worshippers,
and he has unbarred the door of eternal heaven.   1025
Happy are the souls fortunate enough to be born into these times
and now to receive the life they have earned in the sky above!
What did my mind not explore, while I still lived,
as I studied the whole world in all its diverse parts,
seeking to learn what the Gallic Druids, the writings of the   1030
    Samian seer,
and the mysterious forebodings of riddling Tages might reveal,
what the Magi said, and what beliefs the naked Indian put
    forward
as in his dark heart he contemplated the sky,
and what discoveries Thales made, the glory of the Phoenician
    race,
who sits among this number opposite (behold him there).   1035
All the discoveries made by the arcane erudition of the
    Chaldaeans
and by Egypt I was scarcely able to read through in many years.

Dum tenebris densis, dum caeco errore vagarer,
paene mihi summi est Regis lux clara reperta,
1040 namque prophetarum divina volumina legi,
quid dixit Moses, lyrici quid carmina regis,
quid cecinit vates, crudi quem serra tyranni
divisit medium, quidquid Babylonius infans
dixerit, et sanctae quid cantavere Sibyllae.
1045 Sed quis ab aetherio Verbum descendere caelo
crederet in terram, humanos ut vestiat artus,
aequo animo ut ferret quidquid mortalis egestas
producit, frigus, somnos, ignemque famemque?
Accipiens formam servi, de divite regno
1050 descendens pauper, Dominus rerumque Creator
obtulit innumeris sese cruciatibus ultro
ut scelus humanum superi clementia Regis
ablueret vitamque homini pro morte pararet.
Nonnulla in nostris memini posuisse libellis.
1055 Ne mirere: sacris sitiens e fontibus hausi.
Illud non etiam postrema in parte repono,
quod multos Latio nostris incumbere chartis
accepi nomenque meum volitare per ora.
Praecipue colit ante omnes pulcherrima longe,
1060 quam mediam liquidis undis interfluit Arnus,
stirps quondam Romana, tui Florentia mater.
Tu, si quando mei studiosos cernis alumnos,
nostra legant moneas minime contraria sacris
scripta voluminibus. Fidei condita sapore
1065 aspergant. Siqua inveniant contraria, tollant,
sed nihil esse reor. Dubia ad meliora reducant,

While I roamed in dense darkness and blind wandering,
I almost discovered the light of the King most high,
for I read the divine books of the prophets,   1040
what Moses and the songs of the lyrical king said,
what the seer proclaimed whom the cruel tyrant's saw cut in two,
what the Babylonian child told,
and all that the holy Sibyls declared in their utterances.
But who would believe that the Word would descend   1045
from the ethereal heaven to Earth to clothe human limbs
and to bear with equanimity all that mortal need
imposes — cold, sleep, fire, and hunger?
Taking the form of a slave and coming down from his rich
        kingdom
as a beggar, the Lord and Creator of things   1050
even offered himself up to countless tortures,
so that the mercy of the King on high might wash away human
        sin
and secure life for mankind in place of death.
I recall that I put some things in my books.
Do not marvel: in thirst I drank from the sacred fountains.   1055
I also count it not the least honor that (I have heard)
many in Latium pore over my writings,
and that my name flies on men's lips.
I am especially respected in the fairest city of all by far,
through the heart of which the Arno glides with flowing waters, 1060
once Roman stock, your mother Florence.
For your part, if ever you observe pupils with an interest in me,
advise them to read my writings, which are not at all in conflict
        with the Holy Scriptures.
Let them season and sprinkle them with a flavoring of faith.
If they do find things in conflict, let them remove them,   1065
but I think there is nothing. Let them improve upon what is
        dubious,

officioque boni lector fungatur amici;
namque etiam posset divinas carpere leges
perfidus interpres. Quantis vexata procellis
1070   vera fides olim, quam paene sub aequore mersa est!
Sed stetit inviolata tamen, stabitque per aevum.'
    Tunc Medices Cosmus monuit non esse morandum.
'Fata instant, Plato. Superis discedere regnis,
terrestres habitare domos, vitamque sub astris
1075   hunc agitare Deus iubet, et se reddere terrae.
Ne dubites, quodcumque mones sub mente repostum est.'
    Dixit, et in verbo vestigia torsimus illo,
divorumque iterum celeres lustravimus hortum.
Ventum erat ad portam gemmis (mirabile visu)
1080   ornatam (totidem stellas vidisse putares),
quae nobis patefacta fuit venientibus ultro,
rursus et aetherii perlustro palatia Regis
caelestesque domos magnorumque atria divum,
atque iterum Cosmus summi ad penetrale Tonantis
1085   duxit, ubi omnipotens solio Deus aetheris alti
considet aurato, meritis ubi praemia reddit.
Inde gradu celeri retro discedimus unde
venimus et portas tandem superavimus omnes.
Sic quondam fertur magnus Labyrinthus in Ida,
1090   aut, Aegypte, tuus, portas habuisse patentes.
Mille viis thalamis connexa triclinia miris,

and let the reader perform the office of a good friend;
for the treacherous interpreter could carp even at the laws of
    God.
With what great storms the true faith was once beset!
How near it came to being submerged beneath the sea! 1070
But for all that it stood inviolable and will do so for all time."
    Then Cosimo de' Medici warned that there should be no
    delay.
"The fates urge us on, Plato. God commands this man
to depart from the kingdom above, inhabit a terrestrial home,
lead life beneath the stars, and return to Earth. 1075
Have no doubt, all your advice is stored in his mind."
    He spoke, and upon that word we retraced our tracks
and quickly made our way back again through the garden of the
    saints.
We came to a gate that (wonderful to see) was decorated with
    jewels
(you would have thought you were looking at as many stars), 1080
which opened for us at our approach on its own accord,
and again I traversed the palace of the ethereal King
and the celestial homes and halls of the great saints,
and again Cosimo guided me to the sanctum of the Thunderer
    most high,
where high heaven's Almighty God sits on his golden throne 1085
and confers rewards upon the deserving.
From there with swift step we made our way back
along the route by which we had come, and at length we passed
through all the doors. The great Labyrinth on Ida,
or yours, Egypt, is said to have once had such an array of open 1090
    doors.
Through a thousand dining rooms linked to bedrooms by
    wondrous ways,

mille per ambages, quonam vestigia tendas
incertum, pateat cum nusquam egressus in illis,
implicitus fallit connexi tramitis error;
1095   sed duce tam docto sedes peragravimus omnes,
nec via decepit divisa in compita mille.
Vestibulum ante ipsum primaeque in limina portae
duxit, ubi immensum se sustulit aurea turris.
Dein quo quaeque modo devitem immania monstra
1100   Lactentemque Viam, quo sit descensus Olympi
ad terram facilis, ne praeceps volvar ad ima,
edocet atque 'Vale' mihi verba novissima dixit.
Tunc ego, vel rapidis ventis celerique sagitta
vel Iovis irati demisso fulmine dextra
1105   ocior, ad terram labi sum visus ab alto.

through a thousand winding turns (it is uncertain where to steer
    your steps,
since no exit lies open in those chambers)
the intricate meandering of the tangled path misleads you.
But with so skilled a guide we passed through all the dwelling   1095
    places,
and we did not lose our way, though it was divided into a
    thousand forks.
He brought me before the vestibule itself and to the threshold of
    the first gate,
where the golden tower rose massively up.
Then he explained how I might avoid all the terrible monsters
and the Milky Way, and make my descent from heaven to Earth   1100
easy, lest I should tumble headlong all the way down,
and in his final words to me he said *Farewell.*
Then, more swiftly than the rushing winds, a speeding arrow,
or a thunderbolt launched in anger from Jupiter's right hand,
I dreamed that I glided from up on high down to Earth.   1105

APPENDIX I

Summary of Paradise

References are to lines of the Latin text.

1–14. While worrying at midnight about the dangers threatening his homeland, Verino falls asleep and dreams of being transported to heaven.

15–46. In terror he passes monstrous forms (representing various constellations) in his ascent.

47–67. Verino alights in the sky and looks down on the earth, so very small in appearance.

68–75. He hears a choir, the heavens revolve, and the sun appears.

76–88. Verino invokes the Muses and the Holy Spirit as he prepares to describe God's palace, the halls of the saints (the holy dead), and the eternal life that they enjoy.

89–93. A golden chain hanging down from the sky to the earth is observed.

94–122. The towering exterior of God's magnificent palace is described, and Verino marvels at the workmanship visible in the entrance portico/ vestibule.

123–34. Verino sees a doorway leading to the chambers of the saints and to God's sanctum, with a sword-bearing angel on watch as doorkeeper. An inscription forbids entry by a mortal or by anyone who has not deserved a saint's honored status through good conduct in life.

135–53. The poet asks the doorkeeper for admission to God's palace and waits while the doorkeeper ascertains that God permits it.

154–70. The double door is opened for Verino, who is overwhelmed by the sweet fragrance and the bright light.

171–79. Verino tells the reader that he cannot describe God's face and throne, as their brilliance prevented his mortal eyes from looking.

180–90. The poet hears the voice of Cosimo de' Medici, who offers to be his guide.

191–203. Verino duly follows Cosimo, observing that his appearance has changed since death, though his voice is unaltered. Like all the saints in heaven, Cosimo wears white and looks around thirty.

204–23. Verino asks his guide why such great dangers threaten Florence, paying tribute in passing to Piero and Lorenzo de' Medici, Cosimo's son and grandson.

224–75. Cosimo describes the perilous situation facing Florence but declares that God is with the Florentines, predicting victory for them and their allies, in spite of Venetian support for the opponents of the Medici.

276–323. Cosimo recalls what he said just before his death in 1464, when he urged men to justice and warned them to fear God's judgment on them. He reflects how God has saved his son Piero from murder (in 1466) and preserved Florence from the anti-Medici faction.

324–50. As angels (neither corporeal beings nor insubstantial shades, but figures, as in dreams 336–41) serve banquets to the saints, and a prince-archangel guards God's throne, Cosimo shows Verino choirs of cherubim and seraphim, describing to him the hierarchy of angels (342–50).

351–64. The poet sees a seven-headed monster guarding an inscribed book fastened with seven seals (the book of the living promised heaven), which none but God may open.

365–79. A lion, ox, human-faced angel, and eagle (the Beasts of the Apocalypse) terrify Verino. He sees four saints (the evangelists) standing next to these beasts.

380–525. The singing of the angelic choir in the halls of the saints is described. The song recounts God's creation of the world (384–90), of the planets (the Moon, Venus, Mercury, the Sun, Mars, Jupiter, and Saturn, 391–421), and of the angels (428–29). It tells also of the expulsion of Satan's followers from heaven (430–33), of the creation of Adam (435–39) and Eve (441), of their fall (443–45), of man's ascendancy over beasts, plants, and minerals (448–53), of the good and bad guardian angels of each person (454–67), of the long impediment to man of original sin (468–77), of the incarnation of God as Christ (478–81), of the hardships of his time on earth, culminating in his crucifixion (482–98), and of his harrying of hell (499–503). Verino compares the strains to those of Orpheus (506–17). The angels sing of the Twelve Apostles and of the spread of Christianity (518–22). Verino says he may not disclose everything (523–25).

526–605. Cosimo tells Verino about the saints, pointing out for what virtues some of them won a place in heaven (at 568–77 he describes martyrs). Cosimo explains (601–5) that the most worthy shine with the brightest light and are nearer to God than others, but there is no jealousy on that account.

606–31. Cosimo reveals why all the saints look thirty years old, and speaks of how, by God's judgment, the virtuous departed will receive a youthful, shining body in heaven, while the wicked will assume a feeble, lusterless (dull), and aged body for eternal punishment in hell (620–33).

632–46. Cosimo describes the blissful existence of those in heaven, where they enjoy perpetual spring, ever-clement weather, and the constant availability of ripe fruit on trees.

647–62. Addressing the question whether the saints and angelic beings truly eat and drink, Cosimo reveals that they do not.

663–99. Cosimo leads Verino through a gate into God's gardens. The pleasant scene is described. There are no predatory animals (673–87), and trees exude balm uncut (694–99).

700–733. Giovanni de' Medici (Cosimo's deceased younger son) is encountered in the garden. He greets Verino warmly and receives a good report from the poet of how Cosimo's grandsons (Lorenzo and Giuliano) are faring.

734–65. A never-fading wood (with a fountain within it) in the middle of the garden is reached. The song of birds is heard, but there are no ugly birds or birds of prey (753–65).

766–95. Verino asks about a crowd of people in the wood whose faces are not shining, but dark, variously dressed in many colors and speaking diverse languages. Cosimo informs him that they are non-Christians who lived virtuously. He also tells Verino that unbaptized infants are allocated the same place (793–95).

796–879. Cosimo points out within the wood many named pre-Christian figures (mostly great soldiers or statesmen) from Greece (796–825) and Rome (826–79).

880–911. Cosimo and Verino come to a fountain within the wooded area in the gardens, near which the lawgivers Draco, Lycurgus, and Solon are seen (899–911).

912–78. Various Greek and Roman poets are noticed in densely wooded surroundings.

979–1018. Cosimo urges moving on to see more. A shady grove with a fountain is described, where certain figures from philosophy and mysticism are encountered, including Socrates (1009–12) and culminating (1013–18) in Plato.

1019–71. Speaking first, Plato tells Verino of his quest for understanding, involving the study of the thoughts of many non-Greeks, including (1041–44) Moses, David, Isaiah, and Daniel. Plato speaks of Christ's coming to Earth (1045–53) and of how Christians have had a better opportunity than he, living before Christ, to know the full truth. Plato speaks of the study of his works at Florence (1056–71), directing Verino to ensure that it be done in accordance with Christianity.

1072–76. Cosimo warns Plato that Verino must now return to Earth.

1077–105. Verino and Cosimo retrace their steps through the labyrinthine complexities of the way, returning to the threshold of God's palace. They say goodbye, and Verino descends to Earth.

APPENDIX II

Scribal Marginalia

The following notes (other than textual corrections) are found in the margins of the manuscripts stated (for which see Note on the Texts) with reference to the lines indicated, though not always precisely alongside those lines. They mostly just pick out names from the text but sometimes clarify allusions. Unusually spelled names have here been adjusted to the familiar Latin form; occasionally, the irregular spelling is recorded in addition, when thought especially noteworthy. Abbreviations are usually given here in expanded form. In *Fiammetta*, many poems have no marginal notes, and I have found two notes imperfectly legible. In *Paradise*, a few notes in B have had to be recorded as too difficult to make out fully.

Book I

1.1 B Cosmus (8)   1.2 B Sophocles (5), Maro (6), Sappho (8), Alcaeus (11), Prometheus (22), Apelles (23), Cato (42)   1.4 B Phoebus (5), Hippocrene (*Ippocrine*, 44), Sibylla (47), Cornelia (51), Chrysippus (52), Sappho (53), Medea (64), Circe (*Circes*, 67), Admetus rex ("King Admetus," 72), Venus (87), Daphne (99)   1.5 L Propertius, Tibullus, Landinus (3–4)   B Cynthia (3), Nemesis (3), Xandra (4)   1.9 B Pirithous (*Perythous*, 34), Hercules (36)   1.11 B generositas Medicum ("the nobility of the Medici," 42), Orpheus (49), Linus (50)   1.12 B Venus (22 and 34)   1.14 B Maleae scopuli ("the rocks of Malea," 8), Charybdis (*Caribdis*, 11), Scylla (12)   1.15 B Parthus ("Parthian," 2), Hercules (6), Chimaera (8)   1.16 BL Iuno, Pallas, Venus (1–2)   1.17 B Alecto (9)   1.18 B Medea (11), Circe (11)   1.20 L Maecenas (27), Landinus (29)   B Maecenas (27), Landinus (29), Phoebus (41)

1.22 *B* Adonis (23)   1.23 *B* Luna ("Moon," 10), Niobe (29), Pentheus (32), Daphne (33)   1.25 *L* Medea (17), Circe (*Circes*, 21), Ulixes (26), Hercules (29)   *B* Medea (17), Iason (19), Circe (21), Ulixes (26), Hercules (29), Phoebus (33)   1.26 *L* fatum ("fate," 17)   *B* Erato (*Herato*, 13), quid sit fatum ("what fate is," 17), Erinys (*Herinis*, 47)

Book II

2.1 *B* Callimachus (17), Sappho (18), Gallus (19), Tibullus (20), Propertius (21), Ovidius (22), Vergilius (25), Horatius (27), Petrarca (29)
2.2 *L* pompa ("procession," 15)   2.5 *L* Scala (20)   2.10 *B* Attis Phrygius (*Athis Frigius*, "Phrygian Attis," 2)   2.22 *B* Python (*Phiton*, 21), Phoebus (22), Daphne (34)   2.23 *B* Horatius (1), Alcaeus (3), Sappho (3), Pindarus (5), Homerus (5), Vergilius (5)   2.28 *B* Cato (2)   2.32 *B* Zeno Citieus (*Cythieus*, "Zeno of Citium," 3), Cato (3), Curius (5), Fabricius (5)   2.33 *B* . . . (*unclear*)   2.37 *B* Ganymedes (*Ganimedes*, 7)   2.38 *B* Hesperides (2), Martius anguis ("Mars' snake," 3)   2.40 *L* Pollux (12), Themistocles (14), Pirithous (*Perithous*, 15)   *B* Pylades (11), Pollux & Castor (12), Scipio (13), Laelius (13), Theseus (15)   2.41 *L* Sforza Franciscus (7), Galeactius (= Galeazzo, 7)   *B* Caesar (6), Galeactius (7)   2.42 *B* Plato (55), Aristoteles (56), Cicero (56)   2.43 *L* Lucretia (29), Eriphyle (*Heriphile*, 38)   *B* Helena (3), Apollo (8), Iuno (14), Gratiae ("Graces," 24), Iuppiter (26), Alcmaeon (38), Eriphyle (*Eriphilis*, 38), Calliopea (48)
2.45 *L* Alexander (17), Solon (21), Tyrtaeus (*Tyrrheus*, 25), Alcaeus (27), Vergilius (31), Dantes (77), Saturnus (86), orbis terrae ("the world," 90), metaphysice (-ica?, 93), moralis (95), Zeuxis (*Zeusis*, 101), Phidias (103), Apelles (103), Cosmus (133), Petrus (134), Maecenas (135)   *B* Nicias (13), physica (85), astrologica (85), antipodes (91), Christus (92), metaphysica (93), moralis (95), politica (95), d . . . ica? (*perhaps, but not legibly,* domestica, 95), ethica (95), logica (97), Zeuxis (*Zeusis*) pictor ("Zeuxis the painter," 101), Phidias sculptor (103), Aurea Saecla ("Golden Age," 110), Maecenas (135)   2.46 *L* Aristides (13), Africanus M. (= Maior, 15–16), Camillus (19), Themistocles (23)   *B* Aristides (13), Africanus (15–16), Hannibal (17), Camillus (19), Themistocles (23)   2.48 *B*

Flam(m)etta (11)   2.49 B Helena (23)   2.50 L epitaphium ("epi-
taph," 55)   B Apollo (11), Epicureus ("Epicurean," 21–22), Flam(m)
etta (37), distichon ("distich," 55–56)   2.51 L Lycurgus (45), Themis-
tocles (46), Camillus (47), Fabricius (49), Curius (50), Marcellus (52),
Fabius (53–54), Africanus (55–56), Catones (57), Scauri (58), Pompeius
(*Pompeus*, 59), Caesar (61), Apollo (73), Augustus (78), Maecenas
(83)   A Lycurgus (45), Themistocles (46), Camillus (47), Appius
(52), Q. Fabius (54), Pompeius Magnus (59–60)   2.54 B Cosmus
(15)

PARADISE

16 Cancer *AB*   17 Leo *AB*   21 Anguis ("Snake") *AB*   24 Tau-
rus *AB*   27 Aquila ("Eagle") *AB*   28 Ganymedes (*Ganimedes*)
Aquarius *AB*   29 Scorpio *AB*   33 Corvus ("Raven") *AB*
34 Sagittarius *AB*   36 Olor ("Swan") *A*   Cygnus ("Swan") *B*
38 Aries *AB*   Hydrus (*Idrus*) *AB*   Dracones *AB*   40 Orion *AB*
46 Olympus (*Hol-*) *B*   51 Maurus ("Moor") *AB*   Indus ("In-
dian") *AB*   52 Thyle (*Thile*) *AB*   Hyperborei montes ("Hyper-
borean Mountains") *A*   montes Riphaei ("Riphaean mountains") *B*
54 brevitas terrae ("small size of Earth") *A*   57 Florentia *AB*
59 testudo templi Divae Reparatae ("dome of the church of Santa
Reparata") *A*   testudo aedis Reparatae ("dome of the church of
Reparata") *B*   61 Roma *AB*   71 concentus sphaerarum (*sperarum*,
"harmony of the spheres") *B*   72 Phoebus *B*   76 Pierides *B*
77 Parnassus *B*   81 Spiritus Sanctus ("Holy Spirit") *AB*   84 re-
gia Dei ("God's palace") *B*   89 catena aurea ("golden chain") *A*
aurea catena sex gradibus ("golden chain in six steps") *B*   94 regia
Dei ("God's palace") *A*   aula Iovis ("Jupiter's palace") *B*   99 ves-
tibulum palatii ("vestibule of the palace") *B*

103 pyropus *B*   105 smaragdi *B*   106 amet(h)ysti *B*   hyacanthi
(*iacinthi*) *B*   107 adamas *B*   111–14 altitudo turris ("height of
tower") *A*   116 emblemata *B*   125 conclavia divum ("chambers of
the saints") *AB*   130–31 epigramma portae ("inscription on the

door") *AB*   132–34 cherubim ianitor ("cherubim porter") *A*   cherubim *B*   145 ianitor *B*   157–58 comp(aratio) ("comparison") *B*   162 Panchaia (*Pancheia*) *A*   (*Panchia*) *B*   163 India *AB*   165–70 facies divorum ("faces of the saints") *AB*   171–79 facies Dei ("face of God") *AB*   172 Iuppiter *B*   194 Pallas *B*   195 facies Cosmi ("face of Cosimo") *B*   198 stola candida ("white robe") *AB*

207 Cosmus Medices *AB*   216 Petrus Medices *AB*   220 Laurentius Medices *AB*   222 Florentia *AB*   224 Cosmus *A*   225 Bartholomeus Colleo (Culleo *A*) *AB*   226 Flaminia *AB*   Astorgius Faventinus *A*   Astorgius *B*   227 Veneti *B*   230 Lamonae valles ("valley of Lamona") *B*   233 Veneti *AB*   235 laus Florentiae ("praise of Florence") *A*   Florentini ("Florentines") *B*   241 Mars Florentiae ("warfare of Florence") *B*   245 Sullanus *B*   246 Rex Ferrandus ("King Ferrando/Ferrante") *A*   Ferrandus rex *B*   248 A. . .phonsus (*unclear, presumably* Alphonsus) *B*   250 Galeactius dux Mediolani ("Galeazzo, duke of Milan") *A*   *same with* Mediolanensis *B*   254 Philippus *A*   Philippus Savoiae dux ("Filippo, duke/leader of Savoy") *B*   255 Mantua *A*   Ludovicus Gonzaga *B*   257 Robertus *AB*   258 Dux Federicus ("Duke Federigo") *A*   Federicus Urbinates ("Federigo of Urbino") *B*   260 Sertorius *B*   264–69 navale bellum ("naval war") *AB*   266 Ossa, Taurus [*Thaurus*], montes ("Ossa, Taurus, mountains") *AB*   267 Alpes *AB*   277–81 circa mortem Cosmi ("around the death of Cosimo") *AB*   288 Cicero *B*

300–309 iudicium universale ("the Universal Judgment") *A*   in die ultimi iudicii ("on the day of the Last Judgment") *B*   305–6 mali in Tartara ("the wicked to hell") *B*   307–9 boni in caelum ("the good to heaven") *B*   325 cherubim seraphim *AB*   327–29 prima loca ("first places") *A*   330 archangeli *AB*   342–44 Seraphim, Cherubim, t(h)roni primi ("Seraphim, Cherubim, thrones first") *B*   345–46 potestates, virtutes, dominationes secundi (*sdi*) ("powers, virtues, dominations second") *B*   secunda ("second places") *A*   347 Angelus, tertia ("angel, third place") *A*   348 Deus ("God") *B*   348–

50 tres chori angelici ("three angelic choruses") *B*   350 ordo divinus ("divine order/hierarchy") *B*   351–56 monstrum septiceps ("seven-headed monster") *AB*   359–64 libri inscriptio ("inscription on the book" *A*   *similarly*, epigramma libri *B*   367–73 leo, bos, angelus, aquila ("lion, ox, angel, eagle") *AB*   368 G(a)etulia *A*   369 Achelous *AB*   374–76 Marcus, Lucas, Matheus, Ioannes ("Mark, Luke, Matthew, John") *A*   Iohannes, Matheus, Lucas, Marcus *B*   384–85 creatio caeli et terrae ("creation of heaven and earth") *A*   ordo planetarum ("order of the planets") *B*   390 Phoebus (i.e., the sun) *B*   391 Luna ("Moon") *AB*   393–95 Venus *AB*   396–401 Mercurius *AB*

402–3 Apollo *A*   Sol ("Sun") *B*   410–13 Mars *AB*   414–15 Iuppiter *A*   416–21 Saturnus *AB*   426 Seraphim *B*   428–29 creatio angelorum ("creation of the angels") *AB*   430–33 demonum expulsio ("expulsion of the demons") *A*   deiecti daemones mali ("evil demons cast down") *B*   435 creatio primi hominis ("creation of first man") *A*   Adam *B*   436–38 cur ex humo ("why from earth") *A*   439–40 homo Deo similis factus ("man made like to God") *B*   441 Eva *AB*   442 inspiratio vitae ("breathing in of life") *B*   443–44 propter peccatum mors venit ("death came because of sin") *A*   446–47 quae creat(a) sub luna concidunt ("[all] things created under the moon perish") *B*   448–51 omnia propter hominem ("all things [created] on account of man"), homo propter Deum creat(us) est ("man was created on account of God") *A*   omnia subiacent homini ("all things are subordinate to man") *B*   454 bini custodes unicuique homini bonus et malus ("two guardians for each person, a good and a bad") *A*   unicuique bonus et malus angelus adest ("everyone has a good and bad angel") *B*   463 liberum a(rbi)trium ("free will") *AB*   469–70 immensus amor Dei erga homines ("God's very great love toward men") *A*   472–77 ante adventum Christi nullus adibat caelum ("before the coming of Christ no one used to go to heaven") *B*   478–80 descensio et carnatio Dei ("descent and incarnation of God") *AB*   480 assumptio . . . ("assumption . . . [of human

form?]") B   481 Augustus B   485 Jerusalem (*Hyer-*) AB   486–
91 . . . . . . formam viri accipiens (". . . . . taking a man's form") B
492–95 passio Domini ("passion of the Lord") A   498 Iudaei
("Jews") B   499–502 descensio Dei ad infernos ("descent of God to
those in the world below") A   descensio Christi ad inferos prophetas
et . . . ("descent of Christ to prophets and . . . [patriarchs?] below") B

506 Orpheus AB   511 Cerberus A   515 Eurydice (*Eurydi-
ces*) A   (*Euridices*) B   518–19 Christi apostoli ("Christ's apos-
tles") A   apostoli B   520 evangelia ("gospels") B   521 cessatio
oraculorum ("ending of oracles") AB   527 Cosmus AB   530–
32 sanctorum gaudia ("joys of the saints") B   531–32 causa splen-
doris deorum ("reason for the brightness of the gods") A   537–
38 castus ("the chaste man") A   matrimonia . . .ia ("[faithful?]
marriages") B   539–41 constans ("the constant man") A   pauper
patiens ("the patient poor man") B   542–43 virgo ("the virgin," =
celibate man) B   544–46 liberalis ("the generous man") A   pius
et liberalis ("the pious and generous man") B   547–48 vitae contem-
plativae ("[man] of the life of contemplation") B   550 pius ("the pi-
ous man") AB   551–53 continens ("the abstemious man") B   554–
56 religiosus ("the religious man") B   557–59 iustus ("the just
man") B   560–63 praedicator ("preacher") B   564–67 hic beat(us)
. . . . . . propter timorem . . . Deo . . .? (*long but faded and mostly illegible
note, seemingly*, "this blessed one . . . [abstained from sins?] out of fear
. . . God . . .") B   568–77 martyres ("martyrs") A   martyres
patr. . . (*unclear*) B   580 pius et iustus ("the pious and just man") B
584–85 iustitia ("justice") A   quid sit iustitia ("what justice is") B
587 qui ob patriam pe. . . (*unclear, seemingly*, "who . . . [expend their
wealth?] for their homeland") B   594–97 servatores patriae . . .? (*un-
clear; seemingly*, "saviors of their homeland . . .") B

600 ut sol lunam sic Dei facies beatos illustrat ("as the sun does the
moon, so the face of God lights up the blessed" B   605 nulla invidia
in beatis est . . . (*perhaps abbreviated* quod quisque?) sua sorte
content(us) ("there is no jealousy among the blessed . . . [because each?]

content with his lot") B   606–16 cur omnes divi sint iuvenes ("why
all the saints are young") A   beati et iuvenes . . . ("the blessed and
young . . .") B   615 . . . (*seemingly an abbreviated* non) A   622–
31 corpora resurgent in Die Iudicii ("bodies will rise again on Day of
Judgment") A   resurrectio corporum cum animabus ("resurrection of
bodies with souls") B   626–28 corpora resurrectura in aeternum cum
animabus ut poenas seu praemia perpetuo capiant ("bodies to rise again
for ever with souls so as to be able eternally to receive punishments or
rewards") B   627–31 beati resurgent iuvenes, damnati senes ("the
blessed will rise again as young; the damned, as old") B   649 an
beati cibum capiant ("whether the blessed ones take food") A   utrum
dii comedant ("whether the gods eat") B   651–52 corporis beati qual-
itates ("qualities of the blessed body") B   654 mentes supernae ("su-
pernal minds") B   662–63 (h)ortus caelestis ("celestial garden") B
668–69 de ambulation(ne) divorum ("on the walking of the saints") B
673–88 animalia B   694 balsamum ("balsam") AB   696 Iu-
daea A   regius (h)ortus Iudaeus ("royal garden of Judaea") B

702 Ioannes Medices ("Giovanni de' Medici") AB   708 Verinus B
714 Laurentius/Giulianus Medices B   724–30 laus Laurentii et
Iuliani ("praise of Lorenzo & Giuliano") A   laus nepotum ("praise
of the grandsons") B   736 silva ingens caeli ("heaven's huge
wood") A   silva ingens B   740 Corus i(d) q(uod) Gr(aece) etesias
(*last word unclear*) ("Corus, that is, in Greek, *etesias* [= the trade
wind]") B   741 Boreas B   748 Diana Aricina B   750 fons
("fountain") B   755 psittacus ("parrot") AB (*psytacus*)   757 olor
("swan") AB   760 Philomena A   Philomela B   764 vultur
("vulture") AB   765 bubo ("owl") AB   cornix ("crow") AB
766–77 Cur incolae silvae sint varii homines ("Why the dwellers in the
wood are various people") B   774–75 habitatores silvae dissimiles
veste et ling(ua) ("dwellers in the wood unalike in clothing and lan-
guage") A   778 Florentia AB   782–83 Trinitas Dei ("Trinity of
God") A   Trinitas, Pater, Natus, Spiritus ("Trinity, Father, Son,
Spirit") B   785 Pater et Filius semper una ("Father and Son ever

together") B   789 necessaria fides ("necessary faith") B   792 locus
institutus ("place laid down") B   793 locus infantum ("place of in-
fants") B   795 lavacra ("baths") B   796–803 Epaminondas B
798 Thebae ("Thebes") AB   799 Sparta(e) B

800 Leuctra (*Leucturae*) A   (*Leuctrae*) B   801 Epaminondas A
803 Epaminondas moriens solum unum veru reliquit ("Epaminondas at
death left only one spit") B   804 Pelopida(s) A   Pelopidas The-
banus B   807–10 Codrus rex Athenien(sis) ("Codrus, Athenian
king") A   *similarly with* Atheniensium B   811–13 Miltiades AB
812 Marat(h)onia ("[land] of Marathon") A   814–17 Themisto-
cles AB   818–21 Aristides Iustus ("Aristides the Just") AB   822–
25 Pericles qui caput oblongum habuit in forma leonis ("Pericles, who
had an oblong head resembling a lion's") A   Pericles, cui caput ob-
longum fuit ("Pericles, who had an elongated head" B   826 Ro-
mani AB   831–36 Brutus A   Junius Brutus B   834 Tarquinii
("Tarquins") A   837–38 Publicola A   Publicola Valerius B
839–40 Serranus AB (*Seranus*)   841–42 Camillus AB   843–
45 Papirius Cursor AB   846–47 Valerius Corvinus AB   848–
50 Mallius A   Mallius Torquatus B   851–57 Fabii AB
854 Rullianus Fab. B   855 Q. Fab. Maximus B   857 Hanni-
bal AB   858–60 Fabricius AB   Curius AB   861–62 Attilius
Regulus A   M. Attilius B   863–64 P. Decii Mures A   tres De-
cii ("three Decii") B   864–67 L. Martius (= Lucius Marcius) AB
869–71 Scipiones Africani AB   872–73 M. Marcellus A   M.
Claudius Marcellus B   874 Catones AB   874–75 Rutilius AB
876–77 P. Scipio AB   878–79 Brutus AB   882 fons ("foun-
tain") A   fons magnus ("big fountain") B   884 Penneus amnis
("River Peneus") A   Penneus B   885 T(h)empe B
886 Fons Aganippe ("fountain of Aganippe") AB   896 M. Tul-
lius A   M. Tullius Cicero B   897–98 Demosthenes AB

902 Draco legifer ("Draco the lawgiver") A   Draco Atheniensis
("Draco the Athenian") B   905 Lycurgus A   leges Lycurgi ("laws
of Lycurgus") B   909 Sparta A   910 Solon AB   Croesus rex
Lydiae ("Croesus king of Lydia") AB   917 statio poetarum ("station

of poets") *A*   regio poetarum *B*   922–23 Homerus *AB*
924 Vergilius *AB*   925 novem poetae lyrici ("nine lyric po-
ets") *A*   poetae lyrici novem Graeci ("nine Greek lyric poets") *B*
928 Pindarus *AB*   929 Alc(a)eus *AB*   Sap(p)ho *AB*
932 Horatius *AB*   935 elegi ("elegies") *AB*   936 Ovidius *AB*
937 Tibullus *AB*   938 Propertius *AB*   Callimachus Graecus
("Callimachus the Greek") *AB*   942–43 tragici Graeci ("Greek trage-
dians") *A*   tragici poetae ("tragic poets") *B*   949 Sophocles *AB*
950 Aeschylus (*Eschilus*) *AB*   952 Euripides *AB*   954 Seneca
Latinus *A*   Seneca *B*   955 Nero *B*   959–60 Lucanus *AB*
961–62 Silius (*Silus A, Psilus B*) Italicus *AB*   963–65 satiri Latini
("Latin satirists") *A*   satiri *B*   966 Lucilius *AB*   967 Per-
sius *AB*   968 Iuvenalis *AB*   969–70 nulli vates satirici Graeci
("no Greek satirical poets" *B*   971 Cosmus *B*   972–77 comici
Graeci et Latini ("Greek and Latin comedians") *A*   comici *B*
973 Varro Terentius *AB*   974 Aristophanes *AB*   Cratinus *AB*
975 Plautus *AB*   Menander *AB*   976 Pacuvius *AB*
977 Eupolis *AB*   Acteus (= Actius) *A*   Accius *B*   989 fons
("fountain") *AB*   991–92 theologi prisci ("theologians of old") *AB*
993–95 Mercurius Trismegistus *AB*   995 Moyses ("Moses") *A*
Moises B   996–1000 Orpheus *AB*   999 orgia ("orgies") *AB*

1001–5 Pythagoras *AB*   1006 Dion Siracusanus ("Dion of Syra-
cuse") *AB*   1008 Architas Tarenti ("Archytas of Tarentum") *AB*
1010 Pythagoras *A*   Bias *AB*   1011 Socrates sapiens ("Socrates
wise") *A*   Socrates *B*   Apollo *B*   1013–18 Plato *A*   divus
Plato ("the divine Plato") *B*   1016–18 laus Platonis ("praise of
Plato") *A*   laudes Platonis ("praises of Plato") *B*   1023 Christ *A*
1024 Christiani *B*   1030 Druides ("Druids") *AB*   Pythagoras *B*
1031 Tages *AB*   1032 Magus *AB*   Indus ("Indian") *A*   Gym-
nosophistae *B*   1035 Thales *A*   Thales Milesius ("Thales of Mile-
tus") *B*   1036 Chaldaei (*Caldei*) *B*   1040 prophetae ("proph-
ets") *AB*   1041 Moses *AB*   David rex lyricus ("David the lyrical
king") *A*   David *B*   1042–43 Isaias *AB*   1043 Daniel *A*
1044 Sibyllae (*Sibyllae/Syb-*) *AB*   1045 Verbum ("Word") *B*

1050–53 immensus amor Dei erga genus humanum ("God's immense love toward humankind") *B*   1059–61 Florentia Platonica ("Platonic Florence") *AB*   1060 Arnus (= River Arno) *AB*   1072–75 Cosmus ad Platonem ("Cosimo to Plato") *A*   1089 Labyrinthus *A* 1089–90 comparatio ("comparison") *A*

APPENDIX III

Variant Titles in Fiammetta

B and *L* share titles in poems 1.4, 1.15, 1.19, 1.28–30, 2.3, 2.6, 2.9, 2.11, 2.15, 2.17, 2.27, 2.32, 2.35–37, 2.40. There is no title in *B* for 1.7–9 (text lost), and none in *L* for 1.25 and 2.12. Variant titles are found as follows (I mostly give *B*'s titles in the text, and I read *Flammetta* for *Flametta* throughout):

BOOK I

1.1. Ugolini Verini Flammetta Liber Primus ad Laurentium Medicem [ad Laurentium Medicem Liber Primus *L*] incipit *BL*: *Ugolino Verino's 'Fiammetta' Book One to Lorenzo de' Medici begins*

1.2. Ad lectorem, *To the reader L*

1.3. *I read* festinet *for* festinat *in B*: Ad librum in lucem prodire festinantem, *To his book, in haste to venture out into the light L*

1.5. De Xandra et Flammetta, *On Sandra and Fiammetta L*

1.6. Ad Flammettam de ardore suo, *To Fiammetta on his passion L*

1.10. Ad Petrum Vectorium de duritie Flammettae, *To Piero Vettori on Fiammetta's hard-heartedness L*

1.11. Visio de Geminis, *A vision concerning the Two L*

1.12. Ad Cherubinum, *To Cherubino L*

1.13. Conqueritur quod nimis sit nota Flammetta, *He complains that Fiammetta is too well-known L*

1.14. De exclusione sibi [= sibi de exclusione] ab amica, *To himself, on being shut out by his girlfriend L*

1.16. Tetrastichon sub tabula Flammettae, *A four-line poem beneath a picture of Fiammetta L*

1.17. In Gallam, anum deformem, *Against Galla, an ugly old woman* L

1.18. *I read* tribuat *for* tribuant *in B*: Ad Flammettam nimis duram ne tantum formae tribuat, *To the too hard-hearted Fiammetta, not to set such store by beauty* L

1.20. De liberalitate Petri Medicis in omnes doctos, *On the generosity of Piero de' Medici to all learned men* L

1.21. Ad Flammettam, *To Fiammetta* L

1.22. Ad Cupidinem nimis saevientem, *To Cupid, who is being too cruel* L

1.23. Conqueritur de adversa fortuna in amore, *He complains of adverse fortune in love* L

1.24. Alloquitur se ipsum, *He addresses himself* L

1.26. De somno et infelicibus signis sui amoris, *On sleep and inauspicious signs for his love* L

1.27. Ad Flammettam, quae Bruno nupsit, *To Fiammetta, who has married Bruno* L

BOOK II

2.1. Ugolini Verini Flammetta Liber Secundus ad Laurentium Medicem incipit, *Ugolino Verino's 'Fiammetta' Book Two to Lorenzo de' Medici begins* L & B

2.2. Ad Cupidinem, *To Cupid* L: *titles misascribed in 1940 apparatus criticus*

2.4. De nuptiis Benedicti et Lisae, *On the wedding of Benedetto and Lisa* L

2.5. De Albera puella, quae sub porticu attrita est, *On the girl Albiera, who was crushed beneath a portico* L

2.7. Ad Clio, ut Petrum Caponium Romae conveniat, *To Clio, that she visit Piero Capponi in Rome* L

2.8. De Apollonio pictore, *On the painter Apollonio* L

2.10. Ad Amerigum Corsinum de fugiendo puerorum amore, *To Amerigo Corsini on shunning the love of boys* L

2.12. *I expand the abbreviation* Flo *in B to* Florentinum

2.13. Ad Martellum, *To Martelli* L

2.14. Ad Iustum Florentinum, *To the Florentine Justus* L

2.16. Ad Philippum, *To Filippo* L

2.18. Ad Montanum, *To Montano* L

2.19. Ad formosum, *To a beautiful boy* L

2.20. Ad quemdam ambitiosum, *To an ambitious man* L

2.21. *I expand* Flo *in B to* Florentini: Epitaphium egregii civis Petri Benini, *Epitaph of the eminent citizen Piero del Benino* L

2.22. In Cupidinem, *Against Cupid* L

2.23. De Cherubino, *On Cherubino* L

2.24. *I read* Platinensem *for* Pratin- *in B:* Ad Bartholomaeum Platinensem L

2.25. De saevitia muscipulae, *On the cruelty of a rat-trap* L: *both MSS have* musi- *(corr. Mencaraglia)*

2.26. Ad Naldum de invido, *To Naldo on a jealous man* L

2.28. In Franciscum, *On Francesco* L

2.29. Ad Locterium de maledico, *To Lottieri on a slanderer* L

2.30. Cur palleat aurum, *with same meaning* L

2.31. Ad Nerium, *To Neri* L

2.33. Quid sit optimum factum, *The best course of action* L

2.34. Ad Ciprianum, *To Cipriano* L

2.38. De Francisco paedicone, *On the bugger Francesco* L

2.39. De Lurco, *On Lurco* L

2.41. Ad Clio Mediolanum petentem, *To Clio, making for Milan* L

2.42. Ad Federigum adolescentem, ne Amoris illecebris capiatur, *To the youth Federico, not to be trapped by the allurements of love* L

2.43. Ad Lucretiam Donatam, ut amet Laurentium Medicem, *with same meaning* L

2.44. De Corvino, *On Corvinus* L

2.45. Ad Andream Alamannum, de laudibus poetarum et de felicitate sui saeculi, *with same meaning* L

2.46. Contra Invidiam et susurrones, *Against Jealousy and whisperers* L

2.47. Epitaphium optimi civis et peritissimi iurisconsulti Donati Cochii, *Epitaph of the most excellent and skilful jurisconsult Donato Cocchi* L

2.48. Visio qua Clio se obiurgat ne lucri causa Musas relinquat, *A vision in which Clio seeks to dissuade him from abandoning the Muses for gain* L

2.49. Ad Nicolaum Beninum et ad Ginevram, eius amicam, *with same meaning* L

2.50. Eulogium in funere Lisae, formosae puellae, *Eulogy on the death of Lisa, a beautiful girl* L

2.51. Eulogium in funere clarissimi viri Cosmi Medicis, 'Patris Patriae' a Senatu Populoque Florentino dicti, *Eulogy on the death of the most distinguished gentleman Cosimo de' Medici, called "Father of his Country" by the Senate and the People of Florence* L: In funere Cosmi eulogium (Verini),*(Verino's) Eulogy on the death of Cosimo* A

2.52. Epitaphium Cosmi Medicis, Patris Patriae, *Epitaph of Cosimo de' Medici, Father of his Country* L: Epitaphium Cosmi Medicis, *Epitaph of Cosimo de' Medici* A

2.53. Aliud epitaphium pro eodem, *Another epitaph for the same* L: Aliud in eundem, *Another on the same* A

2.54. De portentis infelicis anni urbi Florentinae, *On the portents of an unlucky year for the city of Florence* L

2.55. Ad Venerem et Cupidinem, ut tandem ab eo recedant et finem elegis imponant, *To Venus and Cupid, that they at last leave him and put an end to his elegies* L

Note on the Texts

༄༅༂༃

The manuscripts consulted are designated as follows:

A   Ashburnham 1703 (1626) at the Biblioteca Medicea-
          Laurenziana in Florence (only poems 2.51, 2.52, and 2.53)
B   MS. Add. 16426 at the British Library in London
L   Plut. 39.42 at the Biblioteca Medicea-Laurenziana in Florence

I have not taken account of a fourth manuscript (called M in Mencara-
glia's 1940 edition, p. 14), Florence, Biblioteca Nazionale Centrale Magl.
VII, 601, as its text of Verino's *Fiammetta* was copied entirely from L itself
some two centuries later by Antonio Magliabechi (1633–1714, librarian to
Cosimo III from 1673). To save space, many discrepancies of spelling;
trivial slips of copying corrected in the manuscripts themselves; and read-
ings readily perceived as mere errors, not serious variants, and clearly in-
ferior to another manuscript's, are not recorded. Where a text different
from that of all the manuscripts is adopted, that is indicated. Abbrevia-
tions in the manuscripts are generally given here in expanded form.
Variations of title can be found recorded in Appendix III. Reference to
readings suggested by reviewers of Mencaraglia's edition (Dionisotti,
Perosa, and Munari, for whom, and also for *Carmina*, i.e., *Carmina illus-
trium poetarum Italorum*, see Bibliography) is generally made with the re-
viewer's name in parentheses after the reading advocated in the review.
Editorial rewriting of lines in *Carmina* (usually done in order to remove
metrical anomalies) is ignored. I have not made reference to my Cheadle
Hulme 1998 edition, as any different readings there are superseded by
those adopted in this present volume.

    On errors in Mencaraglia's edition (some particularly obvious and
plainly unintentional misprints and oversights are not here noted), I
make the following observations. Mencaraglia misreports manuscript
readings in 1.6.4 (*latet* L, not *manet*), 1.26.1 (*somnia nocte* L, not *nocte som-*

nia), 1.26.2 (*hen* LB, not *heu*), 1.26.3 (*ater* L, not *alter*), 2.5.15 (*stamina* LB, not *flamina*), 2.27.3 (*desint* L, not *desunt*), 2.27.12 (*solum* L, not *solam*; Perosa's comments are further confused), 2.43.44 (*pulcher et* LB, not *pulcher est et*), 2.45.88 (*Mercurii* LB, not *Mercuriique*; in both these last cases, Perosa repeats the error for L), 2.46.47 (*carpentia* L, not *capentia*), 2.51.93 (*verior* L, not *verius*), 2.51.110 (*struxerit* BA, not *condidit*), 2.54.13 (probably *danna* B, not *danno*). Mencaraglia tacitly misrepresents the manuscripts by printing a different text without comment in 1.4.14 (*mei* LB, not *mihi*), 1.4.29 (*tua semper* LB, not *semper tua*), 1.8.7 (*deplorat* L, not *deploravit*; thus, misled, Munari wrongly conjectures *ploravit*), 1.10.24 (*invidiosa* LB, not *insidiosa*), 1.11.53 (*cantabimur* LB, not *cantabitur*), 1.14.14 (*adesus* LB, not *adhaesus*), 2.6.2 and 2.7.6 (*numve* LB, not *numne*, though that may be better), 2.16.1 (*tentans* L, not *tentas*), 2.22.38 (*vexat* L and, after correction, B, not *versat*), 2.27.7 (*fastus* LB, not *fastos*), 2.38.7 (*nusquam* L and, after correction, B, not *nunquam*). In 1.18.3, 1.21.7, 1.29.17, 2.18.7, and 2.55.24 Munari is misled into seeing B's readings as "author variants," having mistakenly assumed that Mencaraglia's readings *aeternus, laborum, iura, dignius,* and *sint* in the said lines (all seemingly slips) are L's (in fact L and B agree). In 2.46.24 Mencaraglia accidentally omits *edax* (present *LB*), misleading Dionisotti into a wrong conjecture. In 2.12.17 the readings of L and B are mistakenly interchanged in Mencaraglia's apparatus. There too 2.36.12 (wrongly 2.26.12 in Perosa's comment) is confused with 2.36.10, and readings noted under 1.14.13 belong in part to 1.13.17. Most of these errors are noticed by one or other of the reviewers. They are not genuine manuscript variants or deliberate editorial changes. A few cases where Mencaraglia has silently but justifiably departed from the manuscripts are included below.

Book I

1.13. castigatas L (*gast-* B): castigatus *Wilson*

1.25. Petrus LB (*and Perosa*): Petri (*unnecessarily*) *Mencaraglia*

2.12. iste L: ille B

4.26. tepidus L *and in text of* B (rapidus *in margin, approved by Munari*)

4.97. lac(h)rimabile *L*: miserabile *B*

4.105. hoc Graii hoc *L*: hoc Grai atque *B*

6.12. *B lacks 1.6.12 to 1.9.22 inclusive (not as Mencaraglia states p. 15, as Munari notes)*

6.18. fuit *L*: fui *Wilson*

8.16. imperii *L*: imperium *Mencaraglia (and Perosa)*

8.17. orent *L*: orant *Mencaraglia (rightly, but silently)*

8.32. S (*not* si *as Mencaraglia's apparatus*) *L*: sic *Mencaraglia*: (*alternatively*) sit *Wilson*

9.3. cantemus *L*: cantamus *Mencaraglia (rightly, but silently)*

10.25. proterva *L*: protervam *B*: protervi *Wilson*

11.17–20. *present L*: added in margin *B (Munari corrects Mencaraglia's references)*

11.44. superavit *L*: superabit *B (and Munari)*

12.1. ardentem *L*: audentem *B*

13.4. veh *LB*: vah *Wilson (cf., for example, Landino, Xandra 2.20.35)*

13.5. coepi *L*: cepi *B (reviewers are silent)*

13.17. vellem *L*: mallem *B*

14.14. limes *LB*: imus *Mariotti, (misguidedly) approved by Munari*

14.18. tum *LB*: tu *Munari*

15.11. trisulci *LB (and Perosa)*: trisulco *Carmina*

15.13. pugnas *L*: pugnam *B*

15.15. bilustro *LB*: bilustri *Carmina (and Perosa)*

18.5. et *L*: aut *B*

18.10. reseras *LB*: reseres *Munari*

18.24. iuncta *L*: iuncta *or* vincta (*unclear*) *B*: tori *LB*: Cori (*with false quantity*) *Wilson*

18.29. non *LB*: nos *Mariotti, (misguidedly) approved by Munari*

19.2. legas L (*and Perosa*): leges B (*cf. Landino, Xandra 2.2.2*)

20.8. mergebant LB: vergebant *Mariotti (reported by Munari)*: mergebat *Wilson*

20.12. ut LB: et *Carmina (and Munari)*

20.18. Sullanides (Sy-) LB: Sullanidas *Wilson*

20.24. chorum L *and corrected in margin from* pedes *in text* B

20.35. umbras L: undas (*after alteration of first letter*) B

21.10. unde L: inde B

21.12. invidus L: lividus B

23.1. simili semper L: semper simili B (*and Munari*)

23.34. in lauro LB: in laurum *Munari*

26.2. hen LB (*and Perosa*): hem *Wilson*

26.9. auriga LB: Aurora *Munari*

26.36. retecta mihi (*without* est) L: retenta mihi est B

27.3. sanctum L: sancti (*altered from* sanctum) B (*and Munari*)

27.5. impia L: improba B (*and Munari*)

27.17. formula testis adest (adest *inserted*) L: formula sit testis B

27.30. verba rata L: rata verba B (*and Munari*)

27.34. tanta LB: quanta *Munari* (*comparing 2.22.40*), *perhaps rightly*

28.17. me Scythicis releget potius Florentia terris L: B *substitutes in margin at* iubear potius Scyticas (*last* s *possibly canceled*) discedere ad artho (*stroke over* o; *read by Mencaraglia as* Scytica . . . ad artha): *perhaps* Scythica (*with lengthening at caesura*) . . . arva *or* Scythicas . . . arctos?

29.16. vir tu L: tu vir B (*and Munari*)

29.28. curas cum L: curam cum B

30.8. ah L: *omitted* B

30.25. differt L *and after correction* B (*defended by Munari*): differs (*needlessly*) *Dionisotti*

30.34. fastum B (*and Munari*): factum L: perfidiamque L: stultitiamque B

Book II

1.16. num *LB*: nunc *Mancini, followed by Mencaraglia (and Perosa)*

2.6. dura *L*: saeva *B*

2.35. me qui *L*: qui me *B (and Munari)*

5.1.]am *B*: tam *L*: quam *Wilson*

5.13. occidit *LB*: concidit *Wilson*

6.2. numve *LB (and Perosa)*: numne *Mencaraglia*

7.5. an *L*: aut *B*

7.6. numve *LB (and Perosa)*: numne *Mencaraglia*

9.3. medius *L*: medium *B*

10.2. fixit *L*: flexit *B*

12.17. circunstant *L*: circum instant *B*

14.2. Fluentini *(corrected from Florentini)* nunc decus omne *L*: Fluentini maxima fama *B*

16.1. scis: me *L* (scis? me *Mencaraglia*): scimus *B*: tentans *L*: tentas *B*

19.8. non mens *L*: mens non *B (and Munari)*

20.3. assurgat *L*: assurgit *B*

22.9. iam tunc *L*: iam tum *B*: nondum *(misguidedly) Munari*

22.13. haec *LB*: hanc *Wilson*

22.51. uror ut inmitum quam fervens Ethna Cyclopum *LB*: *changed in margin B to* uror ut accensis fervet Liparea caminis

22.53–54. *omitted L: added in margin B*

22.60. iuvet *LB*: iuvat *Wilson*

22.63. purpurei pensum *L*: purpurei pensi *B*

25.1. rapidae *LB (and Perosa)*: rabidae *Mencaraglia*

27.11. non vis *L and in text B (uncanceled, but* nolis *in margin)*

27.12. solum *L*: solam *B*

28.7. insanus *LB*: infamis *Wilson*

36.3–6. *single line* quod nostros damnes sanctos sine crimine mores *B in text; in margin 3–6 as* L

36.10. minime *(abbreviated, replacing erased word)* L: nulli *B*

37.1. frustrum *LB (and Perosa)*: frustum *Mencaraglia*

43.7. et crine soluto *L and altered from* sit candida virgo *(cf. 2.42.13)* B

43.45. quin *L*: quid *changed to* en *in margin* B

45.33. prosintne (–ve *B*) iuventque *LB*: prosintne iuventne *Wilson (reviewers are silent)*

45.41. tacitae *LB*: tacite *Carmina*: vetustas *L*: senectus *B*

45.110. aurea saecla *L and in margin* B (saecula prisca *uncanceled in text*)

45.111. fuit aequi aut recti *L (possibly corrected to read as* B*)*: fuit recti aut aequi *B (and Munari)*

45.115. tales propter *L*: propter tales *B (and Munari)*

45.127. creatum *L*: *seemingly* creatum est *(abbreviated)* B

45.128. habebis *L*: habetis *B*

45.129. tot *LB*: quot *Wilson*

45.137. es *omitted* L: *present* B

46.36. est *(corrected from* et*)* sibi *L*: et sibi . . . est *(inserted)* pallor *B*

48.33–34. *couplet present* L: *omitted* B

49.1. irrisor *L*: illusor *B*

50.15. fuere *L*: fuerunt *B*

50.27. nil *L*: non *B*

50.27–28. *couplet present in* L: *omitted in text* B *but added in margin*

50.41. desit *LB*: defit *Wilson*: narrare *L*: narrate *B*

51.1. sic *LBA*: si *Carmina*

51.10. colitis *LB*: incolitis *A*

51.18. sonos *LB*: modos *in text* A (sonos *noted in margin*)

51.19. est *before* terris *LB*: *after* ademptum *A*

51.22. quanto *A*: quantum *LB*

51.33. quanta Etruscis *LB*: quantum Tuscis *A*

51.42. cuncta *LB*: longa *A* (*cf. Ovid, Met. 15.446 and Ex Ponto 3.3.81*)

51.44. erat *LB*: erit *A*

51.45. tristem *LB*: sanctum *A*

51.47–48. *text ineptly revised or lines lost; does not construe (Dionisotti, p. 177)*

51.50. ille *LB*: ipse *A*

51.51. Feretro *LBA*: Feretrio *Carmina*

51.56. fama secunda *L*: maxima fama *BA*

51.64. qui talem poterunt *LB*: quis talem potuit *A*

51.76. niveis . . . comis *LB*: capite . . . suo *A* (*scansion: 1.21.12n*)

51.80. ornavit *LA*: affecit *B*

51.81. sciptorem amplectitur omnem *LB*: scriptores diligit omnes *A*

51.92. munera plura *LB*: munera tanta *A*

51.93. verior *LA*: verius *B*

51.158. datur *LB*: venit *A*

51.164. degeneretis *LB*: degeneretur (*abbreviated*) *A*

51.177. credite . . . data *LB*: stant quoque . . . sua *A*

52.4. consilio iustitiaque *LB*: iustitia consilioque *A*

53.5–6. *couplet present LB*: omitted *A*

55.4. vellite *L*: tollite *B*

PARADISE

The manuscripts Plut. 26.21 and Plut. 39.40 at the Biblioteca Medicea Laurenziana in Florence are here denoted by *A* and *B*, respectively. Both are of the fifteenth century. At the end of *B* a note identifies its copyist as P(ietro) Crinito (Verino's pupil, born in Florence 1474/75, died 1507) and gives the date of its copying as June 1489. In compiling the following list, I have applied the same general principles as to what to include or exclude and in dealing with abbreviations as stated for *Fiammetta*. Misprints and oversights in Bartolini's 1679 text are mostly ignored, and where he gratuitously departs from the manuscripts, and in particular rewrites lines to correct metrical errors or remove wording otherwise seen as objectionable in Verino's text, I have generally not recorded his substituted wording. I have not made reference to my 1998 edition for the same reason as stated for *Fiammetta*.

44. comprehenderit *AB*: comprehenderet *Wilson*

56. regni *A*: regni est *B*

100. late longe *AB*: late et longe *Wilson*

147. restet adhuc multum nendum *A*: restet adhuc nendum multum *B*: nendum et adhuc restet multum *Bartolini*: restet adhuc multum et nendum *Wilson*

151. repseris *A*: repperis *B* (*and Bartolini, though apparently meaningless*)

157. ut *AB*: ac *Bartolini* (*thereafter rewriting the line*)

161. flagrabat *A*: fragrabat *B*

187. ac ipsos *AB*: atque ipsos *Wilson*

199. tanta *A*: magna *B*

213. ac aere *AB*: atque aere *Bartolini*

221. q (*abbreviation*) *AB*: qui *Bartolini* (*perhaps rightly*): *alternatively* quam *Wilson*

228. sceleratas *A*: sceleratus *B*: sceleratus at *Bartolini*

230. vallisque Lamonae praedam *A*: praedam vallisque Lamonae *B*

234. credit *AB*: credat *Bartolini*

241. cedit *A*: cedet *B*

271. Tuscis *A*: Tuscos *B*

300. veh *A*: *unclear in B, possibly* vhe: vae *Bartolini*: damnat *A*: damnet *B*

304. sub *A*: ad *B*

307. fiet *A*: fiat *B*

332. cohors *A*: choros *B* (*cf.* cohors *in 479 and 568*)

349. haec *AB*: hi *Wilson*

368. Gaetula *AB*: Gaetulia *Wilson*

374. visum *AB*: visu *Bartolini*

378. aut *A*: ac *B*

459. alius *A*: alter *B*

482. dedignatus *A*: dedignavit *B*

506. ut *AB*: ac *Bartolini*

508. cursum *AB*: cursu *Bartolini*

516. *present A: omitted B, but added in margin*

521. sculptorum *A*: stultorum *B*

607. curvusque *AB*: curvusve *Bartolini*

626. pariter capiat *A*: capiat pariter *B*

652. noto *A*: notis *B*

657. *precedes 658 and 659 AB: follows them Bartolini*

683. rapidae *A*: rabidae *B*

718. Etruriae *AB*: Etruscae *Bartolini*

739–42. *omitted A (as both 738 and 741 end* frondes*): present in B*

740. murmura *B*: verbera *Bartolini*

751. rigabant *AB*: rigabat *Bartolini*

760. Philomena *A*: Philomela *B*

769. dissimiles vestes *AB*: dissimilis veste et *Bartolini*

781. ac omni *AB*: atque omni *Wilson*

833, 834. *so A: in reverse order B, possibly corrected by marks in margin*

848. Mallius *A*: Manlius *B*

906. ac usum *AB*: atque usum *Wilson*

981. Deum *A*: Dei *B*

1006. alterque *A*: Architaque *B*: Archytasque *Bartolini (rewriting line)*

1008. *present A: omitted B (and Bartolini)*

1009. laterique *A and probably B*: lateri qui *Bartolini*

1010. Samii dextra *A*: dextra Samii *B*

1018. novit *AB*: norit *Wilson*

1023. occupet *AB*: occupat *Bandini (see Bibliography)*

1063. minime contraria *A*: non abhorrentia *B (cf. 602n)*

1091. connexa *A*: innexa *B*

1093. incertus *AB*: incertum *Wilson*

1105. visus *A*: iubsus *(for iussus) B*

Notes to the Translations

꽃⁙⁙꽃

ABBREVIATIONS

Bottiglioni
Gino Bottiglioni, *La lirica latina in Firenze nella seconda metà del secolo XV* (Pisa, 1913).

Carmina
Carmina illustrium poetarum italorum, ed. [G. G. Bottari], 11 vols. (Florence, 1719–26).

DBI
Dizionario biografico degli italiani (Rome, 1960–).

Gildersleeve and Lodge
B. L. Gildersleeve and G. Lodge, *Latin Grammar*, 3rd ed. (London, 1960).

Gualdo Rosa
Poeti latini del Quattrocento, ed. F. Arnaldi, L. Gualdo Rosa, and L. Monti Sabia (Milan, 1964).

Kristeller
Paul Oskar Kristeller, *Iter Italicum*, 7 vols. (London-Leiden, 1963–97).

Lazzari
Alfonso Lazzari, *Ugolino e Michele Verino: Studi biografici e critici* (Turin, 1897).

Perosa-Sparrow
Renaissance Latin Verse: An Anthology, ed. A. Perosa and J. Sparrow (London, 1979).

References are to lines of the Latin text. *F.* = *Fiammetta*, *P.* = *Paradise*.

FIAMMETTA: BOOK I

1.1

Addressee: Lorenzo de' Medici (*il Magnifico*, 1449–92), son of Piero (*il Gottoso*, 1416–69) and grandson of Cosimo (*il Vecchio*, 1389–1464) in 8 and 25. On *L's* (otherwise blank) preceding page are (mysteriously) the names of Piero Vettori (1.10n), Lionardo/Leonardo Benini/Benino (1.15n), Lottieri Neroni (1.28n), and Pier Capponi (2.7n).

323

1. "Lydian" lion because the Etruscans supposedly originated from Lydia in Asia Minor.

11–12. See 2.46.54n. Verino disparages the crowd also in 1.3.3, 1.4.23 and 107, 1.24.15–20, 2.18.6, 2.42.54, 2.45.44 and 108, 2.46.54, 2.48.36, 2.55.17. Medici "stronghold": Palazzo Medici in Florence. *Scomma* is Late Latin.

13–14. For *castigatus* (my conjecture), cf. Horace, *AP* 294; for *impleat aures*, Cicero, *Or.* 29.104. Landino, *Xandra* 1.1.17–20 comparably invites correction of his poems by his dedicatee, Piero de' Medici (cf. also his 1.13 [Earlier Redaction 1].16–20). Elegiacs were often humorously called lame (as Ovid, *Tristia* 3.1.11–12), while a particular verse might limp because unmetrical. "Bad feet," Landino jokes, make his book totter unsteadily, unable to run, in *Xandra* 1.13.2 (cf. also *Xandra* 1.32.4 and 3.2.1).

15. Pardoning very youthful years: Landino, *Xandra* 1.2.13.

16. Cf. *semina mentis* ("seeds of inspiration"), Ovid, *Am.* 3.1.59, *Fasti* 6.6.

17–18. A lustrum (luster) was five years. When Horace speaks of closing his eighth lustrum (*Odes* 2.4.23f.), he means at forty. Landino and Verino use *lustra* (poetic plural) with an ordinal (as Martial 12.31.7). Landino, *Xandra* Earlier Redaction 42.7–8 helpfully says a girl who "had added four years to thrice five harvests" (and was thus nineteen) died without seeing her *quinta lustra* ("fifth lustrum"); that is, she never reached *twenty*. Cf. also *Xandra* 3.4.6 (and 2.50.9, below). Verino, born January 15 or 25, 1438 (Introduction n. 1), reached his fifth lustrum (at twenty) in January 1458. What precisely "barely yet" reaching it means here is uncertain. Verino could be speaking loosely and be well into his early twenties, though still short of his sixth lustrum, beginning at twenty-five. The poet Giano Teseo Casopero (*Amores ad Fastiam* 4.21.72), describes himself, in a mock epitaph, as "barely aged (*aegre natus*) twice two Olympiads" (Olympiads in Latin poetry denoting, like lustra, five-year spans; Ovid, *Ex Ponto* 4.6.5–6) when in fact probably about twenty-four. By contrast, Naldi (*Carmina varia* 9.17f. Grant) is very precise in giving the age of Verino's son Michele (b. November 17, 1479; d. May 30, 1487) at death (seventeen and a half): "Jealous Fate barely added two years to three lustra and was barely adding a few months more." A further complication is that "barely" can sometimes mean "not quite" rather than "only just." In his preface to *Paradise* (ca. 1468), Verino describes his love elegies as written in his "boyhood years" (cf. 2.22.9–14). Further evidence of early date is provided by 2.13.11 ("My twentieth year [strictly beginning at nineteen in January 1457] has not yet [*nondum*] fallen to me"). The present dedicatory poem has often been said to date to 1463 (the year when Verino reached twenty-*five*), though, as shown above, that seems to involve a misinterpretation of what reaching one's fifth lustrum means. At least a few poems now included in *Fiammetta* must, however, postdate even 1463. Certainly 2.51–54 must be after Cosimo de' Medici's death (August 1, 1464), and 2.47 after July 23, 1464. Mencaraglia (p. 9) suggests that the poems in which Cosimo is dead were added after this dedication was written, and Perosa (p. 51) endorses that view, which seems reasonable. When in 2.43 Lucrezia Donati is urged to love Lorenzo (b. 1449), the date is probably about 1463 or 1464. See also on 1.11 (after Cosimo's death?) and 2.41 (who rules Milan?). Landino's love for Sandra began at nineteen, in 1443/44, when "he had scarcely added four years to three lustra" (*Xandra* 1.2.17). Twenty-five to thirty years on, a faded Sandra's inner beauty still held Landino "now for the sixth lustrum" (Miscellaneous Poems 6.29). Naldo Naldi's love for Alba (2.5n) began at fourteen in his "fourth from eleven (= fifteenth) year," when "living the time measured by three lustra" (the fourth would start at fifteen). For Verino's *Flammetta* as imitating the second version of Landino's *Xandra* of ca. 1458–60 (a further hint of date), see Introduction (p. viii) and 1.20.31–38 (cf. also 1.5). If the dedication here dates to the early 1460s, Lorenzo, the addressee (b. 1449), was very young.

19–20. The hoof of Pegasus (the winged horse, later Bellerophon's, sprung from blood of the slain Medusa, the Gorgon) created the Muses' fountain of Hippocrene ("Horse fountain," also Pegasus', the nag's, or the Gorgon's fount, pool, etc.) on Mt. Helicon in central Greece. Bathing in or drinking its waters, as also those of the Castalian spring (1.11.45–48n) or the river Permessus (2.17.7–10n), supposedly inspired poets.

21–22. Landino, *Xandra* 3.19.13–14, imitated here (2.24.10 almost = 14 there), declares that if Piero de' Medici approves his revised *Xandra* and the limited tributes to him there possible, that assurance (*fiducia*) will empower him to celebrate Piero more grandly (cf. 1.20.31–32 below).

23–24. Punning on *Laurentius*, "Parnassus' laurel" denotes poetic excellence. Mt. Parnassus in central Greece (with Delphi at its foot and the Castalian spring between its two summits) was sacred to Apollo (whose tree the laurel was; 1.4.99n) and the Muses. *Doctus* ("learned") especially describes a poet. Lorenzo wrote surviving vernacular poetry (2.43n). The last five words of 24 are used of Cosimo in 2.51.86. Cf. 2.45.136 and 140, of Piero. In Landino, *Xandra* 3.17.143, Piero "shows indulgence to the learned, being learned (*doctus*) himself"; Naldi, *Eleg.* 3.8.27f. is similar.

25. *Clementia* ("kindness") of patronage: Landino, *Xandra* 1.1.9 and 3.17.145. Note primary sequence after *praestitit ut*. Cf. Juvenal 6.539f.

26. Rising to the stars through fame (common imagery; cf. especially Ovid, *Met.* 15.875–76): 1.11.38, 1.19.6, 2.1.12, 2.23.11, 2.46.5, 2.51.136; P. 711–13.

1.2

Addresses to the reader were especially favored by Martial (Ovid has some too).

1–2. After Martial 1.4(5).1–2, asking Domitian, if taking up his poems to read, to lay aside his stern look (*pone supercilium*; cf. Landino, *Xandra* 2.1.20; Naldi, *Eleg.* 1.3.15). For *tanges* cf. 1.4.97.

3–4. Ovid, *Her.* 15.7 calls elegy "the tearful song" (Greek *elegos* = "lament"). Cf. also *Am.* 3.9.3–4.

5–12. Models: Sophocles for tragedy; Maro (Vergil), epic; Menander (the Athenian New Comedian), comedy; Sappho and Alcaeus, lyric (they are again compared at 2.23.3–4; for Sappho see also 1.4.53–58, for Alcaeus 2.45.27–30 with note). *Soccus* (7): Comic actor's footwear.

13–14. "Divine" or "holy" poets (also 1.7.13, 1.20.28, 1.21.25, 2.45.42 and especially 53–58, 2.51.77): Ovid, *Rem. Am.* 813, *Am.* 3.9.41; Horace, *AP* 400; etc.

15–16. Cf. the purport of 2.1.9–44.

21 and 24. After Vergil, *Aen.* 6.847–48 (cf. 2.45.105; *P.* 118).

22. Iapetus' son Prometheus made man from clay. The patronymic in Ovid (*Met.* 4.632) and Claudian (*Against Eutropius* 2.49) is Iapetionides. Iapetides (scanned differently), a lyre player's name in Ovid, *Met.* 5.111, is here substituted.

23. Apelles: 2.45.103–4n.

25–26. After Landino, *Xandra* 3.7.153–54. *Aenigmata iuris* again 1.29.19. Cf. *P.* 289 for advocates unraveling "knotty" legal obscurities.

34. After Persius 5.52.

35. After Horace, *Satires* 2.1.27 (*quot . . . vivunt*) and 1.1.3 and 109 (*diversa sequentes*).

38. "Unequal measures" refers to the hexameter and pentameter of elegiacs. Cf. Horace, *AP* 75; Ovid, *Tristia* 2.220; Landino, *Xandra* 2.23.38.

39–40. See 1.10.31–32n and 2.55.13–16.

41–42. Marcus Porcius Cato (the Censor, 234–149 BCE): 2.3.3, 2.13.13, 2.28.2, 2.32.3 and 11, 2.51.57 (there with the younger Cato); *P.* 874–75 (with note).

43–44. Cf. Ovid, *Tristia* 2.353ff. and Martial 1.4(5).8 (imitated 2.13.8), both declaring the poet's life upright, only his writings frivolous or lascivious. Verino's purity: 2.2.38, 2.13.1–2 (with note), 2.46.1–2 and 58.

1.3

Landino, *Xandra* 1.2, Naldi, *Eleg.* 1.2, and Braccesi *A* 2 and 3 Perosa are comparably placed addresses to the book. Cf. also Landino, *Xandra* 1.13 (= Earlier Redaction 1). Ovid, *Tristia* 1.1 is such an address; Martial has many. His 1.3(4), for instance (an influence also on 2.3), warns his book of rough treatment it risks in bookseller's shops rather than safe on his shelves.

1. See 2.3.3–4n.

3. Cf. *ventosae plebis*, Horace, *Epist.* 1.19.37.

5. Very like 2.17.12, itself almost as Landino, *Xandra* 1.1.10 (cf. also 1.32.5 there). As 2.17 is addressed to Pellegrino Agli, *peregrini* here may be a pun

(cf. 2.18.12, playing on Montano's name, and 2.14.5). If so, poems are here sent to Agli. See 2.17n.

1.4

Flammetta = "Little Flame," Italian *Fiammetta* (nondiminutive form *Fiamma*, Latin *Flamma*). I have adjusted the regular manuscript spelling *Flametta*, and all other forms from the root *flam(m)a*, to accord with standard orthography. Naldo Naldi's mother and sister were called Fiammetta, also the pseudonym of Boccaccio's girlfriend.

1. Tranchedini is "your poet" to Lelia (as celebrating her) 1.7.1, and Scala to Albiera 2.5.20; so too Marullo to Hybla in Sannazaro, *Epigr.* 1.42.8.

3–6. "Aonians": Muses (Aonia: 1.20.19–22n). "Gorgon's fountain" (Hippocrene; cf. 44): 1.1.19–20n. Parnassus (5): 1.1.23–24n.

9–10. Love at first sight (anciently Vergil, *Ecl.* 8.41 and elsewhere) is likewise claimed by Landino (*Xandra* 1.3.13–14) and Braccesi (A 4.13–18 Perosa), who speak of their loves for Sandra (*Xandra* 1.2.18) and Flora (A 4.1–12 Perosa), respectively, as also their first (so Propertius 1.1.1–2 of Cynthia). *O pulcherrima rerum* is also in 1.7.1 (the masculine equivalent appears three times in Ovid).

13. Ending almost as Ovid, *Am.* 2.9.51. Cupid's "Acidalian mother" (Vergil, *Aen.* 1.720): Venus, from the Acidalian fountain in Boeotia.

16. Cf. Vergil, *Aen.* 3.637.

17–18. In 2.43.8 Lucrezia Donati's hair likewise surpasses Apollo's locks, as does Sandra's in Landino, *Xandra* 2.4.13–14 (cf. Earlier Redaction 25.1). For Fiammetta's looks see Introduction, p. xii; Lazzari, p. 55.

20. *Nequitia* covers a wide range of "badness." In 1.18.28 it denotes "heartlessness"; in 2.46.12, "wrongdoing" in general; in 1.24.20 and 2.42.53 it probably means "foolish behavior" or "disreputable conduct," as in Ovid, *Am.* 3.1.17–18 (1.24.15–20n). Propertius in his 2.24.6 is labeled *nequitiae caput* ("the height of wantonness"). In 2.1.46 Verino uses *nequitia* as Ovid in *Am.* 2.1.2, both poets of their own *nequitia*. Here a softer meaning than "disreputable conduct" (though note *dedecoris* ["shame"] in 103) may perhaps be deduced from Landino, *Xandra* 2.18.42, where *in extrema nequitia* describes prostrate languishing. In 1.13.8 Fiammetta's eyes (cf. 15 here)

began Verino's *malum* ("affliction"), to which *nequitia* here is perhaps roughly equivalent, describing infatuated lovesickness (note the tears and pains in 19). In a letter quoted by Bottiglioni (p. 195) Verino warns his teenage son, Michele, against lapsing into *nequitia*, guiding him instead toward sobriety, scholarliness, and purity. Above everything, he must guard against all moral corruption, as wisdom will not enter a mind infected by wickedness. He must avoid contamination of his character from friends and rarely go to a banquet, where reins are slackened to pleasure, and chastity's chains loosened. Night must not catch him out of doors, but be spent in rest or study. He must keep his brain occupied lest evil thoughts creep in, stand up to the beginnings of *nequitia* (cf. 2.42.3), imagine God ever present, and people witnessing his every act. All secrets will out. There *nequitia* = "dissipation" or "moral corruption."

21. See 2.22.59–60n.

22. The appealing "purity of life" (*sancti mores*; Verino's own in 2.46.1 and in B's original 2.36.3) here seems Fiammetta's. Cf. 31 (and note). *Forma rapit*: Propertius 2.25.44.

23. See 1.9.15–16n.

24–26. Sailing imagery (much favored by Ovid): 1.12.5–8, 1.14.7–12, 1.23.3–4, 1.24.4–6, 2.1.7–8.

31. Landino, *Xandra* 2.4.27 and 2.23.59 counts "manners attractive in every way" among Sandra's qualities.

33–34. "Church of the Virgin" and "Reparata's temple": Florence's cathedral, Santa Maria del Fiore (St. Mary of the Flower), in Verino's day also informally Santa Reparata, the church it replaced (cf. P. 59; Landino, *Xandra* Earlier Redaction 40.15). Virgin (33): Mary, unless Reparata, virgin and martyr, as Gualdo Rosa suggests.

36. *Vos* ("you" plural) implies "you and your girl companions" (so Gualdo Rosa; cf. 1.10.19). For youths outside Fiammetta's mother's house, cf. .10.21–26. *Turba proterva* ("forward/wanton band") describes lustful satyrs in Ovid, *Her.* 5.136 and *Fasti* 4.142. See 1.10.19–28n.

37–40. After Propertius 3.14's envy of mixed (naked) athletic activities at Sparta and the easy access so accorded.

41. Pierides: Muses, as often.

44. Only three-word pentameter in *Fiammetta*. Hippocrene: 1.1.19–20n.

45. Thalia was a Muse.

47–48. Sibyls were prophetesses (in verse); P. 1044n. The entranced Pythian at Delphi delivered the oracular responses (then versified).

51. Cornelia, daughter of Scipio Africanus, was mother of Tiberius and Gaius Sempronius Gracchus, tribunes of the people, 133 and 123–122 BCE, respectively. Widowed early, she brought up twelve children alone, educating them personally.

52. Chrysippus (280–207 BCE), a stern moralist in 2.32.6 (and Landino, *Xandra* 1.9.6), was the third head of the Stoa. "Learned mother": Cornelia. *Chrysippum* denotes the lesson (high-minded Stoic philosophy).

53. Last five words: Ovid, *Ars Am.* 3.331. Sappho: 1.2.5–12n.

56. "Alternating measures" ("Cupid's measures" 1.2.10) means elegiac verse. Cf. P. 935.

57–58. Phaon (also 2.1.18), a youth of Lesbos whom Sappho loved, eventually spurned her and went to Sicily. In Ovid, *Her.* 15 she pleads that its women may send him back. Trinacrian: Sicilian.

61–62. Love incurable by herbs, etc.: Ovid, *Her.* 5.149, *Met.* 1.523–24; Propertius 2.1.57–58; Tibullus 2.3.13–14. With the following lines cf. Landino, *Xandra* 1.2.25–34.

63–66. The Phasian: Medea (also 1.18.11 and 1.25.17–20), with whose magical aid Jason, in quest of the Golden Fleece (cf. 2.38.3–4), yoked two brazen-hoofed oxen, plowed a field, sowed a dragon's teeth, and dealt with the crop of attacking armed men. Medea then used herbs to lull to sleep the Golden Fleece's guardian dragon. Eventually betrayed for another woman, Medea murdered her rival and her children by Jason (hinted in 66).

67–70. The sea nymph Circe (also 1.25.21–26) turned Odysseus' men into animals before being made to change them back and falling in love with him (Homer, *Od.* 10.210ff.). Odysseus/Ulysses ruled Ithaca (Dulichium/Dulichia being another island nearby). *Circes* (for regular Greek *Circe*) is a Latin third declension nominative form (like *Progenes,* 1.6.38 and Landino, *Xandra* 2.25.70).

71–74. Apollo once pastured cattle (or sheep) for Admetus, king of Pherae in Thessaly (1.25.33–34n), some say as a punishment, by Jupiter's command; others, because he was enamored of Admetus (so Callimachus, *Hymn to Apollo* 49). Landino, *Xandra* 1.23.15–16 makes the reason Apollo's passion for some unnamed mistress, presumably thinking of Oenone in (the disputed) Ovid, *Her.* 5.151–52. Cf. also Tibullus 2.3.11–28, especially 13–14. In 73–74 Apollo, as sun god, controls the seasons (cf. P. 402–9). With 71, cf. Ovid, *Rem. Am.* 76.

75–76. The lover in elegy is typically wasted (or without appetite), sleepless, and pale (e.g., Ovid, *Ars Am.* 1.729–36). Landino is all three in *Xandra* 1.4.1–4; in *Xandra* 1.3.44 he is off food; in 2.7.13–14 there he cannot eat or sleep and has no peace in his whole body. Other relevant passages in *Fiammetta*: 1.18.38, with 1.18.37–38n (paleness); 1.22.15–19, with 1.22.15–16n (wasting); 1.24.14; 2.42.43–44; 2.49.9, with 2.49.9–10n.

77–80. For Ugolino's father, Vieri de' Vieri (1401–80), and family, see Introduction, p. vii. For the family background (and address), see also 2.13.17–20, 2.13.19–20n, 2.17.2–6, 2.17.5–6n.

81–82. After Ovid, *Her.* 8.115–16 and *Ars Am.* 3.668.

87–88. Venus had associations with the Greek island of Cythera. Cf. 2.22.9–16.

89–90. The first syllable of Verino's name scans short (as here) fifteen times in *Fiammetta*; it scans long eight times. In 1.14.4 and 21 both quantities occur within the same poem (comparable inconsistencies: 2.8.5–6n, 2.13.13–14n).

91–92. In Ovid, *Met.* 5.369 Venus speaks of Cupid's power over Jupiter (the Thunderer).

93–94. For being Love's soldier, see also 1.10.2–6, 1.12.21, 1.22.9–10 (with 1.22.8–10n), 2.1.10–14, 2.1.33–35, 2.2.1–20 and P. preface; thus Love's camp, 2.1.11, 2.2.1. Elizabeth Thomas, *Greece and Rome* n.s. 11 (1964), pp. 151ff., surveys the *militia amoris* theme (anciently best known from Ovid, *Am.* 1.9).

97. For *tange*, cf. *tanges* in 1.2.1.

99. Daphne, daughter of the River Peneus, fled from Apollo's advances (1.23.33–34, 2.22.33–34), becoming the laurel sacred to him (Ovid, *Met.* 1.452–567).

100. Fiammetta is *Flammea Virgo* ("Flame Maiden") also in 1.30.24 and 2.22.50; in 1.25.47 and 1.28.2 (and in the poem seemingly Francesco Tranchedini's cited 1.7n), just *Flammea*; in 1.25.46, *Flamma*.

101. After Ovid, *Met.* 1.484 (cf. also *Her.* 4.72).

104. Last four words as Ovid, *Ars Am.* 1.34.

106. Last four words as Ovid, *Am.* 1.13.41.

109. Love "matures through long years" in Ovid, *Am.* 2.19.23.

110. *Nisi* is for *non nisi*. See my note on Angeriano, *Erot.* 31.11 (two instances), and E. Löfstedt in *Coniectanea* (Uppsala-Stockholm, 1950), i.28–32. The very few classical examples once claimed are now discredited.

1.5

Landino, *Xandra* 2.27, echoed here, asserts that when Rome saw Sandra's eyes, the once-witnessed glories of Propertius' Cynthia, Catullus' Lesbia, Ovid's Corinna, and Tibullus' Nemesis were all eclipsed. Cf. also *Xandra* Earlier Redaction 26.

4. For Landino's *Xandra*, see Introduction, p. viii, and 1.20.33–34n.

1.6

1–2. The Arno flows through Florence. Sithonian: Thracian.

3–8. In Horace, *Odes* 1.4.2–3, as spring comes, laid-up ships are hauled down to the water again, "neither does the flock delight in the fold (*stabulis*) nor the plowman in the fire." *Peronatus* (7) illicitly has *e* and *o* short (both long Persius 5.102 and Braccesi E 8.26 Perosa).

12. As 2.24.8 (and almost as 1.20.36). From the end of 11 to that of 1.9.22 *B* is wanting.

13–16. Snowballing could be flirtatious (like throwing apples and other things, as in Vergil, *Ecl.* 3.64; Theocritus, *Id.* 5.88–89 and 6.6–7; Aristophanes, *Clouds* 997; Greek Anthology 5.79 and 80). Landino, *Xandra* Earlier Redaction 33 tells how playing with snow with a previously scornful girl led to her speaking pleasantly. With 15–16, cf. Propertius 2.8.12.

17–18. In 1.29.6 Fiammetta says Verino became foremost among a thousand suitors (same hyperbole 1.10.25), and in 1.21.1–2 he recalls being preferred to a hundred others. Fiammetta's suitors: 1.4.36 (with note) and 1.13.6. For *fui* in L (read by Mencaraglia), I read *fui*, after Vergil, *Aen.* 2.6, *pars magna fui* ("I was a great part"). *Ultimus* = "meanest" or "lowest": Horace, *Epist.* 1.17.35; Landino, *Xandra* Earlier Redaction 7.2. Note the change to direct address after referring to Fiammetta in the third person in 11–16. Cf. 1.13.17–18, 1.14.17–22, 1.21.19–36, 1.23.37–40, 1.28.5–16, 2.50.27 (and Landino, Misc. Poems 1.25, 39, and 75) for some similar changes.

19–22. Verino's heart was cold with horror to see Fiammetta look at rivals, but ablaze with fire out of love, a contrast redolent of Petrarch. Line 20 is after Ovid, *Her.* 1.22.

23. After Propertius 2.24.18.

26. See 1.27.23–24n.

27. After [Tibullus] 3.5.16, itself in debt to Ovid, *Ars Am.* 2.670.

29–32. Aurora, the Dawn Goddess, secured immortality (but not permanent youth) from Jupiter for her beautiful lover Tithonus, who therefore deteriorated into proverbially extreme senility. Nestor (also 2.45.7): Pylos' long-reigning king in Homer. Methuselah (King James Version spelling) died aged 969 according to Genesis 5:21–27. *Mat(h)usalem* (if correct) is (indeclinable) genitive (some editions of the Vulgate have *Mathusalae*, declined genitive of *Mathusala*). Apollo granted the Sibyl of Cumae as many years of life as grains of dust in a pile (Ovid, *Met.* 14.129–53). With 31–32, cf. Propertius 2.24.33 (1.7.5n).

33–34. Elysian Fields: Elysium, Underworld abode of the blessed dead. "Dictaean king": Minos, the Cretan ruler later a judge of the dead (Ovid, *Met.* 8.43; Landino, *Xandra* 2.12.23 and Misc. Poems 1.67); otherwise (as P. 414) Jupiter, hidden as a baby in a cave of Mt. Dicte (in Crete).

37–40. *Tereos* (39): Greek genitive (first syllable illicitly short, as in 1.20.5). *Prognes* (38): Latin third declension nominative form (without classical validity) substituted for the normal Greek nominative *Progne* (1.4.67–70n). Philomela and Progne were daughters of Pandion, king of Athens. Progne married Tereus (a Thracian), who raped her sister. Though he cut out Philomela's tongue, Progne found out and served his young son Itys to him as food. In the prevailing Roman version (see Ovid, *Met.* 6.424–676), followed here, as Tereus pursued, Philomela turned into the nightingale; Progne, the swallow (associated with human habitations). The latter bird's red-marked throat is treated as blood-stained in Ovid, *Met.* 6.669–70 and Vergil, *Geo.* 4.15 (cf. also Landino, *Xandra* 2.25.69). In happy Elysium Philomela can here forget Tereus' actions (likewise Landino, *Xandra* 1.25.14); not so in 1.20.5–6. The spelling Philomena (*L* here and, with *B*, 1.20.5), not ancient, is quite often found in neo-Latin (vernacular Filomena, as Petrarch, *Rime sparse* 310.3). In *P.* 758–60 both *Philomela* and *Philomena* occur in the manuscripts.

41–42. The swan was Phoebus' bird. Parrot "of human speech": Ovid, *Am.* 2.6.37.

48. After Propertius 2.7.19.

1.7

Tranchedini: Lazzari (pp. 53 and 161) thinks the Milanese ambassador Nicodemo (or Niccolò) Tranchedini (or Tranchedino) of Pontremoli (1413–81) is meant, but poems of his son Francesco (b. 1441) to a *Lysia* (= Lisia/Elisabetta; also Lelia here?) survive in manuscript (Kristeller, 1:202). Furthermore, some elegiac verses in *A* (fols. 106v–107) addressed to Ugolino Verino are credibly thought by Kristeller (1:98) to be by Francesco Tranchedini, as the title there is followed by *Tr*, and some other poems in *A* are expressly his (Perosa endorses this opinion in his edition of Landino, p. LI). The said verses, misascribed by Lazzari (p. 61) to Landino, are Doubtfully Ascribed 1 in the ITRL Landino volume (pp. 312–15). They urge Verino to resume writing poems of Fiammetta (*Flam(m)ea*, as in 1.25.47 and 1.28.2 here), once his theme but for some time abandoned. She has returned from far away (27–37; Verino says nothing about her leaving Florence), and Verino should let his former sweet passion return too. Declared beautiful and worthy of his verse, she who gave him his inspiration (*ingenium*) and Phoebus' (poetic) arts (cf. 1.21.27–30 here) should not be denied the benefit of those gifts in deserved praises. Lazzari (p. 55) quotes (from Bartolozzi) part of a letter in Latin from Verino to "his friend" Tranchedini comparing Fiammetta and his addressee's Lelia. Verino declares both truly beautiful, but Lelia affable and very humorous, whereas Fiammetta's modesty and rigid moral strictness preclude hope of success with her, his one consolation being the knowledge that so very chaste a girl spurns many a would-be seducer. Naldi addresses Nicodemo at length in *Eleg.* 2.39 and Francesco in *Eleg.* 2.24. Some other examples of appeals to a friend's (especially a poet's) beloved to "spare" him (cf. 2.43 and 2.49.17–26) include Landino, *Xandra* 1.15 (Earlier Redaction 31); Piccolomini, *Cynthia* 20; Tito Vespasiano Strozzi, *Erotica* 2.14.

1. See 1.4.1n and 1.4.9–10n.

5. *Niger ille dies* = "the black day" of death: Propertius 2.24.34 (1.6.31–32 imitates Propertius' previous line); similarly *atra dies* 1.21.18 (Vergil, *Aen.* 6.429; Propertius 2.11.4).

9–12. Tibullus (*cultus* [cf. 2.1.20] in Ovid, *Am.* 1.15.28) sang of Nemesis; Propertius, of Cynthia (cf. 1.5.3, 2.1.20–21). Propertius is *Nauta* ("the Sailor") also in P. 938 (and Landino, *Xandra* 1.19.17, 2.30.13, 3.7.12), as some manuscripts of his poems wrongly call him Sextus Aurelius Propertius Nauta.

12. Souls drank Lethe's Underworld waters of forgetfulness prior to reincarnation. Figurative submersion (oblivion): Ovid, *Ars Am.* 3.340; *Tristia* 1.8.36 and 4.9.2; [Vergil], *Culex* 214. Cf. 1.20.35–36 and 2.1.32 below.

13–14. Tibullus 2.5.114 bids his girl spare "the holy bard" (1.2.13–14n), himself.

1.8

Ovid often represents women as out to exploit lovers. *Am.* 1.8 attacks a bawd for advising his mistress on making money from men (cf. *Am.* 1.10, *Ars Am.* 1.419–36, etc.); similarly Propertius 4.5.

7–10. The *exclusus amator* ("shut-out lover"), with his pleading song (paraclausithyron) by his mistress's door (see Henderson on Ovid, *Rem. Am.* 35f.), is a familiar figure in the Roman elegiac poets and their neo-Latin imitators (as Landino, *Xandra* 2.20, 2.21, 2.25). As well as 19–28 below, see Introduction, p. xii, 1.9.19–22, 1.14, 1.18.9–10, 18, and 21–36, 2.27.9–14. F. O. Copley, *Exclusus Amator. A Study in Latin Love Poetry*, monograph no. 17 (1955) in the American Philological Association series, examines the theme.

14. See 2.46.47–48n.

15–16. Tricking a replacement for a "lost" jewel from a lover: Ovid, *Ars Am.* 1.432 (an earring).

17–20. Ovid, *Ars Am.* 1.433 says girls ask for many things on loan, but will not give them back. Cf. also Ovid, *Am.* 1.8.101–2. Line 18 recalls Vergil, *Aen.* 4.172, where Dido terms her affair with Aeneas a marriage and "with this name covers up guilt."

19–32. In 1.18.21–36 the shut-out Verino suffers severe weather. Tibullus 1.2.29–30 speaks of gladly braving winter's cold and heavy rain to be admitted. In *Xandra* 2.20 the let-down Landino waits all night in the cold, and in 2.25 there he complains of bitter conditions outside while Sandra lies in her warm bed, deaf to his pleading. Cf. 2.42.29–32 below for being let down in an assignation. *Iubaris* (24) illicitly has first syllable long (2.45.87–88n).

25–28. In 2.27.9–14 a gift is seen as gaining the shut-out lover admission. Ovid, *Am.* 1.8.77 advises girls, "Let your door be deaf to the pleader, but unfastened to the bearer of gifts." Cf. Propertius 2.16, 4.5.47–58, etc. Tyrian purple: 1.11.31–32n.

29–32. Tisiphone was a Fury. Tartarus: P. 49n. Line 30 is after Ovid, *Am.* 1.10.22. With 31–32, cf. 1.30.27–28. I take *eventus* (32) as nominative singular (scansion: 1.21.12n). L's abbreviated first word in 32 (S) may be *sit* ("be") or Mencaraglia's *sic* ("thus"). *Dare* of inflicting punishment: 2.49.19–20n.

1.9

The unnamed addressee may be Vettori (1.10).

1–2. Pierides: Muses. Aonian: 1.20.19–22n. Cf. 1.13.1–2 and 2.42.55–60.

5. Love/love, the Fates, Fortune, or the gods are against the lover also in 1.14.16, 1.21.9, 1.23.6, 2.22.2 and 7, 2.42.36. Here Verino reflects Propertius 1.14.15 ("For who has joy of riches if Love be against him?"). The wider context there (rich bedroom furnishings no proof against sleepless love torment) suggested the following couplet.

7. Attalus III (ca.170–133 BCE), king of Pergamum in Asia Minor, was famed for wealth, especially for cloth-of-gold. Cf. Propertius 2.13.22 and 4.5.24 (and previous note).

8. Last four words: Ovid, *Her.* 8.62, also behind Landino, *Xandra* 1.4.4, 1.5.14, and 3.4.80.

11–12. Based, like 2.22.36 and 2.49.16 (and Landino, *Xandra* 1.2.12), on Propertius 2.17.9.

14. Landino, *Xandra* 1.3.45–52 declares love's agonies a greater punishment than being blasted by Jupiter's thunderbolt or imprisoned beneath mountains.

15–16. Ovid, *Am.* 3.1.19–22 pictures himself pointed out as the one burning with love, unknowingly the whole talk of the city. For being a scandal, see also 1.4.23 and 107–8, 1.24.15–22, 2.42.53–54, 2.55.17; for being pointed out in public, 1.21.5, 1.24.19; for gossip at the crossroads (cf. Ovid, *Am.* 3.1.18; Horace, *Sat.* 2.6.50; Propertius 2.20.22), 1.24.16, 2.42.53.

19–20. Shut-out lover: 1.8.7–10n. Winds commonly carry off (empty or wasted) words in both ancient and neo-Latin verse (cf. 1.24.8 below).

21–22. Jupiter (the Thunderer) was the weather god.

33–34. Pirithous, devoted friend of Theseus (cf. 2.40.15), accompanied him to the Underworld intent on carrying off Persephone, Pluto's wife (Dis = Pluto).

35–36. For the archer Apollo's humbling by Cupid, cf. 2.22.21–34.

37–38. Python (also 2.22.21–34) is the huge serpent killed near Delphi by Apollo (Ovid, *Met.* 1.438 and 460). Hercules slew the Nemean Lion (1.25.27–30n).

1.10

Mencaraglia misidentifies the addressee as Petrus Vectorius, 1499–1585. F. W. Kent, *Household and Lineage in Renaissance Florence* (Princeton, 1977), refers (pp. 55 and 97–98) to an earlier Piero (di Francesco) Vettori, who in 1463 married the daughter of the hugely wealthy merchant and memoirs-writer Giovanni Rucellai (1403–81) and was supplied with a painted cassone by Apollonio (2.8n; see p. 11 of Gombrich, *Norm and Form*, cited in Bibliography under *Studies*). That Piero is listed for the Balia of 1480 (for Santo Spirito, Verino's quarter) in N. Rubenstein, *The Government of Florence under the Medici 1434–94* (Oxford, 1966), p. 311. Lazzari (p. 56) calls the addressee "the future Florentine diplomat." See 1.1n. Mencaraglia omits part of *B*'s title in his apparatus criticus.

2. Love's (Cupid's) soldier: 1.4.93–94n.

3–4. "Crescent-shaped" (*lunata*) of a camp: *Bellum Africum* 80.

7–10. Vettori seems to have urged Verino to curb his passion. Love's chains (cf. 2.2.12, 2.42.10): Ovid, *Am.* 1.2.30, *Met.* 4.677–78; Propertius 3.11.4; Tibullus 1.1.56, 2.4.3–4; etc. (Infatuated) love as servitude more generally (cf. 9–10) is familiar ancient imagery too. In 1.22.8 and 26, below, Verino is Love's slave; cf. also 1.14.15, 1.18.27–28, 1.25.1 and 31–32, 2.2.14 and 26, and 2.42.11 for love as servitude. *Tali servire puellae* (9): Landino, *Xandra* 2.5.7 (cf. Ovid, *Am.* 2.17.1).

11–14. Leaden (not Cupid's usual golden) arrows caused aversion (Ovid, *Met.* 1.468–69; [Vergil], *Ciris* 160). See 2.22.31–32n.

15–18. Hyrcania lay south of the Caspian Sea. The Cyprian's (Venus') bird is the dove.

19–28. See Introduction for Fiammetta's circumstances and age. In line 25, for the manuscripts' *proterva* or *protervam*, I conjecture *protervi*, making the suitors, not Fiammetta's mother, "forward." Cf. 1.4.36 and Ovid as cited thereon, 1.6.47, 1.13.11 and 12, and the forward/wanton youths (*iuvenes protervi*) in Horace, *Odes* 1.25.2. *Protervam* is not, however, impossible ("sought you in your wantonness").

30. Cf. 2.55.16.

31–32. Ovid *Am.* 1.9.4 declares love in old age unseemly; similarly Tibul-

lus 1.1.71–72. Cf. 1.2.40 above (and contrast 1.4.94) and Verino's revulsion
at Fiammetta's marrying "old" Bruno (especially 1.28.2 and 9–12).

33–34. After Ovid, *Am.* 1.3.2–3. Line 6 there inspired 34 (and 1.21.22).

1.11

The two unnamed Medici brothers here seem to be Lorenzo (1449–92)
and Giuliano (1453–78), as they are "the fairest offspring of the Medici"
(37), Cosimo's *gemini nepotes* ("two grandsons"), in P. 725–26, and the
"Two" here are treated as boys (45–48n). Questions are, however, raised.
Their paternal grandfather (*avus*), Cosimo, died August 1, 1464 (recently
dead in 2.51–2.54). Does *fuit* ("was") in 43 show him dead here, or can it
do double duty as "has been" and "was"? And could Cosimo's eventual
outshining by the Two (44) be comfortably predicted within his lifetime?
Another point is that two other Medici brothers were once treated as
Florence's great hopes, namely Piero (1416–69) and Giovanni (1421–63),
mentioned with Cosimo in 2.45.117. They are meant in Landino, *Xandra*
3.15.83, where Cosimo has reared "twofold progeny (*geminam prolem*), two
lights of their homeland (Naldi, *Eleg.* 3.6.43ff. has similar wording), for
them to be the great glory of the house of Medici"; and in P. 718 Verino
calls Giovanni (formerly) "one of the two hopes" of his people. Could
Verino comfortably refer in the terms used here to the younger "Two"
when both the older Medici brothers were still alive? Shortly after
Giovanni's death (November 1, 1463), Pellegrino Agli (*Carmina* 1:126)
calls Lorenzo and Giuliano "the two stars of the Medici, children worthy
of their grandfather Cosimo and their father Piero." An alternative inter-
pretation of Verino's "vision" here is that it may look back a whole gen-
eration to the boyhood of Piero and Giovanni in order to flatter them
(before Giovanni's death) by making Apollo predict their patronage of
the arts as adults in Verino's own time. If *they*, not Lorenzo and Giuliano,
are the Two, that would save the problem of the grandfather mentioned
being Cosimo (living or dead).

3. *Titan* denotes the sun. Cf. 1.20.5–8 and 41–42, 1.26.9–10, and 2.48.1–2
for the time of dreaming (dawn) and see 1.26.9–10n.

5–6. After Propertius 3.3.1–2 (1.12.1–4n), also reflected in 1.20.1. Aonian:
1.20.19–22n. Gorgon's stream: 1.1.19–20n.

8. Equaling gods or goddesses: 2.43.2, 2.51.94.

9–10. Fauns are woodland deities with horns and goats' feet. Dryads are wood nymphs.

16. The Graces were commonly depicted in ancient times (as also in Botticelli's painting *Primavera*) standing one turned away from the beholder toward the other two, facing her.

29–30. *Lumina* = "light" and "eyes," Apollo, god of light, being equated with the sun.

31–32. Tyrian purple, anciently renowned: 1.8.28, 1.20.13, 2.43.15.

43–44. See headnote. The great-grandfather of Lorenzo and Giuliano, in the male line, was Giovanni di Averardo Bicci de' Medici, 1360–1429 (father of Cosimo), Gonfaloniere di Giustizia in 1421. Line 43 recasts Ovid, *Met.* 13.205 and *Fasti* 1.492 (cf. Landino, *Xandra* 3.3.53 and 3.7.42).

45–48. In 2.43.47–48 the Muses (called Castalians, 2.51.69) have reared Lorenzo in their Castalian caves (cf. 2.42.59), and Calliope (the chief Muse) has nurtured him in her arms. Castalian spring (also 2.17.11): 1.1.19–20n, 1.1.23–24n.

49–50. Ismarian: Thracian. Calliope's son is Orpheus; Apollo's, Linus (cf. Vergil, *Ecl.* 4.55ff.), who instructed Orpheus and Hercules. In Landino, *Xandra* 1.29.40 Linus would fittingly sing Sandra's praises. Naldi (*Carmina varia* 8.156–57, p. 160 Grant) speaks of songs "in such number as neither Orpheus previously gave his mother Calliope, nor learned Linus gave his father."

53–54. "Where the Tuscan Lion holds sway" refers to Florence's own territories, whereas "Tyrrhenian cities" takes in neighboring communities over the wider area considered Tyrrhenian.

1.12

Inspired by Propertius 3.3 (1–4n) and Ovid, *Am.* 1.1. Lazzari (p. 52) identifies the addressee (also 2.23; Lazzari p. 60) as Cherubinus Quarqualius Geminianensis, or Cherubino (di Bartolo) Quarquagli di San Gimignano. Poet, grammarian, and musician, and eventually an archbishop, his friends included Ficino and Verino. Meter: Sapphic stanzas (so 1.15 and a few poems in Landino's *Xandra*).

1–4. Propertius (3.3) describes intending to sing of Alba Longa's rulers and its kings' deeds, but being warned off by Apollo. *Ardentem* ("eager") L, but B's *audentem* ("venturing") is supported by the use of *audere* in 2.1.3, 5 and 7; Ovid, *Tristia* 2.337; Catullus 1.5; Landino, *Xandra* 3.7.86–88.

5–8. Sailing imagery: 1.4.24–26n. Here cf. Propertius 3.3.22–24.

9–12. Thebes (as in 2.23.5): Pindar, born there. "Mt. Olympus" here is a hill by Olympia in Elis, called the "Olympic peak" and "Olympus" by Sannazaro, *Elegies* 2.6.5–7. Some believed Pelops (11) buried at Olympia and originator of the games there, though Pindar treats Heracles as responsible. Chaplets of wild olive were the prizes in the Olympic games.

13–16. Smyrna (here plural *Smyrnae*) in Asia Minor was one of several cities claiming to be Homer's birthplace. Cf. 2.23.5 and 2.24.11. Turnus opposes Aeneas in Vergil's (Maro's) *Aeneid* 7–12. Ilion (13): Greek form of *Ilium* (Troy).

17–18. The three-headed Underworld dog Cerberus had snakes as mane or tail. Cf. Horace, *Odes* 3.11.17–20.

22–24. Venus had a temple near Mt. Eryx in Sicily. For her pierced by Cupid's arrows (when she loved Mars, Anchises, and Adonis), cf. 1.22.21–24.

30–32. Fauns and dryads: 1.11.9–10n.

34. *Cypron*: Greek accusative.

39. Helicon (cf. 2.51.13): 1.1.19–20n.

1.13

The theme is suggested by Ovid, *Am.* 3.12 (cf. especially 5–6 of both poems).

1–2. Cf. the opening of 1.9.

3–4. Verino (reflecting his source) playfully pretends substantial circulation of his verses (cf. 1.24.18). *Musa iocosa* ("sportive Muse"): Ovid, *Tristia* 2.354.

5–6. Modeled on Ovid, *Am.* 3.12.5–6 ("Her who but lately was called mine, whom I began to love as her only man [*quam coepi solus amare*], I fear I must share with many"). *Coepi* (*L*), read by Mencaraglia, though in the model, does not construe with *amavi* (*amare* could be read; Gualdo Rosa's translation [see Bibliography] treats *amavi* as though *amare*). I prefer *B*'s *cepi* ("I won"), as 1.25.42 speaks of Fiammetta as lately called Verino's girl, as though "won" at one stage, then lost. See also 1.21.1–14, 1.28.15–16, 1.29.6, and 1.6.17–18n.

10. Similar to Propertius 2.34.2.

17–18. See 1.6.17–18n. In 17, understand *esses* (cf. 1.14.13 and 1.18.9). Line 18 reflects Propertius 2.1.48. Cf. Ovid, *Am.* 3.11.41, and Martial 53.3–4.

1.14

1–6. The shut-out (1.8.7–10n) and vacillating Verino debates whether to go back to Fiammetta's house and try again to gain admission.

7–12. Sailing imagery: 1.4.24–26n. Malea is the dangerous promontory in the southern Peloponnese. Cf., for example, Ovid, *Am.* 2.16.24 (echoed here in 8, as in 2.40.4). Scylla and Charybdis personified hazards faced by sailors in negotiating the strait of Messina between Italy and Sicily. Scylla, a (rock and) female monster with dogs around her loins, plucked men from their ships; Charybdis was a whirlpool on the opposite side (the strait has troublesome currents).

13–14. In debt (as Munari observes, p. 303) to Tibullus 2.4.7–10 ("Oh, . . . how I would prefer to be a stone on icy mountains [*quam mallem in gelidis montibus esse lapis*], or stand as a cliff [*cautes*] exposed to mad winds for the shipwrecking waters [*v.l.* the wrath] of the vast sea to pound!"), and Ovid, *Rem. Am.* 692, *ut lapis aequoreis undique pulsus aquis* ("like a stone beaten on all sides by the waters of the sea"). In 14 Munari correctly reads *adesus* ("eroded") for Mencaraglia's *adhaesus*, but wrongly declares *limes* "absurd," approving Mariotti's conjecture *imus* ("at the bottom"). In the alliterative 14, *lapis* and *limes* seem deliberately balanced. *Limes* (here "boundary"), in apposition to *lapis*, denotes a rock bordering the sea (corresponding to Tibullus' *cautes*). With *ortus* understand *essem* (cf. 1.13.17 and 1.18.9). Take *lapis* with both lines.

1.15

Meter: Sapphic (as 1.12). Ovid, *Tristia* 2.317ff. seems an inspiration. Leonardo (Lionardo) del Benino, otherwise Leonardo Benini (1.1n), is probably son of Piero (2.21) and brother of Niccolò (2.49). The Florentine bookseller Vespasiano da Bisticci (1421–98) says much in his *Le Vite* of a Lionardo di Piero del Benino. We gather (without dates) that Leonardo was of a distinguished Florentine family and proficient in, and enthusiastic for, Latin. A virtuous man who scorned sensuality, and who was morally courageous and of good judgment, he married well and had several children but died relatively young. He regularly entertained the highborn and lettered youth of Florence, his principal companions. For Leonardo's brother Niccolò, see Aulo Greco's (Florence, 1976) edition of *Le Vite* (2:365n). Greco finds Piero attested as a Prior (i.e., a member of the Signoria, Florence's governing council) for September and October 1430.

1–4. Horace, *Odes* 3.5.3–4 looks forward to Augustus adding Britons and Persians (i.e., Parthians) to the empire (he never actually did). Cf. also *Odes* 1.21.15 and 1.35.29–32. For the syntax of 2–4 (especially *ire*), cf. 2.8.1–2 (especially *esse cremata*).

5–8. The fire-spewing Chimaera was part-lion (front), part-goat (middle), part-dragon (rear). Comparison with Horace, *Odes* 4.2.13–16 suggests Pindar in mind here. Alcides: Hercules.

9–12. Jupiter's thunderbolts defeated the Giants when they piled mountains on top of each other to assault heaven. I (hesitantly) retain *trisulci* (manuscripts) in 11 (from *trisulcis*), defended by Perosa (p. 53), as *trisulcis* is attested (very weakly) in late antiquity, though *trisulcus* is the regular form (also Pontano, *Parthenopaeus* 1.10.126), like *bisulcus* for "two-forked."

13–16. The "two-formed" centaurs battled against the Lapiths. Danaan: Greek. *Pergama* (n. pl.): Troy (Pergamum). *Bilustri bello*: Ovid, *Am.* 2.12.9.

17–20. The island of Delos was Apollo's birthplace (cf. 2.51.73). Bacchus/Dionysus and Venus/Aphrodite were often associated (wine and sex). *Veneris sodalem* reflects Horace, *Odes* 3.18.6.

26. The Cyprian: Venus (*Cypridos*: Greek genitive). Cf. 1.10.18.

1.16

1–2. Ida, a mountain near Troy, was where Paris judged Venus fairer than Juno and Minerva.

1.17

An attack (in the tradition of such poems as Horace, *Odes* 1.25 and 4.13; Catullus 43; etc.) on the ugly and old Galla (presumably imaginary; the name occurs many times in Martial, for instance).

1. "Smaller than a dwarf": Landino, *Xandra* 2.17.6.

9–10. Alecto (here Greek accusative) was a Fury. Cf. 2.4.9–10 for the snakes as hair.

11–12. *Cerussa* is white lead, a cosmetic (Ovid, *Med. Fac.* 73; Martial 10.22.2, etc.). *Far* is spelt (a kind of flour), presumably to make a binder, like pulped barley in a paste for the face (including white lead and some red coloring) at the end of Ovid's said work. Verino's "juice in herbs" is probably a reddening agent, like rose leaves and poppies in the Ovidian context. Just as Galla is both "black" (1), i.e., swarthy, and "pale" (12), i.e., "sallow" (thus "pale" gold in 2.30, and in Landino, *Xandra* 2.17.7–8, a "yellowy" face is "paler than saffron"), an unattractive man is "blacker than a raven" and "paler than a Stygian ghost" in Piccolomini, *Cynthia* 17.5. For contempt for an aging woman's ugliness disguised by cosmetics (unlike Sandra's natural beauty), cf. Landino, *Xandra* Earlier Redaction 9 (*Xandra* 1.12 also sneers at artificial color).

14. *Luxuria* can mean "lust" in ecclesiastical writers and in neo-Latin verse (as Landino, Misc. Poems 3.34; of Pasiphae's lust in Mantuan, *Eclogues* 4.161). *Luxoriosus* = "lustful" in Braccesi, App.[1].5.10 Perosa (of an overvigorous pederast).

1.18

4–6. After Ovid, *Ars Am.* 2.113–14 (beauty "a fragile boon" fading with time).

7–8. Vergil, *Aen.* 9.435 has the same imagery.

9–10. Dislike of sallow and swarthy complexions: 1.17.11–12n. Shut-out lover: 1.8.7–10n.

11–12. Medea: 1.4.63–66n. Circe: 1.4.67n (*Circes*: Greek genitive). Thessaly had associations with witchcraft and poisons. Cf. Horace, *Odes* 1.27.21–22; Propertius 1.5.6 and 3.24.10; Juvenal 6.610; and Landino, *Xandra* 1.2.34 and 2.20.23–26, where, if he understood magic powers, Landino would use them to bring an unwilling girl to him (cf. 14 here and Propertius 1.1.19ff.).

17. Cf. Propertius 3.24.2 (Cynthia "made too haughty" by his eyes); Landino, *Xandra*. 2.25.64 (Sandra "made haughty" by his flatteries).

19–20. After Ovid, *Her.* 2.103–4.

21–36. See 1.8.19–32n. Ismarian (22): Thracian.

24. Mencaraglia reads *vincta* ("bound"), but *iuncta* is supported by *iunctas . . . fenestras* ("closed window-shutters") in Horace, *Odes* 1.25.1, *iunge ostia* ("close the double-doors") in Juvenal 9.105, and *iunctos . . . postes* ("closed doors") in Landino, *Xandra* 2.7.19. The manuscripts' *tori* ("bed"), if correct, must (uniquely) mean "bed*chamber*." I risk reading *Cori*, presuming the *o* here illicitly short (credible for Verino). Cf. *P.* 740–41 for Boreas and Caurus/Corus (there correctly scanned) together.

25–26. *Aspideus* ("asp-like") = unhearing, as in Landino, *Xandra* 2.7.26, from Psalms 58:4 (57:5 in Vulgate), where the asp (adder) is deaf and stops up its ears.

27–28. Love's servitude: 1.10.7–10n. *Nequitia*: 1.4.20n.

30. "The Cynthian": Diana (from Mt. Cynthos on Delos, her supposed birthplace), the Moon.

33–34. Landino complains of a frozen cloak in such circumstances in *Xandra* 2.25.30.

37–38. For the lover's paleness, see 1.22.15 and 2.49.9 (with notes); Ovid, *Ars Am.* 1.729–32; Horace, *Odes* 3.10.14; Propertius 1.1.22, 1.5.21, 1.9.17; [Vergil], *Ciris* 225; etc. His distressed state generally: 1.4.75–76n.

1.19

Evidently intended to accompany lighthearted poems offered to Piero. Could there even be a hint that part (Book I?) of *Fiammetta* was originally dedicated to him?

1–2. Landino, *Xandra* 2.1.8 similarly urges Piero, when public duties permit, to read his trifles "with cheery face" (*hilari fronte*; cf. 2.41.14 here), and *Xandra* 2.2.6 has *laeta carmina fronte* (cf. 2.18.10 here). *Leges* is probably future for polite imperative.

3–4. Cf. 1.1.5 above. Mixing serious matters with jokes: Landino, *Xandra* 1.29.6 and 2.1.6.

5–6. Cf. Horace, *Odes* 1.1.36, "I shall strike the stars with my exalted head" (to his dedicatee Maecenas, should he count Horace among lyric poets); Ovid, *Met.* 7.61, *Ex Ponto* 2.5.57, and *Fasti* 1.210. Equation of Piero with Maecenas, probably here implied: 1.20 and 2.45.135; Landino, *Xandra* 2.6 (where Piero [l. 17] is "a second Maecenas on Tyrrhenian shores") and 3.2.2; Pellegrino Agli, *Carmina* 1:122. See, however, 2.51.83–84n.

1.20

Piero de' Medici is again a new Maecenas, a patron and benefactor of poets (cf. 1.19.5–6n and 2.45.133–42), here (29–32) especially of Landino. Gualdo Rosa (see Bibliography under *Anthologies*), pp. 855–57, dates this poem after Cosimo's death (August 1, 1464), arguing that Piero seems Florence's leader in 17–30. Possibly, but he may just be Maecenas to Cosimo's Augustus. In Landino, *Xandra* 2.1.19, Piero is even addressed as "holding the reins of a great people" within Cosimo's lifetime.

1–2. The adjective from *Faesulae* (Fiesole) was anciently *Faesulanus* (or *Fesulanus* with long *e*), but is commonly *Fesulus* (with short *e*) in Verino (cf. 23 below and 2.51.109 and 115) and other Florentine poets of his period, as in Landino's *Xandra*, though Perosa's text sometimes prints the unmetrical *Faes-* (e.g., in 1.24.7 and 55, 1.25.11, etc.). Gualdo Rosa reasonably takes the "noble work of the Medici" at Fiesole to be their villa there (cf. 2.51.105–8n). See 1.11.5–6n.

5–8. Tereus: 1.6.37–40n. For the time: 1.26.9–10n.

7–8. *Mergebant* ("were sinking," manuscripts and Mencaraglia) is rejected by Munari (p. 303, reporting Mariotti's conjecture *vergebant*, "were declining"), as *mergere* is not intransitive in classical Latin (in late Latin he finds only St. Ambrose, *De sacramentis* 1.5.14; add *demergere* of the setting sun in Minucius Felix 34.11). I risk reading *mergebat* (transitive), with lengthening (diastole) at the dieresis (1.21.12n), noting Lucan 1.15 (the west described as "where night hides the stars") and 4.54 ("the [western] sky that immerses/hides the stars," *mergenti sidera caelo*). Cf. Marcantonio Flaminio, *Carm.* 1.8.1ff: "Already night had begun to hide (*condere*) the stars in Tethys' blue waters." Cf. 2.48.1–2. *Caeruleas . . . ad undas*: Ovid, *Her.* 19.191. With 7–16, cf. [Tibullus] 3.4.17–42.

18. The Florentines are commonly called *Sullani* (or *Syllani*, "Sullans") because of the claimed establishment of a colony of veteran Roman soldiers at nearby Fiesole by Sulla, the Roman dictator (138–78 BCE), briefly described by Verino in *De ill. urbis Flor.* (fol. 2, Paris 1583 edition; *Carmina* 10:327). *Sullanidae* ("sons of Sulla") is alternatively used by Landino (*Xandra* 3.5.37 and 3.18.46) and Verino. Here the manuscripts (and Mencaraglia) have (as accusative plural) the third declension form *Sullanides* (*Syll-*). In 2.51.27, however, the nominative plural is *Sullanidae* (first declension like *Atridae, Priamidae*, and all similar formations), making the correct accusative plural *Sullanidas* (so 2.54.25). The editor of *Carmina* rewrites this line, 2.45.126, 2.51.27, and 2.54.25 to remove *Sullanidae* from this work.

19–22. Cirrha, near Delphi, had associations with Apollo. "Aonian groves" refers to the area round Mt. Helicon and the fountain of Aganippe in Boeotia (P. 884–86n). With 21–22, cf. 2.51.103–4. "Thessalian Tempe" (pass between Thessaly and Macedonia): Horace, *Odes* 1.7.4; Ovid, *Met.* 7.222; P. 885. *Tempe*: Greek neuter plural accusative.

23–24. See 1–2n for *Fes-*. The mountains of the Mugello are northeast of Florence. Gualdo Rosa well compares Landino, *Xandra* 3.17.15–18, where the Muse Calliope has left haunts in Greece for the *Fesulos montes* and the *claustra Mugelli. Lavare* (24) is intransitive. Cf. Landino, *Xandra*, 3.17.20 (Muses bathing in the Arno) and 3.2.7–10, where Landino has drunk from a new, Tuscan fountain flowing from the Medicean rock (meaning Piero; cf. 2.24.3–4n).

25–26. For fit reward, cf. 2.45.69–74 and 2.51.82 and 138. Landino too links Piero with appropriate rewarding of poets (*Xandra* 3.17.152) and of merit in general (l. 138 there).

29–30. Medici patronage secured Landino, already (1457) a tutor of Piero's sons, the Chair of Poetry and Rhetoric in 1458. With 30, cf. Ovid, *Her.* 15.28 and *Am.* 1.15.

31–32. See Introduction (p. viii) for Landino's *Xandra*, second version finalized shortly after the death of Cosimino de' Medici, Cosimo's grandson, in November 1459 (lamented 3.18 there). With 31, cf. 2.1.1 (and Vergil, *Aen.* 1.330). Line 32: 1.1.21–22n.

33–34. Verino's aspirations to follow Landino's lead and closeness to him are here explicitly recognized. Line 34 = [Tibullus] 3.4.78.

35–36. See 1.7.12n.

36. Almost as 1.6.12 and 2.24.8.

1.21

3–4. See 1.6.17–18n and 1.13.5–6n.

5–6. See 1.9.15–16n. Line 5 here and 2.48.13 reflect Propertius 1.18.7.

12. With L's *invidus* (but not B's *lividus*) the last syllable of *opposuit* is lengthened (by diastole) at the dieresis. Cf. 1.8.32 (*eventus*), 2.24.12 (*poteris*), 1.20.8 (*mergebat*, my conjecture), and A's text of 2.51.76 (*capite*). Gildersleeve and Lodge (§785) recognize only four classical instances, in Propertius (*vincis* 2.8.8, *ingenuus* 2.24.2) and Martial (*domuit* 9.102.4, *plorabat* 14.77.2). By contrast, Landino's *Xandra* has over three dozen examples, and the license is readily found in Braccesi and Marullo, among others.

13–16. Fortune's wheel and winning or losing in love: Tibullus 1.5.70; Propertius 2.8.7–8. Cf. also Landino, *Xandra* 3.18.7–8. Fortune was often pictured precariously standing on a ball (Ovid, *Tristia* 5.8.7, *Ex Ponto* 4.3.31–32, etc.).

17–18. The Athenian sage, statesman, and poet Solon (cf. 2.45.21–22n; P. 910–11) was once, according to Herodotus 1.32, the guest of the fabulously wealthy king Croesus of Lydia in Asia Minor, who pointedly asked him whom he considered the most fortunate of men, but Solon did not give the expected answer, explaining that no one should be called fortunate until death had precluded a change of circumstances. Croesus later unwisely attacked the Persians and lost his kingdom (546 BCE). Cf. Ovid, *Met.* 3.134–36 ("One must always wait for a person's last day; no one should be called blessed before death and last funeral rites").

19–22. Verino's *fides* ("faithfulness"): 1.30.31–32n. Landino too stresses his true-heartedness (as *Xandra* 1.5.12, 2.8.52, 2.18.51–52), protesting never-surpassed (but unrewarded) *fides* (*Xandra* 2.5.3–4). Several passages of Propertius (e.g., 2.20) declare *fides*. For *perfida* ("faithless") to Fiammetta, cf. 1.18.15, 1.27.2, 3 and 27; her *perfidia* is denounced in 1.30.19–34.

25–28. Verino's closest model is Landino, *Xandra* 1.29.41–42, where Sandra will give the inspiration (*ingenium*) that jealous nature denies (a detail after Juvenal 1.79). Both poets reflect Ovid, *Am.* 2.17.33–34 ("nor shall any woman but you be sung of in my poems [cf. 35 here]; you alone shall provide the inspiration for my skill") and Propertius 2.1.4 (Cynthia provides the poet's *ingenium*) and 2.30.40. Cf. also Piccolomini, *Cynthia* 1.3–4; Braccesi A 5.43–44 Perosa; and what seems Francesco Tranchedini's poem to Verino cited 1.7n.

33. After Propertius 1.12.20, like Landino, *Xandra* 2.25.86 and Piccolomini, *Cynthia* 1.10.

1.22

4–6. In *Greek Anthology* 5.98 Aphrodite is urged to find another target, "for I have not even any room for a wound."

8–10. Love's slave: 1.10.7–10n. Love's soldier: 1.4.93–94n. Here Verino reflects Ovid, *Am.* 2.9.3–4 (Cupid wounding his own loyal soldier). Munari (p. 298, foot) rightly sees several further debts to that poem in this. *Ambitiose Cupido* (9) is again in 2.22.25 (cf. Ovid, *Am.* 1.1.14).

11–12. Imagery of passion involving the Sicilian volcano Etna (again 2.22.54) includes Ovid, *Her.* 15.12 and *Met.* 13.868–69; Landino, *Xandra* 3.19.4.

15–16. A lover's bones fleshless from wasting (1.4.75–76n): Propertius 4.5.64 and Ovid, *Am.* 2.9.13–14. The lover's paleness: 1.18.37–38n. *Pallor in ore* is also in 2.46.36 (and Landino, *Xandra* 1.4.2, after Ovid, *Met.* 8.801; cf. *Tristia* 3.9.18).

21–24. Adonis was a handsome mortal youth whom Venus loved, killed by a boar. *Adona:* Greek accusative of alternative form *Adon.* For Venus wounded by Cupid, cf. 1.12.22–24.

1.23

2. A lucky day was figuratively "bright" (cf. 2.14.4).

3–4. Sailing imagery: 1.4.24–26n. For the Syrtes (sandbanks off north Africa), cf. 2.40.3.

5–8. Clotho was a Fate (or Parca). Line 6 is almost as 2.22.2. For *livor edax* ("consuming jealousy"; Ovid *Am.* 1.15.1 and *Rem. Am.* 389, where see Henderson's note), cf. 2.5.16, and 2.46.1 and 24. For the Fates accused of jealousy, cf. Landino, *Xandra* 3.7.72.

9–12. Latona's daughter: Diana, also the Moon. If the three months meant are those since the very beginning of Verino's affair, the date implied is not after spring 1458 (1.1.17–18n), but *geminavit* ("doubled") probably indicates a *second* assault (rather than a *twofold* one with both torches and arrows), especially as 1.25.1–2 speaks of succumbing anew after an attempt to break away (and Fiammetta seems to have spent some time elsewhere: see Introduction, p. x).

13. Cf. Ovid, *Fasti* 2.766.

15. Cf. 2.42.31. First four words as Ovid, *Ex Ponto* 4.3.29 (*Met.* 3.641 is similar).

16. After [Tibullus] 3.4.58.

17–18. Plowing the shore (of futile activity): Ovid, *Tristia* 5.4.48, *Ex Ponto*, 4.2.16 and *Her.* 17.139; Juvenal 7.49.

26. Landino, *Xandra* 2.7.62 and 2.23.62 both declare no haughty girl pleasing, however beautiful, the latter context then citing women (like Daphne) punished for scorning deities.

29–30. Niobe's children were slain by Apollo and Diana, because she spoke slightingly of their mother Latona. Niobe was changed into an eternally weeping rock.

31–32. Pentheus, ruler of Thebes, tried to suppress worship of Dionysus (Bacchus, Lyaeus), but the female devotees caught him spying, and his own mother helped tear him apart, thinking him a boar in Ovid's version (*Met.* 3.511–733). *Pentheus*, properly disyllabic, is here three syllables.

37–38. Verino's faithfulness: 1.30.31–32n.

39–40. Cf. Vergil, *Aen.* 10.814–15. Lover's death if response too late: Landino, *Xandra* 1.4.18.

1.24

1–2. Adding fuel to fires: Landino, *Xandra* 1.17.2 and 1.28.22. With 2, cf. Ovid, *Am.* 3.8.46.

3–6. With 3, cf. Ovid, *Ars Am.* 1.451 ("To avoid having lost, the gambler goes on losing"). With the sailing imagery (1.4.24–26n), here cf. Landino, *Xandra* 2.7.27–28 ("But now it is time to shorten sail before the fierce wind; let the weary ship make for port!"). *Votiva* (5) implies pledging the ship, if spared, to a deity (cf. the retired vessel in Catullus 4, with Fordyce's opening comments there).

10. Almost as 2.42.18. Cf. also 2.22.9 and 2.42.2. Knowing (or not) what love is: Theocritus, *Id.* 3.15–16; Vergil, *Ecl.* 8.43; Ovid, *Met.* 13.762; Propertius 2.30.34; [Tibullus] 3.4.73 (etc.). Landino, *Xandra* 1.2.18 (pointedly contradicting Propertius 2.34.24) speaks of not yet knowing "what an affliction it is to be in love" (cf. *Xandra* 1.4.6 and 2.25.10).

13–14. Wasting lover: 1.4.75–76n and 1.22.15–16n.

15–20. See 1.9.15–16n. Cf. Ovid, *Am.* 3.1.17–18 ("Wine-quaffing revels talk of your dissolute behavior [*nequitia*; 1.4.20n], the crossroads . . . tell of it") and 21 ("Without your realizing it, you are the scandal on every tongue in the city"); Propertius 3.25.1–2 (his affair making him a laughingstock at banquets). Line 18 (cf. Propertius 2.24.2): 1.13.3–4n.

21–22. In 2.51.23 and 2.54.2, the *Priori* making up the *Signoria* are (like senators in ancient Rome) *Patres* ("Fathers"; also 2.54.9), as, for instance, in Landino, *Misc. Poems* 2.35 ("Fathers and People"). They are serious minded and censorious in 2.3.

23–24. Cf. 1.28.23–24 and 2.22.43 (and the theme of 1.25). In Ovid, *Met.*

7.19–21 Cupid urges one course on Medea (in love with Jason); her rational mind, another. She declares, "I see and approve the better course, but follow the worse."

1.25

1–6. See previous note. Servitude to a girl: 1.10.7–10n. *Subdere colla iugo* ("to submit the neck to the yoke" [2]; cf. 2.51.48) is also (erotically) in Landino, *Xandra* 1.3.38 and Piccolomini, *Cynthia* 16.8 (and cf. Braccesi A 4.12 Perosa). Love's yoke anciently: Ovid, *Rem. Am.* 90; Propertius 2.5.14, 3.6.2, and 3.11.4; Tibullus 1.4.16.

8. After Ovid, *Ars Am.* 2.708.

11–12. Parthian horse archers shot a final arrow on turning to ride off. *Letalis harundo* ("deadly shaft"): Vergil, *Aen.* 4.73.

13–14. Landino, *Xandra* 2.9.1 also declares Love wrongly thought blind.

16. Almost as 2.22.18.

17–20. Colchian maid (17): Medea (1.4.63–66n). Line 20 ends as Landino, *Xandra* 2.7.8.

21–22. Circe (daughter of the Sun, 25), here addressed, and her "guest" Odysseus/Ulysses (26): 1.4.67–70n. Pelasgian (cf. 2.45.21): Greek. Line 22 almost = 2.49.14.

23–24. In Vergil, *Aen.* 4.513–14, "herbs cut with brazen sickles by moonlight" supposedly have special powers to free one of love.

25–26. "Plowed the waters": Ovid, *Met.* 4.706 (cf. Vergil, *Aen.* 5.158; Ovid, *Ex Ponto* 2.10.33).

27–30. The Thunderer's (Jupiter's) son: Hercules. His Labors included slaying the Nemean Lion (cf. 1.9.37–38) and the Hydra of Lerna (a seven-headed water snake), as well as dragging up from the Underworld the three-headed dog Cerberus ("the dog of Tartarus," also in 2.50.16 and Landino, *Xandra* 1.4.12), but he succumbed to love for Omphale (becoming her slave). *Nemaei* (cf. 2.51.123) illicitly has first syllable long.

33–34. Apollo serving Admetus: 1.4.71–74n. Tibullus 2.3.23–28 speaks of Apollo's barely recognizable, unkempt looks while living, at Love's bidding, in a small cottage. Line 34 ends as Ovid, *Ars Am.* 2.239–40. Tito Vespasiano Strozzi, *Erotica* 4.1.37–58 describes Apollo's service at length.

42. Last five words as Ovid, *Am.* 3.12.5, and Propertius 2.8.6.

43–44. Cf. Horace, *Odes* 3.9.4 ("happier than a [proverbially wealthy] Persian king"). In *Xandra* 1.5.15–16, 2.3.23–26, and 2.26.12 Landino rejects Persian riches for having Sandra's love or being the Muses' friend. Line 44 ends as Ovid, *Am.* 2.10.33 begins.

45–46. "Wretched" ambition: Horace, *Sat.* 1.6.129. Cf. 2.31.5. *Flamma* (and *Flammea* in 47) for *Flammetta*: 1.4n and 1.4.100n (see also 2.26n).

48. Cf. Ovid, *Am.* 1.1.28.

1.26

2–4. The second and third omens are from Terence, *Phormio* 706–7; the first may reflect Ovid's "birds not white" in *Am.* 3.12.2.

9–10. Line 9 begins as Vergil, *Aen.* 2.268, and Ovid, *Fasti* 5.497. With *Aurora* for the manuscripts' *auriga* ("charioteer"; see Munari, p. 304), it ends as Vergil, *Aen.* 6.535 (cf. 1.11.1 above). "Old Phrygian" (Trojan): Tithonus (1.6.29–32n). The time (cf. 1.11.1–3, 1.20.5–8, 2.48.1–2) is just before dawn, the hour of the evil dream in [Tibullus] 3.4 (a source here). Ovid, *Her.* 19.195–96 regards dreams then as usually true.

11–12. Cf. [Tibullus] 3.4.1–2.

13–14. Erato: Muse of love poetry (cf. 2.48.4, 2.55.11). "slighted lover": 2.49.19–20n.

17–20. Jupiter here = the Christian God. *Ille opifex rerum* (cf. P. 470): Ovid, *Met.* 1.79. In 19, Munari (p. 303) suggests *esse* for *esset*, with colon before *sibimet* ("He is the Maker of the Universe: being opposed to him, that is making war on the gods!"). *Contrarius* would, however, be ungrammatical (for accusative *contrarium*; Gildersleeve and Lodge, §420), and, though *sibi* often = *ei* in medieval and neo-Latin (as in 30 and often elsewhere in this work), *sibimet* used nonreflexively seems most unlikely. The sense with *esset* is that by opposing the *series rerum* ("succession of things [events]"), God would be thwarting himself as *Opifex rerum* ("the

Maker of things [the universe]"). *Series rerum*: Cicero, *ND* 1.4.9 (cf. Vergil, *Aen.* 1.641). In *Div.* 1.55.125, Cicero defines fate as "the order and succession of causes (*series causarum*)"; Aulus Gellius (6.2.1) calls it "a certain eternal succession of events (*series rerum*) and a chain." Pico della Mirandola, *Eleg.* 2.16 speaks of "a succession (*series*) and immutable order of fate." Cf. *fatorum series* in P. 184. Line 20 ends as Landino, *Xandra* 1.3.48.

21–22. With 21, cf. Ovid, *Met.* 3.405; with 22, *Her.* 7.142.

24. "Old Bruno" (if real) is unidentified. Like Perosa (p. 52) I take *Brunus* as the forename *Bruno*, not the surname *Bruni*.

28. Ending almost as Propertius 2.22.40 (and Landino, *Xandra* 2.7.32).

31. Opening words as Vergil, *Aen.* 5.693 and *Ciris* 283.

37–38. Cf. Landino, *Xandra* 2.11.9–12 (also a "nightmare" poem rebuking Sleep) for pain felt by day felt again by night. Sleep as *ignavus* ("sluggish"; cf. 43): Ovid, *Met.* 11.593; [Tibullus] 3.4.81.

41–42. *Simulacra modis pallentia miris* ("strangely pale phantoms") in Vergil, *Geo.* 1.477 suggests taking *tam miris modis* with *horrida* rather than *terrent*.

45. The (masculine or feminine) Greek word *barbitos*, generally masculine in the singular in Latin, is used with the feminine adjective *ulla* in Ovid, *Her.* 15.8. An unacceptable variant there is *barbiton* (Greek neuter form, used in Braccesi A 22.5 Perosa), though Landino, *Xandra* 3.17.8 and Verino here treat *barbiton ulla* as legitimate, while in 2.50.44 Verino has a feminine participle with neuter *barbiton*. In *Carlias* 7.45 he similarly has neuter *barbiton* with a feminine adjective. See A. Perosa, "Critica congetturale e testi umanistici," *Rinascimento* 1 3–4 (1950): 360–63, and p. 53 of his 1941 review.

47. Erinys, really a general word for "Fury," here seems treated as an individual's name (like Alecto, Megaera, or Tisiphone).

1.27

Fiammetta answers Verino's charges here in 1.29.16–30.

1–2. *Perfida* ("faithless") to Fiammetta: 1.21.19–22n. Braccesi so rebukes Flora repeatedly (in a refrain) in his equivalent poem, A 30 Perosa.

3–4. "So sacred a love": Propertius 2.29.41.

5. B's *improba* (favored by Munari) more closely echoes Vergil, *Aen.* 4.386, *dabis, improbe, poenas* (Dido to Aeneas) than *L's impia* (if read, repeated in 6, like *perfida* in 2–3).

9–10. Verino hints violence or perhaps suicide, expressly envisaged by Piccolomini, *Cynthia* 23.85–86: "Nay, rather may I die, and it is better to end my life with my right hand. Away! Now I will follow you [seemingly Cupid] where my anger may will it." Both imitate Ovid, *Her.* 12.209 ("I will follow where my anger leads"), where the betrayed Medea (1.4.63–66n) threatens Jason. Tito Vespasiano Strozzi, *Erotica* 4.25.21–26 speaks of nearly murdering his forsworn, unfaithful girl in jealous fury, while in 5.2.155–68 he briefly contemplates suicide to excite pity.

14. Cf. 1.30.26 (and 1.30.21–30 with the whole passage here).

16. Cf. 1.30.21–28 and 2.49.19f. (with note). Verino inconsistently combines pagan and Christian thought in speaking here and in those passages of the divine witness and lover-avenger, posing problems for the editor and translator. In 2.49.1f. *deus* ("a god"), not *Deus* ("God"), is clearly right. Here, with the oath in church to follow (where *Numen* in 21 is firmly Christian), the context may appear to favor *Deo*, but we awkwardly have plural "gods" in 13–15. The mention of the divine witness in 1.30.21 seems to look back to this present passage, but the same line also makes (pagan) reference to the lover-avenging deity, who then seems to shift toward fusing with the Christian God in the lines there following.

17. Santa Maria del Carmine (in Verino's quarter of Santo Spirito).

21–22. *Numen*: Christ? *Tu meus unus eris* is also in Pontano, *Parthenopaeus* 1.10.173 and 174.

23–24. Verino's faithfulness: 1.30.31–32n. Line 24 (like 1.6.26 and 2.4.12) is after Propertius 2.20.18.

25–26. Cf. Ovid, *Her.* 19.17 (ending *sola voluptas*, as Landino, *Xandra* 1.29.7) and (for 26) Propertius 1.11.22. *Esse = vivere* ("live"); cf. 1.30.4.

29. Last four words as Ovid, *Am.* 1.7.57.

33. *Varium* and *mutabile* of womankind: Vergil, *Aen.* 4.569.

38. Ovid, *Am.* 1.8.104 ("wicked poisons lie hidden beneath sweet honey")

is imitated also by Landino, *Xandra* 1.3.40; Piccolomini, *Cynthia* 23.90; Michele Verino, *Disticha Ethica* 41.2.

1.28

The addressee (also 2.29) is Lottieri (Lottari, Lotteri) di Nigi Neroni (1.1n). His uncle was Gonfaloniere di Giustizia in 1453. See Cosenza (*Biographical and Bibliographical Dictionary of the Italian Humanists* [Boston, 1962]). Involvement in the anti-Medici conspiracy of 1466 saw the treacherous Dietisalvi (Diotisalvi) Neroni (P. 208–76n), once Cosimo's trusted friend, and some others of his family exiled. Cosenza records Marsilio Ficino (1433–99) as Lottieri Neroni's teacher and friend and says that Verino too taught him, though he seems Verino's contemporary in this work. He is attested from the early 1460s to 1481 (in 1462 he compiled his *Excerpts from Cicero's Letters*). In manuscripts summarized in Kristeller's *Iter Italicum*, he writes to Braccesi (4:100) and (in 1468 and 1474) to Lorenzo de' Medici (4:111) and receives correspondence from others in 1471 (1:74) and 1481 (1:109).

1–2. Propertius 2.8.1–2 similarly complains that his beloved girl is being taken from him, and yet his addressee tells him not to weep. "Ugly old man": Bruno. *Flammea*: 1.4.100n.

6–16. Fiammetta is addressed in apostrophe until, with *tune* in 16, Verino reverts to addressing Neroni. See 1.6.17–18n.

7. After Propertius 2.8.4.

9–10. With 9, cf. Ovid, *Am.* 3.8.11–12; with 10, Ovid, *Her.* 8.114.

11. *Pedore* is a false form for *paedore*.

13–14. With 13, cf. Ovid, *Am.* 3.8.18; with 14 (especially *iacent*), *Her.* 4.150.

17. Scythia vaguely denotes the expanses north of the Black Sea. The textually uncertain line substituted in the margin of *B* (see Notes on the Texts) seems to say, "But may I sooner be bidden depart to the Scythian . . . than (etc.)." The missing word could perhaps be *arva* ("lands"). If, alternatively, it is *arctos*, the literal sense is "Bears," standing for the north.

22. Love is too *imperiosus* ("tyrannical" or "domineering") in Landino,

Xandra 2.5.16 (his tyranny is then described). Cf. also Braccesi A 1.23 Perosa.

23–24. See 1.24.23–24n.

1.29

Now married, Fiammetta has refused to continue seeing Verino. Reflecting (for the reader) on her words, he reluctantly agrees to leave her alone. Landino, *Xandra* Earlier Redaction 40.9–50, a long quoted denunciation of him by Sandra (for betraying her), and Tito Vespasiano Strozzi, *Erotica* 5.2.33–130, reporting his girl's answer to allegations of faithlessness, similarly allow the girl the principal say.

1–2. For Verino's aspirations to marry Fiammetta, cf. 16 and 1.27.19.

5–6. *Salvo . . . pudore* ("without impropriety," as 2.43.51): Ovid, *Ex Ponto* 1.2.66. With 6, cf. 1.6.17.

8. Ovid's reputation is "buried" (by exile) in *Ex Ponto* 1.5.85.

11–12. Cf. Ovid, *Her.* 17.31 (Theseus' *modestia* in taking only kisses from Helen).

14. Cf. Ovid, *Her.* 15.184.

16–22. See 1.27.17–26 for Fiammetta's vow to wed Verino. Here (18 and 25) it emerges that her father had already promised her to Bruno. *Aenigmata iuris* (19) as 1.2.25.

23–24. Cf. how *bene* is used in Ovid, *Am.* 1.2.10.

29–30. Cf. Cicero, *Tusc.* 4.35.75 ("Some consider that an old love has to be driven out by a new one, as a nail by a nail"), and Girolamo Balbi (d. 1535) in *Carmina* 2:12 ("As nail drives out nail, so a second love drives out love, and a new flame old torches"). Ovid, *Her.* 19.104 envisages a new love ending an earlier one (cf. also *Rem. Am.* 462).

1.30

21–26. Cf. 2.49.19–20 (and note there), and see also 1.27.16n. In Piccolomini, *Cynthia* 13.6 the epitaph of a wicked lover eventually struck down finishes, "Though the anger of those above is late in coming, it does not pass over the wicked" (cf. Francesco Filelfo as cited 2.49.19–20n). *Flam-*

mea Virgo (24): 1.4.100n. For "giving words to" = deceiving (26), cf. 1.27.14.

27–28. Jupiter here seems to stand for the Christian God, but see 1.27.16n.

31–32. *Fidus* ("faithful") of Verino: 1.27.23–24, 2.42.39; P. 707. He stresses his *fides* ("faithfulness") also in 1.6.26–48, 1.10.34, 1.18.29, 1.21.20, and 1.23.37 and speaks of himself as *verus* ("true") in 2.15.4 and P. 708. See also 1.21.19–22n. Propertius 3.25.3–4 predicts that Cynthia will regret mistreating a lover of his faithfulness.

33. Cf. Vergil, *Ecl.* 5.89.

BOOK II

2.1

Cf. Ovid, *Am.* 1.1 (beginning *Qui modo*), where Cupid stops the poet from turning to grander verse (also *Ex Ponto* 3.3.31–32).

1. Cf. 1.20.31.

3–4. *Cothurni*, tragic actors' buskins (cf. 9 and P. 942), here symbolize lofty style. See 1.12.1–4n.

5–6. Cf. Landino's declared plans noticed 1.1.21–22n (and the progression from love poetry to celebration of Piero announced in *Xandra* 3.1ff.). Maro: Vergil.

7–8. After Ovid, *Tristia* 2.329–30, where, deeming himself unequal to praise of Augustus, Ovid says a little boat should not entrust itself to the open sea, even if it risks venturing out on a tiny lake. Cf. also Propertius 3.9.35–36; Landino, *Xandra* 2.23.33–34; Naldi, *Eleg.* 3.3.9ff. Sailing imagery: 1.4.24–26n. Thetis, Achilles' mother, a sea nymph, here = the sea (cf. Vergil, *Ecl.* 4.32). For *Thetim*, cf. the acc. forms in *m* not *n* in 17, 20, 25, and 27. See 2.2.9–10n.

9–10. Aeschylus was noted for grandeur of diction ("Aeschylus' buskin": Propertius 2.34.41). Love's soldier (also 33–36): 1.4.93–94n. *Eris* is probably future indicative for imperative (cf. 1.19.2, 2.7.11, 2.18.11, 2.39.13).

13–14. For poets' immortality cf., for example, Ovid, *Am.* 1.15.7–30 with its list of bards. Line 14 ends as Ovid, *Am.* 1.10.62.

15. "Phoebus' love" means poetry.

17–18. Reflecting a discredited interpretation of Ovid *Tristia* 1.6.1, Verino treats a work (mostly lost) lamenting the death of Lyde (the poet's mistress) as by Callimachus, though really by Antimachus of Colophon (cf. Propertius 2.34.45), as Politian knew (*Silva* 4.355–57). Landino, *Xandra* 2.4.1 likewise speaks of "Callimachus" and his lady (meaning Lyde). Phaon: 1.4.57–58n.

19–20. Lycoris was the mistress of Gaius Cornelius Gallus (see especially Vergil, *Ecl.* 10), whose poetry is lost. First Roman governor of Egypt, he was recalled and banished, dying by suicide.

21. Propertius is *blandus* in Ovid (Naso), *Tristia* 2.465 and 5.1.17.

23. Lesbia: Catullus' mistress.

25–26. Alexis (Vergil, *Ecl.* 2.1, etc.) was often thought to represent a real youth beloved of Vergil. See Robert Coleman's (Cambridge, 1977) edition of *Eclogues*, pp. 108–9. The Phrygian (Trojan) leader (26) is Aeneas, with allusion to Vergil's *Aeneid*.

27–28. Horace, born in Venosa (cf. 2.23.1), had a mistress Lalage. Line 28 alludes to his *Satires*.

29–30. Petrarch (Francesco Petrarca, 1300–74), born in Arezzo, wrote sonnets (in Italian) of the (French) Laura.

32. Lethe: 1.7.12n.

33–34. *Volitantis . . . Amoris*: Tibullus 2.5.39. For *signa tulisse*, cf. *signa feret*, Horace, *Odes* 4.1.16.

43. After Ovid, *Am.* 1.9.31, denying the lover a feeble-spirited, idle languisher (*desidiosus*).

46. See 1.4.20n.

2.2

In language appropriate to a discharged soldier recalled to the colors, Verino complains of being made to fall in love again, presumably (here and in 2.22) with Lisia (2.50). Love's soldier: 1.4.93–94n. Cupid's triumph: Ovid, *Am.* 1.2.19ff. (Munari, p. 298, rightly notes many debts to that elegy here.)

7–8. Cf. Ovid, *Am.* 2.9.15–16 (and Landino, *Xandra* 2.9.13–18).

9–10. Thyle (or Thule, also 2.40.7; cf. Landino, *Xandra* 2.26.3–4, where *Thyles*, Greek genitive) was vaguely north of Britain. The manuscripts here have the spelling *Thilem* (likewise both manuscripts at *P.* 52), and *Thylem* is a reading in Braccesi A 17.50 (1) Perosa (apparatus criticus). Both *Thylem* and *Thylen* are found in manuscripts of Claudian, where the accusative occurs thrice. Cf. the *m* forms in 2.1.7 (*Thetim*), 17 (*Lydem*), 20 (*Nemesim*), 25 (*Alexim*), and 27 (*Lalagem*). In Vergil, *Ecl.* 4.32 editions vary between *Thetin* and *Thetim*. The Sarmatians lived between the Vistula in Poland and the Don. Line 9 begins as Ovid, *Am.* 1.2.37.

13–14. Mars as Cupid's "stepfather" (i.e., his mother Venus' paramour): Ovid, *Am.* 1.2.24 and 2.9.47.

18. After Ovid, *Am.* 1.2.34, and Tibullus 2.5.118. For *Io triumphe*, cf. also Horace, *Odes* 2.2.49–50.

19–20. In a triumph, "wagons" (floats) bore representations of the scenes of victory and the like. "Mother's doves": Ovid, *Am.* 1.2.23.

25–26. After Ovid, *Am.* 1.2.22 ("vanquished with arms, unarmed myself"). Cf. 2.22.11 below (with 2.22.9–12n); Landino, *Xandra* 1.2.19 (*armatus inermem*). Love as servitude: 1.10.7–10n.

27. Cf. Ovid, *Am.* 1.2.45.

36–37. Propertius 2.30.24–25 seems the inspiration.

38. Ovid uses *sine labe* ("without blemish") of his own life in several places, as *Ex Ponto* 1.2.145 and 2.7.49, and *Tristia* 4.8.33, while *Tristia* 1.9.43 is similar. See 1.2.43–44n.

2.3

See 1.3n.

1. The "House of the Tyrrhenian Lion" is the *Curia* ("Senate-House," *Palazzo della Signoria*; 2.47.5, 2.51.23, and 2.54.2, with 2.51.23–24n), to which submission of the book seems envisaged.

3–4. Cato: 1.2.41–42n and *P.* 874n. *Parve liber* (little [= young] book; cf. *tener libelle* in 1.3.1): Ovid, *Tristia* 1.1.1; Martial 3.5.2 (with *lascive* in 11); Landino, *Xandra* 1.2.2 and 1.13.25 (similarly *parve libelle* in *Xandra* 2.23.38

and Earlier Redaction II.1). Giovan Battista Cantalizio (*Carmina* 3:123) warns his book, eager to rush off to Florence's learned circle, "There you will find one who will note your errors of expression and one to receive your jokes with humorless ear and be sarcastic about them. There are Aristotles there and stern Platos, and both Latin Catos give censorious judgment." Cantalizio's book is told to go to Cosimo's house for its one hope of finding a defender, as a Maecenas there (probably Piero; cf.1.19.5–6n) will give it a sympathetic reception.

5. Ovid, *Am.* 1.13.3 begins comparably.

8. Cf. the "venerable/grave Fathers" of 1.24.22.

2.4

Mencaraglia loses some of B's title. See *Michaelis Marulli Carmina*, ed. A. Perosa (Zürich, 1951), p. 237, for Benedetto Biliotti, identified by Perosa (with references) as the astrologer whose death is noted with irony by Marullo (ca. 1453–1500), *Epigrams* 4.16 (*On the astrologer Biliotti*): "On guard against the stars for friends facing death, but not against mushrooms (*boleti*) for himself, the astrologer perished." His bride Lisia's family, the Pitti, like the Neroni (1.28 and 2.29), were involved in the thwarted 1466 conspiracy against Piero de' Medici (P. 312–24n), Luca Pitti being one of the chief plotters.

1–2. Venus is invoked as goddess of love; Juno, as goddess of weddings (Juno Pronuba); Apollo, as god of poetry and music.

4. Gorgon's waters (Hippocrene): 1.1.19–20n.

5. Bellona: Mars' sister, a war goddess.

8. Hymen, or Hymenaeus, was the marriage god.

9–10. Megaera was one of the Furies. For their snaky hair, cf. 1.17.9–10.

12. See 1.27.23–24n.

15–16. After Ovid, *Tristia* 4.10.81. Keeping joys within a silent breast: Propertius 2.25.30.

19–20. Cf. Ovid, *Fasti* 6.659. Rope dancing: Terence, *Ad.* 4.7.34; cf. also Livy 27.37.

2.5

Albiera (Albera), a young mother ("barely twenty," 2.6.5) formerly celebrated by Bartolomeo Scala, cannot be Albiera degli Albizzi (d. 1473), lamented in poems of Politian, Naldi, Scala, Verino (*Epigrammi*, ed. Bausi, 476–81 and 595–601), and others, though some have assumed that identification, rightly rejected by Alison Brown, *Bartolomeo Scala 1430–1497, Chancellor of Florence, The Humanist as Bureaucrat* (Princeton, 1979), p. 273. She is the (unidentified) Alba whom Naldo Naldi (2.26n) celebrates as his first love for nine years from when he was fourteen (*Eleg.* 1.16.15ff.; see 1.1.17–18n and Lazzari, pp. 41–42). Lazzari quotes Naldi's *Eleg.* 1.27.9ff.: "She [Alba] was snatched away in first youth, as an unfriendly beam fell on her tender head. What effort would it have been, household gods, to hold up the collapsing wall long enough for the dear girl to make her escape?" As Naldi (by Grant's dating; see 2.26n) reached fourteen on August 31, 1450 (three years later by Lazzari's reckoning), (the younger?) Alba could (loosely) be "barely twenty" in the very early 1460s. Yet Verino names Scala, not Naldi, as Albiera's poet. Bartolomeo Scala (or della Scala) di Colle di Val d'Elsa (1430–97), in Florence from 1450, rose through Medici patronage to be Chancellor (1465). See Brown, op. cit.; Lazzari, pp. 48–49; and C. Kidwell, *Marullus, Soldier Poet of the Renaissance* (London, 1989), especially pp. 178–83 (Michele Marullo married Scala's daughter). In his *De ill. urbis Flor.* (fol. 13, Paris 1583 edition; *Carmina* 10:345; also Brown, p. 210) Verino notices Scala's history of Florence and his lost Lucretius-inspired didactic poem *De rebus naturalibus*. The same works (and Scala's *Apologues*) are lauded in a letter to Verino from his son, Michele (Brown, p. 209). See also Brown, p. 131n. Landino addresses Scala in *Xandra* 1.4, 1.23, and 1.24. Perosa (p. 51) observes that this poem and 2.6 are noticed by Isidoro del Lungo, *La donna fiorentina del buon tempo antico* (Florence, 1926), pp. 243–44. Both poems are cited by Giovanni Zannoni, "Un' elegia di Angelo Poliziano," *Rendiconti della R. Accademia dei Lincei*, ser. 5, 2 (1894): 153–54 (see Brown, p. 273 n. 55).

8. Worded similarly to Landino, *Xandra* 2.8.2.

11. Vergil, *Aen.* 8.192 ends *ingentem traxere ruinam*.

12. *Protegit* illicitly has *pro-* short. I find no classical instance, though *procuro*, for example, has *pro-* short in Tibullus 1.5.13 and Ovid, *Ars Am.* 1.587

and *Fasti* 3.331. Some compounds beginning *pro* regularly shorten the *o*, especially before a vowel or *f*; Gildersleeve and Lodge, §715.4. Alba dies to save her tiny son in 19ff. of Naldi's poem.

13. The manuscripts have *occidit* (perhaps rightly), but I venture to read (the more alliterative) *concidit* in pathetic epanalepsis (cf. *gesta* in 2.1.5–6).

16. See 1.23.5–8n.

18–20. See 2.51.68n. "Your poet": 1.4.1n.

21–22. Elysian retreats: 1.6.33–34n. Dis: Pluto (the Jupiter of the Lower World in 24 and 2.51.132), whose wife was his niece, Ceres' young daughter Proserpina (or Persephone); 1.9.33–34n.

2.6

See 2.5n.

1–2. *Lector* ("reader") is the wayfarer (cf. 2.50.53–56) often imagined reading inscriptions. Line 1 follows Propertius 1.17.11. In 2 (and 2.7.6), *L* and *B* have *numve*, favored by Perosa (*numne* Mencaraglia), though it seems anciently unattested. In Gildersleeve and Lodge, §456n, *numne* is noted as perhaps only in Cicero, *ND* 1.31.88 and *Lael.* 11.36 (both passages disputed; Plautus, *Truc.* 2.6.65 is sometimes added). Unable to parallel either reading elsewhere in neo-Latin, I (uneasily) prefer *numne*.

7–8. *Lector amice* ("dear reader"): Ovid, *Tristia* 3.1.2; Martial 5.16.2.

2.7

Verino sends his Muse (verses) to Piero Capponi in Rome, hoping to elicit a reply. Cf. 2.17, 2.18, and 2.41. Landino has comparable pieces in *Xandra*, e.g., 2.29 (cf. Earlier Redaction 11). The general inspiration comes from various poems of Ovid and Martial to their books, or Muses, when about to be sent off. Interest in preserving Rome's ancient remains rose under Pope Pius II (Piccolomini), whose bull of April 28, 1462, tried to check despoliation of them. The Capponi were prominent in Verino's Santo Spirito quarter. R. Goldthwaite, *Private Wealth in Renaissance Florence: A Study of Four Families* (Princeton, 1968), has a family tree (p. 188), and F. W. Kent (1.10n) speaks of them. Landino, Misc. Poems 2, eulogizes Neri di Gino Capponi (1388–1457). If the (uncertain) addressee here is (perhaps) Piero di Gino Capponi (1446–96; Goldthwaite, pp. 210ff.), he would still be a teenager. A Medici ally, he later became a leading banker and Gonfaloniere di Giustizia, stood up to Charles VIII of France in 1494, and died in the Pisan War. He had a remote cousin Piero di Giovanni (1420–1506). A third Piero, from another branch of the family, died in 1480. Cf. 1.1n.

1–2. *Clio* (2), properly two longs, is here long-short (short-long, 2.41.16). Verino shortens nominative endings in *o* in some other names, such as *Apollo* and *Cupido* (both several times in *Fiammetta*, after Martial; cf. also P. preface 4), and *Cato* (2.13.13); so too *Colleo* in P. 225.

3–6. Diana had a temple on the Aventine hill; Apollo, on the Palatine; Jupiter's temple on the Capitol was particularly famous. The Esquiline lacked comparable associations. Mencaraglia takes the *an* clauses as indirect (perhaps correctly).

5–6. See 2.6.1–2n. *Se Iuppiter ornat* (5): Propertius 3.9.15. Cf. Landino, *Xandra* 2.30.13–14.

8. Almost as Landino, *Xandra* 2.30.4.

10. *Domos* (normally dwelling "houses") denotes the temples. Cf. Landino, *Xandra* 2.30.8.

2.8

The Florentine painter Apollonio di Giovanni (di Tomaso), 1415/16–65, was noted for his cassone panels (1.10n) and illustrations of Vergil's *Aeneid* in manuscripts. In addition to Dionisotti's comments (p. 176 footnote, with references to Paul Schubring's *Cassoni, Truhen und Truhenbilder der italienischen Frührenaissance* [Leipzig, 1915]), and the entry on *Apollonio* in Grove's *Dictionary of Art*, ed. Jane Turner, vol. 2 (1996), see especially Gombrich, "Apollonio di Giovanni" (details in Bibliography). Finding three of the scenes here described on two extant cassone panels and two more of them in Apollonio's illustrations in a Vergil manuscript, Gombrich speculates that this poem attests a single large-scale lost painting by Apollonio that included depictions of the same events. A *tabella* (14; "*the* painting" or "*a* painting"?) is, however, normally small, and several distinct pictures are probably here described. Cristelle Baskins, *Cassone Painting, Humanism and Gender in Early Modern Italy* (Cambridge, 1998), pp. 16–17 and 50ff. includes illustrations of Apollonio's work (and Gombrich's translation of this poem).

1–2. *Maeonides* ("the Maeonian," or else "son of Maeon"): Homer (cf. 2.24.1 and 2.55.24). Apollo supposedly helped build Troy.

3–4. "Maro's grand work": Vergil's *Aeneid. Danai* ("Danaans"): Greeks.

5–6. Apelles: 2.45.103–4n. *Pergamon* (Troy's citadel): Greek accusative. *Apollonius* (6) illicitly has the second *o* short (correctly long in 14). Troy in flames and Aeneas' flight (7) are scenes from *Aeneid* 2.

7–10. Juno's anger (7): Vergil, *Aen.* 1.4 (*Iunonis iniquae: Aen.* 8.292). *Quassas . . . rates* ("battered ships") in 8 adapts *Aen.* 4.53. Neptune's calming of the sea: *Aen.* 1.124ff. *Freta versa* (10): *Aen.* 5.141.

11–14. Faithful Achates: Vergil, *Aen.* 1.192 and 8.521 (1.316 ends *comitatus Achate*). *Dissimulanter* ("secretly," 12): Aeneas entered Dido's Carthage enveloped in a mist provided by Venus (*Aen.* 1.412ff.). *Phoenissa* in 12 (*Aen.* 1.674 and 718) and *Elissa* in 13 (*Aen.* 4.335): Dido, who killed herself when abandoned by Aeneas (*Aen.* 4.663–705). Line 14 ends as Martial 7.84.2.

2.9

Cipriano, in 2.34 a malicious, sly, and untrustworthy person shunned by Verino, is unidentified. Several Florentines of that forename occur at this period. *B's* title of 2.34 describes the addressee there as Cipriano For., which Mencaraglia thinks a slip for *Flor*, i.e., *Florentinum*, though in the titles of 2.12 and 2.21, *B* abbreviates *Florentinum* to *Flo*, not *Flor*. Perhaps "For." could be the start of Cipriano's surname (cf. *be* in *B's* title of 2.31). The name of the poet Bastiano Foresi, a member of Ficino's circle, comes to mind. Poem 2.20 attacks its unnamed addressee in similar terms.

5. After Martial 7.76.6. That poem chiefly inspired this one.

2.10

Amerigo di Bartolomeo Corsini, born 1442 of good Florentine lineage (Bottiglioni, Cosenza, and Mencaraglia wrongly say 1452, but no child here or in 2.27.6), Gonfaloniere di Giustizia 1488, a member of Ficino's circle and a friend of Cosimo de' Medici, died 1501. Naldo Naldi has poems addressed to him (*Eleg.* 1.8, 2.18, and 2.29; 2.27n). See Bottiglioni, p. 42ff. (with brief bibliography), Lazzari, p. 46, and the long entry in *DBI*. Among other things (including love elegies), Corsini wrote a surviving three-book poem on Cosimo de' Medici, noticed by Verino, *De ill. urbis Flor.* (fol. 13v, Paris 1583 edition; *Carmina* 10:346): "Furthermore Corsini has sung of Cosimo's achievements in grandiloquent style." Verino's attitude to male homosexuality: 2.19n. Comparably hostile, Landino, *Xandra* Earlier Redaction 39 rebukes a *paedicator* ("sodomite") for presuming to censure him for burning for young girls. The Office of the Night (established 1432) sought to suppress (prevalent) male homosexuality in Florence.

2. Attis (variously spelled), the Phrygian shepherd beloved of Cybele who became her priest but dishonored his vow of chastity and in madness castrated himself (Catullus 63, etc.), here denotes an effeminate youth. Verino's spelling *Athis* (so manuscripts) shortens the first syllable; Ovid and Catullus use *Attis* (first syllable long).

5–10. Ganymede: P. 27–28n. Here "the love of a Phrygian Ganymede" (Ovid, *Met.* 10.155) means pederasty. Execution for sodomy (10) was possible in Verino's day, though lesser punishments such as fines were regular in Florence. Braccesi, *Epigrammata* 37 Perosa, on a man burned alive for that offense, ends, "Then, you who read this, fly boys, if you are wise!" Naldi, *Epigr.* 174 speaks of public burning for pederasty.

2.11

"Eloquent" Lorenzo Lippi (ca. 1440–85) was born in Colle di Val d'Elsa (province of Siena). He studied in Florence, later teaching oratory and poetics at Pisa (1473–79 and 1482–85), and translated Oppian from Greek. Bartolomeo Scala (same birthplace; 2.5n) and Nicodemo Tranchedini (1.7n) were among his friends (like Verino), and he impressed Cosimo, Piero, and Lorenzo de' Medici. Naldi addresses him (*Eleg.* 2.14; Lazzari, p. 49). See Bottiglioni, pp. 100–104, and *DBI*.

2. *De iusto* = "justly" (as *de improviso* = "unexpectedly," and *de integro* = "anew").

2.12

In theme partly after Petronius, *Satyricon* 6, where Encolpius, lost and unable to find his inn, asks an old woman directions. Unexpectedly conducted to a brothel, he makes a prompt getaway.

3–4. *Nonaria* (Persius 1.133) literally means "a ninth-hour girl" (in Persius' day Roman law forbade earlier soliciting).

6. Last four words as Landino, *Xandra* 3.4.48. Cf. 2.51.126 below.

7–8. *Cellula* means a private cubicle within a brothel (so *cella* in Petronius 8; Martial 11.45.1; Juvenal 6.122 and 128). In Juvenal 6.131–32, the empress Messalina is "befouled with the smoke of the lamp" after an energetic night's service as a prostitute. *Carcer* ("dungeon"): Juvenal 10.239.

9–10. The original Thais (Greek accusative *Thaida*) was a celebrated courtesan of ancient Athens.

12 and 13. *Fertis* is a very bold present indicative for imperative *ferte*, an unclassical license.

15–16. Landino, *Xandra* 2.29.12 speaks of Florence's *lustra lupae* ("she-wolf dens"). *Calidus* ("hot") of a brothel: Juvenal 6.121.

2.13

B's title makes the addressee Braccio Martelli (1442–1513). As line 10 seemingly implies a date not after January 1458 (1.1.17–18n), he would be in mid-teens here. Verino, at eighteen or nineteen, would be pleading youth to someone still younger (though cf. 1.1.15), represented as (unfairly) disparaging his morals, hating him, looking down on him socially (4 and 17), and despising poetry (21–22); yet Cosenza's entry on Braccio Martelli calls him Verino's pupil. Braccio Martelli wrote numerous books (from 1461). He was a friend of Naldo Naldi and Ficino and close to Lorenzo de' Medici, with whom he many times corresponded. In *Eleg.* 1.26 Naldi explains to Martelli why he cannot then write cheery poems (Alba's death: 2.5n), as Martelli urges (hardly hostility to poetry), but will praise Martelli's Marietta when able. Alessandro Braccesi addresses Martelli as his "eloquent companion" in A 24.2 Perosa. Does B's title somehow name the wrong Martelli, or did Braccio's relations with Verino (and attitude to poetry) improve? Verino's detractors: 2.46n.

1–2. See 1.2.43–44n. *Sine crimine mores* ("blameless character") is a variant ending in 2.36.3. Ovid, *Am.* 1.2.13 includes good faith and *sine crimine mores* (also *Her.* 20.225) among his qualities.

5–6. Some poems in this collection *are* personal attacks (e.g., 2.9, 2.16, 2.28, 2.32, 2.34, etc.), perhaps written later.

8. After Martial 1.4(5).8 (1.2.43–44n).

11. See 1.1.17–18n.

13–14. Cato: 1.2.41–42n; *P.* 874–75n. Curius (also 2.32.5 and 11, 2.51.50; *P.* 858): Manius Curius Dentatus (Horace, *Odes* 1.12.41), who defeated various enemies of Rome, including Pyrrhus, 290–274 BCE. Frugal and incorruptible, four times consul, censor in 272, he died in 270. *Curius* here illicitly has first syllable long, as in 2.51.50; in 2.32 it is twice correctly short (as in *P.* 858).

15–16. Ovid, *Tristia* 4.9.8 threatens to take up arms against someone who has upset him unless he repents.

17–18. See 1.4.77–80n and Introduction, p. vii.

19–20. The "great-grandfather" meant (actually great-great-grandfather) was another Ugolino, Gonfaloniere di Giustizia 1360 and 1364. He died February 4, 1366, according to Lazzari's family tree of Verino's ancestors (but "1367," p. 29). Descent to the poet was through a son Vieri, grandson Ugolino, and great-grandson Vieri, the poet's father. In *De ill. urbis Flor.* (fol. 35, Paris 1583 edition; *Carmina* 10:383), Verino says, "The house [of de' Vieri] is not plebeian. My thrice-great-grandfather [actually twice-great] Ugolino received the highest honors out of respect for his virtue. Powerful also through his wealth, he exercised supreme control as Gonfaloniere di Giustizia of our city."

2.14

The unidentified *Iustus* (Justus) is (flatteringly?) treated in 2.15.2 as Verino's dearest friend (after some favor?). Finding no *Giusto* among Verino's friends, I suspect *Iustus* to be a nickname or honorific epithet ("the Just"). From 2 he seems of distinction in some capacity (cf. 2.54.12 of Cosimo de' Medici, and 2.45.137 of Piero).

1–2. Line 1 almost = Landino, *Xandra* Earlier Redaction 10.1 (cf. Ovid, *Tristia* 1.5.1 and 4.5.1, and *Ex Ponto* 4.13.1). *Fluentinus* for *Florentinus* is found in Landino's *Xandra* and commonly elsewhere (e.g., Naldi). Verino (*De ill. urbis Flor.*, fol. 2, Paris 1583 edition; *Carmina* 10:327) derives *Fluentia* (= *Florentia*; see Bruni, *History* 1.3) from the flowing (*fluere* = "flow") of the Munio and Arno near Sulla's colony of Faesulae (Fiesole), the name later changing (fol. 3) to *Florentia* (the *flourishing* city, Naldi, *Volaterrais* 1.18ff.). Cf. Politian, *Letters* 1.2 (cited by Gualdo Rosa, p. 867).

4. See 1.23.2n.

2.15

See 2.14n.

4. Verino puns on *verus* ("true") and his own name (cf. P. 708) to stress his true-heartedness (1.30.31–32n). Paying tribute to Verino's deceased son, Michele, Landino (Misc. Poems 9.13–14) declares the surname apt for one who investigated the nature of God with *true* reasoning.

2.16

Filippo is unidentified. Verino's detractors: 2.46n.

2.17

Reflecting Propertius 1.22 (answering a friend's questions about origins, place of birth, and abode) and the opening couplets of Landino, *Xandra* 1.24, Verino imparts like information to the Florentine humanist Pellegrino Agli, or Allio (1440–ca. 1468), who was away from Florence, mostly at Ferrara, from 1458 till December 1463 and back in Florence from then till November 1464, or a little later. Agli, it emerges, has earlier written with criticisms of poems sent him by Verino, who fears that Agli may still fault the now improved versions (11). See 1.3.5n. Several poems by Agli in *Carmina*, vol. 1, support the Medici. They include a lament and epitaphs for Giovanni (d. 1463), Cosimo's younger son, and an extensive flattering address to Piero (pp. 119ff.). Lazzari (p. 51), calling the addressee here Pellegrino degli Agli, cites a biography by F. Flamini (*Pellegrino Agli, umanista poeta e confilosofo del Ficino* [Pisa, 1893]). A friend of Ficino and Landino, Agli began writing Latin verse in boyhood. In *De ill. urbis Flor.* (fol. 12v, Paris 1583 edition; *Carmina* 10:344) Verino considers that only a very untimely death stopped Agli equaling the ancient poets. Naldi, *Eleg.* 2.27 warns Agli against publishing poems prematurely.

1. *Nescius erres:* Ovid, *Met.* 14.131.

2. For *carmina* = individual "verses" or "lines," cf. Landino, Misc. Poems 1.78.

4. Verino on his family: 2.13.19–20n. See also Introduction, p. vii.

5–6. Verino means the family house is where it was of old, in Florence's Santo Spirito quarter. Lazzari (p. 28) says the street, in the *popolo* of San Felice in Piazza, was called Sitorno (now Via della Chiesa). Line 6 almost = Landino, *Xandra* 1.24.10, giving Landino's (long-established) address to Bartolomeo Scala (2.5n).

7–10. The proverbial notion of proceeding with unwashed hands or feet (acting prematurely or ill-prepared) is combined with imagery of poetic inspiration. The Boeotian river Permessus (the regular form), springing from Aganippe (1.1.19–20n and 1.20.19–22n), was sacred to Apollo and the Muses. *Permessidos:* Greek genitive of *Permessis*, a (disputed) alternative form in Martial 1.77.11 (cf. also his 8.70.3). *Nimium petulans* (9): Landino, *Xandra* 1.1.11.

11–12. Castalian spring: 1.1.19–20n, 1.1.23–24n, 1.11.45–48n. See 1.3.5n for 12.

2.18

Verino bids his Muse take poems to his friend Montano, seeking verses of his in return. Cf. especially 2.7 and 2.41, and also 1.19 and 2.17 (with 1.3.5n). Nicolaus Montanus, otherwise Nicola Capponi or Cola Montano, originally of Gaggio Montano (province of Bologna), died in Florence in 1481 or 1482. He was an editor, a professor of eloquence and later of Latin at Milan (there by 1462, possibly some years before), and (from 1472 or 1473) an early printer there. See the entry in *DBI*.

6. Similar to 2.45.44 (cf. also 2.48.36). Ovid, *Am.* 1.15.35–38 sneers, "Let the crowd admire paltry things," himself choosing poetry.

10. For *laeta fronte*, cf. 1.19.2 and 1.19.1–2n.

11–12. For *comitata*, cf. 2.7.1. *Montano . . . sale* is a pun ("mountain/Montano's wit"). Cf. 2.14.5, 2.15.4, and (I suspect) 1.3.5.

2.19

Verino's attitude to male homosexuality is hostile in 2.10, 2.28, 2.32, and 2.38; here he reflects his model (Horace, *Odes* 4.10 — from a Greek source?).

7–8. Horace's last two lines imagine the boy ruefully lamenting years later, "Why did I not think as I do today when I was a boy, or why do unmarred (= beardless) cheeks not return to match my feelings now?" Delayed *et* (8): 2.26.6n.

2.20

Cf. 2.9 (aimed at Cipriano).

2. In Ovid, *Rem. Am.* 182 *sedula turba* denotes attendant dogs.

2.21

Piero del Benino, or Benini: 1.15n.

2. As Landino, *Xandra* 3.1.48.

5–6. *Templa* means "sepulcher," as in Vergil, *Aen.* 4.457.

2.22

Verino's new love after Fiammetta (see 49–50) is presumably Lisia (2.2n, 2.50n). His feelings seem still undeclared (57–60).

2. Almost as 1.23.6.

3–4. Pliny the Elder (*H.N.* 7.40.41) says Thracians recorded each day as good or bad by putting either a white or a black pebble into a jar, the predominant color eventually indicating whether a completed life had been happy. Alternatively, lucky days were marked white in Roman calendars. Cf. Horace, *Odes* 1.36.10, and *Sat.* 2.3.246; Catullus 107.6; Martial 8.45.2 and 9.52.5; Landino, *Xandra* 1.19.13–14; etc.

9–12. In 9, Munari conjectures *nondum* ("not yet") for *iam tum* in B (read by Mencaraglia) and *iam tunc* in L (both = "already then"). With either manuscript's text, the sense is that Verino was made to know love's agonies even while still a mere boy (thrice, in 9, 10, and 14, he stresses his young age, probably nineteen: 1.1.17–18n). Cf. *iam tum cum* in Catullus 1.5. Though in the similar Braccesi A 4.1–12 Perosa (with *armatus . . . inermem* in 7; 2.2.25–26n), *nondum* clauses initially alternate with *nec . . . dum* clauses, Munari's *nondum* seems misguided here. Cf. Landino as cited 1.24.10n.

13–14. In Vergil, *Aen.* 4.93–95 Juno ironically tells Venus that she and Cupid are winning glory and rich spoils through plotting the defeat of one woman (Dido) by two deities. The two deities here must also be Venus and Cupid (see 15), but *haec* ("*these* two deities"), the manuscripts' reading in 13, is very awkward with Venus not yet mentioned. I therefore conjecture *hanc* (with *palmam*).

15–16. *Arcus* is poetic plural (as in 31). Line 16 borrows from Ovid, *Am.* 1.1.22.

18. Almost as 1.25.16.

19–20. Love all-conquering: Vergil, *Ecl.* 10.69.

21–22. Python: 1.9.37–38n. Haemonia: Thessaly (*P.* 960n).

23–24. *Indignos ore . . . sonos:* Ovid, *Her.* 11.94, and *Am.* 3.6.72. The whole episode of Apollo's sneer at Cupid and the boy's response (21–34) is after Ovid, *Met.* 1.454ff.

25. See 1.22.8–10n.

27–28. In 461–62 of the Ovidian original, Cupid is told to confine his attentions to arousing love with torches and leave archery to Apollo.

29–30. Corresponding to 463–65 of the Ovidian original. With 29, cf. also Vergil, *Aen.* 7.445. *Cytherea proles:* 1.4.87–88n (and cf. Statius, *Theb.* 4.554).

31–32. Cupid's bow-bending: Ovid, *Am.* 1.1.23. In the Ovidian model (*Met.* 1.473), Cupid shoots Apollo with a golden arrow, but Daphne (1.4.99n) with one of lead (1.10.11–14n).

36. See 1.9.11–12n.

41–42. Cf. Plautus, *Merc.* 82, *amens amansque* ("out of my mind and in love"); Terence, *Andria* 218; Propertius 2.12.3 (lovers live devoid of sense).

43–44. See 1.24.23–24n.

49–50. *Nova praeda* ("latest prey"; similarly *praeda novella* 2.37.2): Ovid, *Am.* 1.2.19, and *Her.* 15.51. *Flammea Virgo* ("Flame Maiden"): 1.4.100n. Ovid, *Am.* 2.10.12 ("Was one girl not enough to cause me cares?") suggests taking 50 as a question. As *en age* introduces questions a dozen times in *F.*, I treat 49 too as one.

51–52. *Liparea* (regular form *Lipara* or *Lipare*), an island (Lipari) north of Sicily, was associated with Vulcan's smithy. *Rude . . . opus*: Ovid, *Ars Am.* 3.228. Original version of 51: "How I burn as the ungentle Cyclopes' blazing Etna!" Like Mencaraglia, I read the line substituted in *B*'s margin. *Ignipotens* is Vergilian.

53–54. The Giant Typhoeus was supposedly confined under the Sicilian volcano Etna.

55. Begins as Ovid, *Met.* 1.492 (Apollo becoming afire for Daphne).

59–60. In Ovid, *Am.* 3.10.28 shame (or "modesty," *pudor*) and love pull in different directions. *Pudor* is opposed to love also in *Am.* 1.2.32 (cf. 1.4.21 here). *Quod iuvat* ("what delights") means sex in Ovid, *Am.* 1.10.31 and 3.2.6, and *Ars Am.* 2.308. I have preferred Ovid's indicative *iuvat* to the manuscripts' subjunctive *iuvet* here.

62. After Ovid *Her.* 4.154.

63–64. With *B*'s *purpurei pensi* (read by Mencaraglia) the sense would be "any concern for red-faced scruple or for modesty." As Ovid has *purpureus* of *pudor* (*Am.* 1.3.14 and 2.5.34), I follow *L*.

65. "Unworthy love": Vergil, *Ecl.* 8.18 and 10.10.

2.23

Cherubino (Quarquagli): 1.12n.

1–2. Cf. Propertius 2.34.65. See 2.1.27–28n.

3–4. Cf. 1.2.8–12. *Mascula Sappho*: Horace, *Epist.* 1.19.38; Landino, *Xandra* 3.7.13. Line 4 ends as Ovid, *Her.* 15.30.

5–6. Metonymy. Thebes: Pindar (1.12.9–12n; cf. 2.45.17–20). Smyrna: Homer (1.12.13–16n). Mantua: Vergil (2.45.31–32n). *Chely* is ablative.

2.24

The poet addressed, Bartolomeo Platina (or Bartolomeo of Piadena), 1421–81), alias Bartolomeo Sacchi (etc.), was initially a soldier, but subsequently studied at Mantua and Florence (under Verino's Greek teacher John Argyropoulos). A friend of Ficino, he impressed the Medici. Moving to Rome when Pius II (Piccolomini) was pope (1458–64), he found work as a secretary; but when Paul II (1464–71), antagonistic to humanist paganism, suppressed Rome's Academy, Platina incurred his hostility and suspicion and spent two periods in prison (the longer for a year), experiencing torture. Appointed first prefect of the Vatican Library by Sixtus IV (ca. 1477), Platina is shown kneeling before him in Melozzo's celebrated painting. Platina wrote extensively, including on history (his history of the popes is translated in this series), biography and lexicography.

1–2. See 2.8.1–2n. Carlo Aretino (Marsuppini, 1398–1453) had begun a Latin verse translation of Homer's *Iliad* but died with only the first book completed (Landino, *Xandra* 3.7.87–90 and 111–20, and 3.17.41–42). The young Politian later translated four further books.

3–4. The antecedent of *unde* in 4 (2.26.6n) is *cantus* (1); that of *quem* (3) is *umor* (4). In Ovid, *Am.* 3.9.26 the lips of poets are moistened by Pierian waters (1.4.41n) flowing from Homer as from an unfailing fount.

5–6. Landino, *Xandra* 2.3.29–30 speaks in similar words of making Sandra's beauty deathless. The thinking reflects Ovid, *Am.* 3.9.28.

8. As 1.6.12 (and almost as 1.20.36).

9–10. Line 9 begins as Landino, *Xandra* 3.15.7; 10 almost = *Xandra* 3.19.14 (1.1.21–22n). Cf. Horace, *Epist.* 1.7.44, *parvum parva decent* ("Little things become a little man"). Ovid calls himself "a playful poet (*lusor*) of tender amours" in *Tristia* 3.3.73 (within his supposed epitaph) and 4.10.1; cf. also 5.1.22 there. Landino dismisses friends' suggestions of rising to higher poetry in the opening lines of *Xandra* 3.15 and 3.16. Horace declares another poet far better suited to a task than himself in *Odes* 1.6 and 4.2.

11–12. Homer and Smyrna: 1.12.13–16n. Scansion of *poteris*: 1.21.12n.

2.25

7–8. Quite close to Landino, *Xandra* 2.6.43–44 (where 44 = Misc. Poems 2.6), with a hint of Vergil, *Aen.* 2.746.

2.26

Verino is modest about his abilities in 2.23 and 2.24, diffident in 1.1 and 2.17. Verino's detractors: 2.46n. Naldo Naldi, born August 31, 1436 (so Grant), probably died in 1513. Pro-Medici and a friend of Ficino and Politian, he was much influenced by Landino in his elegies (lauded by Politian, *Latin Epigrams* 24), for which Verino (*De ill. urbis Flor.*, fol. 13v, Paris 1583 edition; *Carmina* 10:346) calls him celebrated. For Alba in them, see 2.5n. Two elegies addressed to Verino (*Eleg.* 1.11 and 1.14) seem to refer to his relationship with Fiammetta. The former speaks of Verino as suffering in love, forced by his *flamma* (cf. 1.25.46) to pour out complaints; Naldi will beseech Venus to make Verino's dear (but unyielding) girl reciprocate his love. The latter poem tells Verino not to add fuel to his fires by persisting in his complaints. Naldi's addressees include Amerigo Corsini (2.10n and 2.27n), Braccio Martelli (2.13n), Lorenzo Lippi (2.11n), and Pellegrino Agli (2.17n). W. L. Grant's edition of Naldi's *Bucolica*, etc. (Florence, 1974) has a Latin summary of his life, a family tree, and some bibliographical references (p. 7). See also Grant, "The Life of Naldo Naldi," in *Studies in Philology* 60.4 (1963): 606–17; P. O. Kristeller, *Studies in Renaissance Thought and Letters* (Rome, 1956), pp. 385–89 (with bibliography). Naldi praises Verino's dead son Michele in *Carmina varia* 9 Grant.

1–2. In Vergil, *Ecl.* 7.25–28, Thyrsis asks to be crowned with ivy to make the poet Codrus burst with envy, or, "if he should praise me to displeasing excess, circle my brow with the nard plant, lest a malicious tongue may do harm to your bard-to-be." Thus Naldi tells Verino in *Eleg.* 2.17.5f., "I warn you to ring your learned brow with the nard plant, lest a jealous tongue be able to harm you."

3–4. "Phoebus' gift": Poetic skill. *Quia* probably = "that" (with object clause), a postclassical usage. Line 4 ends almost as Ovid, *Tristia* 2.172.

6. *Sed* is hugely delayed from the beginning of 5. *Et* in 2.19.8, *unde* in

2.24.4, and *ne* in 2.51.7 are similarly much delayed. Cf. also the position of *verere* in 2.38.9–10.

7–8. *Nemo solus . . . beatus* seemingly = "not a single lucky person" (irony). Perhaps cf. *unus . . . nemo* ("not a single one") in Ovid, *Tristia* 5.7.53 (*nemo unus* occurs in Livy and Tacitus).

2.27

Amerigo Corsini: 2.10n. Describing him as playfully writing of tender love (to Lisa?), Naldi (*Eleg.* 1.8) warns him of ensnarement and becoming unable to write.

7–8. After Propertius 1.5.23–24 (noble birth of no help in love).

9–10. Gifts: 1.8.25–28n. Line 10 draws on Ovid, *Ars Am.* 3.653, and *Rem. Am.* 462, though Verino (very questionably) makes *vincitur* mean "is won" (equivalent to *capitur*).

13–14. Shut-out lover: 1.8.7–10n.

2.28

Francesco (also 2.38), if real, is unidentified. Verino's attitude to male homosexuality: 2.19n.

1–2. Cato: 1.2.41–42n and P. 874–75n. Horace, *Odes* 3.21 treats Cato as too fond of wine (cf. Landino, *Xandra* 2.1.17–18; 1 here reflects 18 there), but Martial 2.89.1–2 is Verino's main model: "I pardon you your delighting in drawing out the night with excessive quaffing of wine: it is Cato's failing that you have there." Martial's poem then excuses his addressee's uninspired poetry, Cicero's fault, and some other bad habits, but asks whose vice he displays in giving *fellatio*.

7–8. In 7, for the manuscripts' less apt (but not impossible) *insanus*, I have conjectured *infamis* ("disreputable"). With 8, cf. Landino, *Xandra* 1.10.4 (inability to name one's grandfather's homeland).

2.29

Lottieri Neroni: 1.28n. Verino's detractors: 2.46n. Mencaraglia combines the titles in *L* and *B* to make *ad Locterium Neronium de maledico*.

3. *Hoc ideo* (both manuscripts) seemingly = "for this reason therefore."

Sannazaro, *Epigrams* 1.23.9 starts *hinc adeo* ("for just this reason"). I cannot parallel either.

2.30

The best-known Cynic philosopher, Diogenes of Sinope (ca. 400–325 BCE), was famously contemptuous of wealth, as was his disciple Crates (cf. Braccesi, *Epigrammata* 13.1 Perosa).

1. *Nimirum* = *nil mirum* ("no wonder"). I know no ancient instance, but cf. Giovannantonio Campano (1429–77), line 11 of piece 34 in Perosa-Sparrow (from his *Opera Omnia* [Rome, 1495] bk. 2, fol. 3). *Nil mirum* so used in full: Landino, Misc. Poems 5.15; Marullo, *Epigr.* 1.23.2; and (beginning an epigram) Bernardino Rota, Naples 1726 edition, p. 171. *Nil . . . mirum* (separately) is one reading in Ovid, *Ex Ponto* 1.1.67.

2.31

B heads this poem *ad Nerium be*, seemingly an abbreviated surname. If *be* could be a slip, perhaps the addressee here is the Neri Bonciani in 2.35. A Nerius Boncanius occurs in Naldo Naldi, *Epigr.* 141 as an admirer (with Landino) of Lorenzo de' Medici's poetry. Verino speaks of the distinguished Bonciani family (*Bonciana stirps*) in his *De ill. urbis Flor.* (*Carmina* 10:277).

5. Similar to 1.25.45.

2.32

The hypocritical Piero Cretico, caught by his wife in a homosexual act (like Martial in 11.43), was apparently a disparager of Verino over Fiammetta. His identity is uncertain, though a (different?) Piero Matteo Camers Cretico occurs (see Kristeller, 3:616b) helping Politian consult a book in a Padua bookseller's shop in 1491. Verino's detractors: 2.46n. Verino's attitude to male homosexuality: 2.19n.

3–4. Zeno of Citium founded the Stoic school of philosophy. Cato: 1.2.41–42n; *P.* 874–75n.

5–6. Curius: 2.13.13–14n, 2.51.50n. Decius (one of three called Publius Decius Mus): *P.* 863–64n. Numa was the lawgiving second king of

Rome. Gaius Fabricius Luscinus, consul 282 and 278 BCE, was celebrated for frugality and for conducting himself nobly and incorruptibly toward his foe Pyrrhus (see also 2.51.49; *P.* 820 and 858–60). Horace mentions him in *Odes* 1.12.40 (with Curius in association); Vergil, in *Aen.* 6.845 (as "powerful with little"). Landino, *Xandra* 1.9.5 attacks an immoral priest for hypocritical stern words, delivered "in the manner of Chrysippus" (1.4.52n).

11–12. Cf. Juvenal 2.3 ("who pretend to be Curii and live out the Bacchanalia"). Sardanapalus, last king of Assyria, was notorious for effeminacy and delicate living. His name denotes an unmasculine man in Martial 11.11.6.

2.33

1–2. Verino treats the famous maxim "Know yourself" as inscribed on the golden tripod on which the Pythian sat at the Delphic Oracle (1.4.47–48n).

2.34

Cipriano: 2.9n. Verino's detractors: 2.46n.

5. Reminiscent of Vergil, *Aen.* 4.630.

2.35

Neri Bonciani: 2.31n. The artist Pietro Vannucci, known as Perugino (ca. 1446–1523), spent some time in Florence years later but would be much too young to be the (unidentified) Perugian here derided for being unmarried, though the artist is *Perusinus* in Verino's *De ill. urbis Flor.* (fol. 17, Paris 1583 edition; *Carmina* 10:352). Perugia (in Umbria) is *Perusia* in Latin.

5. After Vergil, *Geo.* 3.98, where a stallion can no longer perform satisfactorily with mares. Imagery of sexual intercourse as a battle or fight is common in ancient and later literature.

9–10. Even gods dared not break an oath by the Underworld river Styx (cf. Vergil, *Aen.* 6.324; Ovid, *Met.* 2.101).

13–14. *Quartana*, applied in ancient authors to a fever striking every fourth day (counting inclusively) here means "an every fourth day" prostitute.

2.36

Martial 5.60 refuses to name a detractor and so grant the worldwide fame and immortality that he seeks. Verino's detractors: 2.46n.

1–2. Wanting one's name immortalized in a poet's verse: Ovid, *Am.* 2.17.28 (2.48.12n).

3–5. The single line originally in B translates, "Because you condemn my pure and blameless character" (cf. 2.13.1, 1.4.22; 2.46.1).

7. Vergil, *Ecl.* 7.41 has "more bitter than Sardinian herbs," referring to the Sardinian or celery-leaved crowfoot. Pausanias 10.17.13 shows that eating it was felt to explain the Sardonic smile.

13. Very similar to 2.34.12.

2.37

1–2. *Praeda novella* ("latest prey"): Ovid, *Ars Am.* 3.560 (2.22.49–50n). Perosa (p. 53) defends the manuscripts' *frustrum* (= *frustum*), a spelling also in Braccesi E 8.92 Perosa.

6. Cf. the Vergilian passage cited 2.48.19–20 and 31n.

7. Ganymede: P. 27–28n.

2.38

See 2.28n.

1–2. One of Hercules' Labors was to obtain the apples in the garden of the Hesperides, guarded by a watchful serpent.

3–4. Golden Fleece legend: 1.4.63–66n. After carrying the boy Phrixus to Colchis, the flying ram was sacrificed by him there, and its fleece was hung up in a grove sacred to Ares/Mars, where a serpent or dragon guarded it.

5–6. Ganymede: P. 27–28n.

11–12. In *Carlias* 6.200 Hadrian's beloved favorite Antinous is mockingly called "the Roman emperor's *wife*."

2.39

Lurco, cognomen of the gourmand Marcus Aufidius Lurco, denotes a glutton in some ancient writers. *Lurcus* here similarly satirizes Verino's (imagined?) target.

1. In Ovid, *Met.* 3.76 a serpent emits foul breath "from its Stygian mouth."

12. The seal as foul-smelling: Homer, *Od.* 4.442; Aristophanes, *Wasps* 1035, and *Peace* 758.

2.40

The unnamed addressee may be Ricci (2.41).

1. First three words as in Propertius 1.10.1.

3–4. With 3, cf. Ovid, *Am.* 2.16.21. Syrtes: 1.23.3–4n. Line 4 ends as 1.14.8 (Malea: 1.14.7–12n).

5–6. The Hyperboreans supposedly inhabited the far north. *Triones* = the Wain (Ursa Major and Ursa Minor), symbolizing the north.

7–8. Thyle: 2.2.9–10n. *Thyles*: Greek genitive.

11–16. The close friends (cf., for example, Landino, *Misc. Poems* 7.21–26; Politian, *Latin Epigrams* 18) are (1) Pylades and Orestes (Agamemnon's son; Ovid, *Rem. Am.* 589, *Tristia* 1.9.27–28, *Ex Ponto* 3.2.69ff.; Martial 6.11, 7.24.3; etc.); (2) Pollux and Castor (immortality-sharing twin sons of Jupiter by Leda, daughter of Oebalus, king of Sparta); (3) Laelius and Scipio (Cicero alternatively named his *De Amicitia* after Laelius, consul 140 BCE, close friend of Scipio Aemilianus [Scipio Africanus the Younger]; cf. 2.48.53 and P. 869–70); (4) Xerxes and Themistocles (see 2.46.23–24 and 2.51.46, and P. 814–17), who contrived the defeat of Xerxes' fleet at Salamis in 480 BCE but later fled Athens and ended his days in Persian territory after allegedly treasonable dealings with the Persians; (5) Pirithous and Theseus (Pirithous, "the Thessalian hero" [1.9.33–34n], was ruler of the Lapiths; Ovid, *Ex Ponto* 2.6.26, *Tristia* 1.5.19, *Met.* 8.303, etc.). Line 11 = 2.45.65. Line 12 ends as Ovid, *Tristia* 4.5.30; 14, as 3.5.42 of the same.

18. Mostly as Ovid, *Her.* 17.158.

2.41

The Muse Clio is dispatched to Francesco Ricci (unnamed addressee in 2.40?) at the Sforza court in Milan; that is, Verino sends him verses there (cf. 2.7 and 2.18). Mencaraglia misidentifies Ricci as Pier Francesco Ricci, secretary to Cosimo I, grand duke of Tuscany. G. Lubkin, *A Renaissance Court, Milan under Galeazzo Maria Sforza* (Berkeley, 1994), p. 266, lists an earlier Francesco Ricci (*Francisco Rizio*) with the *ducale canzeleria* of Galeazzo's retinue. Kristeller, 1:205 records a *Franc. Rictius* as sending letters to Nicodemo Tranchedini (1.7n), and *Franciscus Rictius* or *Franc. Rizius* occurs elsewhere in Kristeller (e.g., 2:60 as a poet).

1–2. Plains of Bedriacum (an ancient settlement east of Cremona, scene of two battles in 69 CE): Lombardy. "Great son of Sforza": I think Francesco Sforza, duke of Milan (1450–66), a former *condottiere*, meant rather than his son Galeazzo Maria (b. 1444), duke 1466–76, named in 7–8. If, however, the latter is meant throughout lines 1–10, this poem postdates his succession on March 20, 1466. In its margin, *L* names both men.

5–8. Francesco Sforza is a new (Julius) Caesar in Landino, Misc. Poems 2.41 (so too in Beccadelli's epitaph for him, piece 10 in Perosa-Sparrow, ll. 9–10). I think Galeazzo Maria (*P.* 208–76n) may here still be his father's heir-in-waiting. *Ducis* (5) can mean "duke" or "commander."

11–12. *Dicito* is second imperative. Horace (*Odes* 1.3.8) calls Vergil (taking ship for Greece) "the half of my soul." Cf. Landino, *Xandra* 1.29.8.

14. See 1.19.1–2n.

15–16. "Pegasaean waters": 1.1.19–20n. Illicit scansion of *Clio*: 2.7.1–2n.

2.42

The addressee, Federico Donati, has living parents (47), a brother, and a sister (48). Still very young (2, 18), he is attracted to Elisabetta, a Tuscan girl (14). With prospects in public life (45), he is well-versed in philosophy (55–56) and a poet (57–60). A close relative of Lucrezia (2.43)?

1–2. Vergil, *Aen.* 2.776 is closely imitated in 1. For 2, see 1.24.10n.

3–6. Resisting love's onset: Ovid, *Rem. Am.* 91; Lucretius 4.1063ff. and 1141ff.; Landino, *Xandra* 1.2.23, 2.26.19; Piccolomini, *Cynthia* 23.91–92.

11–12. Love as servitude: 1.10.7–10n.

18. See on 1.24.10, almost identical.

20. Ovid, *Fasti* 1.419 declares, "Disdain is in the fair, and haughtiness is attendant on beauty."

21–22. For *voto amoris* ("love's desire") of sexual intercourse, cf. *plenum votum* ("fulfillment of desire") in Ovid, *Ars. Am.* 1.671, and *sua vota* ("his way") in *Fasti* 1.431–32.

29–32. For the dishonored assignation, cf. 1.8.19–32.

37–38. Cf. Propertius 1.5.10.

39–40. "Faithful" Verino: 1.30.31–32n.

43–44. See 1.4.75–76n.

46. The wording reflects Ovid, *Am.* 3.7.72, and *Her.* 15.64.

53–54. See 1.4.20n and 1.9.15–16n.

55–56. Cf. Propertius 2.34.27ff. Presumably Cicero's philosophical works are meant.

57–58. Calliope: 1.11.45–48n. Hippocrene (*Hippocrenes* is Greek genitive): 1.1.19–20n.

59–60. See 1.1.19–20n and 1.11.45–48n. Cf. Persius, prologue 1.

2.43

For this type of poem, see 1.7n. Lucrezia Donati is usually thought to have become Lorenzo's literary "mistress" ca. 1463 or 1464 (Lorenzo was fourteen in 1463 if born January 1, 1449, as generally stated). We know little about Lucrezia, not even named in Lorenzo's poems to her. According to André Rochon, *La Jeunesse de Laurent de Médicis* (Clermont-Ferrand, 1963), p. 94, she was born in 1447, though Hugh Ross Williamson, *Lorenzo the Magnificent* (London, 1974), p. 91, has her only eleven and Lorenzo sixteen when they first met, and Judith Hook, *Lorenzo de' Medici* (London, 1984), p. 16, gives the same ages for when Lorenzo (b. 1450 according to Hook) began writing poetry to Lucrezia. The present poem, however, is likely to be about 1463 or 1464 rather than two or three years later. In Lorenzo's own prose account of his first sight of Lucrezia, she seems treated (as here) as rather more than a little girl, as in Dante's first sight of Beatrice. She married Niccolò Ardinghelli April 21, 1465, after a two-year betrothal. Their first child (of three) was born in 1471. When Lucrezia died (1501), Verino wrote a eulogy. See Introduction, n. 14. This poem (wrongly called 2.42) is quoted in the London 1825 edition of W. Roscoe's *Life of Lorenzo de' Medici Called the Magnificent* (Appendix 15, 1:352).

1–2. After many subordinate clauses with *quamvis* ("though"), the main clause is marked by *non tamen* ("yet . . . not") in 33. Cf. the construction of 2.51.45–63.

3–4. Spartan daughter of Tyndareus: Helen (of Troy). Cf. 2.49.23 for *Lacaena*.

7–8. See 1.4.17–18n. 7 begins almost as Ovid, *Her.* 5.125.

9–10. Cf. 1.4.15 for 9. In 10, *lips* (*labra*), not (as regularly) *eyes*, strangely rival the stars of the sky (*astris . . . poli*, also 1.4.6 and 2.22.22). *Aemula labra* (*rosis*) occurs in Martial 4.42.10, and Girolamo Balbi (d. 1535; *Carmina* 2:13), of rose-like lips (common imagery, as Landino, *Xandra* 2.4.16). Lips are elsewhere likened to rubies, coral, cinnabar, Tyrian purple, or the dwarf-elder's berries, but (unsurprisingly) never to stars. Verino's blunder?

14. For beauty that a deity might envy (again 27–28), cf., for example, Ovid, *Am.* 1.14.31–32 (hair Apollo or Bacchus might have wished for).

15–16. The combination of red-tinted cheeks and white surrounding skin (see 1.17.11–12n for imitation with cosmetics) was greatly admired, anciently and in Renaissance times (cf., for example, Ovid, *Am.* 3.3.5–6, *Met.* 3.423; Landino, *Xandra* 2.23.45–48, and Misc. Poems 1.29–30 and 5.39–42).

18. Arms whiter than snow: Ovid, *Am.* 3.7.8.

21. *Collo* ("neck") is apparently used for *capite* ("head").

23–24. Sirens: mythical part-bird, part-women creatures on the southern coast of Italy, luring sailors to their deaths with beautiful song. *Sirenae* has the first syllable illicitly short.

27–28. See 14n. Juno's majestic gait: Propertius 2.2.6; Landino, *Xandra*

2.23.51–52 (Sandra surpasses Juno's gait and Venus' eyes), and Misc. Poems 5.45.

29–30. Lucretia, a virtuous Roman matron, was raped by Sextus Tarquinius, son of Rome's last king Tarquin the Proud, under threat that, if resisted, he would murder her and a slave and pretend them caught in adultery. She denounced her violator to her husband and father before killing herself. Her avengers expelled the Tarquins.

33–34. For the man as a worthy catch, cf. 2.49.24–26. Landino, *Xandra* 2.23.68 similarly has *ultro rogandus erat* of Apollo, whom Daphne should have *asked* to be her lover, not rejected.

35–38. Alcmaeon's mother was Eriphyle; his father, Amphiaraus. Warned that joining Polynices' expedition against Thebes would be fatal to him, Amphiaraus hid to avoid involvement, but Eriphyle, bribed with a golden necklace, betrayed him, and, forced to participate, he perished when the gaping earth swallowed him. Alcmaeon thereafter killed his mother, as Amphiaraus had directed. *Alcmeonis* (properly *Alcmaeonis*) scans illicitly.

46. Last five words as Ovid, *Am.* 1.6.34.

47–48. Castalian caves and Calliope(a): 1.11.45–48n.

51. Cf. 1.29.5.

2.44

Corvinus, seemingly a wellborn poet of sorts, is unidentified. A few men called Corvinus, Corvini, or Corvino (none particularly credible here) occur at this period.

7. I leave this seven-foot hexameter as Verino's error, as Munari recommends.

2.45

The poet Andrea Alamanni (1421–73), a Florentine statesman who frequented the literary circle of Niccolò della Luna as a young man, was a friend and correspondent of Francesco Filelfo, closely involved in the politics of the Florentine Studio and keenly interested in philosophy. See, for instance, Cosenza and the entry by Perosa, with bibliographical references, in *DBI*. Alamanni held public offices from 1444. Verino has not known him long (1–2), but has evidently been granted access to Alamanni's substantial (manuscript) library (67). Among his writings, Alamanni has a surviving oration on the death of Giovanni de' Medici, Cosimo's younger son, in 1463.

1–4. Ovid, *Tristia* 3.5.1–10, especially 9 and 10, seems in Verino's mind here.

6. Cf. [Tibullus] 3.7.7; Propertius 2.10.6.

7–8. Nestor: 1.6.29–32n.

13–16. Nicias was one of the generals sent to besiege Syracuse in Athens' disastrous Sicilian expedition of 415–413 BCE. Athenian prisoners who could recite passages of Euripides received better treatment, even release. Trinacrian: Sicilian.

17–18. The Pellaean (cf. Claudian, *IV Cons. Hon.* 374): Alexander the Great (born in Pella, capital of Macedonia), who took Thebes in 335 BCE. The manuscripts have *Pelei* (short, short, long) for the true form *Pellaei* (three longs). Munari (pp. 302–3) argues (perhaps rightly) for *Pellei* (= *Pellaei*), scanned as disyllabic by synizesis, but trisyllabic *Pelei* seems credible (as a false form) for Verino, who quite often allows himself license over proper names. He has *Pellei* (= *Pellaei*) as three longs in hexameters of his *Carlias* (1.323, 3.48, and 9.409).

21–22. Solon (1.21.17–18n) feigned madness when he recited verses in Athens' marketplace calling for war with Megara over Salamis (ca. 600 BCE), as mention of Salamis was punishable by death. *Pelasgians* (often = "Greeks" in verse) here means the Athenians in particular.

25–26. The seventh-century BCE poet Tyrtaeus roused the Spartans in the struggle against the Messenians (cf. Horace, *AP* 402–3). Justin 3.5 calls him "lame of foot" and refers to the three Spartan defeats that the Messenians inflicted before the eventual Spartan victory.

27–30. Alcaeus (1.2.5–12n), born ca. 620 BCE, contended as soldier and poet against tyrants of his native Mytilene (on Lesbos). Last five words of 30 as in Landino, *Xandra* 1.24.24.

31–32. Vergil was born at Andes (now Pietola) close to Mantua. In his *Ecl.* 9 there is talk of lands round Mantua and Cremona having been taken for Octavian's veterans, but Vergil's character Tityrus has recovered his in *Ecl.* 1.

33–34. In Horace, *AP* 333–34 and 343–44, poets may wish to benefit (*prodesse*), delight (*delectare*), or both. Thus in 33 *prosint* and *iuvent* are alternatives, whereas in 34 poetry combines beneficial and pleasing elements. In 33, the misused (properly enclitic) *ne* after *igitur* seems redundant. With my readings, that appended to *prosint* means "whether," and that appended to *iuvent* means "or" (*ne . . . ne* in disjunctive indirect questions: Gildersleeve and Lodge, §460.2n2; in a direct question, cf. Vergil, *Aen.* 11.126). For the pattern of thought, cf. Landino, *Xandra* 3.16.27–29, expressing uncertainty whether to admire Cosimo de' Medici more in peace or in war, being admirable in both.

37–42. Landino, *Xandra* 2.6.29–32 similarly stresses how poets save great deeds from being forgotten. *Damnosa senectus* (B in 41): Ovid, *Tristia* 3.7.35. Holy poets (42 and 53): 1.2.13–14n.

44. See 2.18.6n.

49. In Ovid, *Ex Ponto* 4.3.49 divine power "makes sport in human affairs."

57–58. In Ovid, *Ars Am.* 3.548–49 poets have *numen* ("divine power") in them and "there is god in us (poets)" (cf. also *Am.* 3.9.18).

61–62. "Owls to Athens" was proverbial of redundant effort (the owl was sacred to Athena, Athenian coins bore owls, etc.). Adding water to the sea: Ovid, *Tristia* 5.6.44.

63. Last three words as Ovid, *Ex Ponto* 3.4.79.

65. As 2.40.11. See 2.40.11–16n.

69–72. In *Ars Am.* 3.121ff., Ovid rejoices at having been born in his own time. 2.51.138 also speaks of just reward for the deserving (cf. 1.20.25–26 too). Gualdo Rosa (pp. 861–65) translates this poem from 69 onward with useful comments in notes.

73. Cf. Ovid, *Fasti* 6.661.

75–78. Dante Alighieri lived 1265 to 1321. Landino, *Xandra* 3.17.15ff. speaks in vaguely comparable terms of the revival of learning in Italy, mentioning Dante, Petrarch, Boccaccio, etc. Line 76 ends as Ovid, *Ex Ponto* 2.7.70.

83. *Copia fandi* in Vergil, *Aen.* 1.520 and 11.248 = "liberty to speak"; in *Aen.* 11.378 it = "wealth of words."

85–86. P. 418–21 treats the planets Venus and Jupiter as countering harm threatened by Saturn. In Propertius 4.1.83–84, Jupiter's star is "lucky," Saturn's "brings ill on every head." Persius 5.50 speaks of how "we counter (*frangimus*) malign Saturn with our Jupiter." In Horace, *Odes* 2.17 the protection of Jupiter outshines "wicked Saturn" and saves Maecenas. Saturn's star is morose and menacing in Juvenal 6.570. Macrobius, *Commentarii in Somnium Scipionis* 1.19 explains why Jupiter was considered a benign influence, but Saturn and Mars malign.

87–88. Venus (here *Iubar*, the "brightness" of the Morning star, as in Landino, *Xandra* 3.15.27–28; cf. his Misc. Poems 1.4) is seen as a mitigating influence on Mars. Servius (on Vergil, *Geo.* 1.336ff.) speaks of two good planets (Jupiter and Venus), two bad (Saturn and Mars), and one neutral (Mercury). In the manuscript text of 87 (*iubar sidusque*), *iubar* illicitly has first syllable long (as in 1.8.24). The rewriting in *Carmina* (*sidusque iubarque*) makes *iubar* wrongly refer to Mercury. Gualdo Rosa's translation (see Bibliography) unconvincingly takes *iubar* to mean Mars' own light. The god Mercury was associated with thieves and eloquence.

89–92. The geographer (and astronomer) Paolo dal Pozzo Toscanelli (1397–1482) is probably foremost in Verino's mind (Landino, *Xandra* 3.6 addresses Toscanelli). Vergilius (Fergal), archbishop of Salzburg (d. 784), was excommunicated for believing in antipodes (91), an idea (attacked by Saint Augustine, *De Civ. Dei* 16.9) that some (denying the earth's sphericity) thought against the Bible.

93–94. Gualdo Rosa credibly considers Giorgio Gemisto Pletone (Plethon) and Marsilio Ficino, the great Platonic and neo-Platonic scholar, probably most in Verino's thoughts. In *De ill. urbis Flor.* (fol. 13, Paris 1583 edition; *Carmina* 10:345), Verino pays Ficino this tribute: "Furthermore Marsilio must be celebrated with great honor, through whom the Italians now know learned Plato; and he has translated Plotinus too, and expounded the doctrines of Christ, telling what faith is to be held true, what form of worship likewise."

95–96. Matteo Palmieri (1406–75) is probably meant, in view of his (vernacular) dialogue on correct behavior, *Vita civile*, as Gualdo Rosa very reasonably suggests.

97–98. Logicians. I find *constrictus* syntactically difficult. Did Verino mean *constrictum*? Perhaps read that?

101–2. Birds supposedly mistook grapes painted by Zeuxis, the renowned Greek artist of Heraclea, for real ones and tried to eat them (Pliny, *HN* 35.61–66). Verino later equated both Leonardo da Vinci (1452–1519) and Botticelli (ca. 1444–1510) with Zeuxis (see next note).

103–4. Phidias worked on the Parthenon sculptures and the statue of Zeus at Olympia. Apelles (cf. 1.2.23 and 2.8.5) was a distinguished painter of Alexander the Great's time. In *Epigr.* 3.23 (text and Italian translation by Gualdo Rosa, pp. 872–75; piece 61 in Perosa-Sparrow), Verino equates Andrea del Verrocchio (1435–88) with Phidias, Sandro Botticelli with Apelles. Botticelli is "Alexander, the Tuscan successor of Apelles of Cos" in a passage of Verino's *Carlias* discussed by Gombrich, *Norm and Form*, pp. 24 and 27–28. Verrocchio may well be the new Phidias here too (so Gualdo Rosa), and perhaps Botticelli (own studio from ca. 1465) can already be the new Apelles (as Gualdo Rosa suggests). Apollonio di Giovanni is a Tuscan Apelles in 2.8.5–6. Much later, in *De ill. urbis Flor.* (fol. 17r–v, Paris 1583 edition; *Carmina* 10:352; discussed by André Chastel, *Marsino Ficin et l'Art* [Geneva-Lille, 1954], p. 184, with French version appended), Verino equates Filippino Lippi (1457–1504) with Apelles. There Verrochio matches Lysippus (not Phidias); Botticelli, Zeuxis (not Apelles); Leonardo da Vinci, Protogenes (in *Epigr.* 3.23.25–26 Leonardo is equated with Zeuxis). The pairings vary. *Pictura* (normally a painting) denotes a carving in relief in the Vulgate (3 Kings 6:32).

105–6. See 1.2.21 and 24n.

109–10. In the Golden Age (cf. 2.51.77–78; *P.* 731), when Saturn ruled, times were easy and blissful. With 109 (2.51.40 is similar), cf. Ovid, *Tristia* 5.12.45.

111–12. Martial 11.5.1 lauds Trajan's *recti reverentia . . . et aequi*.

117–18. Cosimo's two sons: Piero and Giovanni (1.11n). The latter died November 1, 1463, aged forty-one.

121–25. Quirinus (125): Romulus (deified). Vulcan is "the Lemnian Father" in Vergil, *Aen.* 8.454; "the Lemnian" in Ovid, *Met.* 4.185. Bacchus, who found Ariadne on Naxos and married her, was worshipped there (Vergil, *Aen.* 3.125, for example). Minerva/Athena was patroness of Athens. Jupiter/Zeus was hidden in a cave on Mt. Dicte in Crete when in danger of being eaten by his father Saturn/Kronos (1.6.33–34n). Cybele/Mother Earth was "the Phrygian Mother" (Vergil, *Aen.* 7.139, and Ovid, *Fasti* 2.55, etc.). Thus her son Hyperion (father of the Sun) is associated with Phrygia here. *Hyperiona* (125) should have only the *i* long (Ovid, *Met.* 4.192, etc.; Politian, *Silvae* 3.522 and 4.340; Marullo, *Hymns* 3.1.24 and 4.2.10), but here illicitly scans long, two shorts, long, short.

126. *Sullanidae* is dative ("for the son of Sulla"), singular for plural. See 1.20.18n.

127–28. Verino means that both Alamanni and the Medici may ultimately descend, by different lines, from Aeneas' son Iulus (supposed ancestor of Romulus). *Iuleos* can scan as three longs or a short and three longs. With 128, cf. Ovid, *Fasti* 4.124 (Augustus Caesar's "Julian" ancestry).

129–30. Buildings (many ecclesiastical) generously erected or restored by Cosimo de' Medici are listed in Appendix 10 of C. S. Gutkind's *Cosimo de' Medici, Pater Patriae, 1389–1464* (Oxford, 1938); see also D. Kent, *Cosimo de'Medici and the Florentine Renaissance: The Patrons' Oeuvre* (New Haven, 2000). The Monastero di Santa Verdiana (Vallombrosian nuns), restored in 1460, was probably one place in Verino's mind here. Cf. 2.51.95–98 for Cosimo as benefactor of ecclesiastical buildings.

131–32. *Maxima causa* ("a very great cause"), in apposition to the sentence (or clause), should properly be accusative (Gildersleeve and Lodge, §324). The reference to providing needy girls with dowries seems rightly taken by Gualdo Rosa to be to the *Monte delle fanciulle* or *Monte dei doti*. Vergil, *Aen.* 8.412 lies behind 132.

135–36. Cf. 1.1.24 and 2.51.86 (and 140 herebelow has similar flattery).

Piero equated with Maecenas: 1.19.5–6n and 1.20n. Line 136 is after Ovid, *Ex Ponto* 2.5.64.

137–38. Cf. the similar sentiment in 1.20.25–26 (and Landino, *Xandra* 2.1.1–2).

141. *Consortes studii* ("sharers in my pursuit") of fellow poets: Ovid, *Tristia* 5.3.47.

2.46

Other poems rebutting detractors: 2.13, 2.16, 2.26, 2.29, 2.32, 2.34, 2.36.

1–2. See 1.23.5–8n. Verino's purity (also 58): 1.2.43–44n.

13–14. See P. 818–21n.

15–18. Scipio Africanus Major (P. 869–71n) ended his life a virtual exile because of political difficulties in Rome. With 16 (close to Landino, *Xandra* 3.17.72), cf. 2.51.55.

19–20. Marcus Furius Camillus: 2.51.47–48; P. 841–42 (with notes).

23. *Themistocles* (2.40.11–16n) illicitly has first syllable long.

27–52. After Ovid, *Met.* 2.775ff. There Jealousy feeds on snakes (769ff.; 35 and 37 here); is pale (775; 36) and poison tongued (777; 34); delights in seeing pain (778; 45); is sleepless (779; 39–40); constantly beset by cares (779; 39); displeased at people's successes (780–81; 29); gnaws and is gnawed (781; 29); and is self-punishing (782; 28). Cf. also Landino's description of Phthone (invented from Greek *phthonos* = "envy") in *Xandra* 1.24.45–72.

36. *Teter* (correctly *taeter*) illicitly has first syllable short (long in *taetri* in 1.12.18 and *taetrior* in 27 here).

37. Cf. Vergil, *Geo.* 2.528. *Cratera*: Greek accusative. Viper's blood: Ovid, *Ex Ponto* 4.7.36.

39. After Ovid, *Ex Ponto* 1.2.55.

41. *Discordia* personified: Vergil, *Aen.* 8.702. Tisiphone: 1.8.29–32n.

43–44. *Pallida* may qualify *Mors*, as in Horace, *Odes* 1.4.13, or *tempora*.

47–48. *Felle madent* ("drip with gall"), also in 1.8.14: Ovid, *Ars Am.* 2.520 (of Love's arrows).

49–50. *Turpis amor* ("shameful love"): Ovid, *Am.* 3.11.2, *Rem. Am.* 64, *Ibis* 297.

54. Last four words as Landino, *Xandra* 1.33.6. Cf. 1.1.11 and 1.4.23 above.

57–58. Cf. 1.8.31–32. Seemingly treat *crimine graviore* as if governed by *de* or *pro.*

2.47

The Florentine Donato Cocchi Donati (b. 1409), a man of law learned also in philosophy, died July 23, 1464. See L. Miglio's long entry on him in *DBI* (with extensive bibliography). His father (Gonfaloniere di Giustizia 1434 and 1438) played a part in Cosimo de' Medici's return from exile and assumption of domination in Florence. The son, after studying at Bologna, taught civil law in the University of Florence (from 1439) and during his life was several times consulted by the Signoria (*Curia* here). In September–October 1456, after civic service in several lesser capacities, Cocchi Donati was himself Gonfaloniere di Giustizia.

1–2. Servius Sulpicius Rufus and Quintus Mucius Scaevola were leading jurists of Cicero's time.

3. After Ovid, *Rem. Am.* 395. Cf. the structure of 2.53.

5. *Curia* (Signoria): 2.51.23–24n.

2.48

Verino became a notary on July 9, 1464, according to Lazzari (p. 64). The title in *L* calls the Muse *Clio*, not *Erato* (named in 4).

1–2. Memnon's mother is the dawn goddess Aurora. *Oceanos* is adjectival, a usage disputed in Juvenal 11.94 and 113. *Lacus* is (awkwardly) accusative of goal of motion (for *in* or *ad* + accusative). *Compulit* is perfect for imperfect. Cf. 1.20.7–8.

3–4. Erato: 1.26.13–14n.

9–10. The Muses are *Pegasides* (1.1.19–20n; cf. also 2.41.15) in Ovid, *Her.* 15.27, and Propertius 3.1.19. Calliope: 1.11.45–48n.

12. After Ovid, *Am.* 2.17.28.

15–18. Cf. Ovid, *Am.* 1.15.5–6 (*verbosas leges*); Propertius 4.1.134 (*insano*

. . . *Foro*); Landino, *Xandra* 1.29.13–14 ("I am forced to learn the laws of the mad forum [*insani . . . fori*]"). There (15ff.) Landino always returns at once (from his notary's duties) to the Muses "when the bothersome crowd has gone quiet and, with the lawsuits adjourned, all the court precincts are silent." In *Xandra* Earlier Redaction 21 Landino blames poverty for making him foresake the Muses to learn the laws of the forum. The young Verino evidently shared Landino's attitude. *Latrare* (lit., "bark") of ranting orators: Cicero, *Brutus* 15.58.

19–20 and 31. After Vergil, *Aen.* 3.56–57. Cf. 2.37.6.

21. Almost as Lucretius 2.14.

23–27. Cf. Horace, *Odes* 1.3.9ff. (the courage of the first man to venture out on the sea). In 25, "five fingers'-widths" refers to the thickness of the ship's planks (cf. Juvenal 12.57ff.). Ovid, *Ibis* 288 ("food for greedy snakes") partly inspired 27.

28. Scylla: 1.14.7–12n.

29–30. *Amor nummi* ("love of money"): Juvenal 14.139. *Cura peculi* ("concern for wealth"): Horace, *AP* 330.

36. See 2.18.6n.

39–40. Take *per* with *fugit* by tmesis (cf. P. 124); *in* governs *tenuem . . . aera*. The conjectures of Munari (p. 303) and Mariotti (footnote there) are unnecessary. Munari sees imitation of Vergil, *Aen.* 9.656–60, citing also (the rather closer) Ovid, *Ex Ponto* 3.3.93, among other passages.

2.49

Niccolò del Ben(n)ino: 1.15n. Pleas to a girl for a friend: 1.7 (Tranchedini; 1.7n), 2.43 (Lorenzo de' Medici). Warning of love's cares: 2.42. Ginevra here seems unlikely already to be Ginevra de' Benci (b. 1457, m. 1474), famously painted by Leonardo da Vinci. She had a platonic "affair" in 1475–76 with Bernardo Bembo (1433–1513), the Venetian ambassador, about which Landino (Misc. Poems 3–8), Naldi (*Epigr.* 121), and Braccesi (E4, E5, and E6 Perosa) wrote poems at the time (E6 tells of her grief at Bembo's leaving in 1476), while Braccesi E3, lauding her beauty, is vaguer in date. Mencaraglia omits the second *ad* in L's title.

1–2. Propertius 2.2.1 begins *liber eram*. His 1.9.1ff. addresses someone who once mocked him for being a prisoner of love. *L* has Propertius' *irrisor* ("mocker"); *B*'s post-classical *illusor* produces alliteration. Line 2 is after Landino, *Xandra* 3.7.76.

4. Apollo's golden locks are "snowy" (only of white hair in classical Latin) in 2.51.76 (though *A*'s text discards that strange description), and Naldi (*Eleg.* 1.29.77f.) speaks of "snowy hair that might surpass Apollo's locks" (cf. 2.43.7–8 for the comparison). In his *Eleg.* 1.21.11ff., the golden hair of a youth likened to Apollo is "snowy."

9–10. The lover's paleness: 1.18.37–38n. His generally distressed state: 1.4.75–76n. With 9, cf. Propertius 1.5.21. Being burned by slow fires: Ovid, *Ars Am.* 3.573 (there of more mature love).

16–17. For 16, see 1.9.11–12n. For "spare" in 17, cf. 1.7.1 and 14.

19–20. Cf. 1.26.14 and 1.30.21 (and 1.27.16n). Ovid, *Am.* 3.8.65 ("some god who avenges the slighted lover") inspired 19. For this avenger god, cf. also Landino, *Xandra* 2.23.86. In 20 I prefer (with Munari) *B*'s *mei* (genitive of *ego*) to *L*'s *mihi* (*contempti . . . mei* syntactically matches *neglecti . . . amantis*). *Poenas dare*, normally of *being* punished (cf. 1.30.24), here denotes *inflicting* punishment (cf. 1.8.32), as in Francesco Filelfo, *Sat.* 4.9.66, where God awaits "what punishments he may give (*det*) in time."

21. After Ovid, *Her.* 16.328.

23–24. Helen of Troy is meant (as in 2.43.3). Cf. 2.43.33–34.

2.50

Lisia (Lisa), dead at seventeen, Verino's unidentified new love after Fiammetta (2.2n and 2.22n), evidently had both parents living, and a brother and a sister (25–26). Mencaraglia (p. 117) notes Landino, Misc. Poems 1, lamenting the sudden youthful death, seemingly from bubonic plague, of a chaste and pious poetess called Lisa, the beloved "lady/mistress" of an unnamed "friend" of Landino. It seems too risky, however, to presume her Verino's Lisa (not here called a poetess), for the date of Landino's poem is uncertain, Landino had numerous friends, and Florence many Lisas. *B*'s title calls the girl *Lisia* (cf. ll. 1 and 55); *L*'s, *Lisa*.

1. Elysian Fields: 1.6.33–34n.

4. Ending as Ovid, *Am.* 3.9.44 (of the flames that cremated Tibullus).

5–6. Cf. Landino, *Xandra* 3.7.17–18.

9–10. Lustra: 1.1.17–18n. Line 10 = line 70 of Verino's long eulogy for Albiera degli Albizzi (d. 1473), for whom see 2.5n.

11–12. Apollo was a god of healing, as well as of music. Mencaraglia treats the question here as indirect (perhaps correctly), though, like Munari, I make it direct (cf. 1.21.20 and 2.7.3 for *dic* so used).

16. See 1.25.27–30n.

19–20. *Candide lector* ("good reader"): Ovid, *Tristia* 1.11.35 and 4.10.132; Martial 7.99.5.

21–22. Being moved to doubt the gods' existence: Ovid, *Am.* 3.3.23–24 (with *stulta . . . credulitate*) and 3.9.36 (cited 2.51.1–6n). Cf. also Vergil, *Ecl.* 8.35 ("and you do not believe that any god is concerned with mortal things"). *B*'s marginal note calls the thought Epicurean. Epicurus held that gods existed, but without involvement in human affairs.

23–24. Cf. Tibullus 1.1.70 ("Death with head all covered in gloom"), and 2.46.43 above.

27. For the change from second to third person, see 1.6.17–18n.

30. After Ovid, *Fasti* 5.40.

31. Ovid, *Am.* 3.9.6 has *corpus inane* of Tibullus' lifeless body on the pyre (cf. Landino, *Xandra* 3.7.24, and Misc. Poems 1.60).

37. Landino (Misc. Poems 1.61–62) declares the Lisa there second in beauty only to Sandra.

39–40. A vocative to oneself, unexceptionable with the second person (as in 1.14.4), sits very awkwardly with the first person here.

41. Treat *L*'s *narrare* as epexegetic after *spiritus* ("breath to tell"). Cf. *vires . . . pellere* ("strength to drive away") in Ovid, *Her.* 1.109. I read *defit* ("fails") for *desit* ("would fail").

42. Parnassus: 1.1.23–24n.

44. See 1.26.45n.

50. For the earth smiling, cf. Ovid, *Met.* 15.205; Lucretius 1.8, 2.559, 3.22, 5.1005 and 1395; Vergil, *Ecl.* 7.55; Landino, *Xandra* 3.17.78.

52. *Vernet avis* ("let a bird salute the spring"): Cf. Ovid, *Tristia* 3.12.8.

2.51

Cosimo died August 1, 1464 at his Careggi villa. A dying speech to Piero (129–78) also figures in Naldi's long poem on his passing, *Eleg.* 3.11 (ll. 43–92). Cosimo's country is there his grieving daughter.

1–6. Cf. Ovid, *Am.* 3.9.35–41, beginning, "Since the wicked fates carry off the good . . . I am tempted to think there are no gods." Ovid (lamenting Tibullus) then reflects that death spares none. In Naldi's already cited poem (ll. 109–12), Cosimo's country/daughter, rebuking the Fates, declares even Jupiter's death credible, if Cosimo can die. In a poem to Cosimo (*Eleg.* 3.7) on his son Giovanni's passing (November 1, 1463), Naldi infers that even Jupiter's offspring may now seem at like risk. Politian, *Eleg.* 7.226 shows similar thinking. Atropos (6) is a Fate.

9. Gorgon's pool (and Helicon, 13): 1.1.19–20n.

13–14. After Propertius 2.10.12 (telling the Muses "there will now be need of mighty lips"), and Vergil, *Aen.* 7.641 and 10.163 (bidding them "open now Helicon"). Landino, *Xandra* 3.7.6 ends as 14 here (cf. P. 79). There are several borrowings from that poem in this.

15. Does this line (very oddly) mean that the Muses would even have come back from the dead to lament Cosimo, or is it miswritten (like 2.43.9–10)? See on 47–48 for possible imperfect revision.

17–18. The Muse Calliope (1.11.45–48n) is bareheaded in mourning (as Apollo in 76). Her following lament seems partly suggested by that which she delivers for Carlo Marsuppini in Landino, *Xandra* 3.7.59–132.

19–20. Landino, *Xandra* 3.7.7–8 seems half-echoed.

23–24. The *Curia Patrum* ("House of Fathers") is the Signoria, also mentioned in 2.47.5 (and title of 2.3) and contrasted (as *Curia sancta Patrum*) with the commons in 2.54.2. Landino, *Xandra* 3.18.48 has *Curia sancta, Patres,* and *Curia* is used of the Signoria also in *Xandra* 3.1.33, 3.3.15, 3.3.22, 3.17.46 and 172, with *Senatus* denoting the same body in *Xandra*

3.5.27, 3.7.139, and 3.16.41. Politian too has *Senatus* of the ("purple-clad") Signoria (*Latin Epigrams* 34.5). Here, therefore, take *Curia Patrum* and *Sanctus Senatus* (awkwardly) as synonymous and *certatim* (cf. 12) of those within the Signoria vying with one other in displaying grief.

25. Ending as Ovid, *Met.* 4.9.

27–28. See 1.20.18n. With 28, cf. Landino, *Xandra* 3.7.52.

33–36. Cf. 2.54.9–10 for the financial crisis at this time. Shortly after Cosimo died, Piero called in many debts owed to the Medici. Lydian = Etruscan: 1.1.1–2n. With 34, cf. Ovid, *Nux* 94.

45–46. Lycurgus (cf. 2.53.2): P. 905–9n. *Neoclides* (= Themistocles, son of Neocles, 2.40.11–16n), in Ovid, *Ex Ponto* 1.3.69 a short syllable followed by three longs, is here illicitly long, two shorts, long. From 45 (excluding 47–48; see next note) there are many *although* clauses in succession, till *non tamen* (63) begins the one-line main clause. Cf. 2.43.1–34.

47–48. *Camillus* in the margin of *L* means Marcus Furius Camillus (2.46.19–20 and P. 841–42 with note), who (ca. 395 BCE) took Veii by arms, whereas the Falisci (cf. Ovid, *Am.* 3.13.1–2, for instance) surrendered to him voluntarily, impressed by his honorable rejection of treachery proposed by a local schoolmaster (Livy 5.27). Sons of Aeneas: Romans. As Dionisotti perceives, this couplet does not construe within the surrounding *although* clauses. Perhaps it has been left in by oversight after revision of this passage, or some text may have been lost around here.

49–50. Gaius Fabricius Luscinus and Pyrrhus: 2.32.5–6n. Manius Curius Dentatus: 2.13.13–14n.

51–52. Marcus Claudius Marcellus (consul 222 BCE and four times thereafter during the Second Punic War) won the *spolia opima* ("Rich Spoils," arms stripped from a slain enemy commander by a Roman general who had killed him in single combat, and dedicated in the temple of Jupiter Feretrius). See Propertius 4.10.39–48 and also P. 872–73. *Feretro* (all manuscripts) seems to be a metrically convenient shortened form of *Feretrio*. The latter (printed by Mencaraglia) could, however, scan with synizesis of *io*. Cf. *Gaetul(i)a* in P. 368.

53–54. Fabius Maximus Cunctator: *P.* 851–57n. "Foe": Hannibal. Libyan: Carthaginian.

55–56. See *P.* 869–71n. Cf. 2.46.16.

57–58. Catos: 1.2.41–42n, and *P.* 874–75n. Marcus Aemilius Scaurus famously put on magnificent games as aedile (58 BCE). Cf. Horace, *Odes* 1.12.37 for the Scauri as eminent. The first *i* of *aedilitate* is illicitly short.

59–60. Pompey the Great (106–48 BCE), called Gnaeus Pompeius *Magnus* from 81 BCE, celebrated three separate triumphs.

61–62. Gaius Julius Caesar conquered Gaul in the 50s BCE. He subdued the Hiberi (Spaniards) in defeating the Pompeians in Spain in the Civil War. The Pompeian ally Juba, king of Numidia in north Africa, killed himself in 46 BCE after Caesar won the Battle of Thapsus.

68. Drinking *pocula nigra* of Lethe (in death; cf. 2.5.18): Landino, *Xandra* 3.4.68.

69–71. Castalians (1.11.45–48n): Muses (cf. *Castalides* in Martial 7.12.10). With 69, cf. 2.50.35.

72. *Triste ministerium* (also Landino, *Xandra* 3.7.46): Vergil, *Aen.* 6.223.

73–74. See 1.15.17–20n.

76. See 2.49.4n.

77–78. Golden Age: 2.45.109–10n (of Augustus: Vergil, *Aen.* 6.792–94).

81–82. See 1.20.25–26n.

83–84. "Tuscan knight" (cf. Martial 8.56.9): Maecenas (1.19.5–6n, 1.20n), normally equated with Piero, not Cosimo.

86. Cf. 1.1.24 and 2.45.136.

87–88. See 2.45.93–94n.

89–90. *Rhetoras*: Greek accusative plural.

95–98. Naldo Naldi (*Eleg.* 3.11.287ff.) also lauds Cosimo's benefaction to ecclesiastical buildings, mentioning the Badia at Fiesole (109 here), the church of San Marco (99 here), and that of San Lorenzo with its glorious ceiling (111 here). Cosimo built also in Paris and Jerusalem (Gutkind [2.45.129–30n], Appendix 10); hence Verino's overstatement "in all parts of the world." Landino, *Xandra* 3.3.103–6 evidently inspired 97–98. There Landino declares that if all the variously located churches built by Cosimo were concentrated in one place, "scarcely would the site once sacred to Tarpeian Jupiter enclose them with the Capitoline citadel's walls" (cf. 113 below). Remus and his twin, Romulus, were supposedly of Trojan descent (from Aeneas); sometimes Roman poets spoke of Remus as Rome's founder.

99–100. For Cosimo's generosity to the Church and Monastery of San Marco (restored 1437–43), see Gutkind, Appendix 10, and also Kent, *Cosimo de' Medici*. There Cosimo created, it is said, Europe's first public library (101–2n). Thus in *De ill. urbis Flor.* (fol. 18, Paris 1583 edition; *Carmina* 10:353), Verino calls San Marco "a home of the Muses," stressing the quantity of Greek and Latin religious works held. There too he mentions San Lorenzo, "which the pious Medici have built" (111–12n). Cf. Landino, *Xandra* 3.15.71–74 for San Lorenzo as made proud at Cosimo's own expense and for San Marco.

101–2. Dionisotti (p. 177) thinks the Badia at Fiesole meant, but Cosimo founded libraries elsewhere too, including San Marco. See 99–100n and 109–10n.

103. See 1.20.19–22n.

105–8. Lucius Licinius Lucullus (ca. 117–56 BCE), Roman commander before Pompey against Mithridates, king of Pontus, became a byword for luxurious living. He was particularly fond of a kind of marble. At one property of his at Naples, the sea was brought in to make a moat and fishponds around his house, he had structures built out on the water, and he also tunneled through hills there. In *De ill. urbis Flor.* (fol. 18, Paris 1583 edition; *Carmina* 10:353), Verino says, "Why should I mention the Medici's proud residences built at Careggi and Trebbio or on the rock at Fiesole? You would swear they were Lucullus' proud villas." Rich Romans "building on the sea" and "leveling off mountains" figure in Sallust, *Cat.* 20 (145–48n).

109–10. Dionisotti (p. 177) reasonably considers the Badia at Fiesole meant, though he finds difficulty with the sequence of thought in 91–116 and speaks of apparent contamination by combination of two versions of the passage (see 47–48n). The Badia (originally eleventh-century) was rebuilt for Cosimo (who provided a library stocked by the bookseller Vespasiano da Bisticci). Scansion of *Fesulis* (here and 115): 1.20.1–2n.

111–12. For Cosimo's close association with the church of San Lorenzo in Florence, see Kent, *Cosimo de'Medici*, and also the collection *San Lorenzo: A Florentine Church*, ed. R. W. Gaston and L. A. Waldman, forthcoming in the I Tatti series. Cosimo continued reconstruction originally commissioned by his father (1.11.43–44n). The finished church was consecrated in 1461. In Book IV of his *Theotocon* (text in *A*), Dominico Corella (ca. 1403–83) praises Cosimo's aid to churches, including his making San Lorenzo golden at his own expense after the previous century's neglect. Verino here admires the coffered ceiling of the nave. See also 99–100n.

113–14. See 2.7.3–6n.

115. Cf. the wording of Landino, *Xandra* 2.6.23–24.

118. Landino, *Xandra* 3.15.55–56 says of Cosimo, "I shall think him . . . like not to a man but to the gods above."

121. After Calliope's lament, a flashback account of Cosimo's end begins.

123–24. See 1.25.27–30n, *P.* 20n. Line 123 ends as Landino, *Xandra* 2.8.13.

126. See 2.12.6n.

129. An echo of Dido's words in Vergil, *Aen.* 4.653.

131. Reused as line 5 of Verino's long eulogy for Albiera degli Albizzi (d. 1473; see 2.5n). After Propertius 2.28.58.

132. See 2.5.21–22n.

137–38. See 1.20.25–26n.

139–40. After quitting Earth (Ovid, *Met.* 1.150), Astraea, goddess of justice in the Golden Age, became a constellation, Virgo or Libra. Naldi, *Eleg.* 3.11.347ff. sees Cosimo's promotion of peace as on the way to bringing back Astraea and the Golden Age. Cosimo's deathbed speech in *P.* 282–309 is principally concerned with justice.

145–48. The notion of rich men stringing together a row of houses is from Sallust, *Cat.* 20.11 (105–8n).

157–58. Mars is "common" (i.e., liable to favor either side) in [Vergil], *Ciris* 359, and *Cat.* 9.50 (cf. Landino, *Xandra* 3.4.49).

161–62. The *condottiere* Niccolò Piccinino (d. 1444), at the instigation of Filippo Maria Visconti, duke of Milan, invaded Florentine territory in 1440 with a Milanese force accompanied by exiles from Florence, hoping to overthrow the Medici. Piccinino reached Fiesole, but Florence stood firm, and he had to withdraw, subsequently suffering defeat at Anghiari (June 29, 1440). Landino, *Misc. Poems* 2.15ff., and Naldi, *Eleg.* 3.11.191ff. recall events.

167. In Vergil, *Aen.* 6.854, the Romans are "to spare the vanquished and bring down the proud."

173–76. A marble slab (no monument) beneath the dome of San Lorenzo records, "Cosimo de' Medici is buried here, by public decree Father of his Country." The body is buried in the vault below.

179–80. Line 179 begins as Vergil, *Aen.* 5.693, and *Ciris* 283. "Seeking the stars" at death: Ovid, *Tristia* 2.57 (of Augustus). Empyrean: P. 913–16n.

2.52

Written (like 2.53 and 2.54) soon after Cosimo's death (August 1, 1464).

2.53

1–2. Cf. 2.47.1–2 and see 2.47.3n. Cicero was called *Pater Patriae* ("Father of his Country"), for saving Rome from Catiline (63 BCE). Lycurgus (also 2.51.45): P. 905–9n.

2.54

2 (and 9). See 2.51.23–24n.

7–8. Being pitiable even to an enemy: Ovid, *Met.* 6.276 and 9.178.

9–10. Cf. 2.51.33–36n.

12. Cf. 2.14.2 and 2.14n.

25–26. See 1.20.18n. Jupiter here denotes the Christian God.

27–28. *Florens* is used (as, for instance, by Landino and Naldi) for *Floren-*

tinus ("Florentine"). *Series . . . malorum* ("succession of ills"): Ovid, *Met.* 4.564, and *Ex Ponto* 1.4.19 and 2.7.45.

2.55

Much influenced by the last poem of Ovid's *Amores* (3.15), as Munari (p. 297) observes.

1–2. In spite of 2.1.5–6, Verino here and in 23–24 treats Piero's achievements as his intended theme for grander verse after moving on from love poetry. Cf. Landino's intentions in *Xandra* 3.19 (1.1.21–22n, 1.20.31–32n). "Tender elegies": P. preface 3.

3–4. Venus/Aphrodite is often "golden" in ancient literature. Line 4 (with L's alliterative *vellite*) is almost as Ovid, *Am.* 3.15.16, though Munari sees B's *tollite* as Verino's later improvement.

5–6. Ovid, *Am.* 3.15.18 ("A greater racing ground must be pounded by great horses") inspired 5 (cf. *Fasti* 4.10). Horace's lyre is "unwarlike" (*imbellis*) in *Odes* 1.6.10 (and cf. 1.15.15 there); see also 11–12n.

8. After Propertius 2.11.2, "Let him who sows seed in barren earth praise you (= Cynthia)."

10. "Many thousands" of lover's poems: Ovid, *Am.* 1.8.58.

11–12. Ovid, *Am.* 3.15.19 ("Unwarlike elegies, congenial Muse, farewell") suggests that *versus genialis* here is in apposition to *Erato* (1.26.13–14n). *Abito* ("Be gone") is second imperative. *Iam satis est* (11) occurs in Horace, *Sat.* 1.1.120 in rounding off the poem.

16. Ovid, *Fasti* 4.9 speaks of fittingly giving his first years to erotic verse. Cf. 1.2.37–40.

17. Being a scandal: 1.9.15–16n.

19–24. Munari (p. 298) rightly perceives *increpuit* in 19 ("rebuked") as from the Ovidian model (*Am.* 3.15.17) and credibly detects the influence of *Am.* 3.1.15–30 (where Tragedy chides Ovid for being too reluctant to move on from love poetry) in the reproach that follows.

23–24. Ovid, *Am.* 1.3.19 lies behind 23. "Maeonian": 2.8.1–2n. L marks the end with *FINIS*; B uses the equivalent Greek word, *telos* (written in Greek script).

PARADISE

The title is amplified in both manuscripts as follows: "*Paradisus* de rebus supernis [superis *B*] et de beatorum splendore et maxime de his qui optime rem p⟨ublicam⟩ administrarint, Ugolini Verini" ("*Paradise*, on things above and on the splendor of the blessed ones and especially on such as have governed their state very well, the work of Ugolino Verino"). The meter of the Preface is elegiac couplets. The main poem is entirely in dactylic hexameters. False quantities are found in *basis* (100), *ether* (156), *caritate* (199), *Echionia* (805), *Atilius* [*Att-*] (861), *Solon* (910), *Euripides* (952), *Ovidius* (936), *Dion* and *Platonis* (1006), *Plato* (1016 and 1073), *triclinia* (1091); see also on *antea* in 724 and 795, and *semiaperta* in 142. *Archytas/Archyta* (1006 and 1008) takes two different forms for metrical convenience. The Index to *Fiammetta* notes false quantities there under *scansion, anomalies of*.

Preface 1–4. Verino refers to *Fiammetta* (where see 1.1.17–18n). Being Love's soldier: *F.* 1.4.93–94n. Scansion of *Cupido* (4): *F.* 2.7.1–2n (similarly *Scorpio* in 29 below).

Preface 6. As Ovid, *Tristia* 1.5.56.

Preface 9–10. *Divi*, here translated "saints," is the term chiefly used by Verino for the Christians in heaven, the holy dead (occasionally it means saints in the special sense of canonized persons, as in 561, which refers to churches of the saints). *Beati*, here translated "the blessed," is more sparingly employed in this work, but has similar meaning. Both *divus* and *beatus* are commonly so used elsewhere. Verino refers to the celestial (angelic) beings in heaven as *dei* ("gods," sometimes used also of the holy dead) and *caelestes* ("heavenly ones"). There is also *caelicolae* ("dwellers in heaven"). Angels are called gods in, for example, Milton, *Paradise Lost* 2.391, where Satan calls his assembled fallen angels "synod of gods" (cf. 1.116, 1.138, 2.352, and elsewhere there, and similarly 2.11, "deities of heaven").

1–3. Latona was mother to both Apollo and Diana. The former, as god of light, was equated with the sun, while one of Diana's three forms was the moon. I translate *Olympus* as "heaven" throughout this work (where it never refers to the actual mountain).

7. Bellona: *F.* 2.4.5n. Latium: Italy. See 208–76n for the situation.

12. *Grave Martis opus* ("the stern work of Mars"): Vergil, *Aen.* 8.516.

15–43. The wonders or monsters seen (*miracula* in 15 [cf. Ovid, *Met.* 2.193], *monstra* in 42) are various constellations (Cancer, Leo, etc.). Nemean lion (17–19): *F.* 1.9.37–38n.

20. The sun enters the constellation Leo at the hottest time of year (in the northern hemisphere). Cf. 913–16, and *F.* 2.51.121–24.

21–23. The constellation Draco (the Dragon) lies in part between the Great Bear and the Little Bear (cf. Ovid, *Met.* 3.45) and coils around the North Pole. There is also a different constellation called Anguis (the Serpent) in another part of the sky. Nevertheless, Vergil, *Geo.* 1.244–46 confusingly speaks of Anguis as coiling between the two Bears, there actually meaning the Dragon, *anguis* and *draco* often being treated as synonyms = "snake." That identification seems to explain 23, as Verino's "twofold pole" presumably refers to the two Bears (cf. *geminos Triones,* "the twofold Plow Oxen," Vergil, *Aen.* 1.744; Silius Italicus 3.193f., where Anguis encompasses the *geminum sidus,* or "twofold constellation," of the two bears). In Verino's *Carlias* 7.10 the Snake (*Serpens*) is "stretched out with its long body between either pole (*inter utrumque polum*)." The (many-headed) Water Serpent in 38 (Hydrus, also Hydra; *F.* 1.25.27–30n) is commonly equated with Anguis (though not here). The green snakes (*dracones*) in 38 are probably its heads.

24–25. Europa was carried off on the back of a bull (Jupiter in disguise).

27–28. The eagle (here a constellation) was Jupiter's bird, bearing his thunderbolts (cf. 373; Ovid, *Met.* 15.386). The beautiful Trojan boy Ganymede (sometimes equated with Aquarius) was carried off by the eagle to serve as Jupiter's cupbearer (cf. Dante, *Purg.* 9.19ff.). See *F.* 2.10.5–10n and 2.37. Ida: *F.* 1.16.1–2n.

29. Verino's Latin oddly makes the Scorpion's claws, not its tail, poisonous. In Ovid, *Met.* 2.198 the Scorpion is "dripping with the exudation of black poison," but threatens wounds with its curved tail.

34. The centaur Chiron: Sagittarius.

38. See 21–23n.

49. Dis: *F.* 2.5.21–22n. Tartarus: Underworld's place of torment.

52. Thyle (Thule): *F.* 2.2.9–10n. The Rhiphaean Mountains were in northern Scythia (*F.* 1.28.17n).

53. For the sense of *parvo discrimine*, cf. Ovid, *Met.* 6.62.

54–57. Cf. Dante, *Paradiso* 22.135 (and commentators' notes thereon) for the earth seen as tiny and unimpressive when viewed from the sky. Dante is there in debt to Cicero's *Dream of Scipio* (*Somnium Scipionis*), which includes (end of *Rep.* 6.16) the following observation, echoed by Verino here: "Now the very earth seemed to me so small that I grieved for our empire, through which we make contact with the merest dot (or "mathematical point," *punctum*), as it were, of that earth."

56. Cf. Ovid, *Met.* 13.758–59.

59–60. See *F.* 1.4.33–34n. For the awkward syntax of 60, cf. 805.

64. *Discordia demens* ("mad strife"): Vergil, *Aen.* 6.280.

66. *Iugerum* in the singular is normally second declension, not third as here, but *iugero* would not scan.

68. Partly after Ovid, *Am.* 1.4.61.

71–72. A marginal note in B takes *concentus* to refer to the harmony of the spheres, a Pythagorean idea spoken of in Cicero's *Somnium Scipionis* (*Rep.* 6.18), but that supposition seems dubious, as *divinum carmen* in 422 and *concentus carminis* in 425 refer to angelic choir singing. Cf. the revolving of the heavens in Vergil, *Aen.* 2.250 (there as day changes to night, here the reverse).

76–77. Pierides: Muses. Parnassus: *F.* 1.1.23–24n.

79. See *F.* 2.51.13–14n.

81–83. The Holy Spirit is invoked for inspiration (as well as the Muses in 76–80 and 87–88). Milton too invokes the Holy Spirit, in *Paradise Lost* 1.17ff. and in *Paradise Regained* 1.8ff. Vida does the same in the opening lines of his *Christiad* (as also in 5.205 there), and such an invocation is found in numerous places elsewhere (see the Vida volume in this series, translated by James Gardner, 1.2n).

85–87. Like Bartolini, I take all from *quosque* in 85 down to *vidi* in 87 as depending on *narrate* there. In 85 I understand *vidi* from 87 to govern the accusative and infinitive construction.

89–93. In Homer, *Iliad* 8.18–27 Zeus declares that if a golden rope were lowered from heaven to Earth, he would win a contest of strength with it ("tug of war" style) against all the other deities combined. The existence of an *actual* golden chain in the sky is briefly spoken of in Plato, *Theaet.* 153C, and Euripides, *Or.* 982. The idea eventually passed via the Neoplatonists to the medieval alchemists, figuring (in changed form) in their mystical beliefs about the cosmos. Milton's mentions of a golden chain in the heavens (*Paradise Lost* 2.1005 and 1051) palely reflect the tradition. In 91 the reflexive *se ligat* (lit., "ties itself") is equivalent to a passive.

99. The vestibule (*vestibulum*) here (and in 1097) and the entrance portico (*primum tectum*) in 115 refer to the same structure fronting God's palace. The tower in 111–12 is mentioned again in 1098.

100. *Basis* illicitly has the *a* long here. See Preface headnote.

103. Pyrope is a fiery red (crimson) gemstone, a kind of garnet (note the precious stones in 106–10), though a gold-bronze metal alloy is probably meant by *pyropus* here. Cf. Ovid, *Met.* 2.2 (similarly on a door); Lucretius 2.803; Propertius 4.10.21. Translations of, and notes on, those passages show some uncertainty and disagreement over the interpretation of *pyropus*.

118. See *F.* 1.2.21 and 24n.

124. The tmesis in *circum . . . lustro* is after Lucretius 5.1437.

128. *Vectes* is a false nominative singular form for *vectis* (cf. *periuria* in 498).

132–34. Cf. the angel at the gate of St. Peter in Dante, *Purg.* 9.76ff.

142. *Semiaperta* has to scan as five syllables. *Semiadaperta* (with the synizesis of *ia* normal in similar compounds, like *semianimis* in verse) is found in Ovid, *Am.* 1.6.4 and could possibly be read here. *Semiaperta*, however, occurs in Navagero, *Lusus* 39.5 (with synizesis of *ia*, though with illicit shortening of the first syllable).

147. *Clotho* (*F.* 1.23.5–8n): Greek dative.

148–49. Purification by the purging of sin (in Purgatory) is normally necessary before admission to heaven is possible, according to 363–64.

150. *Divum* ("of the saints") should be taken with *sedes* ("dwelling places"); cf. *sedes beatum* ("dwelling places of the blessed") in Preface 9. It may also go with *numine* ("divine help").

151. Bartolini reads *repperis* with B, though no licit form either of *reperio* or *repo*. A has *repseris*, the future perfect or perfect subjunctive of *repo*, normally "creep," but here, it seems, "make one's way."

156. *Aether* illicitly has *er* short. See Preface headnote. *Machina mundi* (Lucretius 5.96) is also in 478.

157. *Non secus ut quondam* is read by both manuscripts here and in 506, but I cannot parallel *ut* for the regular *ac* after *non secus*. Perhaps Verino somehow (wrongly) thought it legitimate, but it seems better to read *ac* for *ut* in both lines (so Bartolini, who here rewrites the line).

162. Panchaia (four syllables) was a fabulous island east of Arabia famed for incense, myrrh, and gems.

181. The voice is that of Cosimo de' Medici (207), who died August 1, 1464. Thereafter, his son Piero the Gouty (l. 216) ruled Florence till 1469, succeeded by his son Lorenzo the Magnificent (220).

187. With a vowel following, I have preferred *atque* to *ac* (manuscripts) here and in 213, 781, and 906.

196–97. Cosimo died aged seventy-five. Why all the blessed dead look around thirty is explained 606–16.

199–200. See 780–95n for the notion of the Holy Spirit bonding together those in heaven, seemingly hinted here (and cf. the communion/fellowship of the Holy Spirit, 2 Corinthians 13:14). *Caritate* should have first syllable long. See Preface headnote.

202–3. Cf. 605 for this contented absence of jealousy.

208–76. I take 216–21 to refer to events of September 2, 1466, a day of great crisis, when, amid the political unrest surrounding the Pitti conspiracy to overthrow Medici rule, a *parlamento* of the citizens of Florence was held in the Piazza della Signoria, and a vote was passed creating a *Balia* empowered to amend the constitution (which ensured continued

Medici control of Florence). On that occasion, Lorenzo, fully armored (cf. 220) and on a horse, was among three thousand pro-Medici troops who surrounded the square. Thereafter, some of the conspirators, whose lives Piero had generously spared, attempted to find foreign armed support to oust him. In particular, Dietisalvi (or Diotisalvi) Neroni and Niccolò Soderini went to Venice and persuaded the authorities there and the great *condottiere* Bartolomeo Colleone (or Colleoni; see 225), at the time Venice's captain general, to help them bring the Medici down in 1467. Borso d'Este (who controlled Ferrara) also backed their cause, while Milan, under Duke Galeazzo Maria Sforza (250), and Naples, under King Ferrante I (246), were Medici allies. Roberto (or Ruberto) San Severino (a Neapolitan noble, 257) commanded the Florentine troops, while the count of Urbino (Federigo da Montefeltro, 258) held the supreme command of all the pro-Medici forces. Colleone crossed the Po to begin operations May 10, 1467. Eventually, after much maneuvering, he was defeated at the Mulinella within the territory of Imola in the Romagna (July 23/24, 1467), and the war was concluded by a peace made in April 1468. Verino seems to have written this passage in expectation (or knowledge) of the eventual success of Florentine arms (cf. 271–76).

225. *Colleo* has its final *o* shortened; F. 2.7.1–2n.

226. Astorgio Manfredi, lord of Faenza, had undertaken to hold the pass of the Lamone valley (230) for Piero but put Florentine troops within his territory in danger by defecting to the other side. See F. T. Perrens, *A History of Florence, 1434–1531* (London, 1892), 1:256 (with sources in footnote there). Colleone invaded Florentine territory from the direction of Faenza. Martial (8.75.2) and Juvenal (1.171) use *Flaminia* for the Flaminian Way (Gaius Flaminius conquered Cisalpine Gaul ca. 224 BCE). Flaminia occurs as a judicial district from the second century CE. In *De ill. urbis Flor. (Carmina* 10:335), Verino describes how the *Marcicolae* (Venetians; 233n) under Colleone "filled the cities of Flaminia with great terrors" but suffered defeat. There *Coleo* scans short, short, long.

228. Cf. Vergil, *Aen.* 2.576.

230. The Lamone flows southwest into Florentine territory from the neighborhood of Faenza.

233. The "foe who venerates St. Mark" is singular for plural. Venice was the Republic of St. Mark.

235. "Roman stock" (cf. 245 and 1061): F. 1.20.17–18n.

241. "Sons of Mars": Mars was father of Romulus and Remus, and the Florentines claimed to be "Sullans" (and thus of Roman ancestry, as stated in 244f.)

245. See F. 1.20.18n.

248. Lydian Lion (emblem of Tuscany): F. 1.1.1–2n. The eldest son of the king of Naples (Alfonso, duke of Calabria) commanded the Neapolitan contingent that served against Colleone.

251. "Gallic towns" here means those of the ancient Cisalpine Gaul, that is, Italy north of the peninsula (including Lombardy and Venice's territories in the region).

254. Philip of Bresse, brother of the duke of Savoy, menaced Florence's ally Milan but was driven back by Galeazzo Maria Sforza after the defeat of Colleone. Perhaps there were unfulfilled hopes of his coming over to the Medici cause. See Perrens (as cited 226n), pp. 258–59.

255. Lodovico Gonzaga, marquis of Mantua (1444–78), is meant.

257. Roberto: 208–76n. *Coniunget castra* is, literally, "will join camps" (= combine forces). The singular verb serves two singular subjects (*Robertus* and *dux*), as often in Latin.

258. If by *dux* Verino means "duke" (*A* has *Dux Federicus* in its margin), Federigo da Montefeltro was not formally such until 1474, though lord or count of Urbino since 1444. *Dux* here may mean only "leader."

260. Sertorius was a capable Roman general who fought Pompey the Great in Spain in the 70s BCE.

261–62. The "unspeakable people" are the Venetians; the "brigand commander" is Colleone.

265. Illyrian Gulf: Adriatic Sea.

266. Ossa and Taurus are mountains in Thessaly and southeastern Asia Minor, respectively.

282. Cf. Cosimo's deathbed speech to similar effect F. 2.51.129–78.

286–309. Christians believe God the Son will make the Last Judgment (see also 620–33) as mediator.

288. For Marcus Tullius Cicero (106–43 BCE), Rome's greatest orator, see 893–96.

305–6. Cf. Matthew 25:41. The context there is of Christ separating the sheep (to the right, verse 33; cf. 308 here) from the goats (to the left) at the Last Judgment.

307. Reading the jussive subjunctive *fiat* (B) for the future *fiet* (A), as Bartolini does, makes this line (wrongly, I think) part of God's words.

312–24. Thwarted assassination plans laid against Piero in August 1466 seem to be in point. Lorenzo is said to have saved his father from an intended ambush by warning him to change his route into Florence. The chief persons then seeking the overthrow of the Medici were Luca Pitti, Agnolo Acciaiuoli, Niccolò Soderini, and Dietisalvi Neroni. See 208–76n.

315–16. See 728–29n.

333. For eating and drinking (or not) in heaven, see 535, 553, and 647–62.

334. For the eyes on angelic wings, cf. Ezekiel 10:12 (his vision of cherubim). Milton (*Paradise Lost* 6.755 and 11.130) follows Ezekiel in this detail.

336. *Fuerant* is pluperfect for imperfect (for metrical convenience), as is *astiterant* in 375. Cf. also *exspoliaverat* in 868 (pluperfect for perfect).

342–43. Verino here uses the indeclinable *seraphim* and *cherubim* as (collective) singulars. They could formerly be so used in English too (seraph and cherub are now the normal singular forms). Cf. 426. *Seraphim* is said to mean "Burning Ones," and so *igneus* ("fiery") in 343 may qualify *seraphim* (cf., for example, "fiery Seraphim" in Milton, *Paradise Lost* 2.512) but goes better with *cherubim* (cf. "flaming cherubim" in 6.102 of Milton's same work). *Summi sapientia Regis* (lit., "the wisdom of the King most high") is in apposition to *seraphim* (cf. *nuntius* [= "messenger"] of the angel in 347), treating the seraph as symbolic of God's wisdom/intelligence (sometimes the cherub was so regarded). In Dante's *Paradiso* (28.97ff.), there are three triads (hierarchies) of angels. Dante there follows the order and number of the types of angel as they had been fixed in the *Celestial Hierarchy* once attributed to Dionysius the Areopagite, while briefly noting (28.135ff.) that Pope Gregory the Great suggested a (slightly) different order. In the arrangement in *Celestial Hierarchy*, the highest triad is of seraphim, cherubim, and thrones (so Verino here). The second is of dominations, virtues, and powers (cf. 345 here, naming only the last two, though B's marginal note also mentions dominations). The lowest triad in *Celestial Hierarchy* is of angels, archangels, and principalities (cf. 347, where Verino has angels below virtues and powers but does not mention archangels or principalities). Pope Gregory put principalities in the second triad, relegating virtues to the third; otherwise he agrees with *Celestial Hierarchy*. In *Convivio* (2.6), Dante has a rather different grouping of the nine orders, with thrones, angels, and archangels in the lowest triad, and powers, cherubim, and seraphim in the highest, the middle rank being given to dominations, virtues, and principalities.

349. Both manuscripts (and Bartolini) have *haec* (with *mandata*), but *hi* (= *hi secundi*) is required.

355–62. For the book with seven seals, cf. Revelation 5:1–9. There the Lamb, seven-horned and seven-eyed, opens the seals.

363–64. In 148–49 the unpurified Verino was told that contact between the impure and the pure was (normally) great sin, though an exception would be made for him.

365–73. The four beasts round God's throne (known as the Beasts of the Apocalypse) are from Revelation 4:7, where (in the King James Version), "The first beast was like a lion, and the second beast like a calf, and the third beast had a face as a man, and the fourth beast was like a flying eagle." Cf. also Ezekiel 1:10, and see further, 374–79n. In 368, scan *Gaetulia*, if read (*Gaetula* manuscripts), as three syllables. Cf. *Feretr(i)o* in F. 2.51.51.

369. The Achelous (now the Aspropotamo) is the longest river in Greece. One story associated with its like-named river god (see Ovid, *Met.* 9.1–100) is that he lost a horn in a fight with Hercules.

372–73. I take *astabat* to be equivalent to *aderat* (*stare* being quite often a substitute for *esse* in neo-Latin verse). See 27–28n for the eagle.

374–79. The four Beasts of the Apocalypse (365–73n) were traditionally taken to symbolize the evangelists (the lion, ox, angel, and eagle being held to stand for Mark, Luke, Matthew, and John, respectively). Verino thus has the four men standing next to the beasts associated with them. See the Sannazaro volume in this I Tatti series, *DPV* 1.407n and especially Appendix I, for extensive related comment by the translator there, Michael C. J. Putnam. For *astiterant*, see 336n. In 374 I have (like Bartolini) preferred *visu* as in Vergil, *Aen.* 12.252 (cf. also Ovid, *Fasti* 3.31) to *visum* (manuscripts).

383–433. The heavenly choir takes its basic theme, of course, from Genesis I, with elaborations concerning the various planets (391–421) and the angels, including the fallen ones (428–33). *Ut* (= "how") in 384 (depending on *cantabant*, "they sang," in 383) is repeated numerous times in the passage down to 421 to add further details of the song. In 409, however, *ut* = "when."

391–421. The "planets" here include the Moon and the Sun, as regularly at this period, and are treated as being associated with particular characteristics in people. Cf. Dante's ten heavens in *Paradiso*, where the first seven are those of the Moon, Mercury, Venus, the Sun, Mars, Jupiter, and Saturn, each tenanted by appropriate kinds of spirit (e.g. Venus by those too inclined to sensual love, Mars by those who fought for the Christian faith). The outer planets Uranus and Neptune were yet to be discovered in Verino's time. *Cytherea* (393; cf. 418): Venus (*F.* 1.4.87–88n). Atlas' grandson (396) and the Cyllenian (400): Mercury. For the sun (Phoebus) as controlling the seasons (402–9), cf. *F.* 1.4.74.

414. The "Dictaean King" here is Jupiter (*F.* 1.6.33–34n).

417. Saturn completes its orbit in 29.46 years.

418–21. Planets restraining or canceling-out others: *F.* 2.45.85–86n and 2.45.87–88n.

426. *Seraphim* as singular: 342–43n.

430–33. The expulsion of Satan and his followers (fallen angels) after their attempt to overthrow God is meant. *Tartarus* is used for hell.

435–36. *Adam* is indeclinable (here accusative). Adam's creation from dust (cf. 474): Genesis 2:7.

436–38. *Superbia* in 436 is subject of the verbs in 438. Take *inflatos* and *feroces* predicatively.

440. The idea seems to be that God did not want man to have a mind/soul incapable of rising above the petty, mundane preoccupations of human existence, even if his body, made from mud, was intended to act as a restraint on his becoming too arrogant.

441. Genesis 2:21–22 describes Eve's creation from a rib of Adam. Understand *ut*.

443. Cf. Genesis 3:3 and 19 for death being the consequence of the sinful eating of fruit of the tree of knowledge, implying that Adam and Eve would otherwise have been immortal.

454. For guardian angels, cf. Matthew 18:10.

463. See F. 2.26.6n for delayed *sed*.

474. See 435–36n. The "dark prison of mud" is the body. Cf. 601 and 709–10 for the prison image, as well as Cicero, *Rep.* 6.14 (*Somnium Scipionis*), "those who have escaped from the chains of their bodies as from a prison."

477. The impediment of man's original sin, stemming from Adam, is meant.

481. Augustus was the Roman emperor 27 BCE to 14 CE.

483. Christ is called a slave again in 487 and 1049, following Philippians 2:6–7.

491. Both manuscripts have *verbere* ("lash"). Bartolini's substitution *vulnere* ("wound") presumably seeks to remove any possible implication that Christ died *during* the flogging he received, but perhaps Verino just wrote a little loosely here.

497–98. Christianity's hostility to the Jews as supposedly guilty of Christ's blood is evident here, albeit briefly (Vida makes far more of blaming them rather than Pilate in his *Christiad*). Only in 1965 did the Vatican declare it wrong to blame Jews now for Christ's death. *Periuria* as nominative singular is unattested (*periurium* is the true form), hence Bartolini's substitution of *violentia*. See 128n.

499–503. The reference is to Christ's withdrawal of some patriarchs from Limbo (1 Peter 3:19; Dante, *Inf.* 12.38–9, where he is the Mighty One who rescued them) in his harrying, or harrowing, of hell. Vida (*Christiad* 6.121–293) deals with the theme at length.

506–15. Orpheus descended to the Underworld to ask permission to bring back his dead bride, Eurydice. Granted his request, he violated the condition forbidding him to look on her until the Upper World had been reached, and she was therefore reclaimed by the realm below. For 506 see 157n.

508–9. *Firmare* ("to make firm") does not usually = "cause (rivers) to stop," but Verino stretches its meaning here to achieve extra alliteration.

511. Cerberus: F. 1.12.17–18n.

518–19. The "Divine Ardor" denotes the Holy Spirit, called *Spiritus Ardens* ("the Ardent Spirit") in 783 (see 780–95n). Acts 2:3 describes the Holy Spirit's descent upon the apostles at Pentecost in the form of cloven tongues "like as of fire."

531–32. See 606–15 for the reason the blessed dead all look about thirty.

535. For eating and drinking in heaven, see 333, 553, and 647–62. Here the saints feast on ambrosia and nectar (and are sated with ambrosia 553), but 647–62 (where see note) denies that they and angelic celestial beings truly eat and digest at all.

572. The Roman emperor Nero (54–68) notoriously made the Christians the scapegoats for the Fire of Rome in 64. *Dira Neronis . . . tormenta* is also in 955–56.

602. This line does not scan unless hiatus be allowed after *fraude*. I suspect that Verino by oversight scanned *abh-* long (as in B's unmetrical reading *abhorrentia* in 1063). Bartolini rewrites the last three feet, but, as the error seems to be Verino's, not a copyist's, I let the line stand.

605. Cf. 202–3.

606–16. Christ was traditionally about thirty-three when crucified, having begun his ministry at around thirty. In 613–16 Verino declares death in youth, before one's physical and mental powers decline, a blessing.

625. See also 293–309 for the theme of divine judgment. Vida, *Christiad*

4.1019–22 makes it clear that until the Last Judgment no one, except for those few brought to heaven by Christ at his resurrection, will have a body there, but will be purely a soul.

629. Avernus here denotes the Underworld, where the Styx flowed.

630. *Obscurum* must mean "dark/dull," as opposed to bright, like the forms of those in heaven.

647–62. For eating and drinking (or not) in heaven, see also 333, 535, and 553 (and Psalms 78:25). Milton, *Paradise Lost* 5.407ff. treats angels as eating (and digesting and defecating), but some had argued from Tobit (in the Apocrypha) 12:19, where Raphael says that he has neither eaten nor drunk but been only a vision, that angels only *appear* to eat, a view expressly rejected by Milton (5.434ff.).

654. "Supernal minds" seems to be used as a general term for angelic orders not already specified. There are no minds as such in the angelology of pseudo-Dionysius or Pope Gregory (342–43n).

675. For *damma* treated as masculine, cf. Vergil, *Ecl.* 8.28, and *Geo.* 3.539 (both *timidi*).

692. The image "purer than amber" is after Vergil, *Geo.* 3.522.

694–99. Verino probably has in mind the biblical balm of Gilead. An Arab tradition said that the queen of Sheba presented the tree from which it was extracted to Solomon, who planted it in his Jericho gardens.

701. *Amoena virecta* (cf. 880) is from Vergil, *Aen.* 6.638.

702–3. Giovanni de' Medici (1421–63) was the younger son of Cosimo and brother of Piero.

708. There is a pun on *Verinus* and *verus* ("true"), treating Verino's name (alternatively *de' Vieri*) as an English speaker might treat *Tru(e)man*. Cf. *F.* 2.15.4 (and n). Note how the appositional nominatives *fidus* (707) and *dictus* (708) are mixed with the vocatives *fautor* and *Verine*. The practice is seen in classical verse (e.g., Vergil, *Aen.* 8.77).

711–14. Poets often spoke figuratively of their fame carrying them to the stars. Giovanni means to ask whether Verino's poetry has taken him to the stars before death (gentle humor?). See *F.* 1.1.26n.

714–15. The two grandsons (of Cosimo) are Piero's sons, Lorenzo (1449–92) and Giuliano de' Medici (1453–78). See F. 1.11n.

724. *Antea* (properly long, short, long) is here and in 795 either a (long, long) disyllable (Verino perhaps had in mind the treatment of *anteambulo* as four syllables in verse; *antehac* is disyllabic in Horace, *Odes* 1.37) or illicitly counted as a dactyl (long, short, short). See Preface headnote.

728–29. *Prudentia velox* (Persius 4.4) is used of Cosimo's shrewdness in Verino's *De ill. urbis Flor.* (fol. 16, Paris 1583 edition; *Carmina* 10:350). *Prudentia* in 729 after *prudens* in 728 may seem undesirably repetitive, though *pectore* occurs twice in 832–33, as does *murmura* in the transmitted text of 740–41 (see 740n). Note also *exitiale* and *exitium* in 315–16 (Bartolini substitutes *excidium* in 316), *cruce* and *cruces* in 494–95, and *vitiis* and *vitiorum* in 965–66. Comparable repetitions in F. 1.2.31–32, 1.8.26–27, 1.11.27–28, 1.11.49–50, 1.13.11–12, 1.21.27–28, 1.23.13–15, 1.27.36–37, 2.1.5–6, 2.2.12–13, 2.5.13–14 (see also 2.5.13n), 2.12.12–13, 2.22.35–36, 2.22.37–38, 2.32.2–3, 2.46.17–18, and 2.51.22–23 show Verino willing to tolerate them or sometimes employ them for effect.

731. Saturn ruled the gods (before Jupiter) in the Golden Age (F. 2.45.109–10n), though here longevity (wished for the invalid Piero de' Medici) is chiefly in point.

740. *Verbera* (Bartolini) avoids having *murmura* at the same point in successive lines (so B, the sole manuscript here) and enhances alliteration (cf. Lucretius 5.955, *verbera ventorum vitare*, and 6.115, *verberibus venti versant*), though the twofold *murmura* is not incredible (728–29n). Cf. F. 1.18.23–24.

746–47. With *annosae* ("ancient") understand (a little awkwardly) *arbores* ("trees"), implied in *silva* ("wood") in 744. Bartolini rewrites this couplet to make the wood continue as subject.

748. Near Aricia in Latium there was a famous grove sacred to Diana.

758–60. See F. 1.6.37–40n.

765. Minerva's hostility to the crow (her attendant till degraded in favor of the owl for offending her by tale-telling): Ovid, *Met.* 2.542ff. "The crow hateful to Minerva": Ovid, *Am.* 2.6.35.

768. The people in the wood are called dusky faced (cf. 790), in that they lack the bright gleam of the Christian saints in heaven. They also wear clothes of various colors, not the brilliant white worn by all the saints. Compare how the damned in 630 are given by the divine Judge a feeble, *lusterless* (dull), and aged body, not a young and brightly shining one, such as the virtuous receive. *Induta colores* ("dressed in colors") is from Ovid's description of Iris (the rainbow) in *Met.* 1.270.

769. The syntactical awkwardness of the manuscript reading *dissimiles vestes* is removed by Bartolini's conjecture *dissimilis veste et* (or perhaps read *dissimilis veste* with lengthening at the caesura).

771. The brightness may be God's (with *Dei*) or a god's (with *dei*).

780–95. The people referred to in 765–79, Cosimo explains, are those who lived without sin, but neither knew nor denied Christ (as they had no knowledge of Christianity). With these in 792 are associated sinless infants who died unbaptized. Both are in Limbo in Dante's *Inferno* 4.33–39 (there Circle 1 of hell). By contrast, Verino here treats their abode as celestial and thus later sets such as Homer, Horace, Ovid, and Lucan (all met by Dante in Limbo, *Inferno* 4.88–90) in the world above. In 782–86 Verino refers to the doctrine of the Trinity, stressing that Father and Son have always existed and always will, and that both are eternally begetting and being begotten (a doctrine known as eternal generation). For the sense in which the Holy Spirit unites the Father and Son (783), cf. Vida, *Christiad* 4.40–42: "Furthermore, the love by which both [Father and Son] are united [*iunguntur*]—for a mutual ardor proceeds, breathing forth jointly, from each—we equally call both an omnipotent divine power and God." There "mutual ardor" (cf. Lucretius 4.1216) means love for each other. Maffeo Barberini, Pope Urban VIII (r. 1623–44), in his *Ad Divinum Spiritum hymnus* (*Poemata* [Antwerp, 1634], pp. 87–91), calls the Holy Spirit "the indissoluble bond (*vinculum*) between Son and Father," as well as "lovable burning (*ardor*) of the heart," and begs the Holy Spirit to burn his heart with fire. See also 518–19n. In 782 Bartolini reads *quae*, not *qui*, making *fides*, not *Christi*, the antecedent, but, though B there has simply *q*, A has *qui* in full, and *qui* in 784 and *quem* in 787 must have *Christi* as antecedent.

789. By "the stars," Verino here means the part of heaven accessible only to the blessed Christian dead. The virtuous non-Christians and unbaptized infants are, of course, in their own special part of the skies (but denied the sight of God). Note that, when (from 796 onward) Verino identifies numerous people in this special area (his version of Limbo), they are all from the ancient world. No virtuous non-Christians of later centuries are named.

792. The fourth-century bishop and theologian Gregory of Nazianzus (*Orat.* 40) described infants dying unbaptized but without sin of their own commission as being neither glorified nor punished after death, the essential notion behind Verino's "place with no glory but without punishment" here. Some other views of the fate of unbaptized infants (and virtuous non-Christians) after death were harsher.

795. See 724n.

796–803. The great Theban general Epaminondas defeated the Spartans at Leuctra in 371 BCE, so wresting the hegemony of Greece from Sparta (which a few years earlier had even had a garrison in Thebes). Pelopidas (804–6) was another leading Theban of the same period, commanding the Sacred Band of three hundred men (pairs of lovers) that was the flower of the Theban army.

798. The Thebans supposedly sprang from a (snake's or) dragon's teeth.

801. Argives here = Greeks in general.

803. Epaminondas' honesty and frugality resulted, we are told, in his leaving only one spit behind him to inherit, as B notes in the margin.

805–6. Echion, a Theban hero (father of Pentheus), sprang up from the earth when Cadmus sowed dragon's teeth. Echionian thus = Theban. Verino illicitly scans *Echionia* with the *o* the sole long quantity; the first *i* should be the only long. See Preface headnote. With the manuscript text (*quo nullo*), the literal meaning is "in none more than in whom." For the syntax, cf. 60.

807–10. Codrus, the last of the kings of Athens, is said to have sacrificed his life (traditionally in 1071 BCE) to secure victory in his city's struggle against the Heraclidae. An oracle had foretold that the side that lost its king would triumph.

811–13. Miltiades is meant. As an Athenian general, he defeated the Persians at Marathon in 490 BCE.

814–17. Themistocles is meant (F. 2.40.11–16n).

818–21. Verino refers to Aristides the Just (F. 2.46.13–14), the upright Athenian statesman unfairly ostracized in 483/82 BCE, who, after his recall, assessed the contributions in ships and men or money to be made by the members of the anti-Persian Delian League formed in 478/77 BCE and led by Athens. For Gaius Fabricius Luscinus (820), see F. 2.32.5 (with note) and 2.51.49, and also 858 below. Pelasgians (819) here = Greeks (cf. 969).

822–25. Pericles (d. 429 BCE), the Athenian statesman, orator, and general, made speeches helmeted to conceal his somewhat pointed head. Before his birth his mother supposedly dreamed that she brought forth a lion (Plutarch, *Life of Pericles*). Warrior Maiden (825): Athena (Minerva), patroness of Athens.

831–36. Lucius Junius Brutus was instrumental in the expulsion of the last king of Rome, the tyrannical Tarquin the Proud, traditionally in 510 BCE. As consul in 509 BCE, he had his own sons executed before his eyes for conspiring to restore the Tarquins (cf. Vergil, *Aen.* 6.819ff.). For the repetition of *pectore* in 832 and 833, see 728–29n and 740n.

837–38. Publius Valerius Poplicola, or Publicola, helped Brutus drive out the Tarquins and was reportedly four times consul. His cognomen (interpreted as "Carer for the People") supposedly came from supporting their rights. When criticized for his towering house, he ordered it pulled down overnight (Plutarch, *Publicola*). These lines (837–40) are the first of several narrative comments interspersed by Verino within Cosimo's quoted words. There are repeated (mostly unstated) switches from narrative to quotation and back again.

839–40. Serranus = C. Atilius Regulus, supposedly summoned from the plow to hold the consulship of 257 BCE (cf. Vergil, *Aen.* 6.845).

841–42. Marcus Furius Camillus (cf. F. 2.46.19–20 and 2.51.47–48 with note) saved and restored Rome after its capture by the Gauls in 390 BCE. When the invaders were being paid an agreed weight of gold to go away, the Romans objected that the weights were fraudulently over-heavy, whereupon the Gallic chieftain Brennus threw his sword too into the scale pan and cried *vae victis!* ("Woe to the vanquished!"); Livy 5.48. Vergil, *Aen.* 6.825 refers to Camillus' recovery of the standards.

843–45. Lucius Papirius Cursor (= "Runner," from prowess as such), dictator 325 and 309, and five times consul, harried the Samnites in Rome's second war against them and is treated by Livy as a general equal to Alexander the Great (9.16, 9.38–39).

846–47. Marcus Valerius Messalla Corvinus (64 BCE–8 CE) was consul with Octavian (the later Augustus) when Antony and Cleopatra were defeated at Actium (31 BCE). He was an orator, historian, and patron of poets (including Tibullus), as well as a soldier and statesman. *Corvus* = "raven."

848–50. Titus Manlius Torquatus reportedly won his cognomen by despoiling a huge Celt of his collar (*torques*) after killing him in a duel in 361 BCE. As consul for the third time, he sternly sentenced his own son to death for fighting the enemy in disobedience of his orders (cf. Vergil, *Aen.* 6.824).

851–57. Fabius Maximus Rullianus (855), five times consul, censor, and dictator (315 BCE), celebrated triumphs over Samnites, Etruscans, and Gauls. The consul, censor, and dictator Quintus Fabius Maximus Verrucosus Cunctator (856; cf. *F.* 2.51.53–54) famously used delaying tactics against Hannibal and avoided pitched battle after Rome's severe defeat at Cannae in 216 BCE. The former Fabius was actually the *great*-grandfather of the latter. Cf. Vergil, *Aen.* 6.846ff. For *excoluere* (853), cf. *Aen.* 6.663.

858. Fabricius: 818–21n. Curius (Manius Curius Dentatus): *F.* 2.13.13–14n.

861–62. Attilius (wrongly so spelled to lengthen the first syllable; see Preface headnote) is Atilius Regulus, a consul in the First Punic War. He invaded Africa but was captured by the Carthaginians, who sent him to Rome to secure them a peace, but instead he urged the Senate to fight on. He still honored his promise to return to Carthage, suffering torture and death (Horace, *Odes* 3.5).

863–68. The three Decii meant (father, son, and grandson, all Publius Decius Mus) devoted themselves to death to save the Roman cause in 340, 295, and 279 BCE, in wars against the Latins, the Samnites, and Pyrrhus, respectively. Cf. Vergil, *Aen.* 6.825 (and *F.* 2.32.5).

864–67. Lucius Marcius took command in Spain in 212 BCE, after the two Roman generals previously in charge had been defeated and killed by the Carthaginians. Spain (where the *Hiberi* lived) seemed lost, but Marcius rallied the forces still left and captured two Carthaginian camps in one night (Livy 25.37–39). Livy describes how, as Marcius addressed his troops, a flame miraculously burst from his head without harming him.

869–71. "Two Scipios" (869): Publius Cornelius Scipio Africanus Major and Minor. The former fought in Spain for some years from 210 BCE, gradually undermining Carthaginian control there, and eventually defeated Hannibal at Zama (in north Africa) in 202. The younger Scipio Africanus presided over Carthage's destruction in the Third Punic War of 149–146 BCE. Vergil (*Aen.* 6.844) calls the two *clades Libyae* ("the defeat/disaster of Libya").

872–73. Marcus Claudius Marcellus and *spolia opima*: *F.* 2.51.51–52. With *Feretri* understand *Iovis*.

874. Publius Rutilius Rufus, consul 105 BCE and a virtuous Stoic, was unfairly condemned in 92 BCE for allegedly plundering the province of Asia as governor, having in fact honorably tried to curb the excesses of profiteering Roman businessmen there. The two Catos (both Marcus Porcius Cato) are Cato the Censor (234–149 BCE) and his great-grandson Cato of Utica (95–46 BCE), both of rigidly upright character. Cf., for example, Horace, *Epist.* 1.19.12ff. for the elder as a man of stern-faced, bare-footed, and scant-robed austerity. See *F.* 1.2.41–42n for him. The younger Cato was the uncompromising republican who eventually committed suicide at Utica in north Africa (46 BCE) rather than survive Julius Caesar's victory in the Civil War.

876–77. Publius Cornelius Scipio Nasica, later consul (191 BCE), was appointed by the Senate, because of his purity of life, to receive the statue of the goddess Cybele that was brought to Ostia, Rome's harbor, from Phrygia in 204 BCE. She is the Idaean Mother (Ida being a mountain near Troy).

878. This second Brutus (Marcus Junius Brutus; see 831–36n for the first), one of Julius Caesar's assassins in 44 BCE, is evidently seen as a praiseworthy tyrannicide, not a common murderer.

884–86. Construe both *Peneius* (quadrisyllabic) and *Aganippeus* with *liquor* in 886. The Peneus River flows through Thessaly (Haemonia), including the Vale of Tempe (*F.* 1.20.19–20n). Aganippe is the fountain on Mt. Helicon in Boeotia that was sacred to the Muses; its waters inspired poets.

893–98. The greatest Greek orator, Demosthenes, is imagined with Cicero, the greatest Roman orator.

902–04. The laws of Draco, the Athenian lawgiver (621 BCE), were later described by the orator Demades (Plutarch, *Solon* 17) as "written in blood," in that they made almost every offense capital.

905–9. The Spartans were said to owe their severe militaristic system to Lycurgus (cf. *F.* 2.51.45 and 2.53.2), whose laws allowed only iron spits as money to discourage accumulation of personal wealth.

910–11. See *F.* 1.21.17–18n. *Solon* illicitly has first syllable long (see Preface headnote).

913–16. The Empyrean (cf. *F.* 2.51.180) is the highest (fiery) heaven in Dante. For the sun (Phoebus/Titan's chariot/Apollo) in Leo, see 20n.

919–24. The two preeminent poets are Homer and Vergil (who was born in Mantua). Line 922 refers to the *Iliad*, 923 to the *Odyssey* (for Dulichian, see *F.* 1.4.67–70n). Verino expressly names many more Latin and Greek poets as being in this region of heaven for virtuous non-Christians and unbaptized babies than Dante describes as being in Limbo (*Inf.* 4.67ff., and *Purg.* 22.10–114). Note that in 922, Homer, like Aeschylus in 950 and Pacuvius in 976, is treated as old in appearance. The virtuous non-Christians and unbaptized babies are not transformed into thirty-year-olds in looks, unlike the blessed Christian dead in heaven, for whose uniform age see 197–98 and 606–16.

925–30. The Nine Lyric Poets of Greece (one a woman) reckoned canonical by Alexandrian critics included Pindar (928), Alcaeus (929), and Sappho (929), as well as Anacreon, Alcman, Stesichorus, Ibycus, Simonides, and Bacchylides. Sappho, incidentally, is the only woman explicitly mentioned as a denizen of heaven (albeit the part for virtuous non-Christians) in *Paradise*. The many nameless Christians cataloged in 533–605 as in heaven for their worthiness are represented only by male examples. In 573 even the martyrs are called *viros* (usually just "men," very occasionally "people," as in 414 and 448). Pindar flowing like a river (928): Horace, *Odes* 4.2.5–8.

935. "Alternating verse": F. 1.4.56n.

936. The *o* in *Ovidius* should be short (cf. the Ovid in Martial 7.44.1 and 7.45.6). See Preface headnote.

936–38. Propertius as *Nauta*: F. 1.7.9–12n. *Cum vate Tibullo Nauta* is treated as equivalent to *Tibullus et Nauta* (hence the plural verb; see Gildersleeve and Lodge, p. 285, n. 2, for ancient instances, notably in Sallust and Livy). Callimachus (the Alexandrian poet) is thus considered outshone by Propertius and Tibullus (Ovid, *Am.* 1.15.13–14 acclaims Callimachus' fame as undying worldwide, but for his art rather than his inspiration). Bartolini unsatisfactorily punctuates to make Propertius and Callimachus the two equals, leaving the identity of *solus* in 938 unexplained and failing to perceive that the change of tense in *lustrabat* (939) shows direct quotation ended with *Nauta*.

942. *Cothurni* ("buskins"): F. 2.1.3–4n. *Syrma*: Tragic actor's robe.

950–53. Aeschylus left Athens in old age to die in Sicily; Euripides died in Macedonia. Euripides' name should have the second syllable long. See Preface headnote.

954–56. Seneca, the Stoic and tragic poet, had been Nero's tutor but was forced into suicide by him.

960. Haemonia: Thessaly, where Julius Caesar defeated Pompey at Pharsalus in 48 BCE. Lucan wrote of the Civil War in his *Pharsalia*.

961–62. Silius Italicus wrote the *Punica*, describing the Second Punic

War. Italy ("Latium") suffered devastation by Hannibal, north Africa ("Libya") in Rome's invasion of Carthage's homeland late in the war.

963–68. One Roman satirist, Horace, has already been mentioned in 931–32, following the writers of Greek lyric. Lucilius lived ca. 180–102 BCE. Persius composed only one book of satires. Juvenal (meant in 968) was born at Aquinum in Latium. For *vitiis . . . vitiorum* in 965, see 728–29n.

969. Quintilian famously said (*Inst.* 10.1.93), "Satire is entirely ours" (Roman). Pelasgian = Greek.

971–77. Cratinus (974) was an Athenian Old Comedy poet of the generation before Aristophanes, though the two competed for a while in the 420s BCE. Eupolis (977) was a more contemporary rival of Aristophanes. Menander (975) was the greatest exponent of the Athenian New Comedy. Plautus (975) and Terence (973) followed in that tradition with their Roman plays. Marcus Terentius Varro (116–27 BCE) is mentioned here (973) for his *Menippean Satires*, only partly in verse. The "old man" in 976 is Marcus Pacuvius (220–ca. 130 BCE), who died at Tarentum, primarily a tragic poet, though there are reports that he also wrote some satires. Accius in 977 (170–ca. 85 BCE) is known to have written some Sotadic satire, but he too was principally a tragedian. Tarentum is "insolent" in Juvenal 6.297, seemingly with reference to an insult to a Roman envoy just before war with Rome began in 281 BCE.

993–95. The "glory of Memphis" (where the kings resided in Egypt) is Hermes Trismegistus ("Hermes thrice-greatest"). The Greeks identified the ibis-headed Egyptian deity Thoth, the father of all knowledge, with their god Hermes, and Hermes Trismegistus was considered the author of the very extensive ancient "Hermetic" writings (some of which survive in Greek or Latin form), partly philosophical and theological (greatly interesting Neoplatonists), but also dealing with occult subjects such as astrology, magic, and alchemy (the "Hermetic art"). In 995, Hermes Trismegistus is supposedly "the agreeable friend of Moses," a strange statement, though in the account of Moses' life by the Jewish romancer Artapanus (second century BCE), Moses himself is assimilated to Hermes/Thoth and treated as imparting knowledge to the Egyptians, including inventing their hieroglyphics. See, for instance, G. Fowden, *The Egyptian Hermes* (Cambridge, 1986), p. 23. For Ficino's translation of pseudo-Hermes works, see *Mercurii Trismegisti Pimander sive de potestate et sapientia Dei*, ed. M. Campanelli (Turin, 2011).

996–1000. Orpheus in legend was torn apart (on the mountain range of Rhodope) by Thracian women (or Maenads) after introducing orgiastic rites to Thrace. *Rhodopes* (998) is Greek genitive.

1001–2. The philosopher Pythagoras believed in successive reincarnation of the soul within various animals or even plants, until it could win release by achieving total purity. He was born on Samos, but immigrated ca. 531 BCE to Croton in the "toe" of Italy. The Calabrian Gulf is evidently the Gulf of Tarentum. In 1002 *quae . . . vocata est* agrees in number and gender with the complement *Graecia Magna*, not with *Sinus Calabros*, the antecedent, a permissible violation of normal concord (Gildersleeve and Lodge, §614.3b).

1006. Dion (ca. 408–354 BCE), formerly a minister of the tyrannical Dionysius I of Syracuse, tried unsuccessfully, with Plato's help, to turn that ruler's successor, Dionysius II, into the perfect philosopher-prince. After years of exile in Greece (and association with Plato's Academy), Dion returned to Sicily and took control of Syracuse for two brief periods, but he became arbitrary himself and was murdered. Archytas of Tarentum (alternatively called *Archyta* in 1008 for the meter), a well-regarded philosopher of the Pythagorean school, distinguished in mathematics, geometry, and mechanics (Horace, *Odes* 1.28.1–6 recognizes his standing), flourished in the first half of the fourth century BCE and was visited by Plato. Verino (like Naldi, *Eleg.* 2.41.11, 61, and 85) wrongly gives Plato's name a long *a* here, in 1016, and in 1073 (correctly short Horace, *Satires* 2.4.3). *Dion* here wrongly has the *o* short. See Preface headnote.

1008. *Syracusis* is ablative of origin, balancing the genitive *Tarenti*.

1009–12. The philosopher Bias of Priene was one of the seven sages of Greece. Socrates (469–399 BCE) was told by Apollo's (Pythian) oracle at Delphi that he was the wisest of men, which he eventually deduced referred to his knowledge of his own ignorance (see Plato's *Apology*). Socrates was condemned to death by hemlock poison for corrupting the youth and for heterodox religious views. Conspicuously absent here is Aristotle, who figures unnamed in Dante's Limbo (*Inf.* 4.130ff.).

1013–18. Plato (ca. 429–347 BCE) is given prominence among the philosophers and actually made to address Verino (1021–71) because of the great interest in him at Florence, where Marsilio Ficino and his circle interpreted Plato's thought in Christian terms (cf. 1058–71 for Platonic studies at Florence). Plato's name (nickname) means "broad" (as hinted in 1015).

1018. Sense and syntax require a (consecutive) subjunctive (I suggest the perfect *norit*) for the indicative *novit* in the manuscripts. Bartolini's *nosset* (imperfect) is a greater change.

1022. Note the unclassical use of *inquit* as if *dicit* or *dixit*, occasionally seen in neo-Latin poets.

1030. The Samian seer is Pythagoras (cf. 1001).

1031. Tages, an Etruscan deity, supposedly taught the Etruscans the art of divination (e.g., Ovid, *Met.* 15.558–59). "Blind" (cf. 1038) presumably means unseeing of the full truth in Christian terms.

1032–33. A *Magus* was a wise man or magician among the Persians. The Gymnosophists ("Naked Philosophers"), ancient Indian ascetics, lived lives of contemplation as (traditionally unclad) hermits.

1034–35. Thales (of Miletus), the presocratic philosopher who saw water as the basic element in the physical world, was one of the seven sages of Greece. He is one of those in Dante's Limbo (*Inf.* 4.134). Thales is said by Herodotus (1.70) to have been of Phoenician descent.

1036. The Chaldaeans (of Assyria) had a reputation for knowledge of astronomy and astrology.

1041. "The lyrical king": David (for his psalms).

1042–43. The prophet Isaiah is said to have been sawn in half inside a tree in the reign of Manasseh.

1043. "Babylonian child": Daniel, a boy-captive in Babylon (1 Daniel), where he rose to be chief among the wise men in the palace (his interpretation of the king's dreams is particularly celebrated).

1044. Sibyls were prophetesses. The sibyl of Cumae is Aeneas' Underworld guide in Vergil, *Aen.* 6.

1045. The Word: Christ (as in John 1:1).

1049. See 483n.

1060. Arno: *F.* 1.6.1–2n.

1061. Cf. 235 and see *F.* 1.20.18n.

1079. Presumably the gate meant is that by which the garden was entered at 664–65.

1089–90. Line 1089 refers to the Cretan Labyrinth with the Minotaur (Ida being a Cretan mountain). Ariadne helped Theseus slay the beast and retrace his path through the maze of ways. The less famous Labyrinth built by Psammetichus on Lake Moeris in Egypt is meant in 1090. It had three thousand chambers.

1091. *Per* in 1092 seems to govern *triclinia*. *Miris* could go with *thalamis* or *viis*. *Triclinia* should have the first *i* long. See Preface headnote.

1093. I read *incertum* as object of *fallit* (1094) with *te* understood, or else *incertum* can be taken as neuter nominative singular. With *incertus* the sentence does not construe (perhaps by Verino's oversight).

1105. After this line in *B*, the copyist Pietro Crinito follows the word *telos* ("the end" — in Greek script) with the date (June 1489) and then a short message about himself, as follows. *P. Crinitus parvulus. Quod opus scripsi admodum puer, quum essem tum Ugolini ipsius auditor; quo quidem tempore Musarum sacris candidari occepi, avi haud arbitror fusca, sed hoc, ut cetera, exitus approbabit*; that is, "Little [i.e., young] P. Crinito. I wrote [= copied out] this work while still a boy, being then a pupil of Ugolino himself, at the time when I began my candidacy for the rites of the Muses [i.e., started training as a Latin poet], under no gloomy auspices in my opinion, but the outcome will establish the truth of that, as of all other things." He then adds *telos* (in Greek script) once more.

Bibliography

TEXTS AND EDITIONS

FIAMMETTA

Bandini, Angelo Maria. *Specimen Literaturae Florentinae Saeculi XV.* 2 vols. Florence: sumptibus J. Rigaccii, 1747–51. Quoted from *Fiammetta*: (1: 100) 1.20.29–30; (1: 120) 1.5, 2.5.19–20; (2: 35) 1.20.

Ugolini Verini Flametta. Edited by Luciano Mencaraglia. Florence: Olschki, 1940. Mencaraglia's edition is reviewed and discussed (with many corrections and improvements suggested) as follows:

> Dionisotti, C. *Giornale storico della letteratura italiana* 116 (1940): 175–77.
>
> Munari, F. "Note sulla *Flametta* di Ugolino Verino." *Maia* 2 (1949): 297–306. This article, besides reviewing Mencaraglia's edition, lists very many debts to classical poets.
>
> Perosa, A. *La nuova Italia. Rassegna critica mensile della cultura italiana e straniera* 19.2–3 (1941): 51–54.

Ugolino Verino: Flammetta. Edited by Allan M. Wilson. Cheadle Hulme, 1998. Text, translation, commentary, full word index (554 pages in all). Seven copies were privately produced (at Cheadle Hulme, Cheadle, Cheshire, England) in March 1998, following a preliminary version of 546 pages provisionally bound up for proofreading purposes in late 1997. One copy was donated to each of the John Rylands University Library, Deansgate, Manchester; the Biblioteca Medicea-Laurenziana, Florence; and the library of the Katholieke Universiteit, Leuven, Belgium.

PARADISE

Bandini, Angelo Maria. *Catalogus Codicum Latinorum Bibliothecae Mediceae Laurentianae.* 4 vols. Florence, 1774. Substantial extracts from the text of *Paradise* are given. In vol. 2, pp. 774–79, lines are quoted (from *A*):

prefatory poem, 1–16, 55–87, 180–92, 206–92, 702–33, 1013–29, 1056–76, 1105.

Ugolini Verini Poetae Florentini Poematia ex manuscriptis . . . Antonii Magliabechi . . . nunc primum edita a Nicolao Bartholini Bargensi. Lyons, 1679. Within this work Bartolini includes *Ugolini Verini Poetae Florentini Paradisus ad Laurentium Medicem.* In places he rewrites Verino's text to remove metrical problems.

Ugolino Verino: Paradisus. Edited by Allan M. Wilson. Cheadle Hulme, 1998. Text, translation, notes (120 pages in all). Of six copies privately produced, one each was donated to the same libraries as detailed for the 1998 *Flammetta.* Now wholly superseded by this present volume.

OTHER WORKS

Ugolino Verino: Carlias. Ein Epos des 15. Jahrhunderts. Edited by Nikolaus Thurn. Munich: Fink, 1995.

Ugolino Verino: Epigrammi. Edited by Francesco Bausi. Messina: Sicania, 1998.

TRANSLATIONS

Fiammetta and *Paradise* are fully translated into English in the 1998 editions listed above. For six poems translated into Italian by Lucia Gualdo Rosa, see *Poeti latini del Quattrocento* under Anthologies below.

ANTHOLOGIES

Carmina illustrium poetarum italorum. [Edited by Giovanni Gaetano Bottari.] 11 vols. Florence: apud J. C. Tartinium and S. Franchium, 1719–26. Seventeen poems from *Fiammetta* are given in vol. 10, as follows, beginning on the pages stated: (p. 395) 1.15; (p. 396) 1.19, 1.20; (p. 397) 2.7; (p. 398) 2.8, 2.11, 2.17; (p. 399) 2.21, 2.24; (p. 400) 2.45; (p. 403) 2.47; (p. 406) 1.1, 2.46; (p. 408) 2.51; (p. 413) 2.52, 2.53, 2.54. Some lines are partly rewritten by the editor to correct the meter. The same volume includes all of Verino's *De illustratione urbis Florentiae.*

Poesie di mille autori intorno a Dante Alighieri. Compiled by Carlo del Balzo. 15 vols. Rome: Forzani, 1889–1904. Poem 2.45 is included in vol. 4 (1893), pp. 272–77, with a biographical note and a few annotations.

Poeti latini del Quattrocento. Edited by Francesco Arnaldi, Lucia Gualdo Rosa, and Liliana Monti Sabia Milan: Ricciardi, 1964. Pages 841–65 contain the text with Lucia Gualdo Rosa's Italian translations, some footnotes, a three-page general introduction on Verino, and a brief bibliography. *Fiammetta* poems included: 1.4, 1.6, 1.13, 1.20, 1.27, 2.45.

Renaissance Latin Verse: An Anthology. Edited by Alessandro Perosa and John Sparrow. London: Duckworth, 1979. Pages 88–90 contain the text of *Fiammetta* 1.13 and 1.27 (pieces 58 and 59, respectively) with a few footnotes and a brief general introduction on Verino.

COMMENTARIES

Thurn, Nikolaus. *Kommentar zur "Carlias" des Ugolino Verino.* Munich: Fink, 2002

STUDIES

Bausi, Francesco. "Ugolino Verino, Savonarola e la poesia religiosa tra Quattro e Cinquecento," *Studi savonaroliani. Verso il V centenario. Atti del seminario di studi savonaroliani. Firenze, Accademia di scienze e lettere "La Colombaria," gennaio 1995,* 127–35. Florence: SISMEL, 1996.

Bottiglioni, Gino. *La lirica latina in Firenze nella seconda metà del secolo XV.* Pisa: Nistri, 1913. Pages 33–41 quote portions of Verino's *Fiammetta* (with some errors) as follows: (p. 35 n. 1) 1.1.13–18; (p. 36 n. 2) 1.29.31–2; (p. 36 n. 3) 1.26.25–30; (p. 36 n. 4) 2.27.10; (p. 37) 1.19.5–6, 2.22.19 and 43, 2.48.19–20; (p. 38) 2.46.27–46; (p. 41 n. 1) 2.13.1–8; (pp. 203–5) 1.4; (p. 205–6) 1.6.

Gombrich, E. H. "Apollonio di Giovanni: A Florentine Cassone Workshop Seen Through the Eyes of a Humanist Poet." *Journal of the Warburg and Courtauld Institutes* xviii (1955): 16–34. Reprinted in his *Norm and Form* (London, 1966), pp. 11–28 (with a version of *F.* 2.8 on p. 12).

Lazzari, Alfonso. *Ugolino e Michele Verino, Studi biografici e critici.* Turin: Libreria C. Clausen, 1897. The main work devoted to the life and poetry of both Ugolino Verino and his son, including substantial consideration of the content of *Fiammetta*, the citations from which are as follows: (p. 28 n. 3) 2.17.5–6; (p. 30 n. 4) 2.13.17–18; (p. 36 n. 1) 2.45.101–4; (p. 42 n. 2) 2.5.5–14; (p. 42 n. 3) 2.6.5–6; (p. 53) 1.7.1–4; (p. 54 n. 3) 2.55.1–2; (p. 55) 1.4.23–24; (p. 55 n. 1) 1.4.15–20; (p. 56) 1.10.5–6 and 1.13.5–6; (p. 56 n. 1) 1.4.29–32; (p. 56 n. 2) 1.4.33–36; (p. 57) 1.27.17–26 and 1–5; (p. 57 n. 1) 1.21.2 and 5; (p. 58) 1.27.6–7 and 9–10, 1.28.1–2 and 5–8; (p. 58–59) 1.29.1–20 and 25–32; (p. 59 n. 2) 1.20.31, 33, 35–6; (p. 60 n. 3) 2.23.1–4; (p. 61) 2.23.5–14; (p. 62) 2.36.1–16, 2.46.50–52. Lazzari's sources include the Latin biography of Verino by Lorenzo Bartolozzi da Figline preserved in manuscript (Florence, Biblioteca Riccardiana, MS. Ricc. 910).

Morrone, Stano. "*Excerpta* epistolari di Ugolino Verino in una biografia cinquecentesca a lui dedicata." *Interpres*, ser. 2, 14 (2010): 215–28.

Index to Fiammetta

ॐ᠋ॐ᠋ॐ᠋

References are to book, poem, and lines of the Latin text or, when they end with *n*, to the notes, as 2.8.11–14n (headnotes have *n* immediately following the number of the poem, as 2.8n). References to notes marked + lead to further references within the note. Roman numerals indicate pages in the Introduction. Sometimes the person or place is alluded to in context rather than expressly named. Some trivial and merely incidental mentions in notes are omitted. Titles are indexed only where especially of note and are indicated with a *t.*

2.46.54n; *2.1*, 1.2.1–2n,
1.19.1–2n, 1.19.3–4n, 1.20n,
2.28.1–2n, 2.45.137–38n; *2.2*,
1.19.1–2n; *2.3*, 1.25.43–44n,
2.24.5–6n; *2.4*, 1.4.17–18n,
1.4.31n, 2.1.17–18n, 2.43.9–
10n; *2.5*, 1.10.7–10n, 1.21.19–
22n, 1.28.22n; *2.6*, 1.19.5–6n,
2.25.7–8n, 2.45.37–42n,
2.51.115n; *2.7*, 1.4.75–78n,
1.18.24n, 1.18.25–26n,
1.23.26n, 1.24.3–6n, 1.25.17–
20n, 1.26.28n; *2.8*, 1.4.33–
34n, 1.21.19–22n, 2.5.8n,
2.51.123–24n; *2.9*, 1.25.13–
14n, 2.2.7–8n; *2.11*, 1.26.37–
38n; *2.12*, 1.6.33–34n; *2.17*,
1.17.1n, 1.17.11–12n; *2.18*,
1.4.20n, 1.21.19–22n; *2.20*,
1.8.7–10n, 1.8.19–32n, 1.18.11–
12n; *2.21*, 1.8.7–10n; *2.23*,
1.2.38n, 1.4.31n, 1.23.26n,
2.1.7–8n, 2.3.3–4n, 2.43.15–
16n, 2.43.27–28n, 2.43.33–
34n, 2.49.19–20n; *2.25*,
1.4.67–70n, 1.6.37–40n,
1.8.7–10n, 1.8.19–32n,
1.18.17n, 1.18.33–34n,
1.21.33n, 1.24.10n; *2.26*,
1.25.43–44n, 2.2.9–10n,
2.42.3–6n; *2.27*, 1.5n; *2.29*,
2.7n, 2.12.15–16n; *2.30*, 1.7.9–
12n, 2.7.5–6n, 2.7.8n,
2.7.10n; *3.1*, 2.1.5–6n,
2.21.2n, 2.51.23–24n; *3.2*,
1.1.13–14n, 1.19.5–6n,
1.20.23–24n; *3.3*, 1.11.43–44n,

2.51.23–24n, 2.51.95–98n;
3.4, 1.1.17–18n, 1.9.8n,
2.12.6n, 2.51.68n, 2.51.157–
58n; *3.5*, 1.20.18n, 2.51.23–
24n; *3.6*, 2.45.89–92; *3.7*,
1.2.25–26n, 1.7.9–12n,
1.11.43–44n, 1.12.1–4n,
1.23.5–8n, 2.23.3–4n, 2.24.1–
2n, 2.49.1–2n, 2.50.5–6n,
2.50.31n, 2.51.13–14n,
2.51.19–20n, 2.51.23–24n,
2.51.72n; *3.15*, 1.11n, 2.24.9–
10n, 2.45.87–88n, 2.51.99–
100n, 2.51.118n; *3.16*, 2.24.9–
10n, 2.45.33–34n,
2.51.23–24n; *3.17*, 1.1.23–24n,
1.1.25n, 1.20.23–24n,
1.20.25–26n, 1.26.45n,
2.24.1–2n, 2.45.75–78n,
2.46.15–18n, 2.50.50n,
2.51.23–24n; *3.18*, 1.20.18n,
1.20.31–32n, 1.21.13–16n,
2.51.23–24n; *3.19*, 1.1.21–22n,
1.22.11–12n, 2.24.9–10n,
2.55.1–2n

Xandra, Earlier Redaction: 1,
1.1.13–14n, 1.3n; *7*, 1.6.17–18n;
9, 1.7.11–12n; *10*, 2.14.1–2n; *11*,
2.3.3–4n, 2.7n; *21*, 2.48.15–
18n; *25*, 1.4.17–18n; *26*, 1.5n;
31, 1.7n; *33*, 1.6.13–16n; *39*,
2.10n; *40*, 1.4.33–34n, 1.29n;
42, 1.1.17–18n

Miscellaneous Poems: 1, 1.6.33–
34n, 2.17.2n, 2.43.15–16n,
2.45.87–88n, 2.50n, 2.50.31n,
2.50.37n; *2*, 1.24.21–22n,

Index to Paradise

ༀ༇༈ༀ

References are to lines of the Latin text or, when they end with *n*, to the notes, as 369n. Sometimes the person or place is alluded to in context rather than expressly named. Some trivial and merely incidental mentions in notes are omitted.

Publication of this volume has been made possible by

The Myron and Sheila Gilmore Publication Fund at I Tatti
The Robert Lehman Endowment Fund
The Jean-François Malle Scholarly Programs and Publications Fund
The Andrew W. Mellon Scholarly Publications Fund
The Craig and Barbara Smyth Fund
for Scholarly Programs and Publications
The Lila Wallace–Reader's Digest Endowment Fund
The Malcolm Wiener Fund for Scholarly Programs and Publications